VICHY.

Contemporary French Culture and Society

edited by Richard J. Golsan, Mary Jean Green, and Lynn A. Higgins

VICHY

An Ever-Present Past

Éric Conan and Henry Rousso

TRANSLATED AND ANNOTATED BY NATHAN BRACHER

FOREWORD BY ROBERT O. PAXTON

Dartmouth College
Published by University Press of New England
Hanover and London

Dartmouth College

Published by University Press of New England, Hanover, NH 03755

© 1998 by the Trustees of Dartmouth College

The original edition of this book was published by Librarie Arthème Fayard in 1994.
The afterword to the 1996 Editions Gallimard "Folio Histoire" edition has been integrated
into the English-language version of the text.

Printed in the United States of America

5 4 3 2 1

CIP data appear at the end of the book

This work, published under the auspices of the program for publications,
benefits from the support of the Ministry of Foreign Affairs and the Cultural Services
of the French Embassy in the United States.

Cet ouvrage publié dans le cadre du programme d'aide à la publication
bénéficie du soutien du Ministère des Affaires Étrangères du Service Culturel
de l'Ambassade de France represente aux Etats-Unis.

Our inheritance has not been preceded by any will.

RENÉ CHAR

Contents

Foreword

ROBERT O. PAXTON

Ten years ago, Henry Rousso produced a landmark book about how the French remember their grim experience of World War II: *The Vichy Syndrome*.[1] He mapped out definitively the phases in which successive French memories of this painful past have been constructed. First, at the moment of Liberation, the bitter wounds of defeat and Nazi occupation could not be healed by a normal collective mourning. Opinions differed too radically about which heroes could be legitimately celebrated: Was it those who had rashly fought on, with de Gaulle and the Resistance, or those who had sought some prudent accommodation with the apparently victorious Nazis, along-side Marshall Pétain and his French State at Vichy? Nor was there agreement about which of the many dead could legitimately be mourned: the soldiers who had lost the war in 1940, the resisters hunted down by the Vichy police or the Gestapo, the collaborators summarily executed in the heat of Liberation, the victims of Allied bombings, the anti-Communist volunteers who died in Nazi uniform on the Russian front, or the Free French soldiers who arrived in 1944 as part of the Allied liberation armies.

Despite this "failed mourning," as Rousso calls it, by the early 1950s a kind of national unity had been achieved around a useful fiction. The Gaullists and Communists who had triumphed at the Liberation succeeded, independently but in tacit complicity, in imposing a version of history according to which France had resisted almost unanimously, from the beginning. In this perspective, Vichy had been limited to a marginal handful of traitors. This version's "invented honor" was generally accepted for twenty years. Vichy aroused no serious debate; collaboration was, Rousso says, a "repressed memory."

In a third phase that began in the early 1970s, according to Rousso, the "mirror broke." Its comfortably consensual image was shattered by iconoclastic works like Marcel Ophuls' film portraying an overwhelmingly collaborationist France, *The Sorrow and the Pity*, and by the arrival of the rebellious generation of 1968. Since that time, in Rousso's account, France has been gripped by the urge to expose the ugly side of collaboration and the compromises of the fathers.

Rousso's *Vichy Syndrome* should have laid to rest a myth that seems all but invincible in the United States: that the French are still "covering up"

Vichy's collaboration, particularly its complicity with the Nazis' arrest and deportation of Jews. On the contrary: For the past two decades many French people have dug almost obsessively into the hitherto taboo parts of their World War II past. Every few months a new "revelation"—often of matters already fully public—sets off another spiral of shocked amazement, debate, and recrimination. Books, films, scholarly dissertations, television specials, and articles in the daily or weekly press pick away steadily at the Vichy experience.

This third phase is still swelling in intensity. Therefore Rousso, in association with Éric Conan, journalist with *L'Express* and author of a poignant classic about the deportation of Jewish children from France in 1942,[2] have produced this sequel about the "syndrome's" latest fevers.

One of the sequel's major accomplishments is a series of lucid accounts of the most recent memory wars about Vichy. Working with exemplary rigor and care, the authors set straight several complicated stories around which emotion and misinformation have gathered. A particularly perceptive chapter brings up to date recent revelations about the late President François Mitterrand's participation in the Vichy regime before joining the active Resistance in the spring of 1943. Conan and Rousso perceive that Mitterrand personified a whole French generation whose relationship to Vichy was complex, and who were reluctant to probe very deeply into their own evolution from early enthusiasm for Pétain to later opposition. This chapter provides one of the most enlightening explanations in print about why reticence about Vichy extended beyond the far Right to the Center and even moderate Left in postwar France.

A provocative chapter examines France's first, and, so far, only trial of a French citizen for crimes against humanity—the trial of Paul Touvier in the spring of 1994. Conan and Rousso explore the legal and historical shortcomings by which the Touvier trial became diverted from the long-awaited official penalization of Vichy's own autonomous project of excluding and segregating Jews into something much more conventional: punishing French cooperation with the Nazis' far more murderous project. We see the full text of President Jacques Chirac's apology on July 16, 1995, for French "collective responsibility" for Vichy's complicity in the Final Solution, following years of tortuous evasions by Mitterrand.

There is, finally, meticulous refutation of charges that French schoolchildren do not learn about the Collaboration, and that French archives are closed to research on Vichy. Conan and Rousso are right to stress how genuinely French archives have been opened to research since 1979, an evolution that has gone much further than some people wish to admit.[3] They pinpoint very precisely the nature of the obstacles that remain—most important, the veto possessed by the documents' originating bureaux—and concede that "tracasseries," administrative foot-dragging, can still make research slow and difficult.[4] One might have wished for a more explicit comparison here with other Western countries where—it must be admitted—research into all aspects of World War II except intelligence is still easier than in France.

This work is more than a mere updating of *The Vichy Syndrome*, however. The very word "syndrome" had already suggested something pathological about the mounting fever to uncover Vichy's secrets. Now Conan and Rousso criticize what they see as excesses in the way the "duty of memory" is being put into practice. Veterans of the historical polemics of the 1990s, the two authors use these pages to flay their enemies. One French reviewer called this book (mostly with admiration) a "paving-stone thrown through a shop window."[5] It attacks the sensationalism and ignorance that, according to Conan and Rousso, increasingly poison what should have been a salutary facing up to the complexities and verities of the past.

Their targets are the public's craving for "revelations" about Vichy and its readiness to believe the worst, a younger generation that seems infinitely eager for vindictive exposure of their elders' failings, media that inflate and distort each new debate, and "intellectuals of the eleventh hour" who rush into the fray without the most elementary knowledge or research credentials. They expose the weak evidence underlying such recent "revelations" as the allegation that Resistance leader Jean Moulin was simultaneously a Soviet agent.

Having themselves published distinguished work exposing the dark face of Vichy France, Conan and Rousso certainly have no desire to return to hiding it. They want the past to be fully explored, but with scholarly rigor, acceptance of the past's complexity, and regard for civic healing. "The duty of memory is an empty shell unless it is based on scholarship," they say, unless it is "yoked to a duty to truth."

The French are not alone, of course, in struggling to "master" their World War II past.[6] Every European nation, in its own way, has experienced in recent years a weakening of taboos and a more transgressive probing, with youthful insouciance, of old wounds. Even in Britain, long blessed with Europe's most comfortably consensual image of a heroic and successful war, some younger historians now accuse Churchill of having squandered the British Empire's resources and subordinated it to the United States in a vaingloriously limitless crusade against Hitler.[7]

It is in France and Germany, among European states, that the World War II past seems particularly "unmasterable." Not that these two countries are strictly comparable. Germany's World War II legacy is uniquely heavy, and the Federal Republic (West Germany), at least, was forced by defeat to accept—however reluctantly—the trial of its wartime leaders and the "denazification" of its ruling elites. The Federal Republic's constitution explicitly recognizes German responsibility for Nazi war crimes and forbids the expression of Nazi doctrine.[8] The West Germans, at first quite skeptical of the Nuremberg trials and of the Allies' "denazification" proceedings, came around, by the 1960s, to their own war crimes prosecutions. A brilliant West German historical school studied the Third Reich with great fruitfulness.[9] West Germans coped reasonably well, too, in the 1960s and 1970s, with the problem of the experts and civil servants still in active service who had once served the Third Reich. Even so, West Germany experienced a momentously bitter public debate in 1986—the "historians' quarrel," *Historikerstreit*—about whether Nazi crimes had not been a preemptive response to comparable Stalinist crimes, and whether the time had not come to close the books on the Nazi legacy and consider contemporary Germany an ordinary nation.[10] In 1996, Germans—now including the hitherto complacent Easterners—were shocked all over again, as if all their historians' labors had been in vain, by the sadism revealed in Daniel Jonah Goldhagen's *Hitler's Willing Executioners*.[11]

The particularity of the French memory wars is their late beginning, and their continuation, with mounting intensity, two generations after the fact, as "repressed memory" returns. It seems to be accidental that Conan and Rousso chose a title for the original French edition of this work—"Un passé qui ne passe pas"—identical to that by which Ernst Nolte set off the German *Historikerstreit*.[12] The French *Historikerstreit* is quite different. Not only are the stakes lower, but the French can also lay ultimate responsibility at German feet. While the German quarrel mobilized primarily professional historians and sociologists, the French memory wars of the 1990s have involved a challenge by journalists and amateur historians to what they regard as an over-cautious "official history"—a challenge that Conan and Rousso spiritedly reject.

So high a pitch of denunciatory energy cannot last forever, of course. French citizens' agitated memory of World War II will grow calmer; this past will pass, as have all the others. The cycle of fiftieth anniversary commemorations is over. The generation old enough to have been actively engaged in public life during the dark years is long retired from responsible positions; it is now rapidly disappearing. The secretive François Mitterrand has been replaced as French President by Jacques Chirac, who was only seven years old in June 1940. Another generation may well be less judgmental about its increasingly remote ancestors. But not yet.

For now, the scandals continue to bubble up. Several reasons explain the continued agitation. One is that French national identity is at stake. In the middle 1990s many French people have suffered acute anxiety about the decline of their culture, language, and way of life under the onslaughts of economic and cultural globalization. To lose the memory of having earned a legitimate place among the victors in World War II would be particularly hard to bear now.

Another reason the agitation will continue is that a few skeletons still remain in Vichy closets. Since this book appeared, new "revelations" have included the probable French manufacture of Cyclone-B gas for the Nazis, the allegation (dubious) that some celebrated resisters were secretly "turned" by the Gestapo, and the discovery of additional wartime police files of Jewish names and addresses in provincial archives. One hitherto taboo subject with immense destructive potential is the disposition of Jewish property confiscated during the Occupation, or bought at knock-down prices, and neither returned nor reimbursed after the Liberation. A corner of the veil was lifted in early 1997 when it turned out that French national museums still possess considerable seized Jewish property. Finally, the trial for complicity in war crimes of Maurice Papon, once a high Vichy civil servant and later a Resistance leader and Gaullist minister, opened in October 1997.

A third reason why the fever does not subside is that mastering the past raises profound issues which are hardly grasped by the public, let alone resolved. Are there legitimate limits to the "duty of memory," imposed by community solidarity, a concomitant "duty to forget," and a necessity to close the past and face current issues? Should the exploration of the past be left to scrupulous specialists, or open to enthusiastic amateurs? Why is the general public astonished over and over again by information already known to scholars, but somehow not effectively transmissible today without media bombast?

For the foreseeable future, the French memory wars will continue, and Conan and Rousso are our most judicious and rigorous guides to the facts and issues at stake.

Preface to the American Edition

The first version of this book was published in France in early September 1994. At that time, one of the biggest controversies over the memory of the Occupation was on the verge of breaking out: this one was about the past of François Mitterrand, then President of the Republic. This coincidence influenced the reception of the book in France, in that our assessments could appear to be an attempt to stem the tide of events. In spite of that, we did not, except for the addition of an afterword devoted specifically to the Mitterrand affair, change anything for the second edition, a paperback destined for a wider public and published in January 1996. The American translation has come from that second edition. The afterword of the 1996 edition has been incorporated into the main body of the text and, in order to take into account the latest developments of 1996 and 1997, we have added some new information, particularly in the chronology at the end of the book. And there are many such developments, because the history of the "Vichy Syndrome," that of the recurrent echoes of the memory of World War II, sounds indeed to French ears like a broken record that no one thinks of stopping. The purpose of this book is to understand why.

ÉRIC CONAN & HENRY ROUSSO

Acknowledgments

We are grateful to all those who have helped us in our study, who were willing to give us their testimony, and who made it possible for us to correct a few inaccuracies contained in the first edition: former President of the Conseil Constitutionnel Robert Badinter; Attorney General Pierre Truche and magistrates Marc Domingo and Jean-Pierre Getti; attorneys Georges Kiejman, Arno Klarsfeld, Serge Klarsfeld, Henri Leclerc, Joe Nordmann, Roland Rappaport, and Jacques Trémolet de Villers; Madame Chantal Bonazzi, Honorary General Curator of the National Archives; retired Colonel Françis Masset; Maurice Bouvet; Adam Rayski; Serge Barcellini, Inspector General in the office of the Secretary of State for War Veterans; Paul Thibaud; philosophers Luc Ferry and Daniel Lindenberg; historians Jean-Pierre Azéma, François Bédarida, Robert Belot, Serge Berstein, Jacques Delarue, Jacques Dupâquier, Anne Grynberg, André Kaspi, Pierre Laborie, Dominique Lerche, Denis Peschanski, René Rémond, and Olivier Wieviorka; journalists Sorj Chalandon, Laurent Greilsamer, and Annette Lévy-Willard, as well as Marjolaine Auricoste; Simon Pinto, President of the Union of Jewish Students of France; Denise J. Lorach, curator of the Musée de la Résistance et de la Déportation in Besançon; as well as Claire Keith and Gordon C. Squire, for information coming from the United States.

Jean Astruc and Anne-Marie Pathé, of the library of the Institut d'Histoire du Temps Présent (CNRS), as well as Marianne Ranson, provided us valuable assistance.

We also warmly thank Marc Alekan for his painstaking proofreading.

Finally, we would like to express our gratitude to the respondents of the IHTP was well as to the teachers who were kind enought to respond to our questionnaire over lycées and middle schools, or who circulated it to their colleagues: Madames and Messieurs Baboulenne, Annie Bacchus, Philippe Barlet, Jeannie Bauvois, Gilbert Beaubatie, Marc Bergère, Jean-Pierre Besse, Gérar Boeldieu, Maryvonne Braunschweig, Jean-Henri Calmon, Bruno Carlier, Pierre Chapoutot, Hélène Chaubin, Michel Chaumet, Claude Cherrier, Dominique Chtourou, Françoise Darmois, Declas, Marie-Françoise Dehu, Gil Emprin, Jean-Louis Étienne, Thierry Fabri, Roger Falcon, Christian Font, Rémy Foucault, Christiane Gachignard, Rémy Gaudillier, Geneviève Gaufillet, Jeanne Gillot-Voisin, Michel Goubet, Alain Grunberg, Jeannet, Claire Jullien, Jean Larrieu, Jean-Louis Laubry, Jocelyne Laurans, Lessous, Claudine Maenhout, Jean-Claude Marquis, Robert Mencherini, Nadia Michel, Million, Alain Monchablon, Ch. Nérisson, Paitry, Jean-Louis Panicacci, Julien Papp, Bernard Pénisson, Jean-Charles Perdriel, Pierre Péré, Éric-Charles Pielberg, Marie-Agnès Pitois-Dehu, Michel Roche, Christine Rousseau, Danièle Rousselier, Pierrette Ruchier-Berquet, Semroud, Jean-Paul Thibaudeau, Évelyne Torre, and Marie-Hélène Velu, as well as several other teachers who wished to remain anonymous.

VICHY

Introduction

Memory All Bent Out of Shape

Our nation's conscience is obsessed with memories of the Occupation. The observation has become a commonplace. More than twenty years ago already, these buried memories and this past, scantly known or disregarded by younger generations, suddenly resurfaced in the memory of the French people. They are now part of our political and cultural surroundings. They almost fit into our everyday routine. Controversies follow closely on the heels of revelations, as commemorations give way to legal proceedings. These four Dark Years[1] have come to occupy a place that is disproportionate with respect both to the context of French history and to that of the present international scene, which nevertheless has no lack of tragedies. The presence of this past is a symptom of unfinished mourning. It is also a warning signal for the future of French identity and the strength of its universalist values.

France is not the only nation to be thus confronted with the memory of World War II. Germany and the countries that were subjected to Nazi occupation are experiencing the same recurrent trauma. Ever since the fall of the Berlin Wall, the former Communist-bloc countries have been forced not only to face up to the outcome of their Stalinist past, but also to reevaluate and even revise what Stalinist discourse had for half a century said about the past, and in particular about World War II. Not even Israel has escaped growing protests over the mythologies which not long ago served in its foundation.[2] In France, discussion of these memories is too conflictual and painful for us not to be induced to question ourselves once more about the meaning of this constant retrospection.

In a work first published in 1987, *Le Syndrome de Vichy*,[3] which was intended to be a history of the memory of the Occupation since 1944, one of the authors of this book had already taken up the issue.[4] His conclusion was that in the seventies and eighties, reminiscences of the war era had resulted in an increasingly obsessive presence of that past. However, unlike quarrels over other periods of French history—the French Revolution, for exam-

I

ple—discussions about Vichy or the Resistance no longer oppose two or more clearly identified ideological camps each bearing rival accounts of what happened. In the case of the Occupation, there are no partisans of "1789" fighting against defenders of "1793," nor are there any "jacobins" fighting against "vendéens."[5] The legitimacy of the Resistance—if not of all the members of the Resistance—is not at issue for a majority of French people of all ages, on the Right as well as on the Left, even though the memory of the Resistance has for several years suffered revisionist assaults and its status within the context of national memory seems less prominent than before. As for the Pétainist[6] view—the myth of the "protective shield" —it remains confined to the extreme Right and a handful of isolated intellectuals. The official rehabilitation of Vichy has never been in the making, even if those who ardently desire it are speaking out with fewer inhibitions than before.

The real issues lie elsewhere. The inevitable question is that of the general attitude of the French people *on the whole* during World War II. What continues to weigh heavily in the balance are the consequences of the arrival of a regime that, after the collapse of 1940, sought to break with republican tradition, for in the beginning Marshall Pétain—if not his government —enjoyed a wide consensus. As in other European countries, the defeat and the Nazi occupation brought on various forms of civil war. But the internal fractures were not only ideological. They were equally social, cultural, and psychological. They were not limited to a confrontation between "resisters" and "collaborators," but split an entire country. That is what accounts for the gravity of the aftermath.

It could be said that this tragic period spared no social group, no political player, and not a single French citizen. Every family still bears the marks of sufferings endured, be they physical or moral: deprivations, the prolonged absence of a prisoner of war, or loss of a loved one during military battles, including those on the French mainland in 1940, those in Africa and the Middle East from 1940 to 1943, as well as the campaigns of 1944 to 1945. Suffering also came from racial and political repression and persecutions, as well as from bombing, not to mention the deaths occurring during the Liberation fighting. Many French have retained the sometimes embarrassing, sometimes shameful memory of large and small acts of cowardice, which were characteristic of the time when people fed on rutabagas and Jerusalem artichokes: they did have to live with the enemy and survive the ordeal. These memories live side by side with those that have become less common in recent years: memories of courage, even heroism, which were much more widespread than is commonly believed.

Granted, the emphasis—historically justified, but belated—on the singular nature of the genocide of the Jews forbids us from putting all the victims on the same level, or rather it forbids us from putting all the crimes committed together with all the sufferings endured. But individual memory often ignores or is unaware of hierarchies (which are moreover variable) imposed by collective memory. This ever increasing tension, between those who bear a memory now largely recognized and maintained and those who sometimes feel left out, further explains part of why present quarrels just will not go away. It is as if the entire array of victims along with the entire array of heroes, not to mention the others—the great majority—still had not been given the places that they respectively deserve in our nation's memory.

Here again, this is not a new observation. But in recent years, the "Vichy syndrome" seems to have evolved. The present obsession is being fed by a two-fold feeling of guilt maintained not only by voices belonging to younger generations, but also, at times, by some of those who lived through the period and have forgotten that they were of an entirely different mindset at the close of the war. The French are supposedly "guilty": guilty of having accepted a regime and worshiped its leader, both of which either committed or allowed abominable crimes for the sake of a certain idea of France; but the French are also supposedly guilty of not having managed, or not having been able, or not having been willing, to deal "otherwise" with the aftermath of the Occupation. At times, nothing is said in this two-fold accusation about the basic fact—namely, the Nazi occupation—which singularly limited the possible choices, including those available to the Vichy regime: aside from its ideological presuppositions, one of the aims of state collaboration was precisely the desire to loosen the occupant's stranglehold, by accepting defeat and bargaining for a place, however modest, in the Nazi Europe that was to come. Nowadays it is sometimes even forgotten that the major crimes of the period, beginning with the extermination of the Jews, were premeditated by the Nazis and not by Vichy, which was in this matter only an accomplice, albeit an active accomplice, which leaves it entirely responsible. The present-day accusation also loses sight of the fact that at the time of the Liberation the matter of long-term repercussions was not dealt with in either a serene or light-hearted manner, but resulted from compromises painfully worked out on the spur of the moment and in the heat of events, sometimes before the war had ended. These are some of the facts presently making up new blind spots in our nation's memory. The children or grandchildren of the war generation, who, now that the tragedy has been overcome, have been constantly denouncing the lack of lucidity or the cowardice displayed by their elders, are all the more free to do so since they have been spared the fury of a world war and since they are lucky never to have been faced with such grave decisions.

Along with this partial reading of history, in the past few years, has come the desire to try or retry Vichy and the politics of Collaboration, as evidenced by the recent Touvier and Papon trials. This results in an implicit criticism of the way in which the purge was conducted, or in the rejection, this time explicit, of the desire to "turn the page" and remain silent, which was the attitude toward some aspects of these traumatic events that a majority of the French had maintained up until the end of the 1960s.

The "duty to remember" has led to a total denial of the legitimacy of the "right to forget." In such a view of things, this right, which had been affirmed for more than forty years, has supposedly just been an extension of the ambivalences and ambiguities stemming from the war, thus almost a self-declared collective amnesty. Present-day claims are thus coupled with the illusion that we can redo history and make up, albeit belatedly, for what *today* are felt to be the failings, gaps, and reductive mythologies that appeared after 1944. It is a process which is forgetting that the lapses of memory were serving useful purposes, and that not only collaborators on the run but also the great majority of the French, including some of the victims of the Nazis or of Vichy, were demanding such lapses of memory. It is a refusal to admit that, beyond morality, forgetting is an integral part of any construction of memory.

We make this observation not to plead secretly for sweeping away or pardoning crimes, which is the prerogative of only the victims, but rather to urge that there be a reflection on the uses of the past, on the sometimes ambiguous forms that the maintenance of memory can assume, and even more on ways of accepting the burden of the past without falling into empty lip service or compulsive rehashing of the same old story.

The authors of this book, both born ten years after the war, have not always avoided the pitfalls pointed out herein, particularly in their previous works, whose effects they have moreover not managed to control. The historian[7] had not foreseen that his attempt to provide a scholarly analysis of the nation's memory and of the uses of the past might in turn become an instrument used no longer to help understand a social phenomenon, but to denounce it in retrospect. Neither had the journalist[8] foreseen that his investigations and his concern for making regularly available to the public historical information about Vichy—often unknown to most people—would also help serve some causes that, while commendable, nevertheless abandon the search for truth that their promoters claim to follow. But even if we had been fully aware of these risks, we would not have changed at all the tenor of what we said.

That is one of the motives that have led us to undertake this essay. But denouncing the aberrations of memory, or rather what is aberrant in some discourses about Vichy, was only worthwhile if the endeavor went beyond simple criticism to try to analyze the current obsession. The nature of this obsession has not really changed for twenty years, but it is now much more stridently expressed. Quarrels about the memory of Vichy, the Resistance, or Genocide are having more and more concrete effects: they are calling the highest governmental officials to account and requiring them to take a position, to give full public disclosure of such and such event, to unveil some true state secrets and to refute the phony ones; they are mobilizing the media, who are devoting an increasing portion of their pages and programs to the subject; they are setting into motion cumbersome and complex legal proceedings, which are to decide the fate of individual lives; they are having repercussions on teaching and research; they are influencing, both locally and nationally, the policy of commemorations, the creation of museums, the official placing or unauthorized removal of plaques and stone monuments. They sometimes have a paralytic effect: a countless number of our politicians have gotten caught up with slips of the tongue or blunders and then have had to do an about-face as soon as they were confronted with the issue. This work attempts to shed light on the matter by studying some cases in point which have highlighted current events in recent years, ranging from the government's handling of the genuinely false "Jewish card indexes," to the flap over the flowers sent on behalf of the president to the Ile d'Yeu.[9] Not only does this past still weigh heavily upon our present, it is moreover still helping to make up the world of our imagination. It would be only a slight exaggeration to say that never since the end of the forties has the debate over Vichy been so heated. Never has this past given a stronger impression that it could not manage to go away.

One might object that it must not "go away," that "vigilance" requires unrelenting exercise of the "duty to remember," and that amnesia is an unforgivable sin. We unhesitatingly agree: our respective books and articles testify to the fact. But the duty to remember does not entail a right to ignorance. Maintaining memory does not imply that what is said in the name of memory can escape criticism. Granted, commemorations or devout observances have their legitimacy, and it is fitting that critical distance or historical nuance not always be included in them. Nevertheless, one cannot demand that a nation look its past squarely in the face while at the same time making the duty to remember into a dogma. For some years now, memory has regained its rightful place. The term has even experienced a real success in the press and the media. But if this is accomplished to the detriment of history and truth, it is an empty achievement: one cannot forget or disregard history and truth for the sake of fighting against the lapse of memory.

Reminders

Since 1944, the memories and representations of World War II have gone through several phases. Four of these phases have been highlighted in *The Vichy Syndrome*.[10] The first, "Unfinished Mourning," extended over the years immediately following the war up until the mid-1950s: this was a period marked by the necessity of getting rid of the stigma of the war, the enemy occupation, and infighting.

On that score, it seems absolutely necessary to recall that, throughout this first phase, the purge constituted a political and social event of great proportions. This is a factor that, especially in justifying recent crimes against humanity proceedings in the courts, is completely underestimated when it is not purely and simply forgotten, as is the case when certain commentators state that "Vichy has never been brought to trial."[11] Granted, this purge was inconsistent; for example, it hit collaborationist[12] intellectuals harder than those in business, yet the assistance furnished by businessmen (whether because of pressure, necessity, or tactical maneuvering) was infinitely more substantial for the Reich's war effort. The purge was incomplete, since on the one hand it allowed a number of collaborators whose record was particularly loaded to escape, while on the other hand it produced flagrant injustices. The purge failed to understand fully the specific nature of French anti-Semitism and to evaluate properly the role Vichy played in the application of the "Final Solution" in France—even if there again, this omission is now being exaggerated in order to justify court cases against former collaborators or Vichy officials.[13] Some current discourses on the subject are moreover not aware of the extent to which the refusal to make distinctions between resistance victims, Jewish victims, even others (such as those enrolled in the "Service du travail obligatoire" [STO],[14] who were by their own desire called "work deportees" at the time) was widely shared in public opinion, even among the victims themselves. This is a point that we will come back to repeatedly in this book, for it shows the discrepancy between the demands of the past and those of today.

In spite of its weaknesses, the purge was an event of indisputable breadth. Out of one hundred cases examined by the High Court[15] that judged Vichy officials, forty-five resulted in dismissal of charges or simple acquittal, fifteen in national degradation (including seven sentences suspended because of acts of resistance, as was the case in 1949 for René Bousquet), twenty-two in prison sentences and forced labor (including five in absentia), eighteen in death penalties (including ten in absentia), of which five (including the death sentence given to Philippe Pétain) were commuted and three were carried out: the executions of Pierre Laval, Joseph Darnand, and Fernand de Brinon. The toll from sentences handed down by criminal courts ("cours de justice") and civilian courts ("chambres civiques") (which had to evaluate a new legal definition: that of "national indignity," which could lead to the sentence of "national degradation," loss of civil and political rights) is clearly heavier: 310,000 cases involving 350,000 people, in other words almost one French citizen out of a hundred, were examined. Out of these cases, 140,000 were dismissed prior to investigation (lack of evidence) and 43,000 afterward (charges declared void or without merit). The remaining 127,000 cases resulted in 58,000 decisions in criminal courts and 69,000 decisions in civil courts. The criminal courts handed down acquittals in 12 percent of their cases, national degradations in 6 percent of their cases, prison sentences or forced labor in 70 percent of their cases (including 4 percent in absentia and 4 percent for life without parole), and death sentences in 12 percent of their cases (including more than half in absentia), out of which 767 were followed by execution. The civil courts decided on national degradations in 67 percent of their cases, acquittals in 28 percent of their cases, and suspended sentences on account of resistance activity in 5 percent of their cases.

To these results must be added those of the military tribunals, whose operations remain little known, but which condemned to death and executed nearly 800 people. This means that the number of *legal* death sentences carried out was about 1,500, double the official figure, which concerns only the criminal courts. In all, the judiciary purge together with the on-the-spot, extra-legal purge (which created about 9,000 victims, mainly before the Allied landing and during Liberation fighting) took the lives of 10,000 to 11,000 people. In addition, more than 30,000 (and not 11,343, the official number) civil servants, magistrates, and military personnel were sanctioned in their professional life, as were many executives and employees in the private sector. This general toll can be deemed light or on the contrary heavy. That is a matter of opinion. But at the very least it deserves to be taken into consideration before one writes that Vichy has never been brought to trial.[16]

The dilemmas facing the political authorities of the time, even though these authorities came from the ranks of the Resistance, which had made the punishment of traitors one of its priorities, are underestimated even more than the purge's physical toll. Were they to abide by the letter of the law at the risk of making the purge slow and ineffective, or could they skirt sacred principles at the risk of favoring vengeance over justice, and thus going against the restoration of rule by law, which was one of the priorities of the Resistance? For how long, to what degree of responsibility, and according to what scale of punishments and sanctions were they to carry out the process, knowing that striking a balance was an absolute social necessity? An overly mild purge could have led to social explosion; an excessive purge, especially during the time of 1945 to 1946 when things were returning to normal, could have led to a similar result. Was it possible to remove tens of thousands of civil servants, magistrates, company heads, in other words, sanction the cream of the country without necessarily being able to replace them, when the reconstruction of a country devastated by war was also a priority?

It is in this context, and in taking into account the widely varying objectives that the provisional government had assigned to the purge, that one must evaluate its shortcomings and omissions. To claim that collaborators could have been judged according to criteria that only the perspective of hindsight, a better knowledge of history, and a sharper awareness of the peculiarities of the time can offer, is simply nonsense.[17] This is nevertheless an extremely widespread idea these days. It is amazing that the real issues of the purge, which went beyond the simple concern for punishing the guilty, are so poorly known, especially since we have for several years witnessed similar dilemmas in the new states or regimes springing up from the disintegration of the Soviet bloc. By insisting—most often to no avail—that the past must enlighten the present, we forget that the present can sometimes allow us to better understand the past.

Likewise, it is first in the context of the Liberation, and then in that of the Cold War, that we must understand what was said and done to weld national unity back together. General de Gaulle, a good number of political leaders, and the majority of the French people were agreed on downplaying the homegrown character of the Vichy regime and on hiding the fact that it fit into a long ideological tradition in France. The domestic and international imperatives of the postwar period thus favored a patriotic view of the tragedy that had occurred: in the purge, collaborators were judged as traitors more than as French fascists and the Vichy regime was termed the "de facto authority," whose legality and legitimacy were completely denied. Collaboration on the whole was considered an incidental digression, a dramatic event due to a minority, since the Resistance had exemplified the values of the "Eternal France." At least that was the dominant view of the period, which moreover General de Gaulle had articulated beginning with his first appeals in 1940.[18]

From the years 1944 to 1945 on, the nation's memory was polarized by the Gaullist memory on one side and by the Communist memory on the other. Even though they were implacable adversaries, Gaullists and Communists, who made up the two main political currents in postwar France, shared a certain view of history, since, like the Gaullists, the Communists stressed that Collaboration had been a criminal but marginal occurrence, and since they defined the Resistance both as a patriotic reaction of the masses and as an alliance of social classes. However, Communist discourse also contained a "revolutionary" component that, in 1944 to 1945, was also found in the discourse of other resistance movements, but which was absent from the Gaullist account.

These two memories were to forge the myths of the fifties and sixties. They left aside whole groups of people who did not fit into their heroic scheme of things—for example, prisoners of war, which is an important thing to recall when one thinks of the itinerary followed by someone like François Mitterrand—or else they cast a shadow on others who at the time did not wish to be different from the rest of the nation or who were not perceived as categories of people who suffered a specific fate. This was of course the case for the Jews, particularly those who survived the Genocide, who were less outspoken than resisters who had been deported. Up until the end of the sixties, the memory of Nazi barbarity was embodied at Le Mont Valérien or at Oradour, not at Le Vél' d'Hiv' (which was even destroyed) nor at Izieu (a place almost nobody knew).[19] It was symbolized by Buchenwald, the concentration camp, and not Auschwitz-Birkenau, the extermination camp. The distinction between Nazi camps to which opponents and resisters, beginning with Germans who had fought against Hitler, were deported, and those where Jews as well as Gypsies and "asocial" people were exterminated, is really very recent.

This period of "repression," the second phase of the "Vichy syndrome," which spanned the years between 1954 and 1971, began right after amnesty laws had been passed in the heart of the Cold War between 1951 and 1953. Legal pardon was accompanied by the return to the political arena of former Vichyites who helped rebuild the conservative and reactionary right wing, which in 1944 had been discredited by the support it had given to Pétain. But the contingency of such decisions should not make us overlook the ineluctable necessity of promulgating such measures sooner or later: even if these laws stirred up violent opposition at the time, they nevertheless conformed to an ancestral tradition, which has been used in France after every crisis of national unity. Whether this is deplorable or commendable is once again a matter of conscience. But contemporary commentary, only interested in seeing abstract but immanent government imperatives in the very principle of amnesty, tends to overlook this aspect of things. This is forgetting that the laws of 1951 and 1953 were passed by Parliament at the initiative of the two largest parties that came out of the ranks of the Resistance (the "Mouvement républicain populaire," of Christian-democratic leanings created in 1944, and the "Rassemblement du peuple français," founded by General de Gaulle in 1947), and contrary to the wishes of the Communists and Socialists, although the latter group was not hostile to the idea of amnesty itself. And these amnesty laws were originally intended to wipe individual offenses off the slate more than to eliminate the memory of Collaboration as such. But one has to believe that they corresponded to a deeply felt social need, to such an extent that they ushered in a long phase of national amnesia.

Once the Algerian war was over, de Gaulle's Fifth Republic[20] sought to avoid saying anything in official statements that might recall the internal divisions of the recent past, including both the divisions occasioned by the Occupation as well as those arising from decolonization. This domestic policy was coupled with the foreign policy of Franco-German reconciliation and of the creation of the European Community. In this respect, it is worthwhile to recall that the "résistancialiste" myth[21] created as early as

1940 by General de Gaulle, had repercussions beyond the domestic scene. It allowed France to be a part of the great victorious alliance and thus to be subsequently offered a seat on the United Nations Security Council, even though it also owes this especially to Churchill and his stormy support of de Gaulle. This position in the international community owes its origin more to the Gaullist vision of history, which throughout the war had been imposed on the three other countries (the United States, Great Britain, and the USSR) that had to bear the real burden of crushing the Third Reich, than to its actual influence on global affairs.[22]

Along with the policy of remaining silent about Vichy, the memory of the Resistance became one of the pillars of the new regime. In December 1964, the ashes of Jean Moulin, "the unifier," were transferred to the Pantheon; he was thus officially recognized as an ecumenical figure over other heroes of the clandestine struggle. In cinema, in literature, on television, which was taking off dramatically at the time, and even in works of history, the Resistance took up all the space, while leaving huge gaps: Collaboration, the National Revolution,[23] French anti-Semitism, French internment camps, or even the role of foreigners in the Resistance, to cite only a few of the topics that are on the contrary widely discussed today.

The third phase, that of the "broken mirror," came about in the beginning of the 1970s. The scandals caused by Marcel Ophuls' iconoclastic film *The Sorrow and the Pity* and by Georges Pompidou's pardon of a former member of the Milice,[24] Paul Touvier, an unfamiliar figure for most French people, set in motion a tidal wave. Then, the consequences of May 1968,[25] the departure and subsequent death of General de Gaulle, his successor's abandonment of the "résistancialiste" tradition, and the younger generations' questioning of such traditions exploded postwar myths.

It is with the last phase beginning in the 1970s that the Dark Years start to be an issue in obsessive memory. The awakening of Jewish identity, which for the first time since the Liberation claimed its "right to be different," sharpened the focus on the memory of the Genocide: from then on, this would be at the heart of every discussion about World War II, in the same manner as it would in other countries at that time. The direct and decisive result was a series of indictments for crimes against humanity. The memory of those Dark Years also invaded political debate. It became once again, if not for the first time, a classic means of disqualifying adversaries, whoever they might be. Throughout the eighties, allusions to some official's past intruded into almost all the big political debates: on the eve of the first European elections in December 1978, Jacques Chirac, directing his fire at President Valéry Giscard d'Estaing, denounced the "foreign party" in his "call of Cochin"; in the 1981 presidential campaign, before the Left came to power, the followers of both candidates tried to smear their opponents with stories about the Pétainist past of either the rival candidate or his family; in 1984, during the Parliament's debate over the press, first Robert Hersant and then François Mitterrand were both targeted, the former by the Left and the latter by the Right; for over ten years, the past of Georges Marchais, who was a volunteer worker in Germany during the war and not a forced laborer, made the headlines; just recently in January 1992, activists for the Socialist party brought up the subject of Vichy's "special sections"[26] by inviting to their party seat, rue de Solférino, the examining magistrate who had come to investigate in the context of the Urba-Graco affair; while in July 1993, when for the first time the nation was observing a day commemorating the massive Vél' d'Hiv' roundup, Bernard Tapie spoke of the "Gestapo" to denounce the methods used by the courts in the soccer scandal involving the teams "Olympique de Marseille" and "Valenciennes." The permanent presence in the political arena of a nationalistic, xenophobic, and anti-Semitic extreme Right ultimately helped keep references to Vichy in the limelight, since the National Front party[27] could not or would not rid itself of the cumbersome legacy of fascism and Collaboration, in spite of the wishes of some of its young leaders.

Phony Taboos and Historical Fantasies

For twenty years, Vichy has thus been the object of nationwide dispute. Yet never has so much been made of "taboos" as it is today. Some media sources, hungrier for sensationalism than for investigative reporting, cannot bring up a single court case, controversy, or book involving World War II without claiming that their news stories have been put together in spite of attempts to hush them up, even though the facts in question, available in scores of historical works, are at the same time making the headlines of all the papers! Never has access to public archives of that era been so often denounced as impossible, although in fact these archives have never been more frequently opened and studied, thus supplying the raw material for the decisive historiographical breakthroughs that have been made over the last fifteen years.

This ritual engagement in pseudo-revelations dealing with phony taboos seems like a reminiscence of the seventies and eighties. Beyond the publicity-stunt aspect of the matter, which is lost only on the naïve, it shows how difficult it is for some people to identify accounts which did come to light during those years and which did indeed often remove taboos and shed light into murky matters. Not all of today's valorous activists can even come close to being able to boast of the tremendous work of documentation achieved by Serge Klarsfeld and his assistants, not all reporters can claim to match the scoop made by Jacques Derogy (who in 1972 revealed the pardon granted to Paul Touvier the previous year), nor could every filmmaker equal the exploit of Marcel Ophuls in 1969,[28] nor every historian have the same impact as the American Robert Paxton in 1973, nor, finally, could every writer have the talent of Patrick Modiano. Though that might grieve certain belated militants for memory, one has to admit that today the Dark Years are anything but taboo. What this time period needs is not for its secrets to be revealed but for the mass of information thrown out to stir up public opinion to be organized and put into perspective.

Historical work on the subject is constantly moving forward and becoming more diversified: one only has to browse through bookstore displays to be convinced of that fact. And that is not just the result of the commemorative boom; it is already an old story. Thus the *Bibliographie annuelle de l'histoire de France* notes the fact that between 1982 and 1987 the number of references on the subject (including French books and doctoral theses, French and foreign scholarly articles) averaged some 427 per year, in other words 3 to 4 percent of *all* scholarly publications devoted to French history. Between 1988 and 1992, this average rose to 881 references per year, with the portion of historical publications about World War II increasing regularly from 4.5 percent in 1988 to 8.2 percent in 1992![29]

Similarly, one has only to switch on television and flip from one channel to the next to realize that, whether in terms of fictional narratives, documentaries, panel discussions, history programs, not to mention the news whenever a story takes a dramatic new turn, the amount of broadcast time devoted to the subject of World War II has increased exponentially over the last few years. Between 1994 and 1995, the two major public networks (France 2 and France 3) alone devoted almost a hundred hours, half of which were regional programs, of fictional narratives, documentaries, and live broadcasts (the commemorative ceremonies on June 6 and August 25, 1994) to this period.[30] We have come a long way from the "censure by inertia" to which *The Sorrow and the Pity* fell victim in the seventies! Granted, the quality of programs is uneven, and they convey the most widely spread clichés of the moment. But some (like *Les Brûlures de l'Histoire*[31]) are of high quality. Documentaries such as the film *Haute-Savoie*, made in 1992 by Denis Chegaray and Olivier Doat, and which deals with the history of the Maquis and the extralegal purge in the region, now take up the least known subjects. Other documentaries, such as Blanche Finger's and William Karel's *Opération Vent Printanier*, which is about the fate of children who had escaped the Vél' d'Hiv' roundup and which was shown during *La Marche du siècle*[32] on June 10, 1992, give an original and accurate treatment of subjects that have now been aired many times.

This prime-time program, one of the most faithfully watched in its category, is moreover characteristic of the way in which television can deal with these subjects: the best is found side by side with the worst. Between June 1992 and February 1994, its producers devoted no less than six features (a record number) to World War II: "Fifty Years Ago: The Vél' d'Hiv' Round-up" (June 10, 1992); "Spies Above Suspicion" (February 3, 1993), which was devoted to Thierry Wolton's sensational book, *Le Grand Recrutement*, and which suggested that Jean Moulin be regarded as a "Soviet agent";[33] "Resisters Speak Out" (May 19, 1993), which was an attempt somehow to make up for the damage done by the calumnies uttered during the previous program; "The Duty to Remember" (June 30, 1993), devoted mainly to the issue of the archives of the war years; "Justice, History, and Memory" (September 8, 1993), a program which screened the film that Paul Lefèvre had made from footage of the Barbie trial; and finally, "A Handful of the Righteous[34] Against the Holocaust" (February 23, 1994), a program devoted to Steven Spielberg's film *Schindler's List*. The programs about the Vél' d'Hiv' roundup, Klaus Barbie, or Oskar Schindler and other "righteous individuals" provided poignant testimony and information presented with a suitable amount of historical rigor for a prime-time broadcast. They indisputably contributed to a better knowledge of the war years and helped make the events of the time more "true to life" in a positive way. Two of them, however, in going along with the scandals of the moment, ended up misinforming the public. Such was the case for the program devoted to "spies": Thierry Wolton was permitted to speak all he wanted, while Daniel Cordier, Jean Moulin's erudite biographer (and also his secretary), invited at the very last moment, could hardly get a word in without being rudely cut off by the announcer. The same is true for the program dealing with the National Archives, during which a documentary based on pure intellectual fraud managed to give credence to the notion that the public archives dating from the Occupation were being kept in a secrecy worthy of Fort Knox.[35] This edition of the program *La Marche du siècle* also featured another "taboo," that of the plight of the mentally ill during the Occupation: it recirculated the idea that tens of thousands of mental patients had been deliberately exterminated by Vichy, as were the patients euthanized by the Third Reich.[36] One could even hear in the commentary of the report devoted to the subject that "In the Vichy regime, Alexis Carrel administrated a good number of psychiatric hospitals," a detail given by the TV producers and consisting of a pure fabrication. There again, the program was relating the latest theories. Not content with making up a "genocide," some people claimed to have found the one responsible for it in the person of Dr. Alexis Carrel, who is known for his theories about eugenics and who in recent years has become a fashionable new diabolical figure.[37] In fact, Alexis Carrel was never part of the Vichy regime and absolutely never had anything to do with the policies implemented in psychiatric hospitals at the time. As for his inspiration, he derived it more from American eugenicists (he was in the United States until 1940) than from the Nazis.[38] It is one thing to find that some of his theories are nauseating; it is quite another to claim that they were the cause of a mass crime that Vichy premeditated and then covered up, when in fact this crime is imaginary.

This is one example among countless others that shows to what extent a television program, a quality one at that, can blow out of proportion unfounded controversies which, without the TV cameras, would only have a limited and inconsequential impact if they ever reached the public at all. Such polemical debates have proliferated during recent years, spreading false information at the same time.[39] We find ourselves in a situation which is exactly the opposite of a "taboo," since we are often seeing history rewritten according to fantasies. Far from contributing to a heightened awareness, this rewriting only spreads confusion, making it impossible to sort out the real advances in historical research from the phony ones.

Our book comes out of an encounter of a journalist and an historian. While our respective viewpoints, investigative tools, and methods of analysis differ, we share a common interest in the Occupation era. Our professional vocations moreover provide us a special vantage point on the subject. But our book is above all the result of a convergence of mind and of perspectives common to our generation.

We have been following the erratic leaps and starts of memory for several years. We have each in our own way participated in current debates over Vichy, its shadowy areas, its blank pages, which remain, or at one time still remained, to be written. But we feel that what is commonly said about the period is increasingly leading people astray and is running the risk of leading to an impasse. The growing insistence on the duty to remember, which is now proclaimed right and left, as well as the solemn calls to "vigilance," often relegate the concern for truth and the necessity of critical perspective to the background.

Our work attempts to describe this dangerous turn of events by analyzing some recent symptoms: the controversy over the commemoration of the Vél' d'Hiv' roundup in the summer of 1992; the scandal of the "Jewish card file," which broke out in November 1991, and which still has not come to closure; the Paul Touvier trial, which took place in the spring of 1994, and to which we devote a large part of the book. Our book also takes up some of the highly charged symbolical issues of memory: access to archives, the running of archives, the social role of historians, the place now given to the teaching of the history of World War II in secondary schools, as well as the role played in these matters by François Mitterrand, the President of the Rebublic, responsible for national unity—thus for national memory— and François Mitterrand the politician, typical of a generation that lived through the tragedies of the Occupation and its aftermath.

In some ways, this book constitutes an extension of *The Vichy Syndrome,* since it covers a chronological sequence subsequent to the one (from 1990 through 1994) included in the latest edition of the book and since it uses the same system of interpretation. But in other ways, it sets itself clearly apart. It does not claim to be a scholarly work and has not sought to give an exhaustive treatment of the subject. We intend for this book to be a joint effort in reflecting and taking a politically committed intellectual stance on the burning questions which concern us as journalists and historians as much as citizens. We felt it was urgent to get away from the sanctification of the memory of World War II that we have been seeing recently: in our opinion, that is the biggest favor we could do for it.

1

Vél' d'Hiv'
Or the Impossible Commemoration

It was supposed to be a great occasion, a once-in-a-lifetime event. July 1992: Would the fiftieth anniversary of the massive police roundup at the Vélodrome d'Hiver make it possible to make a clean breast of memory? On July 16 and 17, 1942, 13,152 Jews—including 3,118 men, 5,919 women, and 4,115 children—were arrested by French police, on the basis of agreements reached a few days before between René Bousquet, Secretary General of Police with the Vichy government, and Karl Oberg, head of the SS and of German police in occupied France. The massive Vél' d'Hiv' roundup had been preceded by other mass arrests of Jews, which began in May 1941. But for the first time, it was women, children, and elderly people who were targeted, and not just men siezed under the pretext of "terrorism." Entire families were thus deported in the context of the "Final Solution," which, since the beginning of 1942, had been hitting the occupied territories in the West.

This event has become the symbol of Vichy's complicity in the Genocide. Its fiftieth anniversary was expected to be a very special occasion for the memory of the nation, and not just for the memory of the victims. This was to be the high point of a sensitivity that had increased with time, especially because of stalled legal proceedings against former dignitaries of the French State:[1] René Bousquet and his assistant Jean Leguay, organizers of the mass arrest, and Maurice Papon, former Secretary General of the Prefecture of the Gironde region, in the occupied zone. The dismissal of charges granted to the former member of the Milice Paul Touvier by the Court of Appeals in Paris on April 13 of that same year, 1992, had moreover given a special significance to a commemoration that was to take place in a setting of scandal and revolt against a ruling seen as iniquitous, even at the highest levels of the state.

But for the French, this new rendezvous with their history failed to live up to its promise: instead, it once again stirred up misgivings and controversy. People saw a President of the Republic booed during a memorial observance. People saw the development of an anachronistic "constitutional" dispute. People saw frustrations cropping up without the prospect of any immediate relief. The long-awaited tribute took place amid confusion and embarrassment, as if serenity were no longer possible. The hope of seeing the resolution of this conflict, which continued to pit France against its past, once again sank in a crisis of memory.

"Just Make a Gesture, Mr. President!"

The occasion had been preceded—and followed—for several weeks by a little drama: the quest for a "gesture," the object of a more and more abstract desire. A few people were hoping for such a gesture, some requested it, while still others demanded it from the President. People expected him to make a symbolic act in order that Vichy's responsibility in the "Final Solution" might be acknowledged. François Mitterrand first evaded the problem, then became angry and stated that the gesture that people were trying to impose upon him was not in the offing. When the controversy soured, he let it be known that he was thinking of an initiative, but that it would come in its time. It came indeed, but after the fateful day of July 16.

At first, only a few isolated voices had put forth the idea of a gesture as a sort of remedy to judicial delays, or even as reaction to the ideological aberrations of certain magistrates. Above all, it was a matter of transferring the charge of acknowledging Vichy's crimes against the Jews to the political realm. Whether it was justified or not, this expectation by much of the public was real. Some people brought up such a possibility while recalling the gesture of King Juan Carlos, who came on behalf of Spain to ask forgiveness for the expulsion of Jews in 1492. Others recalled the memory of Chancellor Willy Brandt, kneeling spontaneously before the monument to the victims of the Warsaw ghetto on December 7, 1970. At this point, it was a matter of expressing a desire, not an explicit request. That did not mean that the Republic was held accountable for the deeds of Vichy, but that the nation was now ready officially to accept all aspects of the history of the Occupation. If it had been spontaneous—the Republic was after all Vichy's first victim—such a gesture might have had a significant effect. At least that is what a certain number of us thought.[2]

However, events took another turn. The desire was quickly transformed into a haughty demand. As usually happens in France, this demand was expressed in the form of a petition initiated by a "Vél' d'Hiv' 42 Committee" and signed by over two hundred artists, university professors, and writers, and published by the newspaper *Le Monde* on June 17, 1992, with the paper's backing. Here is the complete text of the petition:

At the end of the Second World War, a few high officials of the Vichy French State were rightly condemned for treason and collaboration with the enemy. However, the highest authorities of the government of the Republic have not always officially acknowledged or declared that this same Vichy French State persecuted the Jews and committed crimes against them for the sole and unique reason that they were Jews.

Thus it is that in public speeches and on the rare commemorative plaques, the Jews who were deported from France and murdered in Nazi camps most often appear as victims of only the barbarity of the German occupying forces, even though they were pursued, rounded up, and handed over to the Germans by the French State just because they were Jews.

It was indeed by its own authority, and without the German occupying forces having requested it, that the Vichy French State separated the Jews from the national community by enacting the "Jewish Statutes," signed and promulgated by Philippe Pétain, "Marshall of France, Chief of the French State," on October 3, 1940.

The same Vichy French State then applied a policy of systematic discrimination against the Jews, including the establishment of police files, confiscation of property, exclusion, extortions, and humiliations.

It ordered their arrest by French police and *gendarmes*, who worked in close collaboration with the Gestapo and units of the German *Feldgendamerie*. Then it crowded them together in camps such as those at Drancy, Pithiviers, Beaune-la-Rolande, Gurs, Rivesaltes, Argelès, Saïda, etc.

Finally, it handed over, or facilitated the Germans' arrest of 75,000 Jews from France (including 24,000 French nationals and 51,000 foreigners and denaturalized citizens), men, women, and children of all ages who were then deported and murdered in Nazi extermination camps.

On the occasion of the fiftieth anniversary of the Vél' d'Hiv' roundup next July 16 and 17, we ask that the head of state, the President of the French Republic, officially declare and acknowledge that the Vichy French State is responsible for persecutions and crimes against the Jews of France.

This symbolic act is demanded by the memory of the victims and by their descendants. It is also a demand of France's collective memory which suffers from this silence.

Ultimately, it is the very idea of the French Republic, faithful to its founding principles, which is at stake.[3]

For a number of those who drew up this text, their interest in the memory of Vichy was quite recent and at times very naïve. "I wondered why hadn't we had this idea before" (Viviane Forrester). "I discovered this incredible gap consisting of the non-recognition of Vichy's responsibility" (Paul Otchakovsky-Laurens). "We must be unrelenting about Vichy, because I recognize in our current political life so many attitudes, gestures, and words that recall the National Revolution" (Jean-Marc Roberts). "A step such as the one we are requesting will really forge anew the Republic" (Jean-Pierre Le Dantec). "There must be an official, historicized acknowledgement of Vichy's role, one that institutes a polemical relation, bearing truth, with the effect of breaking France's history in two" (Christian Jambet).[4]

A generational effect might well explain this belated militancy for the sake of memory, which over the last few years has become a new war horse for intellectuals, especially for certain veterans of May 1968 and the like. Hence a certain pomposity, which is not without ingenuousness: these intellectuals were finally taking things into their own hands, denouncing the "silences" and "taboos" which supposedly still hung over Vichy. As sincere as it might have been, this initiative posed a series of problems that are characteristic of present aberrations in discussions of the past.

First of all, the petition leaves out the purge, which is reduced to the judgment of "a few high officials" of Vichy. It "forgets" the Liberation trials and transforms their inconsistencies, weaknesses, and inequities, which have been underlined many times before, into a total vacuum that supposedly needs filling fifty years after the fact. The very first draft did not include the slightest allusion to the purge, and it took extensive negotiations for it to be in the final text. Further, nothing, not one single line, explains why Vichy's anti-Jewish policies were not taken into consideration in these trials, which focused only on treason and collaboration. Nothing reminds us that this was a reflection of the dominant mindset of that time and of a general feeling shared by all sectors of public opinion, and not an indication of some imaginary state imperative. That is why legal documents are silent about the subject. That is what explains the stances of that time, which are characterized by the almost total lack of any protest *specifically* concerning anti-Semitic crimes and persecutions. This protest came much later, since it cropped up in the 1970s.

Thus when the petition speaks of a "symbolic demand on behalf of the memory of the victims and of their descendants," it is really expressing the viewpoint of the latter: in other words, that of a good part of the petition writers themselves, thus of *another* generation. But by including the victims themselves, it cheats a bit with history by hiding the fact that this political demand had not been that of the survivors or of postwar Jewish institutions. Their priority had been to wipe out all aftereffects of the exclusion to which they had been subjected for four years. With the exception of a few isolated actions, French Jews like foreign Jews did not, after the Liberation, wish to demand justice for the crimes of Vichy and the collaborators as Jews per se. They did not want to be distinguished from the rest of the nation nor from other groups who suffered from the Occupation, even though they were not able at that time to measure the extent to which this aspect of the Occupation would be hushed up and what the consequences would be in the long term. Today's request is precisely a belated reaction to this silence. It is a request that does not belong to that time, even though it was signed by former resisters and deportees.

The petition implicitly conveys another current cliché: it gives the impression that the mass roundups of the summer of 1942 were undertaken upon the sole initiative of Vichy for ideological reasons in the logic of state anti-Semitism. In reality, they were first and foremost the consequence of the application by the occupying forces of the "Final Solution" in France, with Vichy agreeing to lend the decisive aid of the French police and administration to a demented plan that was not its own. The Vichy regime never had the intention of exterminating the Jews. It was content to exclude Jews and to give itself the possibility of detaining—often in inhumane and deadly conditions—foreign Jews (according to legal texts of 1940 to 1941). It is by virtue of a strategy, that of state collaboration, that it accepted—without any soul searching—a role in the "Final Solution," without asking any unnecessary questions about the destination of the trains that French police were loading. As in the case of the children which the Nazis were not then demanding but who were handed over, its reasoning did not follow a logic of extermination but of cold politics and bureaucracy, inconsiderate of human life. It moreover set up a discrimination between foreign Jews, handed over en masse, and French Jews, although almost 24,000 French Jews, including 8,000 children born in France to foreigners and 8,000 Jews denaturalized by Vichy, were also deported. We recall these facts not out of unbridled interest in nuance, but to reestablish the hierarchy of responsibilities. By harping on the crimes of Vichy alone, one ends up writing a history that writes off the one holding the primary responsibility, the Third Reich. In a petition addressed to the highest authority of the state and which moreover articulates "demands," respect for historical truth should have been an essential preoccupation.

When all is said and done, to claim that "France's collective memory [is supposedly] suffering from this silence," in other words from official non-recognition of Vichy's anti-Semitic crimes, is to give considerable weight to official memory. As if collective memory with its plurality need the pronouncements of the state to know, in 1992, what was the extent of Vichy's crimes. By transforming this desire of spontaneous recognition modeled after the gesture of Willy Brandt or that of Juan Carlos into an aggressive political demand, the petitioners themselves made it impossible for their demand to achieve its goal in the short term. By appearing to stigmatize a sort of collective, and thus general and indeterminate, guilt, or by pointing to the state as the only one reponsible for past silences, they were stirring up anachronistic controversies.

Should the Liberation Be Redone?

Gradually, this petition gained momentum, gathering signatures even among the President's followers. Tension mounted noticeably when, in the beginning of July 1992, the press disclosed that every year since 1987, the President of the Republic had regularly had flowers placed on the grave of ex-Marshall Pétain on the Ile d'Yeu.[5] This was not really a scoop, for the annual placing of flowers was not totally unknown. Nevertheless, the frequency of this tribute and the conditions surrounding it remained poorly known and few people had been interested. The presidential team refused to see anything but a strange, almost inexplicable, but unimportant insistance in the matter. The Élysée[6] brushed aside the few rare questions about this curious placing of flowers, specifying that it concerned a "republican tradition" which François Mitterrand was following as his predecessors had. Within the ranks of the Socialist party, curious reporters were regularly put off by the irritated embarrassment of their interlocutors. Those who knew had in fact chosen not to ask questions about a little matter so discrete and apparently minor that it was easy to forget. In July 1992, the context was obviously completely different.

This tribute, strangely termed "republican," had nothing traditional about it concerning Pétain. The habit was a recent one introduced by François Mitterrand himself. In the past, General de Gaulle had only had an arrangement (of chrysanthemums) placed on the tomb once, on November 10, 1968, for the fiftieth anniversary of the victory of 1918. He had had flowers placed on the graves of the victorious generals without excluding Philippe Pétain. This gesture was not well appreciated at the time . . . by some of Philippe Pétain's faithful followers. One of them tore the ribbon bearing General de Gaulle's name off the flower arrangement. As for Georges Pompidou, he had had flowers (anemones and mimosas) placed on Pétain's grave on only one exceptional occasion: on February 20, 1973, when Pétain's coffin was buried a second time. The coffin had been removed a few days before by an extreme right wing commando led by Hubert Massol, with the intention of transferring it to the ossuary at Douaumont:[7] this had long been the demand of those defending Pétain. But the coffin was found in the suburbs of Paris and brought back to the Ile d'Yeu. As for Valéry Giscard d'Estaing,[8] he also had consented only to a single tribute, on the occasion of the sixtieth anniversary of the end of World War I, on November 11, 1978. This initiative, however, aroused numerous reactions of indignation, for it came at a time when a number of reminiscences linked to the Occupation were in the air. Only a few days before, the newsmagazine *L'Express* had just published an interview with Louis Darquier de Pellepoix, former head of the General Commission on Jewish

Questions.[9] This was also when the public was discovering Robert Faurisson's negations of the Holocaust and the emergence of the "New Right."

It was in fact François Mitterrand who inaugurated the annual tradition. He had red roses placed on Pétain's grave on September 22, 1984, the day he shook hands with Chancellor Helmut Kohl at Verdun, and then again on June 15, 1986, on the occasion of the seventieth anniversary of the battle of Verdun, and then, since 1987, every year without exception on November 11.

In July 1992, after charges against Paul Touvier had been dismissed and while the controversy over the upcoming fiftieth anniversary of the Vél' d'Hiv' roundup was at its height, the disclosure of this habit of the President struck a nerve. In order to clear up these misgivings, the Élysée announced on July 10 that François Mitterrand would take part in the ceremony commemorating the fiftieth anniversary of the roundup on the sixteenth and would place flowers at the site of the regular gathering of Jewish organizations, where the stadium used to be. He had nevertheless previously indicated that his schedule would not permit him to attend. But the annoyance caused by the Comité Vél' d'Hiv's petition no doubt gave way to the concern for putting an end to disputes over his manner of handling the memory of the Dark Years. The rumor then began to be spread: the President would speak.

And indeed, he spoke. Not on the sixteenth, but on the fourteenth, Bastille Day. And he spoke clearly. After the military parade, during his traditional talk with reporters, François Mitterrand declared that the demands that had been addressed to him for several weeks were unreceivable:

> Throughout its entire history, the Republic has consistently adopted an attitude of complete openness, considering that the rights of citizens were to be applied to anyone recognized as a citizen and to French Jews in particular. So don't come asking this Republic to account for its deeds! It has done what it was supposed to. For two centuries during which different republics succeeded each other,[10] it was the Republic that decided on practically all the measures granting equality and citizenship. It was the Republic that decided the Algerian Jews would no longer be considered to be a sort of inferior race . . . The Republic has always been the one that offered its hand in order avoid racial segregation. So don't come and ask the Republic to account for its actions! But in 1940, there was a "French State," which was the Vichy regime, not the Republic. And this "French State" must be asked to account for its deeds: of course I will grant you that, how could I not grant it? I share completely the feeling of those who are petitioning me. But for that very reason, my point is that the Resistance, then the government of de Gaulle, and afterwards the Fourth Republic and the others were founded on the refusal of this "French State." We must be clear on this point.[11]

The response of the Comité Vél' d'Hiv' came without delay:

We knew that the State was dumb, now we see that it is deaf . . . According to
the President, we have no business holding the Republic accountable, since it
was the Republic that, in 1790, integrated the Jews in France as full-fledged
citizens . . . But how can the President of the Republic seriously suspect the
thousands who signed the Vél' d'Hiv' committee's appeal of being unaware
of all that? He would have people think that we supposedly want the Republic
to accuse itself of crimes that it has not committed. But there is no basis in the
text of the appeal for this confusion. We know well that before it perpetrated
its crimes, Vichy began by abolishing the Republic and doing away with its
motto. Similarly, no one thought that the gesture of Willy Brandt kneeling
at Auschwitz [sic] was directed against the Weimar Republic or the Federal
Republic.

We are told that Vichy's doings do not engage the responsibility of the
Republic, and that this State was only French in name. But it was nonetheless
served by French administrators, French magistrates, and French police who
massively accepted to swear an oath of loyalty to Pétain, to carry out inhumane orders and at times to take criminal initiatives themselves, forgetting
that they had been named to their position by a republican state. For everything that was done in France's name, the French State is accountable today.
To proclaim it formally is one way of remaining faithful to the republican
ideal and to the memory of all those who resisted the Nazis and their accomplices. Who better than the President of the Republic can put an end to the
official silence which has lasted for fifty years over one of the most sinister
pages in French history?

That is why we are reiterating our appeal for the president of the Republic, head of state, to deliver a formal declaration on the 16th of July at the very
site of the Vél' d'Hiv' roundup. Neither the placing of flowers during this
ceremony nor even eventual legal condemnations of individuals could take
the place of a political act involving the entire Nation.[12]

This response was in fact a new, more explicit petition. At the end of the
text, the signatories seemed to feel that henceforth the trials were less important than a political act. They went so far as to claim that any eventual
convictions would not engage the responsibility of the nation, forgetting
that some of them had themselves been demanding these trials for a long
time and, furthermore, that justice is theoretically rendered in the name of
the French people. More important, the petitioners, whether consciously
or not, had subtly gone from demanding an official condemnation of
Vichy's *anti-Semitic* crimes to demanding a *global* condemnation of the regime, there again forgetting that this condemnation had been massive and
general at the time of the Liberation. That is the whole difference between

the gesture that they were demanding of François Mitterrand and that of Willy Brandt: German crimes had been of a totally different dimension and the Third Reich had been the instigator of the Genocide, not an accomplice in a subservient position. But above all, the condemnation of Nazism was first of all the doing of the Allies before being that of the Germans. When German Chancellor Willy Brandt kneeled down in front of the Warsaw monument (and not at Auschwitz), he was in a way symbolically continuing the principles of Nuremberg, on a different level and for the sake of the new Germany.

By declaring itself this time to be acting no longer for the sake of remembering Jewish victims, but for the sake of resisters, the Comité Vél' d'Hiv's appeal was changing in nature: What was being requested was indeed a new condemnation of Vichy, a half a century later by a new generation, as if for this generation it were a matter of reenacting the script of the Liberation, and reenacting it better than their elders had, by avoiding their mistakes and their omissions. This was an attempt to redo the history of 1945 with the mindset of 1992.

July 16, 1992

The long-awaited day finally came. It turned into a disaster. At the site of the former Vélodrome d'Hiver, on the sidewalk of the Boulevard de Grenelle in the fifteenth arrondissement,[13] in an almost nonexistent place jammed between the elevated metro and a few dull-gray buildings, an immense crowd had gathered. There had never been as many people in previous years. For a long time, the solemn yearly gathering on July 16 had been observed quietly and without official support. The commemoration was of a private nature, since the Council Representing the Jewish Institutions of France (CRIF), which organized it, refused all official aid (and it had invited one government minister, the Minister of War Veterans, for the first time only in 1992). For the fiftieth anniversary, the Republic had come in royal style: the presidents of the National Assembly and the Senate, several ministers and members of Parliament, the president of the Constitutional Council, the police prefect, the regional prefect . . .

People listened silently to Louis Mexandeau, Secretary of State for War Veterans, who was speaking of the role of the French administration, "of which we can never stress enough that, save for a few exceptions, it lacked courage and honor," when the President of the Republic suddenly appeared. Whistles and jeers rose up immediately from the crowd: "Send Mitterrand to Vichy!" There were numerous and startling cries of the sort, which in a few seconds made the memorial ceremony sway over into a political incident. Some people tried in vain to cover the jeers with applause, and Henry Bulawko, the president of the Union of Resisters and Deported French Jews and vice president of the CRIF, who was presiding over the ceremony, cried out at the top of his lungs from the podium to denounce the "offense of the memory of the dead" and to demand that the demonstrators agree to "greet the President of the Republic with dignity." The President continued to walk forward in the middle of the crowd, his face frozen in a rigid smile. Jean Kahn, president of the CRIF, hastened to thank François Mitterrand for his presence which "confirms that republican France has no intention of hiding the dark hours of the Occupation and Collaboration." But when the President rose to go place flowers, shouts and whistles sounded again, smothered this time by the applause led by the organizers.

Robert Badinter then took the podium and gave his reaction with exceptional virulence. From this ceremony, newspapers and TV networks would retain the image of the president of the Constitutional Council, shaking the lectern and, in a sudden fit of anger, addressing the disturbers: "You have made me ashamed! You have made me ashamed! Be quiet or leave this place of prayer and solemn meditation! You are dishonoring the cause that you intend to serve!" He then delivered a short speech, specifying right away: "I am not assuming any official duty here, and what I have to say is not in the least tied to my position in public life." After having recalled Vichy's crimes, he took up once again, in his concluding remarks and more firmly, the argument developed two days earlier by François Mitterrand:

> A great nation, whose destiny has often been tragic, has nothing to fear from the truth. And there is no shame in exposing the secret wounds of an ever more distant past. Granted, with respect to either Jews or resisters, the Republic could not be held accountable for the crimes committed by Vichy's men, which were its enemies. But it owes their victims the highest tribute that we can pay them: the teaching of the truth and the force of justice.[14]

François Mitterrand thus did not speak. Some people found consolation by saying they were glad he had come and pretending to believe that he had spoken through the words of his friend Robert Badinter. Others found that this "wasn't enough."[15] Still others, such as the leaders of the Comité Vél' d'Hiv' 42, were outraged at his silence and issued a new communiqué that began with this truly astounding sentence: "The truth about the crimes of the Vichy French State has finally come out into the open in the press and the media."[16] This seems to confirm that the members of the said committee had not paid much attention to these issues until the day when they decided to take things into their own hands. The rest of their communiqué asserts that the speech given on his own behalf by Robert Badinter should have been "given officially" by the President of the Republic.

The long awaited symbolic gesture thus remains to be done. The Comité Vél' d'Hiv' 42 reaffirms the necessity of such a gesture and reiterates the purpose of its appeal: Today we turn to the nation's representatives and request each member of Parliament to work for the passage by the National Assembly of a law making July 16 a national day of commemoration for the persecutions and crimes perpetrated against the Jews by the Vichy French State.[17]

This time the proposal was clear and the gesture expected was directly whispered in the President's ear. Moreover, the Comité once again took up an old idea that had resurfaced at that time. But during this controversy, the liberty taken with history that accompanied the fulfillment of the duty to remember and the open hostility of some toward François Mitterrand postponed the conclusion of this affair.

An Anachronistic "Constitutional" Debate

Throughout the last few months, the discussion had been raging even among those former deportees or resisters, intellectuals, and activists who agreed on the necessity of fighting against lapse of memory. Who was accountable for Vichy's crimes? France? The French? The State? The Nation? The Republic? Who then was to acknowledge them officially, and above all, *how*, since the half-truth that they never had been acknowledged had lodged itself in public opinion? And thus, fifty years later, the crucial debate that had sprung out of de Gaulle's decision to split away from the official government in June 1940 was reopened. Once again, the question of the nature and even of the legal existence of the Vichy regime was posed. Indeed, in order for the head of state to acknowledge and assume responsibility on behalf of France for the crimes committed by the "French State," it first of all had to be granted that they had been done by a legal, recognized authority. That, however, amounted to undoing what General de Gaulle, Free France, and the Resistance had put together in the heat of the events themselves, and in the midst of tremendous tensions and dilemmas.

There again, we find ourselves before a contradiction between memory and history, which gives rise to unending anachronisms. The Gaullist vision of the Occupation, which has been contested for twenty years, founded itself on hindsight and on a memory based on a certain political will, and also on the natural implications of the fundamental choice made in June 1940 by de Gaulle and his handful of followers: i.e., the choice to deny the legitimacy of the government that had been formed on June 16 and 17, 1940, and which had signed the armistice on June 22. The decision to put Vichy in parentheses in official memory after the war was a direct result of the refusal by Free France and the Resistance to accord it any legality whatsoever, and still less any sort of legitimacy, during the war.[18]

However, a new generation finally placed the Vichy episode back into a continuum, thus emphasizing along with historians (and first of all Robert Paxton) the Vichy regime's specificity, its degree of autonomy, and the projects stemming from the National Revolution itself. For some twenty years, there has been no doubt as to whether "the Vichy regime existed."[19] But this evolution of thought raised an unexpected problem which exploded in 1992. Did reaffirming the importance and the autonomous existence of Vichy imply retrospectively giving it a different political and legal status?

That was the gist of a provocative article published by Dominique Rousseau in November 1992, shortly after the controversy over the Vél' d'Hiv'.[20] This constitutional specialist observed that the demand for an official acknowledgment of Vichy's crimes should be accompanied by an abrogation of the ordinance of August 9, 1944, "concerning the reestablishment of republican legality over the territory of mainland France." This founding text provided that:

Article number 1. France's form of government is and remains the Republic. Legally, it has never ceased to exist.

Article number 2. Accordingly, all constitutional, legislative or regulatory acts, as well as the rulings made as to their execution, under any form whatsoever, that were promulgated in mainland France after June 16, 1940, and up until the reestablishment of the Provisional Government of the French Republic, are null and void. This nullification must be explicitly observed.[21]

In a few sentences, Vichy had thus been wiped off the map with one stroke of a pen, and the Provisory Government of the French Republic proclaimed itself to be the sole legal, legitimate authority. It nevertheless left itself the possibility of maintaining or nullifying the texts as it wanted, in view of a optimal handling of state affairs. Let us recall, however, that this ordinance stemmed directly from the very first positions taken by de Gaulle's Free France and expressed right after the defeat. On October 27, 1940, in his famous Brazzaville manifesto, General de Gaulle had indeed clearly stated that "there no longer exists a truly French government." He added: "The entity located at Vichy and which claims to bear this name is unconstitutional and subservient to the invaders." On the same day, Free France's first ordinance instituted a "Defense Council for the Empire" and organized "public authority in all parts of the Empire that have been liberated from enemy control [. . .] on the basis of French legislation prior to June 23, 1940."[22]

The demand for an official condemnation of Vichy's crimes by a current of public opinion was tantamount to abolishing these ordinances. In his article, for example, legal scholar Dominique Rousseau feels that the legality of the last government of the Third Republic, which held its last session be-

tween June 16 and July 10, 1940, with Pétain as leader, was not disputable.
"[This] entails recognizing the legal validity of the armistice and, by the
same standard, puts the legal realm out of step with the political sphere,"
in other words, with the very foundations of the efforts of de Gaulle's Free
France and the Resistance, and, by extension, with the republican regimes
that have followed Vichy. He goes on to refute the argument that, from July
10, 1940, on,[23] the new regime supposedly had no constitutional legitimacy:
"Article number 1 of the ordinance of August 9, 1944 [. . .] is strictly mean-
ingless on legal grounds."[24] Furthermore, Olivier Duhamel, another highly
regarded constitutional scholar, agrees with him on this point: "There was,
in 1940, hardly a doubt as to the formal legality of the new regime."[25]

Actually, this discussion of the real issues has been going on for almost half
a century. In this respect, we can recall the arguments put forward right after the defeat by the very first followers of de Gaulle, beginning with René
Cassin.[26] In the first place, the vote taken on July 10, 1940, presented serious irregularities: death threats were made against members of Parliament;
it was impossible for some opponents of the constitutional revision, such as
the Deputy Vincent Badie or the twenty-seven members of Parliament (including such highly regarded figures as Pierre Mendès France, Édouard
Daladier, Georges Mandel, Jean Zay, and others) on board the ship "Massilia" (that was deliberately prevented from returning to mainland France)
to take the floor during the debate; the debate was not published in its entirety in the *Journal officiel*, and so forth. In the second place, even if we concede along with Olivier Duhamel the validity of the National Assembly (the
Chamber of Deputies in joint session with the Senate) decision to delegate
constitution-making authority to Marshall Pétain, thus asking "the government of the Republic, under the authority and signature of Marshall Pétain, to promulgate a new Constitution to be ratified by the nation and applied by the Assemblies thus created,"[27] we have to observe the fact that
Philippe Pétain did not comply with the terms of the decision made by the
National Assembly on July 10, 1940, in that he signed Vichy's constitutional acts in his very own name ("We, Marshall of France, head of the
French state . . .") and not in the name of the government. Also, he never
had these acts ratified (and for good reason!).

Furthermore, one cannot simply write off the fact that the signing of the
armistice even by a legal government nevertheless constituted a formal violation of the accords of March 28, 1940, with Great Britain, which forbade
any separate cessation of hostilities.

Finally, we must reject the cliché stating that it was "the Popular Front
Parliament" that scuttled the Republic. This cliché has long been propa-
gated by the extreme Right in order to condone the Pétainist regime, and it

has more recently been taken up by those contending that the Republic must assume responsibility for Vichy's crimes, since the Republic had its share of responsibility in the advent of the new regime. This assertion, often repeated in the course of the controversies of 1992, is inaccurate (even if it contains some truth, in that there had been no legislative elections between May 5, 1936,[28] and July 10, 1940). First, this contention underestimates the political evolution that had occurred between 1936 and 1940, the fragility of the coalition of radicals, Socialists, and Communists, and also the divisions created in 1938 by the crisis of Munich. Above all, this notion completely ignores the presence in the casino at Vichy of 245 Senators who, to say the least, were in their vast majority hardly favorable to the Popular Front, since it was the Senate that had toppled Blum's first government. And then, it must be remembered that out of a total of 907 Deputies and Senators in 1939, only 670 were present at Vichy. A significant number had been excluded: 61 Communist members of Parliament who had been stripped of their office on January 20, 1940, subsequent to the German-Soviet pact, 176 "absentees" (including the 27 on the ship *Massilia*), 17 members of Parliament who had died, and a large number who, because of the war, were unable or unwilling to get to Vichy.[29]

Nevertheless, de Gaulle's contention that the last government of the Third Republic was illegal is disputable on numerous points. As for the discussion over the nature of the Vichy regime and its legitimacy, it is indissociable from the context of that time. The legal issues weighed little in comparison with the scope of the military defeat and the widely held idea that it was necessary to put an end to combat in mainland France in any manner possible, even if this defeatist choice led to the splitting away of de Gaulle, whose movement was but a small minority in the beginning. Moreover, the idea that Vichy was illegal was at the time based on errors of judgment, such as the notion that there had been a plot against the Republic before the defeat. Similarly, even if the Republic as such was not involved in the Vichy escapade, the responsibility of the upper echelons of society—members of Parliament, magistrates, clergy, and others—that made this regime possible, is overwhelming. Finally, the personal legitimacy of Philippe Pétain—the man, the military commander, if not the head of the "French State"—was quite real in public opinion, at least at the beginning.

And yet, that is not the essential point, in that the discussion is rather pointless when it goes beyond the historical debate and aims at refounding a doctrine. What good is this belated legal scholarship ruling on a case that has been decided? (Furthermore, Dominique Rousseau admits this himself.) What benefit could the France of 1992 gain from a review of the legalities and/or of the respective legitimacies of Vichy and the Provisional Government of the French Republic, if it abolished the latter and formally reestablished the former in order to be in a position to condemn its crimes?

None, other than the truly incongruous situation of denying the achievements of de Gaulle and the Resistance on the pretext that their memory of
the Occupation had led to distortions after the war!

> If the ordinance of August 9, 1944, were no longer recognized as valid, Charles
> de Gaulle would be nothing but a general stripped of his rank, a deserter, and
> a man condemned to death in absentia. Léon Blum would be nothing but a
> tarnished politician responsible for the defeat. The resisters would be noth-
> ing but terrorists. The Jews who escaped the massive roundups would be
> delinquents, having placed themselves outside of the law. The men of the
> Milice and of the LVF[30] would be war veterans, and the men of the Maquis
> or Free France would be rebels. [. . .] If France mistook itself for Vichy during
> four years, then it finds itself, along with Germany, Italy, and Japan, among
> the fascist or protofascist countries that were defeated in World War II.
> France would then bear a sense of being stigmatized. More concretely, its
> seat as a permanent member of the Security Council, with the power of veto,
> would no longer be justified.[31]

Jean-Pierre Chevènement, the author of these lines, perfectly draws the
conclusions from this absurd debate, which was a kind of paroxysm of the
intellectual aberrations of the seventies and eighties which made Vichy into
the very essence of the "French ideology," to paraphrase the title of a fanciful book by Bernard-Henri Lévy. Behind the demand addressed to the
head of state loomed this idea of a sort of unavowed continuity between
Vichy's crimes and the Republic's silence, a continuity that could only
be explained by the "state" whose nature was by definition sinister. Hence
this responsibility which was indirectly attributed to it, as if the state had no
history, as if the French State (i.e., Vichy) and the republican state had
stemmed from one and the same root. Hence the anachronistic anti-
Gaullism denounced by Paul Thibaud:

> De Gaulle winds up being nothing but the great illusionist (or even the great
> liar) who made the French believe that they had all been resisters. The fact
> that he had first of all fought and discredited Pétain has no importance, since
> when all is said and done (it was finally said at the time of the fiftieth anniver-
> sary of the Vél' d'Hiv' roundup) France was (and still is) not de Gaulle, but
> Pétain: Cardinal Gerlier was right![32]

The Flowers

Inasmuch as François Mitterrand had long since adopted the Gaullian view
of government institutions as his own, there was nothing surprising about
his response to the Comité Vél' d'Hiv'. In assuming the legacy of the Fifth

Republic, he also assumed in his own way the official interpretation of
Vichy that had been prevalent since August 9, 1944, which moreover did
not prevent in any way an official gesture, freely assumed in the name of the
continuity of France, and not of the state. On November 6, 1992, Jean Le
Garrec, a Socialist deputy and president of the Finance Committee in the
National Assembly, took up the idea of a day of commemoration for the
Vél' d'Hiv' by introducing a bill to this effect which was signed by some
sixty Socialist deputies. The initiative is followed in the Senate on November 10, by a proposal from the Communist Charles Lederman.

However, not only did the gesture demanded not come, what came was
another gesture which made the controversy flare up all over again on November 11, 1992. To the astonishment of all, the President once again had
flowers placed on Philippe Pétain's tomb. In its communiqué, the Élysée
specified: "Flowers have been placed on the tombs of the Marshalls of
France who distinguished themselves in their commands during the First
World War: Fayolle, Foch, Franchet d'Esperey, Gallieni, Joffre, Lyautey,
Maunoury, and Pétain." The Élysée indicated that in paying tribute to all
of France's Marshalls of the Great War, the head of state had intended to
"draw the lessons from the controversies" caused in the beginning of the
summer by regular placing of flowers on Philippe Pétain's tomb: "Let it be
quite clear that it is for the sake of activities during the war of 1914–1918
that these flowers were placed there."

The conditions of the tribute paid to Pétain added to the virulence of the
reactions. The prefect of the Vendée waited for the departure, on the last
boat, of the delegation of the Union of French Jewish Students (UEJF) who
had come in the company of Serge Klarsfeld, to stand in front of the cemetery of Port-Joinville to make sure that there would be no official tribute. It
was only after they had left the premises that the prefect, who came in a navy
helicopter in late afternoon, placed the flowers sent by the President beside
those from Jean-Marie Le Pen, from the Association Pétain-Verdun, and
from the Italian Social Movement, the neo-fascist party.

The Association of Sons and Daughters of the Jews Deported from
France (Serge Klarsfeld's organization) expressed its indignation. "After
having honored the victims of Pétain's anti-Semitism, the President of the
Republic wound up taking the scandalous decision of honoring once more
the memory of their executioner. [. . .] Under these circumstances, during
Mr. Mitterrand's upcoming visit to Israel, our association does not think it
desirable that the President of the Republic be at the memorial for the deportation of the Jews from France.[33] The CRIF spoke of a "wound inflicted
on the families of the victims" and the National Federation of Deported
and Interned Resisters and Patriots spoke of an "insult to Pétain's victims."
The Comité Vél' d'Hiv' 42 indicated that, as far as it was concerned, "this
tribute to Pétain reopens the wound that Vichy was guilty of inflicting

when it cut France in two."[34] Only the extreme Right approved of the President's gesture. Jean Madiran hailed it in the daily paper *Présent* and stressed that, every year, he "officially chips away at the protective mask of historical lies that has been imposed on France by a moral violence that is inadmissable."[35] Responding to the call of the Union of Jewish Students of France, several hundred demonstrators placed at the site of the Vélodrome d'Hiver an arrangement of red and white carnations in the form of the Francisque[36] bearing the inscription, "To François Mitterrand, with all my gratitude: Philippe Pétain."

The affair of the flowers quickly took on a political twist. During a luncheon meeting at Champagnole (in the Jura region) on November 13, Jacques Chirac, asked if this gesture went along with the duties of being President, replied: "Honestly, I don't think so." He stressed to a former resister who said he was shocked by the attitude of François Mitterrand: "I can only share your feeling. [. . .] Anything that seems to minimize the attitude of those who, while forming such a small minority in the beginning, had the honor of France in their hands is utterly repugnant to the values that we represent. [. . .] I am sorry for these gestures, whatever they may be and whatever be the reasons why they are made, which are liable to maintain a certain confusion in this area."[37] Édouard Balladur chose irony: "In the list of rituals begun by François Mitterrand, I prefer the climbing of the rock of Solutré."[38]

Within the Socialist party, embarrassment quickly gave way to disavowal. It was the first time in twelve years that one of François Mitterrand's initiatives was subject to a public condemnation by party barons. The party's first secretary, Laurent Fabius, did not hesitate to request that "this gesture not be renewed, [for] Pétain had an eminent role at Verdun, but he was also and first of all the man responsible for collaboration with the occupier, with the Nazis. A man is responsible for everything he does, and the judgment we pass on him is on his life in its entirety." Henri Emmanuelli, president of the National Assembly, simply declared that he "didn't understand." And Lionel Jospin pointed out that the Pétain of World War I was "wiped off the slate" by the Pétain of Vichy: "If a choice must be made, the choice must be made for the condemnation of what Vichy was and what the man who carried Vichy was. [. . .] We must decide once and for all and express our shame for what happened, and say that the Pétain of 1914 was unfortunately swept away by the Pétain of 1940."

The reactions took a turn such that, within the Socialist party, the steering committee, which was to meet on November 15, planned to express its disapproval publicly. In an attempt to cut off the increasing indignation, the Élysée published, already on November 13, the transcript of an interview that François Mitterrand had given "Radio J," a Jewish community radio, and which was to be broadcast on November 22. The President admitted that he should in the future "handle differently" the "fundamental contradiction" that existed between the tribute to the victor of Verdun and the memory of the "shame" of the massive roundup of Vél' d'Hiv' in 1942:

> Here we are before a typical case of the contradictions of History, which in turn places us in contradictions that are really unbearable. [. . .] We will never be able to tear out the pages on which is written the greatest battle that France has ever experienced and won, the battle of Verdun, nor will we ever be able to delete from the history of France those who fought and led it twenty-five years before the Vél' d'Hiv' roundup. [. . .] I would not want the misunderstanding to grow. [. . .] If the French nation had been involved in this sad escapade of the Vichy government, this apology would be in order. That is what Willy Brandt did in Germany's name. [. . .] But the French nation was not involved in that affair, nor was the Republic; it was a new, different, occasional regime. The French State that took on that terrible responsibility marked by acts of racism, anti-Semitism, outside of other really French aspects, was the Vichy regime. It is practically intolerable. When I was asked: "Will you apologize in France's name?" I really did not understand this manner of speaking. [. . .] What happened at that time, particularly at the Vél' d'Hiv', is something not only intolerable but also unbearable for the mind, thus essentially to be condemned.[39]

The President then declared that he was "quite ready to make" a gesture, which remained to "be determined." In this important pronouncement, aimed at preventing incidents during his upcoming trip to Israel (from November 25 to 27) and at putting an end to the growing complaints coming from within the Socialist party, he retreated, yet without yielding anything on the substance of the matter.

The choice of a Jewish radio station to offer an explanation of the flowers placed on Pétain's tomb insidiously reinforced the idea that the expected gesture concerned only the Jews, as if keeping memory alive was exclusively a community matter. In this presidential choice, as in a number of stances on these issues, the memories of anti-Jewish persecutions were supposedly only the concern of the victims and their loved ones, and not a national concern. This presidential attitude was exactly opposite of the request that some had made for the Republic to acknowledge the said persecutions in the name of the French nation. Those opposed to such a tendency were very few at the time. Among them, Daniel Mayer, head of the clandestine Socialist party under the Occupation, declared at the awards ceremony for the 1992 Shoah Prize given by the Fondation du Judaïsme: "I am completely hostile to the placing of these flowers. It is not first of all as a Jew, but as a resister that I am displaying this complete opposition." Similarly, the historian André Kaspi wrote: "When the memory of the nation runs into a detestable past, Jews must not be sent to the front line and abandoned there all alone."[40] Along with others, he was behind a text signed this time by numerous French historians working on the Occupation and who deplored the President's placing of flowers. This text explained that it was not possible to separate the Pétain of Verdun from the Pétain of Vichy, since the latter never could have existed without the former. It was indeed in the name of his past glory that Pétain was able to impose the National Revolution and state collaboration, thus betraying the "trust that French men and women had placed in the victor of Verdun in 1940."[41]

A few days before his departure for Israel, François Mitterrand granted, on November 20, an interview to the Tel Aviv newspaper *Yedioth Aharonoth*: "As for me, I lived through the period of World War II and the ensuing trials. They were not particularly kind. Then, there was a long period when this kind of problem slipped into the background. There is an awakening today. Actually, people did not know very well how it had happened. France was a country occupied by the Nazis. It was rather difficult to sort out the responsibilities that were specific to the government, and to the administration of the French State. Today, they *appear* to be very heavy in that matter."[42]

In the end the presidential trip to Israel went off with no serious incident even though the matter of the flowers was regularly mentioned, even by the Israeli president in his conversations with François Mitterrand. But Mitterrand had immediately brushed aside Israeli criticism, contending that it was a matter of "a complicated area, which concerned [his] country and its internal affairs," an answer that Israeli television termed "revolting," judging the attitude of the French President "arrogant." The principal daily newspaper of the country, *Haaretz*, reacted bluntly: "Under the Vichy regime, 80,000 Jews from France were sent to extermination camps. This does not involve an internal affair. Human rights can never be an internal matter in any country."[43]

A New Commemoration

It was only on February 3, 1993, when nobody was expecting it, a few weeks before legislative elections and after following a long round-about path, that the President finally yielded to pressure by deciding to institute a "National Day for commemorating racist and anti-Semitic persecutions committed under the de facto authority of the so-called 'government of the French State'."

Michel Charasse, an advisor to the President, had for a long time been in favor of granting the demand of the Comité Vél' d'Hiv', which, three months earlier, the socialist deputy Jean Le Garrec had translated into a bill. Since in all probability the President would have to offer the promised "gesture" before the end of the year 1992, it was in December that the proposed decree was put into final form. But the principle of the decree divided the President's entourage. Some advisors, hostile toward this idea, pointed out that there already existed, on the last Sunday in April of every year, a National Day for remembering deportation, dedicated to all those deported. Having been reformed in 1985 and 1988, this day paid tribute precisely both to deported resisters and to Jewish victims deported in the "Final Solution" (which was not the case when the day was instituted in 1954, chiefly in memory of deported resisters).[44] The government minister Louis Mexandeau thus proposed to add an explicit condemnation of Vichy in the official heading of the law on the National Day for remembering deportation. Other advisors defended another solution, put forward by Théo Klein. "Uninterested in a declaration from the President of the Republic, who, besides, refused to make one during the summer of 1992," the former president of the CRIF suggested instead the idea of a joint declaration by the National Assembly and the Senate. This initiative, according to him, presented two advantages. First, it would bring together the votes from the Right and the Left, which "would have a value, an impact that a declaration from just the President of the Republic might not have in present-day France." Second, "it would make formal reparation for the error and weakness of those who, on July 10, 1940, placed the Republic in the hands of Pétain."[45]

On the eve of the last Ministry Council meeting of 1992, the decision was made . . . not to decide on anything. The President was in fact waiting to see the effects of the publication of the memoirs of the former director of the Izieu boarding house, as François Mitterrand had given a short preface in which he specified: "The Republic, through my office, pays tribute to the memory of martyred children of the Izieu boarding house."[46] But these few words went almost unnoticed, and the Élysée went out once more in quest of a new "gesture." Weary from these battles, the President resolved to execute the aborted plan for a specific day of commemoration.

The decree of February 3, 1993, published the next day in the *Journal officiel*, thus instituted July 16 as a national day of commemoration. The text maintained the tradition of refusing to grant Vichy any legal basis. At the same time, it eluded the question of the regime's responsibilities: while Jean Le Garrec's bill mentioned the "racist, anti-Semitic, and xenophobic persecutions and crimes perpetrated *by* the Vichy French State," thus adopting the strange wording used by the Comité Vél' d'Hiv' 42 (the "French State" was the official term used by the new regime, which in common parlance was quickly called "Vichy"), the text of the presidential decree announced the commemoration of the "racist and anti-Semitic persecutions committed *under* the de facto authority of the so-called 'government of the

French State.'" Moreover, the notion of "de facto authority," which denied that the Vichy regime had any legality, would thus continue to be the official language to the great disappointment of those who wanted to undo what the Liberation had hastily put together while emerging from the tragedy.

If exception is made of the hostility of the Lepénist daily newspaper *Présent*, which spoke of an "act of civil war,"[47] the event was greeted with relief and eagerness as the acceptable outcome of a controversy that had already gone on too long. Serge Klarsfeld decided on a cease-fire and took note of a condemnation that "put an end to a misunderstanding with the Jewish community and the national community" and that "will prevent any tribute to Philippe Pétain." "We have a formal, explicit condemnation of Vichy's crimes. We cannot ask for much more."[48]

At the meeting of the Ministry Council on February 8, Louis Mexandeau justified the institution of this national day of observance by the fact that "fifty years later, the time has come to affirm the full responsibility of the Vichy regime." On a practical level, the decree provided for the national day of observance to be organized on July 16 if that date fell on a Sunday, or if not, on the closest Sunday thereafter. It was at the same time decided to institute a "National Committee for defending the memory of the racist and anti-Semitic persecutions committed under the de facto authority of the so-called 'government of the French State'," charged with conceiving and erecting a monument at the former location of the Vélodrome d'Hiver, in Paris, and two stone markers, one at the site of an internment camp and the other at the Izieu boarding house, whose memorial museum was to be inaugurated by François Mitterrand on April 24, 1994. This committee was also to draft the texts to be inscribed on the Paris monument, on the two other stone markers, and on the memorial plaques that were to be placed at the administrative headquarters of each department. This committee, placed under the high patronage of the President of the Republic, was made up of five ex officio members—the national leaders of the CRIF, the MRAP, the LICRA, the League of Human Rights, and the Social, National, and International Evangelical Gypsy Association; of ten representatives of State and Regional Administrations, including the Mayor of Paris and the Mayor of Izieu; of nineteen representatives "of the leading organizations whose purpose is to preserve the memory of the victims of racist and anti-Semitic persecutions as well as the memory of internment and deportation"; and finally of twelve "qualified personalities," whose number included only one historian, René Rémond. The absence of Serge Klarsfeld from this list is to be noted.

The job of this national committee consisted mainly in drafting the sentence—a crucial and supposedly identical sentence—to be inscribed on the memorial stone markers and plaques. The inscription placed on the Vél' d'Hiv' monument, inaugurated Sunday, July 17, 1994, by François Mitterrand, Prime Minister Édouard Balladur, and the Mayor of Paris, Jacques Chirac, reads as follows:

> The French Republic pays tribute to the victims of racist and anti-Semitic persecutions and of crimes against humanity committed under the de facto authority of the so-called "Government of the French State" (1940–1944). Let us never forget.

In the case of Izieu, this inscription raised a thorny problem in that it forgot to specify that the Jewish children from the Izieu boarding house were arrested and deported by the German Klaus Barbie. That was the main reason for his condemnation to life in prison in 1987 and it is the reason why Izieu has since become a place of memory. The Vichy government, in this particular episode, played absolutely no role, except for the fact that, as was the case for most of the foreign Jews that were going to be deported, the boarders of Izieu and their parents had transited beforehand through several French internment camps. They had subsequently been taken in by Mr. and Mrs. Zlatin who lodged them at Izieu, with the active support of the subprefect of Belley (in the Ain region), Pierre-Marcel Wiltzer, who was therefore taking risks in view of his official capacity.[49]

The remark—one of simple common sense—about the respective responsibilities of the Nazis and Vichy in this affair brought about sharp verbal exchanges between the scholarly council of the museum and the national committee, or at least with some of its most active members. Finally, in order to respect the terms of the presidential decree while at the same time taking the situation at Izieu into consideration, the national committee agreed to add a clarifying sentence and revised the first draft of the inscription it had originally proposed. The inscription on the stone marker at Izieu thus reads as follows:

> Here, on April 6, 1944, the Gestapo arrested and deported forty-four children and seven adults because they were Jews by birth. Fifty were exterminated at Auschwitz II and Reval. The French Republic pays tribute to the victims of racist and anti-Semitic persecutions and of crimes against humanity *with the complicity* of the Vichy government, the so-called "government of the French State" (1940–1944). Let us never forget. [Italics added.]

At least the historical facts and the role of Barbie were recalled. Nevertheless, what is singularly paradoxical is that in a place (Izieu) where crimes in which Vichy played no role are commemorated, mention is made of its "complicity," while at the Vél' d'Hiv' monument, which is supposed to recall Vichy's overwhelming responsibility in anti-Semitic persecutions, only crimes against humanity committed "under" its reign are mentioned!

The organization of the first ceremony resulting from the presidential decree on July 16, 1993, was up to the Right, which had returned to power in March. It had thus been necessary to wait fifty-one years for a leader of the Republic, Édouard Balladur, to pronounce, without provoking any controversy, the simple words recalling that the Vél' d'Hiv' roundup had been "the scene of one of the most painful tragedies that have saddened our country's history." Its victims "bear in their bodies and souls the marks of the tremendous ordeal that [they] have experienced," with the "awful complicity of the regime established under the Occupation. [. . .] Let no one have any doubts about it, France will remain in the eyes of the world the land of human rights. May the men and women who lost theirs in those terrible moments [. . .] know that France is in mourning. With respect to this horrifying ordeal, France remains inconsolable."

In the epilogue to this tense commemoration, a brief communiqué from the Élysée on November 8, 1993, let it implicitly be known that the President had stopped placing flowers on Philippe Pétain's grave. To pay tribute "to the soldiers and their leaders," three flower arrangements would be placed at the sites of the three great battles of World War I, including Verdun.

Although everyone was admittedly relieved, the outcome of this national psychodrama poses a problem. François Mitterrand failed to say the right thing. He said other things in response to pointless quarrels. There was never a public debate on the same level as the demands of history and memory. The decision was made in the heat of the controversy, hastily and with a political aim.

As for the new commemoration, one can wonder about its real meaning. Let us recall that there are now in France three national commemorations tied to the memory of the last war: the National Day commemorating deportation, observed the last Sunday of April, the 8th of May, an official holiday celebrating the German surrender—these two anniversaries are observed in numerous other countries—and July 16.[50] In other words, two out of the three commemorations are related to deportation, and, while the persecution of the Jews is clearly identifiable in this arrangement, the memory of the Resistance still does not appear on the official national calendar: the commemorations on that score are mostly local ones, such as the anniversaries of the Liberation, which vary according to their location, or the celebration of June 18, which is customary particularly in Paris.[51] This is an odd turnabout compared with the period from 1950 to 1970, when in the official and even collective memory, the heroic remembrance of wartime Gaullism and silence about the Genocide and French anti-Semitism predominated.

Furthermore, the memory of the Vél' d'Hiv' roundup was chosen so that the persecutions conducted by Vichy would never be forgotten. This choice, however, even if it indisputably has a strong symbolic value, over-looks the fact that this roundup was indeed perpetrated by the French police, but within the framework of collaboration, and that it was demanded by the Nazi occupant. Only in a very imperfect way is it a "place of memory" of native French anti-Semitism, which is itself much better symbolized by the date of October 3, the day of the first Jewish Statute, promulgated in 1940 without German pressure and more discriminatory than the ordinances concerning Jews that had been decreed a few days before in the zone occu-pied by the Nazis.

In 1992, there was an attempt to do the Liberation over again and to make up for its shortcomings. In the end, the same pitfalls blocked the way: it was more the Vichy of the Collaboration than the anti-Semitic Vichy, more the accomplice of the Third Reich than the French tradition of au-thoritarian nationalism and xenophobia that were symbolically condemned.

Chirac, the State, and France

It was Jacques Chirac, a few months later, on July 16, 1995, marking the fifty-third anniversary of the massive Vél' d'Hiv' roundup, who was to eliminate once and for all the ambiguity that Mitterrand had maintained about the memory of Vichy. He was thus to be the first President of the Re-public to choose to speak during this ceremony. His short speech wiped out several years of confusion, while at the same time opening up new debates. Given its importance and the commentaries that it provoked, we thought it worthwhile to transcribe it in its entirety:

Mr. Mayor,
Mr. President,
Mr. Ambassador,
Mr. Chief Rabbi,
Ladies and gentlemen,
    There are in the life of a nation times that are painful for memory and for the idea that we have of our country.
    It is hard to speak of these times, because we are not always capable of finding the right words to recall the horror and to express our sorrow for those who experience this tragedy: they are forever marked in their soul and in their flesh by the memory of these days of tears and shame.
    It is hard to speak of these times also because these dark hours have for-ever fouled our history, and are an insult to our past and our traditions. Yes, it is true that the criminal insanity of the occupying forces was backed up by French people and by the French State.
    Fifty-three years ago, on July 16, 1942, four hundred and fifty French po-

lice agents and gendarmes, acting under the authority of their leaders, responded to the Nazis' demands.

That day, in the capital and in the Paris region, nearly ten thousand Jewish men, women, and children were arrested in their homes in the early morning and rounded up in police stations.

Horrible scenes were witnessed: families torn apart, with mothers separated from their children, elderly men, some of whom were veterans of the
First World War and had shed their blood for France, were unsparingly
thrown in Parisian buses and wagons from police headquarters.

People also saw some police agents close their eyes, thus allowing a few
escapes.

For all these people who were arrested, then began the long and painful
journey toward hell. How many of them were never again to see their homes?
And how many, at that moment, felt betrayed? How great was their distress?

France, land of the Enlightenment and of Human Rights, land of hospitality and asylum, France, on that day, committed an irreparable act. It failed
to keep its word and delivered those it was protecting to their executioners.

Taken to the Vélodrome d'Hiver, the victims were to wait several days in
what we know were terrible conditions before being led away to one of the
staging camps—either Pithiviers or Beaune-la-Rolande—that had been set
up by Vichy authorities.

But the horror was just beginning.

Other massive roundups and arrests were to follow. In Paris and in the
provinces. Sixty-four trains were to depart for Auschwitz. Seventy-six thousand Jews deported from France would never return.

We retain toward them an unforgivable debt.

The Torah assigns to every Jew the duty to remember. The sentence that
is always invoked says: "Never forget that you were a stranger and a slave in
the land of Pharaoh."

Fifty years after, faithful to its law, but without any spirit of hatred or revenge, the Jewish community remembers, and all of France with it. In order
that the six million martyrs of the Shoah may live. In order that such atrocities may never happen again. In order that the Holocaust may become, according to the expression of Samuel Pisar, the "blood of hope."

When the spirit of hatred, whipped up on one side by fundamentalism,
and fed on the other side by fear and exclusion, and when right here at our
own doorstep, certain little groups, certain publications, certain teachings,
and certain political parties show themselves more or less openly to be pur-
veyors of a racist and anti-Semitic ideology, then this spirit of vigilance which
guides you, and which guides us, must display itself more forcefully than
ever.

In this domain, nothing is insignificant, nothing is commonplace, nothing
is dissociable. Racist crimes, the defense of revisionist ideas, and provocations

of all sorts—little comments with hints and quips—are all drawn from the same sources.

In passing on the memory of the Jewish people and of its sufferings, and of the camps; in witnessing again and again, in acknowledging the sins of the past, and the sins committed by the State; in covering up nothing about the dark hours of our History, we are simply defending an idea of humanity, of human liberty and dignity. We are fighting against the forces of darkness which are constantly at work.

This endless combat is mine as much as it is yours.

The youngest among us, I am happy to say, are sensitive to everything that relates to the Shoah. They want to know. And with them from now on, there are more and more French people determined to face their past head on.

France, as we all know, is not at all an anti-Semitic country.

In this moment of solemn meditation and memory, I would like to choose to hope.

I want to remember that that summer of 1942, which revealed the true face of "collaboration" (whose racist nature, after the anti-Jewish laws of 1940, could no longer be subject to doubt), was to be, for many of our fellow citizens, the time of an awakening and the point of departure for a vast movement of resistance.

I want to remember all the Jewish families who were being hunted and who were sheltered from the merciless searches being carried out by the Germans and the Milice by the heroic and fraternal deeds of numerous French families.

I like to think of the fact that a month earlier, at Bir Hakeim, the Free French under Koenig had for two full weeks heroically stood up to German and Italian divisions.

Certainly, there are the mistakes that were made, there are the offenses, there is a collective sin. But there is also France, a certain idea of France, upright, generous, and faithful to its traditions and its spirit. That France had never been at Vichy. It had long since been absent from Paris. It was in the sands of Libya and everywhere the Free French were fighting. It was in London, exemplified by General de Gaulle. It was present, one and indivisible, in the heart of those French people, those "righteous among the nations" who, at the risk of their lives and in the darkest hour of the storm, as Serge Klarsfeld has written, saved three-fourths of the Jewish community living in France and gave life to the best in this country: the values of humanity, of liberty, of justice, and of tolerance. They are the foundation of French identity and our obligation for the future.

These values, which are the foundation of our democracies, are presently being flouted right under our eyes here in Europe, by the practitioners of "ethnic cleansing." Let us know how to learn the lessons of History. Let us refuse to be passive observers, or accomplices, of the unacceptable.

That is the meaning of the appeal that I have made to our chief partners in London, Washington, and Bonn. If we want to, together, we can put a halt to an undertaking that destroys our values and which gradually risks threatening all of Europe.[53]

For many people, this speech was a surprise, because it had neither been announced nor particularly expected. It was greeted all the more favorably for that reason, both on the Left and on the Right. There were, of course, a few discordant voices, such as Jack Lang, the former Socialist government minister, who did not hesitate to distinguish between "two visions, two conceptions": that of Jacques Chirac and that of his predecessors, "General de Gaulle, President Pompidou, President Giscard d'Estaing, President Mitterrand, who were all patriots and great resisters."[54] Jean-Marie Le Pen, president of the National Front, declared for his part that Jacques Chirac was only "paying his electoral debt with respect to the Jewish community." As for Jean Madiran, the editorialist for the daily newspaper *Présent*, who has always taken pride in his Vichy years, he wrote that "the name of Jacques Chirac will be connected with the fraudulent exploitation of the Shoah against French honor."[55] Significantly, Michel Rocard[56] solemnly stated his approval of Jacques Chirac's declaration.[57] As for Lionel Jospin, the Socialist party candidate who had given Jacques Chirac a run for his money during the presidential election a few months earlier, he would be summoned by Serge Klarsfeld to account for his strange silence after the July 16 speech by Chirac.[58] Jospin did so a few days later and, in order to justify his reservedness, invoked the fact that, being "on vacation for a while," he had decided not to express himself publicly about current events, which was a rather unconvincing alibi.[59] These reactions, which were to say the least varied, show to what degree Jacques Chirac's speech had a bearing on things which went far beyond political cleavages.

Some tried to give the impression that they believed that Jacques Chirac was conceding in 1995 what François Mitterrand had stubbornly refused to do since 1992: to declare, as many had demanded, that the French Republic was indeed accountable for the persecution of the Jews carried out by Pétain's regime. On this key point, however, the new President stuck to the Gaullist reading of things that his predecessor had tactically adopted as his own: it is historically speaking absurd, and morally unjust, to ask the Republic to assume responsibility for the crimes of a regime by which it had been undone and condemned. The break is to be found elsewhere. It results first of all from the fact that, for the first time, a President of the Republic used a language free of the ambiguities, loopholes, and contortions that had up until then characterized most presidential speeches—which in final analysis were rather rare—touching on the question of Vichy.

The break results in the second place from a change in perspective.

Contrary to François Mitterrand, and contrary to Georges Pompidou, who had both, in different contexts, felt that it was necessary to put an end to the "permanent civil war" between the French, Jacques Chirac asserted that it was essential to explain to citizens of all generations that France had experienced "days of tears and shame [. . . which] are painful for memory and for the idea that we have of our country [. . . which] are an insult to our past and our traditions." While Jacques Chirac made no concession on the question of the Republic, he did invoke the responsibility of the "State," and not just of the "French State," to indicate "France's share of responsibility." It was French police agents (granted, under the orders of a supposedly illegitimate regime) that carried out the massive roundups of Jews, who were first penned up in French camps and deported in French trains. While the Republic is not accountable for the crimes of Vichy, the principle of state continuity, especially in a centralized country like France, entails the necessity of one way or another assuming responsibility after the fact for acts committed by the government officials and employees, even if they were at the time following the orders of a "de facto authority." From this point of view, Jacques Chirac's speech does not obey a narrowly legalistic logic, but conforms to an historical reality that is now hard to dispute.

But Jacques Chirac went even farther in his break with the tradition. He felt that "France" was equally involved. He even went so far as to speak of a "collective sin,"[60] a term that is highly debatable morally and that is moreover not admitted in law: it had been refused in 1948 by the United Nations in defining the crimes of the Third Reich; a half a century later, can it define those of an accomplice?

Paradoxically, the strength and accuracy of this speech stem from its fundamental contradiction. The contradiction resides not in the condemnation of the state, the rulers, the higher echelons, and of government employees who committed crimes or let crimes be committed. It rather resides in the repeated reference to "France," thus to the nation, without our knowing exactly which "France" we are dealing with. Indeed, Jacques Chirac stated on the one hand: "France, land of the Enlightenment and of Human Rights, land of hospitality and asylum, France, on that day [July 16, 1942] committed an irreparable act." But on the other hand, he stated a little later in the speech: "But there is also France, a certain idea of France, upright, generous, faithful to its traditions and to its spirit," the France that survived "in the heart of these French people," who, both on the mainland and abroad, did not bow down. Moreover, it is not at all an accident that this last sentence follows the reference to a "collective sin," as if intended to alleviate immediately the effects of this burdensome imputation. Therein lies the insurmountable contradiction: it was indeed the same country that, on the one hand, brought the Vichy regime into being and, on the other, produced de Gaulle and the Resistance. But we are talking about a country that was divided, split, and evolving according to the circumstances. It was a nation that was not only defeated, but split apart, that went through these terrible years—like so many other European countries.

For indeed the problem resides precisely in that aspect, which has been the same for a half a century. While sparing the Republic in order to better condemn the state that at the time enjoyed official legality does not pose any serious problems for our conscience, it appear difficult, however, to keep the nation clear of any responsibility, in that the Occupation was the theater of a civil war and of a confrontation between two and even several legitimate claims to power who all could point out the favor they enjoyed with a portion of the nation's citizens. Jacques Chirac thus finds himself back in the middle of the quandary of the Dark Years, which is that of all civil wars. Now, the settling of fratricidal conflicts (as we have often observed in this book) is the biggest of obstacles. In 1944, and even as early as June 1940, General de Gaulle had solved the problem with the legal and political negation of the governmental teams that had signed and applied the armistice: the only legitimate France was de Gaulle's Free French. Vichy was nothing more than a "de facto authority." These words were an act of faith as are many fighting words. To do away with this founding act is to bring oneself, in another context, back into political, ideological, and moral quandaries.

Among the rare public criticisms of the President's speech, the most serious were precisely those that leveled charges of abandoning his faith, reproaching him for trampling over Gaullist orthodoxy. Irony would have it that this criticism was expressed most bluntly by two who had been the conscience of Pompidou, Pierre Juillet and Marie-France Garaud, although the latter had not until then distinguished herself in defending the spirit of the Resistance. They did not hesitate, moreover, to write that Jacques Chirac had stated that "the Vichy State exemplified the Republic," which is not true.[61]

Actually, even if, strictly speaking, it is true that Jacques Chirac has broken with the Gaullist tradition, it must be admitted that this tradition has not, for almost twenty-five years now, been adequate either to the task of dressing the wound of memory or of calming the consciences that have been awakened. On this level, in spite of its contradictions, Jacques Chirac's speech was right, becaused it responded to one of the expectations of its time, just as the legal fiction invented by de Gaulle fit in completely in the context of "renewal" necessary for defeated France. Politicians express themselves in and act upon their own times. General de Gaulle and Jacques Chirac, each in his own context, have had to confront issues which in every respect are not equivalent, and that makes any mechanical comparison between their statements absurd. As Blandine Kriegel correctly wrote: "while in the past it was necessary to decide that Vichy was not France, we must now have the courage to acknowledge what was the role of Vichy in the State."[62] Jacques Chirac did not have to deal with handling the aftermath of the Occupation, nor with the urgency of Reconstruction. He had on the contrary to face the problem of obsession with Vichy, which for a large part arose out of the rejection of the Gaullist narrative, a narrative that was necessary in the past, but which is now contested. Even though he may find himself back in the quandary of the war years, he has taken on this responsibility in his own way and with other objectives.

In forsaking Gaullist mythology, Jacques Chirac has moreover drawn nearer to historical truth. While he clearly affirmed the overwhelming responsibility of Vichy in the organization of the massive police roundups of the summer of 1942, he also recalled that it was indeed the Nazis who ordered the crime be committed, and that French police agents and *gendarmes*, obeying orders from authority, were accomplices in the deed; as we have seen, this is a hierarchy that people have at times managed to forget. Beyond its respect for the facts, this speech restores their original, and in the strictest sense of the word, historical dimension particularly to General de Gaulle and to all the resisters: they were rebels fighting to make prevalent an idea of France that was different from that of the legal French State.

In short, this speech provided a *contemporary* meaning for the duty to remember. The direct reference to Bosnia, albeit soft-pedaled, made it thus possible to escape from the prison of the past: "Let us know how to learn the lessons of History. Let us refuse to be passive observers, or accomplices, of the unacceptable." The intention was there, and the link between the past and the present was henceforth possible, since the sins of yesteryear had been acknowledged at the highest level.

2

The Archives
They Hide Everything, They Tell Us Nothing

It was one of the best scoops in recent years. On November 13, 1991, *Le Monde* announced on its front page: "Jewish Card File: the end of an enigma. It had been created by Vichy police. It was said to have been lost or destroyed. It is found in the office of the Secretary of State for War Veterans." The huge card file from the census of Jews in the Seine district, the first and the most complete of a long series, had been constituted on the basis of information gathered during the census carried out between the 3rd and the 19th of October 1940 by the Prefecture of the Paris Police, at the request of the occupying forces and within the framework of the first German and French anti-Jewish measures. For more than fifteen years, rumor had it that this file was hidden somewhere.[1] However, the paper revealed, it had just been discovered in the archives of the Ministry of War Veterans by the lawyer Serge Klarsfeld.

The story made a big impact: not only did it put an end to years of controversy and research, but also it seemed to establish a grave governmental duplicity and a will to cover things up completely. Some even saw in this matter the very sign of an infamous continuity of the State, from Vichy to the present day. The revelation created a panic. The Secretary of State Louis Mexandeau, who had an advanced degree in history,[2] confirmed the story immediately, but his ministry was still not spared by the public reaction. During the wild weeks that followed, the scoop made newspaper headlines, while at the same time, there was, as usual, a proliferation of highly serious and definitive declarations. The story would nevertheless turn out to be erroneous.

Thus began the "card file affair," one episode among many others of the incessant quarrels over memory, once more crystallized around Vichy's anti-Jewish policies. This affair indeed constitutes an archetype, not only because of the genuinely phony debates that came into play but also because of the attitudes of the various protagonists. Ultimately, it raises two real problems: How should historical documents from a recent and still hotly debated era be handled, expertly studied, and authenticated while they are at the same time tossed into the public arena under terrific pressure from the media and with unmanageable issues of politics and memory? Under what conditions, and above all, to what ends have these documents been kept, and how should they be conserved?

The Card File, or How to Dispose of It

Having had access to the ministry archives shortly before, Serge Klarsfeld discovered the existence of these documents almost by accident. This discovery was liable to provide him more complete information about the identity of the deported Jews, which was the subject of his fundamental work, *Le Mémorial de la déportation des juifs de France*.[3] Known for his action against Klaus Barbie and René Bousquet, praised for his determination to write a story that had been covered up until the seventies, Serge Klarsfeld, president of the Association of the Sons and Daughters of the Jews Deported from France, inspires respect and fear. Most of the time, he proceeds with all the rigor consistent with his activism; he had moreover informed the government minister of his discovery six weeks before revealing the story to *Le Monde*.[4]

Two officers in the archives section of the Ministry of War Veterans were then summoned by Louis Mexandeau's cabinet. They immediately disputed the nature of the documents disclosed by Serge Klarsfeld: the "card file" in question was, according to them, not that of the census; they maintained that it was not the notorious card file dating from October 1940. That is probably what explains how the cabinet could have declared to Laurent Greilsamer of *Le Monde* shortly before he published his article announcing Serge Klarsfeld's discovery, that the ministry "did not hold this card file in their possession."[5] But in the context of the "affair," their explanation must not have been sufficiently persuasive, since at the time, no one—neither archivists, historians, journalists, nor others—had the possibility of determining with precision the exact nature of these documents. This underlying incertitude required at the least a verification by those in charge, but the Secretary of State thought that, once the affair had been thrown out into the public arena by the press, the only way to save face was to participate in the disclosure. A member of his entourage was later to admit: "The matter was not clear, but there was such pressure from the media that we couldn't say anything else."[6] Louis Mexandeau thus immediately validated Serge Klarsfeld's affirmations in a press release put out on November 12. Announcing that his office had begun an inventory of the documents held in the possession of his ministry, he confirmed that "this inventory will reveal the presence of the card file made from the census of the Jewish population of Paris."[7] In order to prove his willingness to cooperate, the government minister referred the matter to the CNIL. Actually, this step was taken only for appearances, for the card file, whatever its nature or origin might have been, should long before have been declared before the CNIL, in that it contained information of a confessional nature. At the same time, the government minister requested a report on the subject from the General Inspection Office of the Ministry of War Veterans, which turned in the report two weeks later.

Two essential but incomplete pieces of information appeared in this report written in the heat of things. First of all, there was indeed a confusion as to the real nature of this card file: it was composed of three distinct card files, and the total number of cards was just over half that of the card file of 1940, whose exact size was known. In addition, the great majority of cards bore notes such as "sought," "disappeared," "arrested." While the authors of the report did not draw all the conclusions from these observations, they nevertheless declared: "In any case, we can state that this documentation represents only a part of the card files made during the census of the Jewish population in France after 1940."[8] Second, whatever the exact origin of these files might have been, they had in no way been forgotten. Upon the request of the Jewish associations of the time, they had after the war been handed over to the Ministry of Prisoners of War and Deportees (which later became the Ministry of War Veterans), just as similar documents, such as the "Drancy" card file put together by the administration during the internments and which was, as far as it was concerned, perfectly well known and identified by the internees themselves at the time of the Liberation. Up until 1966 and even beyond, these files were used to search for missing persons and to make it possible to establish rights and grant pensions. At the end of the sixties, the authors of the report indicate, the ministry then started having to deal with the curiosity of the inquirers. In view of the policy used at the time by the government administrations and the National Archives, these documents were defined as inaccessible to historians. In spite of the legislation of 1979, which, the authors point out, "challenged the age-old tradition of authority and secret,"[9] liberalized access to administrative documents (cf. below), the inspectors noted that various "illegal" memoranda in the end succeeded "in creating a total secret, even in dealing with people affected by a certain document."[10] Only a few exceptions had been granted to historians, in particular to Serge Klarsfeld. This meant that the card files had been perfectly well known, but virtually inaccessible. In order to "protect the sensitive information about people's behavior during the war, as such behavior might appear in the documents that it held," the ministry had found itself torn between restrictive instructions from higher up and the liberal nature of the new legal codes. And so the archives offices at the ministry had functioned in an "ambiguous situation," and even in a "form of illegality" which, according to the authors of the report, accounted for the confusion and the ministry's repeated missteps at the moment when Serge Klarsfeld made his "discovery."[11] The General Inspection's report above all revealed a classic dilemma, which is one of the complex issues of the matter: "If it is not possible to close the archives for the sake of protecting privacy, it can be feared that opening them up without any control may result in personal accusations."[12]

The report was not made public, but *Le Monde* partially revealed its tenor. The daily newspaper recounted in detail the second part, concerning the relative secrecy that surrounded these documents, without mentioning the first part and the doubts as to their real nature: the article kept on talking about "the Jewish card file from October 1940."[13] However, it did point out, in a footnote, that the Prefect of Police had just responded to a timely question posed by Jacques Dominati, assistant mayor of Paris, that "the Jewish card file from the executive office of the general police" had been transferred to the Ministry of War Veterans on April 28, 1948, and that "the rest of the documents and files" had been officially destroyed: "6,890 kilos" on November 16, 1948, "15,000 notecards and 40 filing cabinets" on December 14, 1949.[14] Did this destruction involve the much-discussed card file of October 1940 that had supposedly been found or a different file? Nothing was specified on this point, and the declarations of the Prefect of Police, in these circumstances, were not likely to be very convincing. In fact, these declarations went almost completely unnoticed. At this point in the story, there was total confusion, which was maintained partly by the fragmentary bits of information coming in from all over. As for the general public, they could at that time base their judgment only on one fact: the card file of October 1940 had supposedly been found, having previously been "secretly" held in the possession of a government ministry.

But the debate had already spilled over into another domain: Should the file in question be kept or destroyed? A few voices spoke out to request total or partial destruction. The writer Michel Drachline immediately sued for non-destruction.[15] At times the debate took odd turns. "The Jewish card file must be thrown into the fire," declared flatly the ecologist Brice Lalonde, Minister of the Environment.[16] "This card file must be destroyed, because, if Le Pen takes power, he will be able to use it"; "these documents are too dangerous to be entrusted to historians." These imperious demands were particularly surprising, coming as they often did from people who were publicly campaigning for a complete disclosure of Vichy's crimes and the fate of the victims.

These knee-jerk reactions were forgetting or ignoring that the desire to wipe out the traces of infamous deeds on the one hand, and, on the other hand, the desire to keep alive both the memory *of the names* of those who had died without receiving proper burial and also the proof of the crime, had constituted the terms of a terrible dilemma after the war. These reactions were neglecting the crucial fact that the latter solution had carried the day, as the General Inspection's report pointed out. Adam Rayski recalled the reasons behind this decision:

> With the return of the survivors from Auschwitz and the other camps, the families were still hoping, but after a very long, long wait, they realized that their loved ones were dead. These families had no choice but to begin a long, sad procedure in order for the death of their relatives to be legally acknowledged, while at the same time at the Ministry of the Interior, it was realized that perhaps they had gone too far in ordering the destruction of the files without any other precaution. On January 31, 1947, a new memorandum emanating from the same ministry and addressed to prefects, requests them to "retain in [their] archives documents concerning surveys, abuses, and arrests of which the persons considered to be Jewish had been victim": this was done in view of "finding persons reported missing and of issuing certificates of deportation or internment."[17]

Most of the associations and personalities consulted quickly dismissed the hypothesis of destruction. At that point, a second debate cropped up. The files should be kept, but where and in what conditions? The CNIL[18] talked first of returning the anonymous file cards, then of dispersing the card file, then of keeping it in the Ministry of War Veterans, and finally of transferring it into the National Archives . . . However, the discussion began to lean toward a simple alternative: either the National Archives or the Center for Contemporary Jewish Documentation (CDJC).[19] Serge Klarsfeld first wanted the card file to be kept at the CDJC, a symbolic place for the preservation of the memory of French Jews. But since he was sympathetic to the opinions of historians and officials at the National Archives, he modified his position and conceded that it would be good if these files were the property of the National Archives, with the proviso that they then be transferred to the CDJC. The CDJC itself, the Consistory, the Union of Jewish Students of France, the League of Human Rights, and the United Jewish Social Documentation suggested in various ways that the card file be kept by one of the two offices and that a copy be kept by the other. On the other hand, the Association of Former Deported Jews from France, the LICRA, the bishopry, the Grand Masonic Lodge of France, as well as four historians officially consulted (François Bédarida, Marc Ferro, André Kaspi, and Pierre Vidal-Naquet) argued in favor of designating the National Archives as the unique depository for such a document, which was an integral part of the nation's memory; however, they did not preclude the idea of having a copy deposited at the CDJC. Finally, a third group, made up of representatives of the Chief Rabbi of France, of the President of the Universal Israelite Alliance, and of the grand master of the masonic lodge "Grand-Orient de France," proposed that the card file be considered as a "collective burial place" and placed in the crypt of the Memorial to the Unknown Jewish Martyr.[20]

In its ruling February 25, 1992, the CNIL tried to reconcile these varying viewpoints. Its author, Senator Henri Caillavet, proposed that the Ministry of War Veterans be stripped of the "Jewish card file constituted for the Paris region in 1940" that it held illegally in its possession, and that the original copy be officially transferred to the National Archives. He suggested that this original copy subsequently be deposited, in accordance with a provisory agreement, "in a symbolic way and by the way of exception," in the crypt of the Memorial to the Unknown Jewish Martyr, with the Center for Contemporary Jewish Documentation having a copy for research purposes.

This solution unleashed fury on all sides. Some pointed out that the proposal of the CNIL might lead to a grave confusion on one point: the crypt of the Memorial to the Unknown Jewish Martyr shelters funeral urns coming from the extermination camps. However, the people who had submitted to the census of that time and who were thus in the card file—*which at this moment was thought to be that of the general census of 1940*—had not all been subsequently arrested and deported, far from it. Some of them were even still alive. Were the two going to be mixed together with the prayer for the dead thus recited . . . for the living?[21]

Others, in particular the great majority of historians and archivists (with a few exceptions), denounced the violation of the principle of a common system for conserving public archives. Even within Jewish institutions, many were opposed to this arrangement of depositing the card file in separate locations. Although it often happens that private French or foreign institutions (beginning with the Center for Contemporary Jewish Documentation) hold documents or objects constituting part of the national patrimony, this formal action would indeed have made official a specific arrangement. This would have been particularly inappropriate in this instance, in that the disputed card file was created precisely on the basis of a partly native policy of "racial" and religious discrimination. Were the Jews, fifty years after Vichy, to remain apart from the national community? Once again came into play—and this was a constant—the perverse effect of the "Judeocentrism" which characterizes most contemporary debates about the memory of Vichy and the Occupation: it is often forgotten, in these debates, to what extent the Jews, both French and foreign, both camp survivors and those saved from persecution, had in the immediate postwar period refused at all cost to appear as victims distinct from the other victims of the Nazis. As revolting as they may be, the Jewish card files do indeed belong to the national patrimony.

Minister of Culture Jack Lang, who oversees the French National Archives, then entered the scene and found a way to smooth over the awkward solution proposed by the CNIL. He felt that the latter had issued a "recommendation" that had not been requested. The matter was not in its purview and thus remained open. He then named an ad hoc commission charged with issuing a definitive ruling on the best possible site for depositing this troublesome file. Its members were chosen for their competency but also for their hostility toward any fragmentation of the nation's memory. Under the direction of René Rémond, who had already headed the commission on the relations between Paul Touvier and the Church, and who equally headed the High Council of French National Archives, the following people were thus named to the commission: Jean-Pierre Azéma and André Kaspi, two historical scholars on Vichy; Jean Kahn, president of the CRIF; and Chantal Bonazzi, conservator general charged with the contemporary section of the National Archives. A few days after the "file" was transferred to the National Archives, on June 2, 1992, the commission would discover the extent of the error that had been sensed intuitively by the General Inspection in November 1991.

Just as had the General Inspection, the commission observed that the number of file cards (at that time evaluated at roughly 60,000) was well below the number of persons who had responded to the census in October 1940: 149,734, including 85,664 French citizens and 64,070 foreigners (these figures are known from other documents).[22] Moreover, it is known that the card file from the October 1940 census contained several entries and was used for various subcategories of files: files by name, nationality, address, profession, and family. The total number of index cards thus had to be considerable (it was estimated to be about 600,000). In addition, the individual index cards only concerned Jews *arrested after October 1940* and not the Jewish population of the Department of the Seine covered by the census of that month. This fact was confirmed when a rush of requests to consult the files was received by the National Archives on behalf of persons who had been covered by the census in October 1940, or from their inheritors, who had been authorized to consult the index cards concerning them or to whom photocopies were given. Indeed, Chantal Bonazzi could only find corresponding index cards in cases where the person or relative had been arrested. She thus confirmed that those who had been covered by the census but not arrested were not to be found in the "newly found" card file that the commission was analyzing. A few additional verifications allowed her to realize this obvious fact in early July 1992: There had been a mistake; this was not the card file from the census of October 1940. What did she have in her hands then? An unusual, mixed-up card file, as yet still poorly identified. This was the same provisional conclusion that the General Inspection had reached in 1991, but at that time its observations had not succeeded in countering the storm of media attention, since the Ministry of War Veterans did not dare react.

Now embarrassed, the Rémond commission decided, in this early part of July 1992, not to make public the news, which for several months was to become an artificially maintained state secret. "I believe that at the time many people would not have believed us," explained René Rémond later in justifying the reasons—political reasons—for this silence. On the one hand, he had not wanted to add to the climate of tension just a few days before the fiftieth anniversary of the Vél' d'Hiv' roundup, and on the other hand, he had not wanted to provide any arguments to the right wing press, which, in his opinion, would have "made hay" of this pathetic matter.[23] The commission nevertheless informed Jack Lang so that he could decide what steps to take. The Minister of Culture accepted the approach suggested by René Rémond: The mistake would only be made public when it would be possible to state clearly what had become of the huge card file from the census. Three other persons were informed by René Rémond: Louis Mexandeau, Serge Klarsfeld, and François Mitterrand, in order to prevent the latter from saying anything "unwise" during a possible speech at the fiftieth anniversary of the great roundup of July 1942, which at the time already promised to be a rather stormy event (see chapter 1).[24]

Before his mistake was announced publicly by the commission, Serge Klarsfeld decided that it was preferable to take the initiative. He chose to explain the matter in his preface to the book by the reporter Annette Kahn on the card file, which was to appear at the outset of 1993.[25] But this initiative only added to the confusion. The book avoided any mention of the mistake and claimed once again to set straight "the story of the Jewish card file from the 1940 census, newly found in 1991." "Why the hell publish a book about such a crucial issue of memory without being able to give any real answers and without having conducted a thorough scholarly analysis of the card file?" protested indignantly Jean-Pierre Azéma, who was on the Rémond commission.[26]

In his preface, Serge Klarsfeld nevertheless admitted his mistake, but in a way that was so elliptical as to be understood only by experts. And he refused all personal responsibility, laying the blame for the mistake on the Ministry of War Veterans, which had poorly done its job of verification, and on Louis Joinet, technical advisor to the Prime Minister, who had taken up the matter with the CNIL. The latter had supposedly "informed him that it was indeed the prefecture's card file." Finally, he charged the CNIL itself, which had "confirmed" the declarations of Louis Joinet. The "accused" defended themselves by condemning these charges as a "crass, bad-faith campaign." Louis Joinet, usually a placid man, flew off the handle:

"Anyone can make a mistake, but it is indecent to refuse to admit it! [. . .] I committed an error in November 1991 in believing that we were dealing with the card file of the 1940 census. We were under fire from various pressure groups. It would have been better to let the controversy go on for a week and entrust the matter to historians."[27]

A few days before the publication of Annette Kahn's book, the newsmagazine *L'Express* announced both the mistake about the card file and the attempted diversion in the forthcoming preface by Serge Klarsfeld.[28] The Minister of Culture then made up his mind to publish an official communiqué confirming that "what had been called the 'card file from the census taken in particular in the administrative Department of the Seine in compliance with an ordinance from the occupying authorities and dated September 27, 1940' was really a card file concerning victims" and that the card file from the 1940 census had been destroyed. This information made "henceforth moot part of the controversy which had sprung up a year ago." The Minister of Culture also decided, in a "spirit of transparency, truth, and serenity," to make public the "pre-report" that he had requested from René Rémond and which had been officially turned in on December 28, 1992, six months after the initial mistake had actually been established.[29]

In the space of five little sheets drafted a few hours before the publication of the article in *L'Express*, René Rémond indicated that, far from being camouflaged anywhere, the huge card file from the census had been destroyed, in the most official and usual way, in 1948 and 1949. On the basis of the ordinance of August 9, 1944, from the Provisional Government that was reestablishing the rule of the law of the Republic in mainland France (Article 3 of this ordinance struck down any and all acts creating discrimination on the basis of being a Jew), a memorandum from the Minister of the Interior, Édouard Depreux, dated December 6, 1946, required prefects to destroy all "racial" files, with the exception of those that might be useful in validating the rights of victims or their inheritors. On November 15 and 16, 1948, in the presence of the chiefs of police from the Saint-Merri and Charenton sections of Paris, 158 sacks, "with a gross weight of 6,890 kilos and a net weight of 6,732 kilos," were thus pulverized at Charenton. The written report of this destruction specified that these "papers, [which] had been declared useless and had been deposited in the annex of the police headquarters, concerned the census of Israelites,[30] including people and property, index cards and dossiers." Sometime between December 20 and 27, 1949, a remainder of about 15,000 index cards would also be destroyed. On April 28, 1948, police headquarters had turned over to the administration of the Ministry of War Veterans a mixed bag of files recording traces of persecutions, arrests, and deportations.[31] These details confirmed the declarations made a year earlier by the Prefect of Paris Police to Jacques Dominati. After considerable efforts, the commission finally gained access to the written reports testifying to these destructions "thanks to the support of the prefect of Paris police and of his staff," indicated René Rémond in his preliminary report. (Such support and staff assistance are quite unusual when requests come from historians going about their normal research.)

Those who were directly or indirectly held responsible tried to make the best of things. "Whether it is the card file in its entirety or large fragments including Jews arrested or sought after in Paris and its suburbs, the tens of thousands of index cards kept in the Ministry of War Veterans were made out by the Prefecture of Police and are part of the Jewish card file," wrote Serge Klarsfeld. The same defense was put forward by Henri Caillavet, on behalf of the CNIL: "We are dealing with part of the memory of 78,000 people who fell victim to the Shoah.[32] These were ignominious, devastating papers, kept up to date for four years by conscientious French civil servants."[33] At that point the eleventh-hour intellectuals appeared on the scene. In an op-ed piece published by the newspaper Libération, Sonia Combe, who presented herself as an historian and producer with the radio network France-Culture, wrote without hesitation: "The Jewish card file is indeed that of October 1940."[34] Even though she had strictly nothing new to add to the dossier (with which she was not even familiar), she accused the commission, beginning with René Rémond, of presenting a truncated version of the facts. She treated the members of this commission as "state historians" of the Soviet brand, whose intent was to further the reasons of state.

This charge was too grotesque to be taken seriously. There nevertheless remained the psychological effect caused by the commission's pre-report. The text itself, of which only excerpts were published at that time, was written in language too dry and too technical to stem the considerable tide of emotion that had risen over the course of several months. The statements pertaining to this text might indeed seem rather murky on one crucial point: While there subsisted some doubts as to the nature of the card file—were we dealing with a card file that had been reconstituted after the war, with all or part of files set up under the Occupation, or even a remainder of the card file of October 1940?—there was no doubt as to the nature of the index cards, which did in fact originate from Vichy police services. This point was obvious for scholars and the members of the commission. The fact that this was so obvious, however, should have been clearly recalled, since, at this stage, a few questions could still be considered unanswered by people of good faith. To be sure, the facts reported by the commission made "moot part of the controversy," as Jack Lang had written in his communiqué, but what was to be made of the remaining "part," of the issue of memory, which had not been entirely resolved by the publication of Rémond's pre-report? Added to that was a sense that university scholars and the activist Serge Klarsfeld were settling a few scores.

From that resulted a sort of stand-off. On the one side, there was a discourse based on the rigorous examination of the facts then available. The content of this discourse, however, could only be obtained with great care, on account of the delicate political stakes as well as the uncertainties that still clouded the exact nature of the documents. On the other side, there was a discourse which admittedly disregarded the material reality of certain facts, and even ventured out onto purely ideological terrain, but nevertheless did pose a significant question: Whatever the nature of these litigious documents might be—and in view of the fact that they originated from Vichy—the problem of determining their destination, their use, and their possible disclosure remained entirely unresolved. In their public statements, those who were then charged with the dossier doubtless should have been alert to that aspect of things, which was at the heart of the problem of memory raised by this affair, even though it had been stirred up on the basis of error.

Who should throw the first stone at the protagonists? The original mistake would have been insignificant if it had been immediately acknowledged and corrected; in this area, no one is exempt from error. What is more serious, however, is the uncontrollable chain of events in this affair, in which the "demands of memory" come up over and over. This demand, which was just as vague as it was imperious, put very strong pressure on a government administration that indisputably had some things to hide—if not the possession of the huge card file from October 1940, then at least the nondisclosure of certain documents, and the "illegalities" mentioned by the General Inspection of the Ministry of War Veterans. It is this same demand that explains—without justifying it—the initial panic as well as the hesitations of the commission of experts, who were embarrassed by the possible exploitation of their discovery: this was the risk that some "vigilant" hidden look-outs kept brandishing in the face of the researchers who were working on delicate subjects. In such matters, the facts are indeed liable to "be exploited by the extreme Right." What should be done? Remain silent? At this point, an ex-leftist on duty shows up to accuse the scholars of being "official historians," while the extreme Right laughs it up when the truth finally comes out. Tough job . . .

In this story, none of the players really comes out of it unscathed. Neither those who refuse to admit their blunder, nor the reporters who want one way or another to protect their scoop, nor the politicians, nor even the historians on the commission, who might have expected an easy victory, since they had had, without restriction, access to all the elements of the dossier, while at the very same time this had been, for right or wrong, one of the bones of contention in the matter. As for the irresponsible commentators, was it really admissible, once the facts had been established, to claim that with respect to state administration, there was no *essential* difference between holding a card file from a criminal census and using a card file of victims to establish rights and pensions, especially since the issue had been settled after the war by those directly concerned?

And finally, the worst part of this whole affair is that most of those who tried to follow its developments and to understand something about it probably remain convinced, even after the publication of the definitive report,[35] that the card file from the census of the Jews remained hidden by the state administration until its discovery in 1991. Or else they will inwardly say that the whole affair is rather murky and that it is difficult to know where the truth lies. All this has come out of a debate that became absolutely irrational and that strengthens one of the most stubborn fantasies in the obsession with Vichy: that of the "hidden archives" of an "impossible history."

"Hot Off the Press! The Latest Archives! Get Your Copy Now!"

Another controversy, the Schaechter affair, quite well illustrated the new ritual that consists of the media's touting disclosures, in the name of "the duty to remember" and, paradoxically, outside of any memory of historians' achievements.

In the spring of 1992, right in the middle of the "card file affair," when the controversy over the fiftieth anniversary of the Vél' d'Hiv' roundup was just beginning, several thousand photocopies of official documents dating from the Occupation and originating from the archives of the regional department of the Haute-Garonne were out loose and roaming about in the wild. And in the offices of newspaper editors. The Archives of France, the administration with jurisdiction over them, was thus taken off guard by one of the most delicate matters that it had ever encountered.

A "transparency activist," Kurt Schaechter, had decided to violate the law in order to place in full public view a big stack of papers concerning the administration of the prefecture in the region of Toulouse during the Vichy years. The undertaking was of unprecedented proportions: within a few months, he succeeded in photocopying more than 10,000 documents. We should specify right away that, in order to have access to these documents, Kurt Schaechter had obtained a whole series of special permissions (we will come back to this point), in other words the possibility of actually consulting documents that the law prevents anyone from obtaining before sixty years from the date they were made. This special permission, often granted for a number of papers from this period, carries with it the prohibition of making photocopies, since the special permission is only accorded on an individual basis.

The perpetrator of this heist wanted to denounce "the French administrative Holocaust" and to make available to the public archives that had been "padlocked for a hundred years": these statements were systematically relayed by the press, but they were untrue, for the very reason that he had routinely obtained the right to consult the archives.

Kurt Schaechter is a survivor of the arrests made in December 1942 in the Department of the Tarn-et-Garonne. His parents, Austrian Jews who had taken refuge in France before the war, had been interned in the French camps, his father at Drancy and his mother at Noé (in the Department of the Haute-Garonne), before being deported to their deaths. He even thought for a while that his mother had been "liquidated on the spot" by French *gendarmes* and that "a mass grave [existed] near Toulouse." Serge Klarsfeld was the one who would prove him wrong on this point and who would provide him proof that his mother had been deported in May 1944.[36] Schaechter himself had been released from the camp at Septfonds (in the Tarn-et-Garonne) thanks to his status as a member of the Foreign Legion and a veteran of the battle of Narvik in 1940. Like many others in a similar situation, he who had not dared—or had not had the chance—to investigate the final moments his parents had spent on French soil, started asking questions when, in the early nineties, the press started speaking of the French internment camps at Pithiviers, Beaune-la-Rolande, and Les Milles. He inquired into the matter, and a reporter informed him that he had the right, as a relative, to consult the papers concerning the internment of his parents in the departmental archives. He made a request which was granted by the administration of the archives and then, with the bundles of old papers, plunged into the language and activities of the Vichy bureaucracy. He was overwhelmed. Without being able to step back and put things into perspective, without much historical knowledge (but who could blame him?), he thought that he was discovering everything and quickly elaborated his very own theory: "The administrative tool has taken itself for the end, has substituted itself for the state, and has taken itself for the state! These mechanisms of horror did not pop up out of nowhere, nor out of the unbridled mind of some high official, nor from some torturer hungry for action, nor some fanatic of the Order of the Legion or from the Milice; we are dealing with a civil, police-like, prefectural administration: smooth, cold, impersonal, without passion or compassion, with limited responsibility, compartmentalized, fearless, self-important, and functioning without constraint." Without his being aware of it, Schaechter's focus on the French bureaucracy went along with an obfuscation of the presence of the Germans and a certain indulgence for Pétain who "perhaps was not aware of all the initiatives that his civil servants were taking." Even though he had been able to consult these documents freely, documents which had already been studied by a number of students and historians, Kurt Schaechter set out on a mission: "To make the secret explode." He had gotten it into his head and kept on repeating that "the state administration prefers to keep these thousands of stinking, nauseous documents, which prove its responsibility, locked up until the years 2039 and 2100!"[37]

The "explosion" began with a generous distribution. Several kilos of choice excerpts were sent to the principal moral and political authorities in France and Europe: the President of the Republic, the Prime Minister, the President of the Senate, the President of the Constitutional Council, the ambassadors of Germany, Israel, the Nobel Prize attribution committee, the Queen of Netherlands, the King of Belgium, and others. All French and foreign newspaper editors were invited to accept delivery of the scoops in stock. In the land of transparency, the *New York Times* would even be tricked into devoting a front page story, reprinted in the *Herald Tribune*, to the "French guilt" and the Gallic penchant for state secrets![38] All this was happening at the very moment when, in the background of the debates aroused by Japan's aggressive trade practices, Americans were finding out about the fate their government allotted during the war to their compatriots of Japanese origin, who were interned in camps beginning in December 1941 and who did not receive any compensation until fifty years later . . .

There was thus in the Parisian press a whole flurry of sensational articles about the "forbidden, inaccessible, and unconsultable archives of the French camps." Reporters were free to shop around among the packets of mixed administrative documents that were presented as previously unknown and secret. There were police memos concerning the arrest and internment of foreign Jews and of "French citizens of uncertain racial origin," of Spanish refugees, and of others. There were texts and registers dealing with the management of the numerous internment camps in the southwestern part of France (Gurs, Récébédou, Noé, Argelès, and others), letters reporting that a train full of people had indeed been "turned over to the German authorities," instructions spelling out the procedure to follow for the "confiscation of all valuables belonging to the internees," and bills sent by the SNCF[39] to the Ministry of the Interior to obtain payment for the trainloads of deportees.

The "wildcat" interpretations of certain documents that Kurt Schaechter offered to the press (which often contented itself with reproducing them) were revealed to be very loose or completely erroneous. For example, the fact that a large number of foreigners were still present under the classification "Jew" or "stateless" or "of doubtful nationality" in 1945 and 1946 in the camps in the southwestern part of France can be explained not—as Schaechter asserted and as some newspapers would report—by de Gaulle's desire to continue Vichy's policies of exclusion(!), but by the political and administrative mess of the Liberation period and by several factors peculiar to that region of France, especially the massive return, in 1945, of Spanish refugees who in October 1944 had attempted to win back their country from under the yoke of Franco.

Several of these documents were widely published in the press, accompanied by more or less hairbrained commentaries. Such was the case with the Château du Doux affair in the Corrèze region, where Jews able to pay the heavy expenses of their stay were interned. The historian Anne Grynberg explained that, contrary to the fanciful theories put forth in several newspapers, that episode could be understood not in the framework of any sort of "ransom" enterprise supposedly sponsored by René Bousquet in person, but in the context of a whole series of efforts undertaken by Jewish and non-Jewish charitable organizations alike which were trying by all means available to get all the Jews who could be saved out of the French camps. Denis Peschanski, another historical scholar on the subject, took on the task of taking apart the assertions made by several reporters, in particular the one about the sum paid by those staying in the Château du Doux: "the current equivalent of 2.9 billion francs" according to the weekly newsmagazine *VSD*[40]—a completely ridiculous figure.[41] These refutations, however, were to no avail. Not only were they rejected with a contemptuous stroke of the pen, but also several newspapers retorted by clearly stating their claim to write the history of Vichy more effectively and honestly than the historians; they thus asserted that history was not the historians' "private property."[42] In point of fact, this is perfectly true, just as is the fact that the right to publish nonsense does not belong exclusively to university scholars.

"Alas, one cannot but observe that Vichy remains a forbidden zone. Silence on this subject still becomes too many people," proclaimed an editorial of the weekly newsmagazine *VSD*.[43] This was in June 1992, seven months after the beginning of the card file controversy, five months after the publication of the report on Touvier and the Church, two months after the huge scandal caused by the court ruling dismissing charges against the same former member of the Milice, and in the midst of the controversy over the upcoming commemoration of the Vél' d'Hiv' roundup. And that was what was called a taboo subject that people only talked about in whispers out in the boonies.

"Free the Archives Now! Free the Archives Now!"

These phony scandals raised the ritual question of the access to the "archives of the Occupation," a thriller series that has continued for fifty years. Sonia Combe wrote:

> The attitude of the French Archives that was revealed in this instance [the card file controversy] is one example among many others evident at present, of the notorious "Vichy syndrome." The fact that it affects the institution

that manages the memory of our nation is a serious matter. We must double our efforts to make Vichy intelligible, so that no magistrate may absolve a Touvier, and so that we ourselves may not slip imperceptibly towards a trivialization of the darkest pages of our history. And as in Moscow, this task is to be achieved through an ethical and political battle for the opening up of our archives.[44]

The same person who had claimed that the card file found in the Ministry of War Veterans was indeed that of October 1940, in spite of the categorical denial of the Rémond commission, was now, a few weeks later, marching off to war against the French Archives, thus taking up where Kurt Schaechter had left off. Had she worked with the documents of this history and had she been refused access to explosive papers? Did she have even a minimum of facts on the subject? "Madame Sonia Combe, an historian, has never had need of the services of the French Archives, she has never registered here, and has never requested the slightest special permission, and in particular not the slightest disclosure [of documents]," pointed out Chantal Bonazzi.[45]

This situation illustrated several aspects of the "Vichy syndrome" poorly understood by those who throw the expression around: the logic of suspicion, which subsists in groups whose ideology does not stand up very well to the test of time; the tendency to favor fantasies, the ignorance of the realities of the Vichy period; and the ignorance of the way in which its memory should be handled and its history should be written. Such mindless diatribes coming from "intellectuals" having absolutely no competence in this field (and nothing interesting to say) have become all too frequent. Unfortunately, they often create a picture so distorted that it is necessary to put things back into perspective a bit.

Access to public and private documents deposited in the National Archives is regulated by the law of January 3, 1979, which brought about an in-depth reform of an archaic system. It was in 1897 that so-called national archives (papers from government ministries and administrations) on the one hand and departmental archives on the other were brought together under the same authority. A decree of August 18, 1945, created one centralized supervisory office for the Archives, which subsequently became the supervisory office for the French Archives (both national and departmental). On that level, the law of 1979 was not very innovative: this supervisory office has control over all public archives, with the exception—as was traditionally the case—of those of the Ministries of National Defense and of Foreign Affairs, which maintained their autonomy in this area. The supervisory office was charged with collecting, sorting out, conserving, and disclosing documents, which *remained under the authority of the respective government offices*

from which they originated—this is an essential point which is too often unknown or ignored, but which is still the key to the problem. The supervisory office assists government ministries in various ways and above all plays
the role of mediator between these government offices and the public,
which is allowed to consult the documents in a center provided for that
purpose, the Center for Reception and Research of the National Archives
(CARAN).[46] Inaugurated a few years ago and completely computerized,
the CARAN is probably one of the most modern of all the centers for the
consultation of public archives in Europe; all the researchers who use foreign centers or who, just ten years ago, still had to make their way around in
the narrow rooms of the Hôtel de Soubise, know it.

Before the law of 1979, the collection and disclosure of these public documents was governed by legislation that was very vague. This legislation
provided that, in theory, any citizen could gain access to public documents
(according to the law of June 25, 1794). Nevertheless, it was not until July
21, 1936, that a decree made it obligatory for the various government offices to save their documents and to place them in the archives. "In practice,
various provisions [including the decrees of July 31, 1962, and November
19, 1970] had considerably limited this theoretical liberty of disclosure."[47]
Before the reform of 1979, all public archives dating from after July 10,
1940, were therefore unavailable for disclosure: this date had been explicitly defined as a barrier marking the borderline between the "modern" period and the "contemporary" period and between the similarly named sections of the National Archives. The fact that this date was that of the birth
of the Vichy regime was not originally due to happenstance. Nowadays,
this separation no longer exists. Public archives from the twentieth century
are divided into two new sections, one going from 1914 to 1958, and the
other from 1958 to the present. The previous dividing line (that of July 10,
1940, and the advent of the Vichy regime) has given way to a different transition: that of 1958, which marks the advent of the Fifth Republic.

This general rule was moreover limited by the status of certain documents. Medical records were undisclosable for 150 years; personnel records (for civil servants, magistrates, and the like), judicial records, notarized
minutes, and the like were inaccessible for 100 years; basic statistical documents (resulting from the data collection) were permanently undisclosable
(this was a radical provision of the decreee of June 7, 1951, which created
the INSEE,[48] and which was not unrelated to fears that had been aroused
by what had happened to certain statistical card files during the Occupation, especially those of the Jewish census . . .).[49] Finally, any document not
fitting into any of the preceding categories and "threatening privacy and
public interest" remained inaccessible for fifty to a hundred years according
to government ministries.

In short, it was almost impossible, or in any case quite difficult, to work on the history of Vichy in the sixties and seventies, because of the lack of extensive, free access to French public sources. The report of the General Inspection of the Ministry of War Veterans, from which we have cited excerpts at the beginning of this chapter, recalled what had been the position of the National Archives of that time with respect to requests to consult documents from the Occupation: "Disclosing documents dating from after 1940 was out of the question"; historians' demands were "intolerable" and the Archives were going to "dig in their heels."[50]

Upon the initiative of Jean Favier, who was then director of the French Archives, a major reform was undertaken from 1975 to 1979, in order both to modernize and unify laws and statutes and to liberalize access to public documents. It should be noted that it was during this time period that the aftereffects of the Occupation that were to mark the two following decades spectacularly resurfaced, beginning with the Touvier affair (1972), the Darquier affair (1978), and the Leguay-Bousquet affair (1979). The policy of liberalization—which did not specifically concern the Occupation era—was carried out during the same time that there was a brutal awakening to what this previously repressed past was. Finally, the archives law took its place in the framework of a new set of rules concerning government administrative offices and those who used them (as set out by the law of July 17, 1978), and concerning the protection of privacy with respect to computerization, which led to the creation of the CNIL (also in 1978).

The law of 1979 both modified and clarified the rules of disclosure. In general, and consistent with international norms in this area, the documents in the public archives would henceforth be accessible at the end of thirty years (according to Article 6). Access to a whole series of documents was, however, clearly more restricted: papers of a medical nature (150 years after the date the person was born); personnel files (120 years after the date the magistrate, officer, or other civil servant was born[51]); judicial and notary documents (100 years after the closing of the file); facts included in public statistics (100 years after the census or survey); and finally, the most debatable point, "60 years after the date indicated on the document for papers that contain information threatening privacy or concerning state security or national defense" (according to Article 7).

This law was passed unanimously by the Senate and by the National Assembly. The Occupation was mentioned only once in the debate, by the historian and Senator Henri Fréville, to demand sanctions against those who . . . might destroy public documents from that era.[52] This piece of legislation had therefore not been at issue during the discussions dealing with the need to balance the right to information against the right to privacy and the necessity of certain state secrets. Furthermore, the list of restrictions in Article 7 basically concerned the protection of individuals, with only one paragraph dealing with state security.

A decree of December 3, 1979, was added to complete this set of rules by first specifying the list of documents that could not be disclosed for sixty years: those concerning the President of the Republic and the Prime Minister; those coming from the Interior Ministry, the National Police, the Renseignements Généraux,[53] the General Inspection of Government Offices, and the tax office *when they touch on private life, national defense, or state security*; those dealing with negotiations or with disputes with foreign countries, with war damages, with mineral rights, and so forth. In other words, they are documents whose "active" lifespan is generally very long (according to Article 1). The decree also stipulated that these conditions of disclosure could—and this was a major innovation—be subject to requests for *special permission* for disclosure, which would be submitted to "the government minister in charge of cultural policy (in the office of the director of the French Archives) which would, after obtaining the agreement from the administrative authority that had transferred the documents or that saw to their storage, issue a ruling." (This was according to Article 2). Such special permission, which would be granted in writing to a specific individual, could apply even to documents less than thirty years old. It could even be generalized, that is to say granted systematically for certain archival sources, once a time period of thirty years expired, which fall under the general rule; this is, for example, the case for the archives from the offices of the vice president of the Council under Vichy, and also for the prefects' reports during that era.

That is the law. Just what, then, is the exact nature of the dispute?

Nobody, except for ignoramuses, disputes the liberality of the 1979 law, and even less the considerable progress achieved in comparison with the previous situation. The administrative procedures and the philosophy of the principle of these special permissions, however, have been at issue. The interpretation of the notion of "privacy" does indeed pose more problems than that of "state security," which is currently rarely invoked in practice, at least not for the Occupation era. Almost all the documents subject to limited access by definition hold information of a "personal" nature; that is, according to the definition given by the Commission for Access to Administrative Documents, a document that carries a value judgment or observation about a person or which includes a description of a person's behavior that might be harmful to disclose. Actually, a large part of the public archival sources for this era, which do not explicitly fit into the legal framework of documents subject to requests for special permission and which therefore might be freely accessible without special authorization, have in practice been considered to come under the rules of special permissions. In other words, the rule of automatic disclosure after thirty years has only been partially applied, by virtue of a wide interpretation of the notion of the protection of privacy. This has been one of the points of contention regarding the 1979

law, which did not really resolve the conflict between the right to (historical) information and the right to protect individual privacy, two principles
of republican democracy that are at times at odds with each other. This was
left up to the government offices in question and to archivists. However,
when added to the bad memories of what the situation had been before
1979, this room for interpretation allowed by the text of the law has come
to be the source of criticisms expressed from many different observers (we
are talking about scholars and reporters acting in good faith here). Many
archivists and historians have moreover pleaded for a simplification of the
rule of sixty years, while at the same time knowing that this would not resolve the problems intrinsic to any disclosure of archives.

The first of these difficulties is that the more liberal the rules are, the
fewer the papers that are deposited by various government ministries, even
though the law requires them to do so. Unless a sort of "archives police"
were put into place or unless one wanted to pretend to be naïve, this is a fact
that is hard to ignore: no state, no regime has ever willingly placed its vital,
sometimes scandalous secrets in the public arena, be it in Paris, Washington, or Moscow. We might believe that there are thick files on the Ben Barka
affair,[54] on torture in Algeria, or that there remain some essential documents pertaining to the *Rainbow Warrior* affair.[55] We can imagine what there
might be or stamp our feet indignantly, but unless we are seriously thinking
about a revolution, it is difficult to see how this entrenched tradition, which
is not at all peculiar to France, is to be changed: it took fifty years for the
World War II archives of the intelligence agencies of the United States, the
country that is always cited as an example of freedom of information, to be
"declassified." The historian's work consists accordingly in getting around
these obstacles by studying a large number of widely dispersed sources.

Those who work on the history of the Occupation moreover meet
rather infrequently with this kind of difficulty, contrary to the stories that
can often be heard on the subject. Indeed, in view of the circumstances of
that time and because of the very early concern for recovering all sorts of
archives (from the Liberation period on), the mass of documents on that
era that are available and that have in fact been deposited in the National
Archives is considerable. While deliberate destructions of documents have
occurred in the past, and the retentive reflex has not disappeared (certain
government ministries, such as the Ministry of the Interior, still hold large
archival sources in their possession), it is more the sheer immensity of the
task that causes problems rather than the access to documents: how many
archival sources, whose classification has been completed after years of inventory, find no researchers to pore over them, even though the National
Archives regularly publish a list of the archives that are deposited there?[56]
One of the major sources for the era, that of the German military administration in occupied France (called the "Majestic," after the Parisian hotel

where its headquarters were located), from which hundreds of linear meters of archives have been recovered, stored, and classified in the National Archives (thanks in particlular to Chantal Bonazzi's predecessor, the curator Pierre Cézard), has until recently been neglected by researchers. It is nevertheless a source essential for making Vichy "intelligible." True, it does present one major drawback: most all of its documents are in German.[57]

The second difficulty is that permission to consult documents is not systematically granted by the particular government office that deposits, classifies, and retains authority over them, even if the attitude of the National Archives is often more favorable. Most of the government offices depositing documents, however, have for the last ten years or so proven to be quite liberal with respect to Occupation period archives. This is true of the Ministries of Justice, National Education, Industry, Finance, Postal Services, Transportation, to name only those subjected to the rule of systematic deposit (let us recall that the Ministries of National Defense and Foreign Affairs have retained their autonomy). This policy of openness has provided the material for a large number of dissertations, books, and theses about the history of Vichy France. There remain, however, little islands of resistance, which are well known to researchers and which gain a good deal of attention: this is the case, mainly, for the Prefecture of Police and the Ministry of the Interior. The latter holds in particular the archives of the territorial administration and those of the former central administrative headquarters of the police (including the National Security police, the Renseignements généraux, and the administrative internment camps). Outside of the archives of the territorial administration and those of the camps—for which special permission is often granted (hence the abundance of historical publications on the subject)—the archives of the other offices of the Ministry of the Interior, as well as those of the Prefecture of Police, remain hard to access, when indeed they have been deposited and are thus physically accessible. And obviously they do concern a crucial aspect of the history of Vichy, even though numerous sources (German archives, or those coming from other government ministries) have in the last few years made it possible to get started with decisive research in this field and to provide a rather clear, if not exhaustive vision of French acts of repression and persecution under the Occupation. The reason cited by the Ministry of the Interior is always the same: it considers itself to be charged with a mission of preserving "domestic peace," and is not keen on complying with what is commonly done in other government ministries. This line of thinking is particularly absurd, since most documents exist in duplicates that are accessible in other archival holdings, especially in German archives. The virulent criticism that has been leveled at the Ministry of the Interior and the Prefecture of Police from all quarters, and above all, the realization that in this area the risks involved in withholding information are worse that those of disclosure, have nevertheless brought about an appreciable change, at any rate with the Ministry of the Interior.

The third difficulty stems from the diversity of situations that exist in the various regional archives. These archives are of a much higher volume than the National Archives, but the principle of special permissions is applied to them much more restrictively. These documents, especially prefectoral archives, are essential for understanding the era, because the division of French territory into zones (including those occupied by the Germans, those occupied by the Italians, the free zone, the forbidden zone, and the reserved zone) created a great diversity of regional and local situations. Now, out of the hundred or so regional archivists, there are only a few who prove to be reticent about issuing special permission. Their attitude is nevertheless less decisive than that of the prefect, who, on a regional level, either grants or refuses permission in the capacity of a state official. And some prefects tend to feel that the disclosure of information about that era presents more risks locally, where memories are closer to the surface and more precise, than nationally. This argument is not very convincing, inasmuch as opening the archives in most regional departments does not raise any serious problems, except when somebody deliberately seeks to create a scandal, for good or bad reasons—although it is true that neither the prefect nor the archivist can gauge the real intentions of those making the request. On that score, one can express some doubts, on the level both of principles and effectiveness, about media campaigns that seek to single out *individual persons* for public condemnation, even if some of these campaigns have justly undermined solid reputations. Morality, justice, and historical truth generally gain very little in such conditions, except for the judicial strategies that are aimed at pursuing someone for crimes against humanity, which is an entirely different matter. It is moreover the proliferation of scandals targeting specific individuals that have made certain prefects and archivists more circumspect with respect to issuing special permissions. This is one of the perverse results of these "transparency campaigns" that has often been pointed out.

The system is thus far from perfect and malfunctions do exist. But if we stick to the facts, the criticisms recently leveled at the National Archives most of the time concern either the archives of the Ministry of the Interior —over which they have no power, even when they issue a favorable ruling on the request for special permission—or certain regional archives, where local officials enjoy a large measure of autonomy, and their personal attitudes often play a decisive role. Questioned by the reporters of the television program *La Marche du siècle* during the broadcast previously cited, Serge Klarsfeld, whom we cannot suspect of being lenient on the subject, gave a clear explanation of this situation: "A year ago, I wrote to some forty archivists requesting documents from them. The regional directors of the archives answered with a variety of responses ranging from 'We don't have any documents' to 'An authorization must be requested in order to consult these documents' to 'Here is a list of the documents requested' and even photocopies of the requested documents which came right away without any authorization ever having been requested." The same program nonetheless highlighted the particularly clear case of a regional depository of archives that was not liberal at all, letting people believe that this was an example of what was generally the rule.

To convince oneself of the magnitude of the clichés about this issue, all one has to do is to take a look at the quantitative aspect of the problem. While unfavorable decisions from prefects or regional archivists exist, although always turning up in the same departments, unfavorable decisions from the officials at the National Archives are rare: Jean Favier mentioned that he had personally issued four in fourteen years;[58] Chantal Bonazzi, the former curator general in charge of the contemporary section, has for her part issued a few during each of the ten years that she has been at this position.[59] However, that is only true for the unfavorable rulings issued *solely* by the National Archives. Every researcher has met with refusal to access certain series of archives once or more *from the various government offices depositing them there*, even though at the same time that they obtained a good number of special permissions. During the same broadcast of *La Marche du siècle*, Rita Thalmann, whom the producers of the show had used almost exclusively as a basis for preparing their indictment of the Archives, explained how the files (about the collaboration between French and German police) coming under the jurisdiction (once again) of the Ministry of the Interior had been refused to her by the Interior Minister of that time, Pierre Joxe, while at the same time the German archives dealing with the same subject and stored in France were available to her. All researchers would agree with her: on a scholarly level, these situations are absurd. We approve when she proclaims that "if the Republic has nothing in common with Vichy, then it should clean up its act," and that the Republic should put an end to the special sets of rules governing certain government offices. But when Chantal Bonazzi, without receiving any denial of the fact, reminds her live on the same program that she (Rita Thalmann) had personally requested special permission to consult 156 boxes and that only 17 (coming from the Ministry of the Interior) were denied to her, one can only conclude that there is a considerable gap between the controversy that she was fueling and the reality of the situation. Actually, Rita Thalmann found herself in the same boat with many of her colleagues, including the authors of this book, with respect to these requests for special permission that were both granted or refused. No more, no less. Yet no one dreamed of taxing her with being an "official historian."[60]

The Duty to Remember and the Duty to Be Responsible

Access to the archives is thus not completely free, even if it has now been greatly facilitated. But on what criteria do government ministries base their decisions to grant or refuse special permissions, and on what basis do archivists issue their rulings? This question is much more important than the bean-counting over the number of boxes obtained or refused—all historians, not just those in France, are used to, if not resigned to, this sort of jumping through hoops.

> It is one thing to desire complete transparency, but it is quite another to know whether the French want their professional files, their marriage and family records, their medical records, and their tax records to be open to anybody. It is easy to speak cynically about this protection of privacy. I believe I know for a fact that the French have on several occasions been deeply disturbed at the risks that the disclosure of confidential information would represent for them.[61]

This observation by Jean Favier, the former director of the French National Archives, went well beyond a simple justification. His line of argument did indeed arouse indignant reactions, since this issue comes up almost only when we are dealing with the Occupation: in that instance, what is the protection of the "privacy" of such-and-such individual worth in the face of memory or history? But what would happen, to take a random example, if one were to disclose, without taking any precautions and without guarantees that researchers would respect anonymity, police documents dating from May and June 1968?[62] Perhaps it would be discovered—this is only an hypothesis—that the attitude of the police forces was not as respectful of republican legality as was claimed in the official statements made after these "events." Maybe it would be also discovered—this is still only an hypothesis—that some of the protesters arrested had not all been the heroes that they were thought to be, and even that some of them, a tiny minority, might have aided the police for one reason or another, perhaps valid, perhaps not. Would there then be nobody to write sensational books and articles on the subject that would highlight entirely marginal cases in order to show the student movement in a bad light? . . .[63]

Contrary to the clichés in circulation, the question of privacy concerns not just "collabos" that some are still trying to protect. It is a serious problem that fortunately only arises for a small number of documents that are still difficult to access. Let us give a few anonymous examples. Can the dossier of a person brought before a court of justice at the time of the Liberation be disclosed to a researcher, *if the person in question is still living*? The historian, caught up in his own logic, and even though subject to the legal obligation "not to divulge anything that might damage the reputation of individual persons," will tend to answer in the affirmative, knowing that certain precautions would have to be taken. The government official or archivist will answer in the opposite way, if only because, according to the law, amnesty precludes the disclosure of any criminal conviction.

If the person is deceased, another difficulty arises: in addition to facts of "historical" value (facts about collaboration for example), there exists in these files a great deal of information about the individual, the individual's family, entourage, and so on. Can documents containing information about the deceased that the latter was not able or willing to divulge be revealed to a son, a daughter, a wife, or a husband who might be unaware of these facts? This is a thorny question, and in this case, it is not professional historians, but relatives or loved ones wanting to consult documents for their own personal information, who run up against the problem.

Even information of historical value can, in this situation, present pitfalls for the archivist. The example of a person persuaded that one of his relatives was a Resistance hero, and who might discover, in examining the documents, that this was far from being the case, if not worse, is not just an hypothesis. The problem is still more delicate when one is dealing not with a collaborator (whose activities are moreover generally more or less noticeable), but rather with an individual, known or unknown, who was a victim of the Nazis or Vichy, and whose memory risks being tarnished by the sudden revelation of a rather shady aspect of the individual's life, which had up until then remained hidden. May we open files on French citizens brought before German military tribunals in occupied France or in Germany without taking any precautions, when they concern neither resisters nor political opponents but individuals accused of other offenses? The Nazis, for example, considered it a crime for prisoners of war or foreign forced laborers to have sexual relations with German women, and some were judged and even deported for that reason. Those are acts that it is no one's business to judge. The fact remains, however, that once this information is divulged, no one, neither private citizens nor public officials, can control the results. Has it occurred to people that the files from the census or arrests of Jews, which are exactly the type of documents which refer to private individuals by name and which are at the origin of the recent controversy, might contain this type of difficulty, while at the same time providing little worthwhile information about the Vichy regime as such?

The history of the Dark Years is not a tale about fairies or witches telling the story of a handful of good guys and bad guys. It is the story of a human, fully human tragedy, in which even now it is still difficult to understand all the gray areas. This tragedy was inscribed in the bodies and minds of human beings. It left painful, tangible wounds in flesh and blood which continue to ooze. To refuse to admit this, to refuse to understand that this suffering exists not only for victims of persecutions but also for many groups, and to refuse to see that this suffering now often affects the protagonists' offspring and no longer the protagonists themselves, is to show an irresponsibility unworthy of an archivist or an historian. We are therefore utterly astounded to see a philosopher, describing the perpetual and disorderly repeat performance of this past, allow himself to write such nonsense as follows:

> [The] process of dissemination of the narrative of the Dark Years and of the Liberation, of the wearing down of its live, cutting edges, nevertheless presents a clear contrast with the reinforcement which, inexplicably, has, since the 1970s, worked only to increase the hold of state power over one of the main sources and one of the most reliable materials that scholarly memory (the work of historians) can base itself on—the *archives*. It is as if a certain "sense of state," effectively transmitted through the corporate atavisms and routine of the archivists, remained the ultimate conservator of a will to make the memory of that era sacred, intent on preserving its tawdry secrets, just as it keeps burning the flame of its most mechanical and stereotyped narratives. The systematic and concerted nonapplication of the legislation on the opening of public archives after a period of thirty years, under the fanciful pretext of protecting individual privacy (a phony justification that is daily ridiculed by the work of newspaper reporters, television reporters, clever people of every stripe, and the well-regarded researchers) gives a free hand to the archaic and leonine system of consultation by "special permission," which is left to the sole discretion of the director of the French Archives.[64]

Our philosopher is either ignorant or, worse, contemptuous of the examples cited above. They are nevertheless real, although relatively infrequent. The principle of consultation by special permission, in other words through screening and mediation, moreover has as its first function, before that of protecting the state, to keep things from getting out of hand: this was precisely the gist of the long debate in the National Assembly in 1978, leading to a unanimous vote.[65] The government employee who grants special permission and the archivist who knows the file and issues a ruling are, just as is the historian, subject to a certain discretion, the former by duty (professional secret, as for magistrates or doctors), the latter by ethics. An archivist questioned by one of the authors of this book thought that he did not feel that he had the right to allow information that could cause a problem to be divulged, even to a member of a deceased person's family: "If that person did not want to say anything, by what right would I provide the means to get the information to the family member?" Is he right or wrong? The principle of consultation by special permission has given to the various government offices that deposit documents, to prefects, and to archivists, the task of evaluating the question in their souls and consciences on a case by case basis. If there is a debate to be had, it is there and nowhere else.

As for historians, their work does not consist of sitting in judgment or in compensating for the failures of the purge, but rather of understanding and explaining. In the case of prominent individuals or high-ranking government officials, secrecy scarcely makes any sense after fifty years, particularly for information fitting into the framework of their public activities: divulging certain documents from the prosecution's files on René Bousquet after his assassination, as did the daily newspaper *Libération* on July 13, 1993, was necessary for the sake of both memory and history.[66] The problem is different when one is dealing with unknown individuals, even if the line between the two categories of people is not always simple to draw. That is what is called exercising a duty to be responsible, which is just as crucial as the duty to think critically or the duty to remember.

Finally, another aspect of the question lies in the trusting relationship that archivists and researchers maintain with each other. That goes for anyone who requests access to documents—the myth of "privileged researchers" (the "official historians") is a product of pure fantasy when it does not stem from a resentment just as paltry as the quality of the writings of those who flippantly utter these accusations. All researchers are in the same boat; all one has to do is to look at who consults what. When a researcher has been the first to obtain a special permission to consult such and such document (or when the researcher was simply the first to have had the idea to request it), this permission is from then on very rarely refused to others—and it must not be refused—in accordance with two basic rules: the equality of citizens before the law and the necessity of being able to verify the sources of information used in writing a work of history. The principle of consultation by special permission, as imperfect or subject to criticism as it might be, has, moreover, paradoxically strengthened the bonds between archivists, who are intimately familiar with their holdings, and historians (this is the "plot" . . .). How many proven young dissertation writers or university students have been oriented by a competent archivist in directions they had never thought of? They are much more numerous than those who have been discouraged by some local guard dog! This fact particularly deserves to be recalled since it is always the historian who receives the honors for making a discovery, and not the archivist without whom this discovery would sometimes never have been possible.

In any case, this controversy, which was in many respects irrational, at least succeeded in bringing about changes in the legislation governing the archives. Indeed, after the report on the functioning of the archives (a report that the government had requested) was submitted in June 1996,[67] Prime Minister Lionel Jospin announced in July 1997, at the time of the commemoration of the Vél' d'Hiv' roundup, that a new law governing the archives would be promulgated: this law is to make access to the archives easier by reducing the amount of time it takes to disclose documents. The concrete result for those who study Vichy France is that they will no longer have to request the old "special permission" and so will be able to work with greater facility. This is more of a technical change than a change of principle, but that did not keep most newspapers, beginning with *Le Monde*, from writing that "Vichy's archives" were "finally" going to be opened up, thus suggesting that—until 1997!—they had been kept hermetically sealed.

The debate over the archives has something unreal about it. In the wave of media clichés or of activists' diatribes, one regularly hears that it is scandalous that the Occupation archives should remain secret, that they should be destroyed (see the controversy over the Jewish card file), or even that nothing can equal the value of direct oral testimony of the survivors of the tragedy. And this is always asserted in the name of fighting against "trivialization" or "lapse of memory." However, these valiant, belated defenders of memory—we are not talking about the generation that lived through the Dark Years here—never pose the only questions that are really valid: What history remains even now impossible to write for lack of free access to documents? In spite of the flood of books, films, and articles about these Dark Years that have recently been produced, of what crucial knowledge are we still deprived? Before claiming that the truth is being hidden, people should read the historical writing, what the philosopher would call "the dissemination of the narrative," on the subject. Granted, it is less fun and more work than barking at the door of the Archives without even thinking of going in.

3

The Touvier Trial

Justice, Memory, and History

On April 20, 1994, in Versailles, a relatively insignificant former member of the Milice was condemned by the circuit court to life in prison without parole for complicity in a crime against humanity. The Touvier trial, a trial "for the sake of memory," will in fact be one of the last episodes of the purge, fifty years after the Liberation.

Between 1944 and 1953, the courts had the delicate mission of working out the aftereffects of the Occupation. In order to put an end to wildcat purge actions, it was to this criminal justice system that General de Gaulle's Provisory Government, whose priorities included the restoration of the rule of law, had entrusted the task of judging Vichy officials and collaborators. It did this after having first carried out a purge of the magistrates themselves, whose legitimacy had been undermined by the role they had played under Vichy. This purge of the magistrates had been perceived to be so severe and unfair as to leave an enduring bitterness among them.[1] After the passage of the amnesty laws in the early fifties, the veil of legal oblivion fell over most crimes committed under the Occupation. It was henceforth up to posterity to judge those who had joined forces with Nazism. The magistrates experienced this transition with particular relief, since the purge, by its excesses and even more by its omissions leading to injustices, had aroused all kinds of virulent criticisms and deep frustrations.

Nevertheless, since the early seventies, the courts have returned to the arena. They have become the vector of memory par excellence, and are considered by some to be the place where the blank pages of this story should be filled in. They have been asked, although belatedly, to try still unpunished crimes, but also—and above all—to teach a lesson in civics.

In a context completely different from that of the postwar period, the courts have been asked to reopen certain cases in order, this time, to find out about crimes against humanity, which have been taken out from under the statute of limitations by a brief bill passed unanimously on December 26, 1964. Invented toward the end of the war and partially applied in the Nuremberg trials, this type of incrimination had never concerned a French citizen. The international texts of law of 1945, like the French law of 1964, were primarily aimed at the major Nazi war criminals. The law removing the statute of limitations was totally forgotten until June 5, 1972, when it was revealed by the weekly newsmagazine *L'Express* that on November 23, 1971, President Pompidou had pardoned a leader of the Milice forgotten and even unknown for the great majority of the French people: Paul Touvier.

From that point on, the criminal justice system was to become a key player in the issues of memory that were resurfacing all around the memory of Vichy. The pardoning of Paul Touvier brought about, in reaction, the filing of the first charges of crimes against humanity in 1973: the concept of crimes against humanity was a vague one that was made even more difficult to handle by the absence of the statute of limitations, something contrary to the French legal tradition. On March 12, 1979, at a time when the Touvier case had already been open for six years, Jean Leguay, the former representative in the occupied zone for René Bousquet (who was Secretary General of the Laval government's police), was indicted for crimes against humanity for his role in the organization of the Vél' d'Hiv' roundup in July 1942. Leguay was the first in France to suffer this fate; however, he would die, indicted, on July 2, 1989, without ever having been tried. Meanwhile, other cases were opened. Paul Touvier, on the run, was subject to an arrest warrant on November 27, 1981, before being arrested and indicted on May 24, 1989. Klaus Barbie, the former chief of Section IV (the Gestapo) of the German Security forces in Lyons, was extradited from Bolivia and indicted in 1983. Tried in Lyons, he was condemned to life in prison without parole on July 4, 1987. René Bousquet was also indicted in March 1991, but was murdered on June 8, 1993, before having been brought before a court. Finally, Maurice Papon, the former Secretary General of the Prefecture of the Gironde region, was indicted in 1983, then, after the nullification of this court action in 1987, was again indicted in 1988 and 1992. His case wandered through the obscure, esoteric legal channels of the Bordeaux courthouse until October 1997, when his trial finally began.

The courts have thus been placed at the crossroads of the principle stages of the history of the memory of the Occupation. The vicissitudes—and there has been no shortage of them—of each one of these cases have relentlessly fueled the debate over Vichy, its responsibilities in the "Final Solution," French anti-Semitism, and Collaboration. The unbelievable delays in these judicial proceedings have been loudly—and rightly—denounced on countless occasions. But at the same time this dragging out of the proceedings has made it possible to keep the memory of the Occupation in public view. The more the courts and the governmental team in power appeared reticent, the more the pressure was kept up, thereby bringing about a periodical reappearance of the subject. Scandalous on the moral and legal levels, these delays have done memory a favor: the more they wanted to hush things up, the more noise was made around the very thing they sought to conceal.

A Debate Poorly Undertaken

The legal delays have left dangling another debate, which is just as essential as the reassessment of the history of Vichy. Could these cases be tried so long after the deeds had been done? Was it possible, within the confines of a courthouse, to reimmerse oneself in the context of that era, and to weigh things against each other retrospectively? How could the demands of equity (giving reparations to the victims or to their descendants) and the ineluctable necessity of approaching this historical era with detachment be reconciled? Could criminal policies and a criminal regime be tried through the cases of individuals who were not all "representative" of what one wanted to condemn? Could what the war generation had with great pain and conflict put back together after 1944 (that is, the recomposition of the fabric of the nation, both in its social body and in its heart and mind) be undone without risk? For better or for worse, prematurely or not, the choice of amnesty had, in spite of all, been an important milestone in the moral reconstruction of the country. Without garnering unanimous support nor calming passions, it expressed a will of the majority to turn the page. Could another generation nullify this choice, inasmuch as it had been ratified by all the presidents of the Fourth Republic and of the early Fifth Republic, from Vincent Auriol to General de Gaulle? Every one of them had granted a number of individual pardons, either at the time of the purge or afterward, as in the case of those issued to the SS chiefs Karl Oberg and his assistant Helmut Knochen, both condemned to death in 1954, pardoned by René Coty in 1958 and freed in 1962 by de Gaulle, on the eve of the signing of the Franco-German Treaty of Cooperation on January 22, 1963.

Once new prosecutions were begun much later, the postwar debate took on another meaning. It no longer fit into the context of the urgency of reconstruction, but into that of the crisis that France has been undergoing since 1973–1974, and which cannot be reduced to an economic crisis. The debate now was putting into the arena at least two generations, one which had experienced the war, the Occupation, and the purge, and the other, too young at the time or else born later, which was belatedly demanding accountability, with a completely different view of things. Their presuppositions were thus quite different from those of the Liberation period. In the first place, the crime against humanity, the only one that could be prosecuted, primarily concerns persecutions and acts committed in the context of the "Final Solution": these are aspects of the war that were not, or were only slightly taken into consideration during the purge. In the second place, and this is almost obvious, such proceedings against a few isolated, elderly individuals, who no longer represent, as they formerly did, any identifiable political faction, no longer threaten "national unity," whereas such was the feeling at the time of the purge. The trial at Versailles[2] did not in the least undermine national unity, no more than a Bousquet trial would have, no more than will the trial of Papon. The issues were elsewhere. They dealt with the way in which a country confronts its past and with the respective status that it gives history, memory, and justice.

The dilemma between the right to forget and the right to remember, between pardons and the need for justice, has resurfaced from several areas, although not without having sometimes been reduced to a simplistic alternative. It has of course been so reduced by a nostalgic extreme Right, which has constantly waved the silly specter of rekindled "civil war." By means of a discourse recalling that used by those sanctioned by the purge in 1945, the extreme Right has especially defended certain Vichy values readapted to current events, such as the racist, xenophobic nationalism of exclusion. From this viewpoint, these calls to forget, and even to negate purely and simply certain historical realities, were a consequence of the "respectability" that the extreme Right has regained since the early 1980s. Some members of the reactionary Right have also lashed out virulently against the very principle of the legal proceedings, but on an ideological and partisan basis. This is the case, for example, with Annie Kriegel and Alain Griotteray, two former resisters who were not at the time on the same side. Annie Kriegel provided inspiration to Paul Touvier's lawyer, Jacques Trémolet de Villers, who reiterated some of her historical arguments.[3] Her writings, which were quite marginal in the historiography of the period, and which reverted back to the obsolete theory of Vichy as having been a protective "shield" against the occupying forces, had already explicitly influenced the magistrates of the Criminal Appeals Court of Paris who had granted a general dismissal of charges against Paul Touvier on April 13, 1992. Alain Griotteray, defending these same magistrates, denounced "the huge trial of France that a cohort of historians followed by an army of useful simpletons are constantly struggling to prosecute."[4] This is an argument we have often heard, which seems to forget that Vichy was not necessarily "France": was not this precisely one of the messages delivered by a great number of resisters, if not by all of them? This argument also overlooks the fact that, among those who were demanding these trials with the most determination, one found the most adamant defenders of the necessary distinction between the "French State" and the French. The very first of these is Serge Klarsfeld, often vilified, but rarely read with objectivity.

These reticences with respect to the legal proceedings in crimes against humanity cases were not, however, confined to the reactionary or populist Right. Far removed from those leanings, a few isolated voices publicly raised questions about the moral impact of these trials. This is notably the case with Simone Veil,[5] who has done so much to keep the memory of the Genocide alive, and who has nonetheless remained faithful to a principle defended since the extradition of Klaus Barbie:

> I have always thought that the work of historians would contribute much more than belated trials, especially in view of the interpretation given to the concept of "crime against humanity." The dramatization produced in a trial due to a certain personalization of the issues doubtlessly has a greater emotional effect. But, as a former magistrate, I remain puzzled as to the means used and as to the exemplary value of a legal system that intervenes long after the crimes, at a time when the witnesses no longer always have very precise memories, and when the magistrates and the members of the jury have a hard time understanding the context of crimes prosecuted. Even Touvier today looks like an elderly man who can have a pitiful appearance and can make people forget the young man who was . . . pitiless. [. . .] I nevertheless retain certain reservations about the notion of removing the statute of limitations, even for crimes against humanity.[6]

Finally, and above all, the debate was kept alive at the highest level of the state. However, this was done by what was left to be read in between the lines and by incidents: this sometimes created a slight confusion between the positions taken personally by certain political officials, beginning with François Mitterrand, and the role that they directly or indirectly played in the legal system's dragging out of the case.

The first example is what occurred on October 19, 1990, in the Bousquet affair, when the public prosecutor concluded that the former Secretary General of the Police could not be tried under common law jurisdiction (in the criminal circuit court). He would have to be tried on the basis of the ordinance of November 18, 1944, targeting the Chief of State, his ministers, and the Secretaries of State as well as Vichy's commissioners and General Secretaries, who had been brought before the High Court. However, the reconstitution of this High Court a half a century later was at the very least problematical . . . In order to justify what appeared to be another attempt by the government in power to buy time—the proposal came from the public prosecutor—the minister delegated to the Ministry of Justice, Georges Kiejman, declared in an interview: "Beyond the necessary struggle against the lapse of memory, it can seem important to preserve domestic peace and tranquillity [. . .]. There are means other than a trial to condemn the cowardice of the Vichy regime."[7] Taken literally, this declaration doubtless deserved to be taken into account, even though "domestic peace and tranquillity" was hardly at risk and even though at issue was not the "cowardice" of the Vichy regime, but rather its crimes, which were the consequences of its choices. But since this declaration had been made by an acting minister delegated to the Ministry of Justice and a son of a deportee, it could not but provoke an uproar: it expressed only too clearly the position of the President of the Republic and constituted an implicit form of interference in a judicial proceeding.[8] Because of the close—and well-known—links between Georges Kiejman and President Mitterrand, the declaration moreover once again raised recurring questions about the real reasons for François Mitterrand's reticence with respect to a Bousquet trial.

The second example, taken precisely from the President of the Republic's declarations, illustrates the consequences of the ambiguity that had been maintained around this issue for many long years. Right in the middle of the Touvier trial, and a few days before the verdict, the press gave reviews of a book by the historian Olivier Wieviorka that came out in April 1994. In this work, devoted to the testimony of former resisters, the historian gave an account of several interviews with François Mitterrand that had been conducted between April 1990 and January 1993, well before the trial. In the book, the President explained at length his feelings about the legacy of the Resistance, the memory of the Occupation, and the aftereffects that can still be felt, including the Bousquet case (Bousquet was still living at the time) and the Touvier case (the most salient aspect of the case at that time was the dismissal of charges in April 1992, about which the President had expressed his "surprise"):

> *Olivier Wieviorka*: In your opinion, should those who served Vichy be tried now?
>
> *François Mitterrand*: I am not inclined to do so from my own instincts. Except for a totally exceptional case.
>
> *Olivier Wieviorka*: But do you put individuals such as Paul Touvier and men like René Bousquet on the same level?
>
> *François Mitterrand*: Under no circumstances. Paul Touvier—I only know about his case through the press—appears to me to have been somebody who collaborated and perhaps turned people in. So he belongs to a sort of political riff-raff. Bousquet is a high official who got caught up in things. He does not personally have the low character that I attribute to Touvier —unless of course a more thorough study should show otherwise. Bousquet constitutes the very prototype of those high officials whose integrity was compromised or who let their integrity be compromised. To what extent . . . That had to be judged. It was judged, moreover, after the war.

Forty-five years later, they are old men. There no longer remain many witnesses and it no longer makes much sense. In French history, it is rare for the trauma of internal strife not to have been swept away in the twenty years that followed by acts of amnesty or willful oblivion. Even the Commune.[9] The Commune was the most traumatic domestic event to happen in France after the Revolution. It claimed more victims than the French Revolution or the religious wars. But, twenty years afterward, those who had participated in the Commune, at least those who had not been shot, were free. One cannot constantly live on memories and resentment.[10]

In the rest of the interview, the President spoke of the extent of the purge and approved the policy of national reconciliation favored by Georges Pompidou. At the same time, the President recalled that he himself had "amnestied the rebellious generals of Algeria"[11] in November 1982. He also stated that he himself had "authorized legislation on crimes against humanity."[12]

Chance would have it that the book came out in April 1994; this modified the implications of these words, which at least had the merit of being consistent and sincere. But the substance of the debate that they could have provoked was at that moment swept away by the controversy. Made public right amid the final pleas of the prosecution, these statements interfered in the course of a trial that was already rather complicated. Whatever his inner motivations might have been, the President's stances nevertheless deserved to be discussed. Whether or not one agrees with them, it was (and remains) difficult simply to brush aside the question of such a belated trial and the argument of national reconciliation, understood not as a reconciliation between resisters and collaborators—nobody, except for the extreme Right, has ever defended that idea—but as the reconciliation of the French with their past. This by no means signifies a lapse of historical memory, and even less any pardon whatsoever for the crimes committed: the right to grant pardon belongs exclusively to the victims, and cannot be given over to a criminal who acknowledges his deeds and asks forgiveness for his offenses. (And over many long years, no one indicted for crimes against humanity has ever done so.) This is the idea defended not too many years ago by Vladimir Jankélévitch: "Maybe the statute of limitations would have less importance if the purge had been more thorough and more sincere, if one sensed more spontaneity and more unanimity in recalling these terrible memories. Alas! The disproportion between the tragedy of these four cursed years and the frivolity of our contemporaries will doubtless turn out to be one of history's bitterest ironies. What business do people have talking about forgiving and forgetting?"[13]

Now, no one has really undertaken a debate of national proportions over whether or not to try these cases fifty years afterward, nor over the respective merits and drawbacks of the statute of limitations and of its removal, nor over the role of the justice system as a vector of national memory. The discussion has either been limited to a privileged few, in particular to the few legal experts capable of deciphering the laws on crimes against humanity, or else it has been of an ideological nature. Nevertheless, expressing reticence about such trials does not mean becoming an objective ally of those who hark back to the Vichy years. This debate was not without legitimacy nor grandeur, whatever might be the positions defended, since it was understood that the renewed condemnation of the anti-Semitic crimes was an indispensable prerequisite, in the eventuality that the trials were abandoned.[14]

One can simply observe, if not regret, that this debate was cut off. But there is an objective explanation for this: once set into motion, the justice system had to decide one way or another. No other authority—unless it be the Parliament, by a new amnesty bill, or the President of the Republic, by a new pardon, to the extent that these channels might be used with respect to crimes with no statute of limitations—could block its course. Delays and inertia were bad solutions in the long run; one cannot on the one hand defend the duty to remember and humanist principles while on the other hand accept that the accused—however serious the alleged crime might be—remain accused until death without being tried, because it keeps up media pressure. This situation is moreover contrary to the European Convention on human rights. As for the dismissal of charges, such as that of April 1992, it was no longer possible, considering the heavy presumptions of guilt which weighed upon the accused. It should be noted besides that the ruling of April 1992, similarly to most of the legal decisions stemming from the various prosecutions, not to mention the Touvier trial itself, provide a perfect illustration of the danger of leaving it to magistrates to write or rewrite history. But once again, this is a rather useless observation. Bringing to trial at least one of the four cases against French citizens will prove to have had at least one advantage: that of deciding the matter conclusively at least once in the eyes of justice, if not in the eyes of memory or history.

The Singularities of the Touvier Affair[15]

Born in 1915, Paul Touvier became the regional chief of the intelligence service (Deuxième Bureau) of the Milice of the Rhône region, thus occupying an important position, in January 1944. Charged with gathering intelligence in the fight against the Resistance, he was suspected of having committed several crimes and acts of violence. Condemned to death in absentia on two occasions, September 10, 1946, and March 4, 1947, by the criminal courts (Cours de Justice) of Lyons and Chambéry on the charges of treason and intelligence with the enemy, he escaped justice for many long years, thanks to the benevolent or charitable complicity of a very large number of high-ranking clergy in the French Catholic Church. With one of these prelates, Bishop Charles Duquaire, the private secretary of the Archbishop of Lyons who was totally devoted to his cause, he managed to obtain the pardon of President Pompidou in 1971 for two of the so-called "secondary" sentences to the death penalty, which had reached the statute of limitations at the end of twenty years in 1967: the confiscation of property and the prohibition of residing in several regional departments including the Savoie. (The third sentence remained in effect: Paul Touvier was still punished with "civic death," which in particular prevented him from voting.) The commotion stirred up by this pardon in 1972 (following the revelations of Jacques Derogy in *L'Express*) obliged Touvier to return into hiding. When a warrant for his arrest was issued on November 27, 1981, subsequent to charges filed on November 9, 1973, in Lyons and on March 27, 1974, in Chambéry, the police unit charged with tracking him down did not pursue the matter very vigorously. He was finally arrested on May 24, 1989, once the investigation had been handed over to the search unit of the Paris *gendarmerie*, which was led by Colonel Jean-Louis Recordon and his assistant, Philippe Mathy. Touvier was then indicted that very same day by the judge Jean-Pierre Getti. After a long, painstakingly precise investigation, the legal ordinance bringing the case before the Court of Criminal Appeals of Paris on October 29, 1991, retained five major charges, including the murder of Victor Basch, President of the League of Human Rights, and his wife, Hélène Basch, on January 10, 1944, and the execution of seven persons, all Jews, at Rillieux (a town that at that time was in the Department of Ain, but now is in the Department of the Rhône and has become Rillieux-la-Pape): Léon Glaeser, Claude Benzimra, Maurice Schlusselman, Louis Krzyzkowski, Émile Zeizig, Siegfried Prock, and one unknown person, who were summarily shot on June 29, 1944. These innocent people paid for the execution of Philippe Henriot, Vichy's Secretary of State for Information and Propaganda, assassinated on the previous day by the Resistance. On April 13, 1992, the First Criminal Appeals Court of Paris, issued, against all expectations, a dismissal of all charges. But this ruling was partially reversed on November 27, 1992. Paul Touvier was thus brought before the Criminal Circuit Court of Versailles, but on only one charge: that of the seven crimes committed at Rillieux. His trial opened on March 17, 1994.

By all accounts, this was an exceptional event. First of all, Paul Touvier was the first French citizen tried for crimes against humanity. He was tried a few months after the assassination of René Bousquet, who had also been indicted, and his trial promised to provide an outlet for the animosities that had been built up over decades by these dangling cases which raised the issue of Vichy's racial persecutions.

Furthermore, the Touvier case, while rather commonplace when one considers the average of all the cases concerning members of the Milice who were brought before a criminal court at the time of the Liberation, ended up directly or indirectly compromising the reputation of an incredible number of dignitaries of the Catholic Church, high government officials, and members of ministry cabinets. Two Presidents of the Republic, Georges Pompidou and François Mitterrand, were virulently criticized for their positions in this matter; although the former's stance was decisive and deliberate while the latter's fortuitous, the two were close to each other. As for the trial itself, it brought forward several former government ministers and Prime Ministers to take the stand and testify: Jacques Chaban-Delmas, Pierre Messmer, and Pierre Arpaillange. The Prime Minister in office, Édouard Balladur, narrowly avoided being called to the witness stand.

There was another singularity of considerable importance in this trial: rarely has a legal case been dissected and analyzed to such an extent in full public view before coming before the Criminal Court. For fifty years, it had been the target of several successive, and sometimes parallel, investigations: the judicial prosecutions of 1945 to 1947; the hunt for witnesses and for the testimonies of Paul Touvier and his protectors (including Bishop Duquaire), between 1959 and 1972; police commissioner Jacques Delarue's investigation and report, expedited by the State Security Court in order to examine the validity of a request for pardon in June 1970, which concluded that the request should be denied; the research into the validity of the charges of crimes against humanity, between 1973 and 1981; the first judicial investigation for prosecution for crimes against humanity, conducted by Judge Martine Anzani, then by Judge Claude Grellier, between 1981 and 1989; the second judicial investigation, conducted by Judge Getti, between 1989 and 1991; the inquiry conducted by the commission of historians into the relations between Paul Touvier and the Catholic Church, presided over by René Rémond, between June 1989 and January 1992 . . . Added to all that is the explosion of media reports, articles, documentaries, and books that have come out since 1972, and finally, the hearings in Versailles, where the entire case was reexamined in the most minute detail.

It is crucial to stress this point, for the proliferation of investigations weighed heavily on the nature of the sworn testimony. Questioned dozens of times, and over a very long period of time, some witnesses ended up constructing veritable "historical" narratives, built not only on their personal experience—which was tragic in the case of Paul Touvier's victims, especially the resisters who had been arrested by him—but also on everything they had been able to read and hear over the last fifty years. And so it was that the Versailles trial saw some of them, after giving poignantly sincere testimony on what went on in the offices of the Impasse Catelin in Lyons, where the intelligence service of the Milice had its headquarters, charge forward into highly problematical historical demonstrations about the strategy of the SS, the Milice, and Vichy. This frequently happens when witnesses respond to historians' questions long after the events have taken place, and it is inconsequential if historians are in a position to give a balanced account of things. But once the concrete reality of the facts had become one of the critical issues of the trial, which was for the most part based on direct witnesses, these witnesses weakened their own testimony, either by straying from what they had seen or suffered in order to talk about what they believed to be the truth, or by trying their hand at historical analysis. This is not the least of the difficulties of a trial of this type; such problems were already visible at the time of the Barbie trial.

While some of the witnesses, in particular the former resisters, had kept their memory (the memory of suffering) intact, others, on the contrary, had clearly adapted their statements to fit the circumstances. A few did so for tactical reasons. But for most of them, this was a consequence of a view of things that had changed over time. Now, the court had at its disposal all of their previous statements, so the sometimes pathetic comparison of what they had said years ago and the testimony given during the Versailles proceedings constituted one of the most interesting aspects of this trial . . . of memory. The examination of Jean-Lucien Feuz, Paul Touvier's former chauffeur, who explained how he had attempted to engage in "double-dealing" between the Milice and the Resistance, and who in the process contradicted himself several times and called the accused by his first name, as if an old complicity still tied them together, was a textbook example in this respect. Just as pathetic was the April 5 testimony of Father Roland Ducret, Touvier's director of conscience between 1953 and 1978, who had reconsidered the positions that he had taken previously: "If I had to give my testimony for a pardon again, I would not do it." [16]

The most famous of these witnesses did not escape the pressure of the courtroom, which led them to contradict themselves. The historian Olivier Wieviorka, in his previously cited book, gathered the opinion of others besides François Mitterrand about the Touvier affair. By the greatest of coincidences, two of the resisters that he questioned were called to the witness stand at the Versailles trial: Jacques Chaban-Delmas and Pierre Messmer. The former was ailing and could not make any trips, but he wrote a letter to the court, which was read during the first hearing on March 17, 1994. In this letter Chaban-Delmas affirmed his unswerving fidelity to the duty to remember: "The persecution of the Jews would not have been able to come about without the participation of the Milice. In the eyes of the French people [. . .], these facts cannot fall into oblivion simply by the force of time." [17] However, four years earlier, he had stated to Wieviorka:

After decades and decades, I believe not only that the men are no longer the

same, but also I do not see on what basis these trials could be an absolute necessity. I really do not see to what it can contribute. Some say: "to recall horrible things." Why not. But where is the truth? How can it be unraveled after
so much time? I find that we should let the dead bury the dead.[18]

As for the presidential pardon of November 1971, he was in favor of it.
At the time, Jacques Chaban-Delmas was still Prime Minister. He was replaced by Pierre Messmer in July 1972, when the Touvier affair had just
blown up.

As Minister of the Armed Forces in 1963, Messmer had at that time refused to reopen the Touvier case to examine a request for amnesty. He too
came to the Versailles trial proclaiming in the session of April 5, 1994,
his refusal to forget: "The men of my generation already have a hard time
forgetting war crimes, and thus, they have an even harder time forgetting
crimes against humanity." Questioned by Olivier Wieviorka in 1990, he had
stated on the contrary:

> These prosecutions are no doubt founded on a legal basis since they are go-
> ing forward, but they are a mistake. When one sees what Germany has be-
> come, I think that the moment has come to cast the veil of oblivion over the
> individual deeds between 1940 and 1945.[19]

Georges Pompidou had used the same expression to justify the pardon
that set off the affair.

One does not run a great risk of being wrong in supposing that what was
freely said to the historian Wieviorka is a better reflection of these men's
thinking than what they stated at the Versailles trial, where the stakes were
obviously different. One can thus gauge the difficulty of assessing a case
whose symbolic value has varied over time. The trial for memory was only
one moment of memory, one step in a history of memory full of surprises.

The real singularity of the Touvier case, however, is of a legal nature. The
matter is unique in more than one way in the history of jurisprudence. Let
us recall that the former member of the Milice was tried and convicted on
three occasions, in 1946, 1947, and 1994: he was condemned to death in
absentia, then to life in prison without parole when he was present at the
trial. Along the way, he benefited from the statute of limitations which was
reached by his main conviction (in 1967), a presidential pardon for two convictions on lesser charges (in 1971), and a general dismissal of charges (in
1992), a ruling which was overturned in that same year for only one of
charges of crimes against humanity that had been brought against him.
This is a highly unusual itinerary.

In the history of French criminal justice, Paul Touvier came to trial longer after the crimes took place than any other accused criminal (except Maurice Papon in 1997). There are two reasons for this delay. First, Touvier continually sought to hide from the courts, even during the time he was to serve for his in absentia conviction; if he had appeared in court in the 1950s, he would have risked only a few years in prison. The second reason for the delay stemmed from the complexity of the notion of crimes against humanity and the delays in judicial proceedings.

Moreover, there is the often forgotten paradox that consists of the fact that Touvier was brought to trial for a crime (the Rillieux affair) that he himself voluntarily acknowledged with the intention of absolving himself. Indeed, it was in 1959 that he revealed, for the first time and of his own initiative, the circumstances of those executions. At that time, he was seeking to obtain a pardon or an amnesty of his main convictions (which at the time were not yet under the statute of limitations) from the Minister of Justice, Edmond Michelet. The Rillieux affair, although not unknown at the time, did not appear in the charges filed against Touvier in 1946 and 1947, and was not considered his doing. By bringing this up spontaneously and acknowledging his responsibility (if not his guilt), Paul Touvier thought he had a solid argument in his defense: he had supposedly been forced to execute some Jewish "hostages" by the regional head of the Lyons Milice, Victor de Bourmont, who himself had been the target of a demand formulated by Werner Knab, the head of the Lyons Sipo-SD (security police), after the assassination of Philippe Henriot.[20] Werner Knab had supposedly demanded "a hundred Jewish hostages" from Victor de Bourmont, who had supposedly managed to bring the sinister contingent down to "thirty," proposing in exchange that it be the French Milice and not the Germans who would take care of the job, since the death of Philippe Henriot was a "strictly French matter." Paul Touvier, after maneuvering to buy time, supposedly "limited" the number of victims to seven. In other words, he had supposedly "saved" twenty-three people from death, not counting the resister Louis Goudard, who was not Jewish and that Touvier did indeed separate from the group just before the execution (which will constitute by converse implication the proof that it was in fact an anti-Semitic crime).[21] More than his accusers, Paul Touvier is the one who is responsible for his fate. The request for and granting of pardon, in 1971, both done supposedly to let time and oblivion heal old wounds, had the opposite effect of stirring up passions on both sides and bringing Touvier out of obscurity into public view. His version of what had happened, far from inspiring forgiveness, ended up sending him to prison for the duration of his life.

Finally, there was one last legal singularity: Paul Touvier saw the legal definition of the crimes he was accused of modified several times. This will prove to be one of the most disturbing characteristics of this trial and the defense's strongest argument.

Can We Overrule History?

When a warrant was issued for his arrest on November 27, 1981, the definition of crimes against humanity was that of the statutes of the International Military Tribunal which was to hold its sessions at Nuremberg. These statutes were annexed to the Interallied Accords of London signed on August 8, 1945, by the Provisory Government of the French Republic, and the governments of the United States, the United Kingdom, and the USSR. Article 6 of these accords gives the definition of the crimes to be prosecuted:

> The Tribunal established by the Agreement [. . .] for the trial and punishment of the major war criminals of the European Axis countries shall have the power to try and punish all persons who, acting in the interests of the European Axis countries, whether as individuals or as members of organisations, committed any of the following crimes.
>
> The following acts, or any of them, are crimes coming within the jurisdiction of the Tribunal for which there shall be individual responsibility:
>
> a) *Crimes against peace*: namely, planning, preparation, initiation or waging of a war of aggression, or a war in violation of international treaties, agreements or assurances, or participation in a common plan or conspiracy for the accomplishment of the foregoing;
> b) *War crimes*: namely, violations of the laws or customs of war. Such violations shall include, but not be limited to, murder, ill-treatment or deportation to slave labour or any other purpose of civilian population of or in occupied territory, murder or ill-treatment of prisoners of war or persons on the seas, killing of hostages, plunder of public or private property, wanton destruction of cities, towns or villages, or devastation not justified by military necessity;
> c) *Crimes against humanity*: namely, murder, extermination, enslavement, deportation, and other inhumane acts committed against any civilian population, before or during the war, or persecutions on political, racial or religious grounds in execution of or in connection with any crime within the jursdiction of the Tribunal, whether or not in violation of the domestic law of the country where perpetrated.
>
> Leaders, organisers, instigators and accomplices participating in the formulation or execution of a common plan or conspiracy to commit any of the foregoing crimes are responsible for all acts performed by any persons in the execution of such plans.[22]

Already at this stage, there was no lack of problems in defining crimes against humanity. The text quoted was accused of being retroactive and of inventing new grounds for incrimination. These criticisms were voiced mainly by the "losers," who were forgetting that murder is in any case a major crime in all the legal systems of the planet, especially when it has been committed on a large scale. Conversely, this text was criticized for being too weak and for having been applied parsimoniously at the Nuremberg trials, which were focused mainly on the two other crimes (crimes against peace and war crimes) defined by the text of 1945. For our purposes here, we shall be concerned only with those aspects that had an impact on French jurisprudence.

The statute of the International Military Tribunal combined both the standard of jurisdiction and the standard of behavior (which defines the violation). About the jurisdiction of this tribunal, the text specifies that this court was created "to try and to punish appropriately and without delay, the major war criminals of the European countries of the Axis." And it could do so in the cases of crimes "without any precise geographical location": for example, crimes against peace, in other words, a war of aggression waged against several countries, or crimes committed in several places (as according to the first and following articles). This standard of jurisdiction thus excluded in the first place war criminals having acted in one single country and in the second place the citizens of occupied countries who had been guilty of the same crimes or who had been an accomplice to those crimes. They were to be tried according to the domestic legal system in place in their country. In France, the ordinance of August 28, 1944, which was prior to the London accords and which provided the legal basis for the purge conducted by the courts, had moreover specified that two groups were to be tried on the basis of French domestic law: first, the French collaborators (for treason, intelligence with the enemy, or breaching the state's security with respect to foreign powers), and second, Nazi criminals who had been active in France. The latter would be tried for war crimes, for which a legal definition already existed in French law. This was the case for a very large number of Germans, Austrians, and nationals of other countries, who were either members of the Wehrmacht or the SS, such as Karl Oberg, the Supreme Chief of the SS and of the German police in occupied France, who was tried and convicted in 1954 by the military tribunal of Paris.

However, while it did lay out the jurisdiction of the Nuremberg tribunal, the 1945 text specifically spelled out that there was a crime against humanity when the acts or persecutions defined were "in execution of or in connection with any crime within the jurisdiction of the Tribunal" (Article 6, paragraph c). In other words, the crime against humanity had to be committed by persons "acting in the interests of the European Axis countries" and in conjunction with a crime against peace or a war crime, the two other legal definitions provided for by the statute. In other words, there was no real dissociation between the standard of jurisdiction and the standard of behavior, since the latter was tied to the former. This lack of dissociation can be explained by the fact that the London accords, which were worked out in haste, were innovative on the levels of both jurisdiction and legal definition. It can also be accounted for by the desire to limit the notion of crimes against humanity or war crimes to those committed by Nazi Germany, and secondarily, by Fascist Italy (the Axis), without making it possible to raise the question of crimes of the same nature which might have been committed during the war by other countries, including those of the victorious coalition.[23]

In practice, that meant that the concept of crimes against humanity was applicable first of all to the citizens of the Third Reich or to accomplices of every nationality acting on its behalf, and that it was up to the International Military Tribunal to try them. However, even though these two elements —the fact that the instigators of crimes against humanity belonged to the Third Reich and the fact that these crimes had to have been committed in the context of another crime falling under the jurisdiction of the International Military Tribunal—were tied to each other, they did not *explicitly* constitute conditions *sine qua non* which would for example prevent any other court from being empowered to deal with such a crime, nor for any other criminal who was not a citizen of the Reich to be tried on the basis of this legal definition. That is the reason why, until the new legal code went into effect in March 1994, French jurisprudence was able to modify, enlarge, and limit, to a certain extent, the original definition.

This definition was adopted by the French law of 1964 which, referring back to the London accords (without, however, citing them in its own text), observed that crimes against humanity were "by their very nature" not subject to the statute of limitations. Moreover, other countries took similar decisions at the same time.[24] This gave rise to debates over the practical application of this law, particularly after the first charges of crimes against humanity were filed against Paul Touvier in 1973. Was this a matter of an incrimination fitting into the framework of domestic law, even when the latter had given no legal definition of it? What court could try these cases, since the Nuremberg tribunal no longer existed? Above all, was this not a retroactive law, since it introduced after the facts a new element, the removal of the statute of limitations, which was not present in the text of 1945 and which had not spelled out anything on this crucial point because it was inspired especially by British and American law (which do not recognize any statute of limitations in criminal cases)? This was the criticism most consistently made by legal experts and the defenders of the accused. Finally, the law of 1964 only removed the statute of limitations for crimes against humanity, contrary to subsequent international agreements, which also removed the statute of limitations for war crimes, and which France has not ratified.[25] In spite of these difficulties, the obstacles to trying a French citizen in the jurisdiction of a domestic court were ultimately removed.

The definition of crimes against humanity was first amended during the prosecution of the Klaus Barbie case. A ruling by the Court of Criminal Appeals on December 20, 1985, a year and a half before the Barbie trial, offered a new definition, which responded to the crucial issues of memory of that time:

> Crimes against humanity not subject to the statute of limitations are constituted, in keeping with Article 6c of the statutes of the International Military Tribunal of Nuremberg, appended to the London accords of August 8, 1945, even when they could be defined as war crimes according to Article 6b of this same text, all inhumane acts and persecutions which, for the sake of a State practicing a policy of ideological hegemony, were committed systematically not only against individuals because they belonged to a racial or religious group, but also against the adversaries of this policy, whatever may be the form of their opposition.

The innovation here is twofold. First, contrary to the more restrictive interpretation in effect up until that time, crimes against humanity no longer concern only those crimes with *civilian* victims, that is to say men and women persecuted for what they are, what they think, or what they believe, but are also applicable to crimes committed against resisters, in other words, combatants having committed acts that brought on repression. According to the Court of Appeals, the harm to which the latter may have been subjected involves not only war crimes, but also crimes against humanity, once these crimes fit into the category of "inhumane acts" (for example, torture and deportation to Nazi concentration camps). At the same time, the Court of Appeals cleared up a confusion existing in the Nuremberg statutes, in which crimes committed against civilians were sometimes defined as war crimes (according to Article 6b)—and thus came under the statute of limitations in 1985—and sometimes defined as crimes against humanity (according to Article 6c). The 1985 definition is thus no longer based on the nature of the victims, but on the nature of harm to which they had been subjected.

Second, the Court of Appeals introduced for the first time the notion of a "State practicing a policy of ideological hegemony," a formula absent from the 1945 text. Two other rulings, dating from March 9 and June 3, 1988, introduced another element to the definition of what constituted crimes against humanity: that of a "concerted plan," whose instigator had to be the "hegemonic State" and not an organization or an individual alone. While the notion of a "concerted plan" was not present explicitly in the 1945 text, it did not, contrary to the interpretation of the Court of Appeals, constitute a restrictive nor even necessary condition, but rather one of a purely secondary nature.

At this stage already, the law seemed to be applying a variable standard in defining crimes against humanity, adapting itself to fit the circumstances of the moment and the specific complexity of each case, namely that of Barbie in this instance. There were a huge number of criticisms of this ruling: they denounced the loss of substance, even the possible "trivialization" of the notion of crimes against humanity.[26]

Nevertheless, the prosecution of the Touvier case, from 1989 to 1991, was conducted within this legal framework and in view of this wording. Judge Getti concluded that certain deeds (in particular the murder of the Basch couple and the Rillieux affair) of which the former member of the Milice was accused fell under the definition of crimes against humanity once the concrete reality of the facts was established; and that Paul Touvier was indeed an appointed agent of the Milice, the official organization created by the Vichy regime and remaining under its authority. In other words, the Milice was considered to be the creation of a state by definition practicing a "policy of ideological hegemony" against its opponents, against the Jews (who had been persecuted since 1940), and against other categories, since it had organized mass roundups in the framework of the "concerted plan," which consisted in the systematic extermination of the Jews decided on by the Nazis.

To everyone's surprise, this prosecution culminated in a dismissal of charges, issued on April 13, 1992, by the Paris Court of Criminal Appeals. The three judges of that court justified their decision by claiming that "no well-defined ideology ruled" at Vichy, that for Vichy the Jews were not considered to be "enemies of the State" as they were in Germany, and that the expression "State practicing a policy of ideological hegemony" applied to Hitler's Third Reich and not to the regime of Pétain, which was termed to be "a constellation of 'good intentions' and of political animosities." While Paul Touvier, as he himself had admitted, had indeed been guilty of the Rillieux slaughter, this was not a matter of crimes against humanity, and therefore those deeds fell under the statute of limitations. As for the other charges, they were dismissed for lack of sufficient proof, since the Court of Criminal Appeals almost systematically disputed the validity of the testimony gathered by Judge Getti.

While this ruling is enough to make one shudder with its pseudo-historical reasoning, which would have caused any university student to fail on a history exam, it nevertheless came off as highly clever on a legal level, in that it slipped through the loopholes that had been left open by the contradictions, incertitudes, and variations of the jurisprudence on crimes against humanity. Moreover, it constituted a real victory for Paul Touvier's defense, for it singularly limited the scope of the trial by reducing it to the dimensions of the events at Rillieux.

Immediately requested to review the case by Attorney General Pierre Truche, the final Court of Criminal Appeals partially overturned this ruling on November 27, 1992. Ruling on the form and not the content, and while confirming the dismissal of the other charges which thus became irrevocable, this court succeeded in removing one major contradiction in the legal interpretation of the Rillieux crimes:

> Whereas . . . according to the terms of Article 6 of the statutes of the International Military Tribunal at Nuremberg, the authors or accomplices of crimes against humanity are punished only if they acted for the sake of a European country of the Axis, the Court of Appeals could not without contradicting itself, declare that the murders being prosecuted did not constitute crimes against humanity while at the same time pointing out that they had been perpetrated at the instigation of an official of the Gestapo, an organization that has been declared to be criminal in that it belonged to a country which had practiced a policy of ideological hegemony.

In other words, Paul Touvier was, if not the instigator, at least an accomplice, in these crimes. This fundamental decision of the court, which in the end made it possible to try the former member of the Milice, was nevertheless decried, for it too influenced the course of the trial by adding new misconceptions. At first glance, this ruling was in keeping with the logic of the text of 1945, which at that time remained the legal basis for all prosecution; until the new French penal code (which included a new, final definition of crimes against humanity in distinguishing "genocide" from "other crimes against humanity") took effect on March 1, 1994 (right before the beginning of the Touvier trial!), crimes against humanity were defined by the London accords. By specifying that "the authors or accomplices of crimes against humanity are only punished if they acted for the sake of a European country of the Axis," the final Court of Criminal Appeals was only adopting the terms of Article 6 of the statutes of the International Tribunal. However—but this is a crucial point!—it made this article a necessary, and thus restrictive condition in a completely unambiguous way. Now, the context was no longer that of 1945, when the crimes of Paul Touvier, even though at that time they were not "crimes against humanity," and even though they did not fall under the jurisdiction of the Nuremberg tribunal, were largely established and sufficiently well defined legally for him to be sent to the gallows by a decision of a French court of justice. If the restrictive condition introduced in 1992 was not clearly and explicitly met, Paul Touvier would benefit from a dismissal of charges, or still worse, would be able rightly to demand his acquittal by the criminal court.

He was thus guilty only if he had been an accomplice to the Germans. If he had acted alone, out of his own initiative, or on the initiative of the Milice, or even on that of the Vichy government from which the Milice emanated, his crime had to fall under the statute of limitations. What a strange form of incrimination: complicity is punishable, but not the direct act! Nevertheless, that is what was spelled out on June 2, 1993, by the ruling of the Court of Criminal Appeals of the Department of Yvelines, which served as a frame of reference for the debates in the Criminal Court of Versailles:

> [The] responsibility [of Paul Touvier] is engaged by the simple fact of his personal dealings, even though he was not himself a national of a European Axis country. It is therefore not necessary to follow the private parties in their argumentation, which attempts to prove that the Milice and the government of the French State, which Touvier served, had themselves been accomplices of the Nazi state in its policies of ideological hegemony.

In its ruling of October 21, 1993, rejecting the defense's appeal of the decision to bring the case to trial, the Court of Criminal Appeals spelled things out in even clearer language:

> Considering [. . .] that it makes no difference whether or not the deeds prosecuted may have been committed during the assassination of a member of the Vichy government who also belonged to the Milice, as long as these deeds were carried out at the instigation of an official of a Nazi criminal organization and involved victims chosen exclusively because they belonged to the Jewish community, the deeds were therefore an integral part of a concerted plan of extermination and systematic persecution of this community that was put into action by the German National-Socialist government.

These last modifications of the legal framework of the case, which came between the close of the investigations and the opening of the trial—something that very rarely happens—seemed in a way to nullify years of work by the examining magistrate. Most importantly, these changes almost completely eliminated from the discussions a crucial problem, that of the degree of autonomy, or even initiative, of a French citizen belonging to the Milice under Vichy's orders. These decisions exhibited a narrow legalism, doubtless unimpeachable on the level of form, but which singularly restricted the "lesson" that the Touvier trial was supposed to deliver. While on the one hand the court had shown in 1985 that it could "adapt itself" to certain issues of memory and not remain indifferent to the demands of certain pressure groups—namely, the associations of resisters—it turned a deaf ear to those who were demanding that the anti-Semitic aspects of Vichy, or at the very least the anti-Semitism of the Milice, should be put on trial, and that in any case there should be a trial of French policy, even if the law in no instance allows the state to be judged, but only an individual. The Court of Criminal Appeals did not consider it worthwhile ("it makes no difference whether or not . . .") to raise a question that, while delicate legally, was nevertheless central with respect to the issues of memory of these last twenty years: did the Vichy regime, through the deeds of one of its operatives, render itself guilty of crimes against humanity? While the French Republic had just (in Februry 1993) acknowledged that such crimes had been committed "under the de facto authority of the so-called 'government of the French State'"—without specifying, moreover, if the said authority was itself responsible for the crimes in question[27]—the French courts, even before the beginning of the trial, let doubts remain by eluding the question. If one were to suppose that such a trial might have an historical interest so long after the events occurred, it was precisely in this context, and not for the sake of proving that the Milice collaborated with the Germans, a fact that can be found in any and every history text!

Did Vichy, *acting on its own initiative*, indeed commit such crimes? The answer is hardly simple. For example, when one of the most subtle legal minds in the field, Attorney General Pierre Truche, was asked whether Vichy's anti-Semitic laws of 1940 and 1941, laws that were genuinely French, made as they were prior to Vichy's participation in the "Final Solution," which began in the summer of 1942 (and even before the Germans put the machinery of the "Final Solution" into operation), were crimes against humanity, he answered in the negative, while specifying that they could rather be considered as "apartheid"[28] crimes. In this case, the historian agrees with the legal scholar: the French anti-Semitic laws did not originally fit into the framework of a process of physical elimination, but reflected the desire to exclude Jews from society. On the other hand, however, the active participation in the massive roundups and deportations from 1942 to 1944 clearly fits into the framework of complicity in crimes against humanity. Pierre Laval's spontaneous delivery of Jewish children less than sixteen years old (whatever his real motivations may have been) during the summer of 1942 might even be a case not of complicity (since the Germans were not requesting the children at that time), but of a direct crime, on the condition that one could solve the question of what knowledge he had—or wanted to have—at that time about the destination of trains of deportees. These are all questions that a Bousquet trial—which doubtless would have also posed great difficulties—might have partially resolved. The "substitute" for this trial, the trial of Paul Touvier, already had significantly fewer chances of clarifying this essential point. But at least the discussion could have been more open and complete without these last minute changes in the legal framework of crimes against humanity cases.

How, in final analysis, should these changes be understood? On the surface, it would seem that the magistrates of the Court of Criminal Appeals stuck closely to the texts of law. The magistrates came back to the imperfections of the 1945 definition and made them even more pronounced, even though they had not hesitated to amend this definition a first time, and in a major way, in 1985. They thus confined the retroactive application of crimes against humanity to deeds committed exclusively by the Third Reich, as the London accords had wished; the ruling of October 1993 explicitly precludes any prosecution of crimes committed after 1945 in Indochina or in Algeria (this was already true in practice since the ruling of December 20, 1985)—forbidding a new ad hoc modification or retroactive application of the new French Penal Code. Neither the former political commissar Georges Boudarel, who had joined the Viêt-Minh during the Indochina war (1946–1954), nor the torturers of the battle of Algiers,[29] should they be targeted, could be termed "accomplices of the Axis powers."

Perhaps the magistrates also wanted to avoid the pitfalls of a new ruling in favor of dismissing charges, which was still possible if not probable. Once things were based on the declarations of Paul Touvier and on the acts carried out "upon the instigation of the Germans," matters were much simpler on a strictly legal level: rather than seeking to determine whether Vichy had been a criminal state, it was better to stick to the fact that Touvier, as member of the Milice, had been the accomplice of the Third Reich, a state that had been defined as being guilty of crimes against humanity since Nuremberg, a fact that could not suffer the slightest dispute, even from a Court of Criminal Appeals that was indulgent and understanding with respect to Vichy's "good intentions."

At the opening of the Versailles trial, we thus found ourselves before a situation which was preposterous from both a legal and historical perspective. Paul Touvier was to be tried on the basis of an accusation completely opposite that of the investigation, which considered any question about Vichy's autonomy "useless," even though that question had for twenty years been the basis for prosecuting French citizens for crimes against humanity. Not to mention two other questions which were very quickly to appear at the core of the debate: had the Milice been a special instrument in the "Final Solution"? Had Paul Touvier told the truth about Rillieux?

A Trial for the Sake of Appearances

What an affair for such a mediocre figure! What appeared most obvious from the first hearings on was this incredible distance between the man and the heavy symbolism with which he had been invested. The hermetically sealed glass cage in which the accused appeared before the court (for reasons of security) would have had one believe that a French Eichmann was in the dock. At the defense's request, the cage was kept slightly open, and the reality of the matter appeared in all its banality: the accused was a withered, broken man of no stature. Morally and physically worn, having given up trying to defend himself, he spoke only in bits and pieces, with slips of the tongue. Although he had always repeatedly denied that the Rillieux crimes had been an act of reprisal for which the Milice itself was responsible, and although he had always maintained that the intention to kill came from the Gestapo of Lyons, he nevertheless, during the March 29 session let this terribly sincere sentence escape his mouth: "It was horrible, for us, that the Germans should be the ones to get revenge for Henriot." The member of the Milice of yesteryear had remained walled up within his commitments: he was a fossil, locked up in a bygone time. Even though he had constantly and against all evidence (including his own previous declarations) denied that there had been any anti-Semitic discrimination in the choice of the victims at Rillieux, he exclaimed during the session of April 6: "I was not in charge of sorting them out!"

At least, unlike Klaus Barbie, Paul Touvier was present during these sessions, and put directly face to face with his victims. He was required to account for his actions. He who had played around so much hiding things away separately, giving fragmentary information to each of his interlocutors, he who in the past had succeeded in charming and convincing so many important people, saw his entire system of defense collapse in the full view of all. Panic-stricken with the fear of prison, which seemed more and more likely as time went by, this was doubtless the worst ordeal that he had to undergo before his judges. In this respect, the trial did end up serving its function of reparation.

In view of the doubts that hovered over this case (about the different versions of what had happened, about the interpretation of these events, about their legal definition), the Touvier trial was a rather open one. Even though now, in retrospect, the maximum sentence seems to have been ineluctable, doubt at times prevailed over the private parties to the case as well as among observers, while the defense kept hoping for a miracle. Doubt had as a corollary the sense that the court was in spite of all fulfilling its duty to examine, analyze, and assess the facts and the responsibility of Touvier the individual.

As for the rest, there was a great discrepancy between the expectations and the results obtained. Unlike the Barbie trial, that of Paul Touvier did not turn out to be a great moment for the witnesses from the very instant that their oral testimony was revived. Certainly, the victims and their descendants were present, attentive, and free of hate, and, true to the image of the sons of Léon Glaeser or of the son of Émile Zeizig, displayed unfailing modesty and dignity. But their voices were often drowned out by rhetorical sparring matches over law and history. This was a trial that was more for the lawyers than for the witnesses. There were nonetheless some very intense moments, and it is doubtless these that will remain in the memory of the participants. The testimony given on April 6 by the former resister Louis Goudard, chief of intelligence for the "Francs-tireurs et partisans" of the Lyons region, who was "spared" by Paul Touvier in the evening of June 28, 1944, because he was a non-Jew, was doubtless one of the most dramatically truthful testimonies. The resister that he had been had kept his memories intact, and not only the facts: "The clandestine life is like a drug, you get hooked on it, you get a taste for it." Responding to the judge who questioned him about the fear of torture, he answered: "The idea that you put into your mind about physical suffering is often more unbearable than the suffering itself." Only those who have experienced such ordeals can find the words to express what it is like.

On April 11, 1994, the face-to-face encounter of Paul Touvier, age seventy-nine, and Attorney Joe Nordmann, age eighty-four, dean of the lawyers of the civil parties, a Communist and noted figure in the judicial Resistance, constantly illustrated the degree to which the memory of the combat of that time was still vivid for its protagonists. Certainly, time had gone by, and the hearings had indeed focused on anti-Semitism and not on the struggle against the Resistance, but the desire for justice in the former resister was at least as strong as the bitter resentment of the former member of the Milice toward his perpetual enemies. This confrontation gave one the feeling that the Touvier trial was indeed one of the last acts of the purge, like a reconstitution in real time with the same actors, a play in which the curtain still had not definitively fallen.

It is likely, moreover, that the members of the jury were not insensitive to this time lag. The average age of the eight men and the sole woman of this jury of lay people was forty-one. Most, however, were younger still, since five of them were between twenty-seven and thirty-three years old, one was forty-two, and the oldest among them were barely fifty-six, sixty, and sixty-three years old. These latter three were, then, six, eleven, and thirteen years old, respectively, at the time of the Liberation. No member of the jury had lived through the period as an adult. Was this rift of experience a factor in the trial? In any case, the interest and curiosity of the members of the jury proved to be constant. Almost all took lengthy notes; some asked often quite relevant questions. As far as the deliberations are concerned, we can only offer conjectures. Certain sources of information (obviously unverifiable) would have it that the youngest proved to be more skeptical as to the legal possibility of convicting Paul Touvier on the basis of then current jurisprudence. Did the fact that the deeds were temporally distant and that the charges upheld were of a limited nature (given the extent of the crimes at the time of the Liberation), have a bearing for a while before the final verdict was issued? After all, it took the jury five hours and thirty-five minutes to reach a decision and answer affirmatively the seventeen questions that it had been asked, although only the last three questions were the subject of debate: the existence of a crime fitting into the framework of a concerted plan, the establishment of complicity with the occupying forces, and the intentional nature of the act (the first fourteen referred to the physical reality of the seven murders at Rillieux, which was never disputed by the accused).

The Touvier trial nevertheless stirred up embarrassment and feelings of uneasiness, feelings that we shared with a number of observers. The court sessions were at times lacking in solemnity. The peak, so to speak, was reached when a former member of the Milice who did not have any direct link with Paul Touvier but who was called by the defense, came to the witness stand and proclaimed, as proud as could be, that he granted the Milice's pardon to the Resistance and that he expected as much to be granted reciprocally to Paul Touvier. This session of April 7 resulted in a general outbreak of giggling, even among the magistrates. The absence of seriousness was doubtless due to the cramped conditions in the courtroom, as well as to the fact that the discussions were at times choppy or too technical, in spite of prosecuting attorney Hubert de Touzalin's concern for "pedagogy." The lack of solemnity was also due to the very personality of the accused, who aroused more disgust than indignation, and to the personality of the accused's lawyer, attorney Jacques Trémolet de Villers. The latter, armed with multi-faceted talents and with a polemical wit traditionally associated with a certain reactionary Right (he was the disciple of attorney Jean-Louis Tixier-Vignancour, whose eloquence was formidable) pulled out all the stops, using a perfect knowledge of the legal dossier to his advantage. The defense lawyer also took great advantage of the spectacle that the thirty-seven lawyers of the private parties put on in spite of themselves.

Among some of these private parties, there was an obvious ignorance of the legal dossier. Among others, there was a disturbing absence of historical knowledge: indeed, during one of the lawyers' arguments, mention was made of "the *attempt* to land in North Africa" (italics added) in November 1942, while during another argument, the armistice was placed in October 1940.[30] This was all filmed and has now been filed away for the benefit of future generations. Several lawyers were only there to make the scene. Such was the case with two eloquent speakers from the bar: one announced that he would argue his client's case without attending any other sessions, except for the opening photo (this lawyer wound up being replaced by a second fiddle who only intervened for a few minutes), while another, a former government minister, argued his client's case even though he had not attended the long weeks of hearings during which the witnesses had given their testimony . . .

Sometimes these lawyers gave the impression of being short of arguments. Witness the overkill on the "green notebook," which was the personal diary in which, up until a recent date, Paul Touvier recorded his personal hates. When it was dug up in a falsely accidental way on March 30, it constituted one of the crucial pieces of evidence in the trial. This nauseous document probably weighed heavily in Touvier's conviction: it provided indisputable evidence that the former member of the Milice was lying when he asserted, "I have never been anti-Semitic." But it did not provide a decisive argument for establishing his guilt. And it hardly differed, by the nature of the things that he would say to himself, from anti-Semitic writings that circulate freely in the extreme Right press, which is available in all the newspaper stands. This "green notebook" was nevertheless cited as a leitmotif in some of the legal arguments, with the risk not only of giving the impression that Touvier's inner personal privacy, as ugly as it might be, was being violated, but also that crimes against humanity were being reduced to the incoherent, repetitious mumblings of an old man.

The lawyers for the private parties have been greatly criticized, and unfairly so with respect to the few of them who did take on their task with talent and conviction. This is probably due to their diversity and their number (almost thirty argued in the case during one week!). But above all and most important, it is due to the fact that they never had a concerted strategy, and for a good reason: this was a trial that took place for lack of anything better. At times the impossibility of trying René Bousquet cast a shadow on things. So the trial of Paul Touvier was a catch-all, into which people tried to fit all the issues of memory that had emerged over the last twenty years. This pitfall, which was partly excusable given the importance of the event, at times made it unavoidably ridiculous. During the moving testimony of Louis Goudard, which was crucial for the prosecution, one witnessed the spectacle of a lawyer standing up to recall, on the pretext that it was April 6, 1994, the fiftieth anniversary of the tragedy, the roundup of the children of Izieu, a crime which had been committed by Klaus Barbie and bore no relation to Paul Touvier or to Vichy. Similarly, we heard one of his colleagues ask the accused's daughter, in a voice just as solemn, and pointing the finger, if she had "heard about the extermination of the Jews?" To this question, Chantal Berthet, born in 1948, whose testimony hardly deserved commentary (she was defending her father) replied that "we heard about it every day." (This took place during the March 25 session.)

That was not the least excess in a trial that some people wanted to make into the trial of collaboration, of the application of the "Final Solution" in France, and of the Vichy regime all at once. It was thus forgotten, in spite of the reminders of the defense and of the court, that at Versailles a man was on trial. Equally forgotten was the fact that the accused represented a marginal element in relation to the Vichy regime, since he was certainly less representative than a René Bousquet, even if he was much more fanatical. While the former member of the Milice could be reproached for murdering at least seven people, and doubtless for numerous resisters and Jewish civilians either killed or handed over to the Gestapo, René Bousquet, by his actions during the years of 1942 and 1943, was one of those responsible for deporting 59,000 out of the 76,000 French Jews that were deported for the sake of a deliberate policy of political collaboration.

On several occasions, the frustration of having only a Paul Touvier on the witness stand was openly expressed, as if those abominable crimes could find no other outlet for mourning than a court of justice, even if it were during a trial whose arguments were obviously of little significance with respect to memory.

A Legal Truth, an Historical Lie

Paul Touvier was convicted. And that is all well and good. France has finally had its trial for crimes against humanity; it will no longer be accused of running away from its past, except by someone of considerable bad faith. It nonetheless remains that Paul Touvier was convicted on the basis of a lie. Granted, it was his own.

Vichy France was never part of the Axis. In order to be found guilty of such a crime, Paul Touvier thus had to have made himself an accomplice to a heinous crime of German origin. This is what stemmed from last minute changes in the legal definition of crimes against humanity used in the trial, as analyzed above. Now, the only elements corresponding to the idea of a German intervention in the Rillieux affair were the declarations made by the accused himself. In all the fifty-two boxes of the legal dossier, neither the lawyers, nor the prosecuting attorney, nor the court, nor the examining magistrate found the slightest trace of a clue that would have supported the accused's declarations. Further, most of these documents are items dating from the postwar period (originating in particular from courts of justice) and not from the Occupation. Paul Touvier and the Milice of Lyons destroyed their archives at the time of the Liberation. As for the German archives, they proved to be of little interest, except for a few documents. Aside from accused's own assertions (the other two protagonists had died in 1945), there was nothing else found that would substantiate the fable of the hundred Jewish hostages demanded by Werner Knab, the head of the Sipo-SD of Lyons, a figure which was then reduced to thirty by Victor de Bourmont, the regional head of the Milice, and finally brought down to seven by Paul Touvier.

During the investigation, Judge Getti had moreover remained particularly determined to demonstrate that Paul Touvier was lying on this point. At that stage, the issue was to prove that he had indeed acted alone. It was imperative to stop cold all attempts by the defense to hide behind the "order that had been received" (or rather the "pressure of the occupying forces"), which might have resulted in the finding of extenuating circumstances, or even in the clearing of the former member of the Milice. That is why the final indictment of October 7, 1991, went back over the conclusions of the examining magistrate on this crucial point:

> First of all, Paul Touvier would have no basis for maintaining that the execution of the seven Jewish hostages at Rillieux had been imposed on the Milice by the German authorities, in reprisal for the assassination of Philippe Henriot.
>
> This line of argument is indeed completely unconvincing in that there is no reason why the Germans would have involved the Milice (and particularly de Bourmont) in this operation, in view of the fact that they held at the Montluc fort [in Lyons] a very large number of Jewish prisoners, whose immediate execution would have been much simpler and just as symbolic in the eyes of the public.
>
> In reality, it does indeed appear that the killing of the seven hostages at Rillieux is directly and solely attributable to the Milice alone, which thus tried to take vengeance for the death of Philippe Henriot, who was also a member of the Milice, and whose many famous speeches over the radio were at that time forcefully and virulently stigmatizing the imperious necessity of defending the National Revolution facing its enemies (this was a basic theme of the ideology of the Milice).[31]

Moreover, in accordance with historical analyses, the investigation demonstrated that not only did the Germans not get involved in the reprisals that followed the death of Henriot, but that the Laval government disapproved of them.[32] The occupying forces did not take part (although they had no objection), for actions of this sort fit right into the logic of Nazi policy, for which the Milice was at the time the main support in France. On the other hand, Pierre Laval, who had created the Milice but who then no longer controlled it, vigorously protested against such massacres committed by official forces of order; three weeks before the Allied landing in Normandy, he feared the reactions of a public whose opinions had already largely been won over to the cause of the Allies and the Resistance. Thus it was that he condemned an act of reprisal quite similar to that at Rillieux, which was committed on the very same day at Mâcon, by order of the head of Milice Clavier. (There was, however a difference, which is critical for us now, but which was not really significant in the eyes of the members of the Milice at the time: the seven victims who were shot at Mâcon were not, except for one, Jews but constituted a sort of macabre "sampling" of all those categories of people that the Milice, of its own accord, considered to be its enemies.[33]) Joseph Darnand, the chief of the Milice, was admonished by Pierre Laval, who himself had been alerted by the prefect and was furious

that his prerogatives were being flouted by the men of the Milice. Following these killings, Joannès Clavier was locked up in the Montluc fort, before being freed on the orders of the regional director of the penitentiary
office of Lyons, who was also a member of the Milice, on August 21, 1944.
Not knowing that Clavier had thus been freed thanks to the complicity of a
fellow member of the Milice, the district attorney's office of Lyons had on
August 22, 1944, sent to the (Vichy) Minister of Justice a request that the
Clavier case be taken up by the State Tribunal (a special court created by
the Pétainist regime to bring resisters and opponents to trial quickly). Meanwhile, Paris was liberated and the Minister of Justice had departed on the
paths of exile, towards Sigmaringen.[34]

This episode illustrates not only the difficulty of distinguishing, within
the context of that time, the reprisals made by the Milice against the Jews
from other categories of reprisals, it also shows to what degree the situation
during the weeks preceding the Liberation was complex and changing.
While the installation of the provisory government's administration was
becoming clearer and clearer throughout the land, the rivalries between
the members of the Milice on one side and the judicial and administrative
system in place on the other were reaching the height of their intensity.

At this stage, already, it was a particularly delicate matter to "try Vichy" by
means of the incident at Rillieux. If the complexity of history were to be respected, one would have to be able to distinguish between the responsibilities of a regime that had accepted the collaborationist commitment made
by an official entity of the state which became, by the will of Pierre Laval,
an instrument of the police's collaboration with the Nazis, and the specific responsibility of the Milice and its members, whose criminal attitude
stemmed from a largely autonomous political commitment. In 1944, the
Milice was both an outgrowth of Vichy resulting from its ideological evolution after the summer of 1940 (and which was partially rooted in the prewar context), and a distinct entity which was extending its sway over the
machinery of the state. In final analysis, even though the Laval government
had wanted a *French* force of order to fight against the Resistance in the
name of protecting the sovereignty that it claimed, and even though the
regime had given birth to the Milice, it would nonetheless have preferred
to avoid incidents such as the events at Rillieux or Mâcon. Was it possible
to explain these historical subtleties, which were after all essential, in the
context of a trial taking place fifty years after the events happened? Did
these subtleties even have a chance of being heard, much less understood?

Judge Getti's investigation, without skewing historical reality, had in
part skirted the obstacle by basing itself on the legal definition of crimes
against humanity that was then prevalent, according to the precedent of

1985. Ultimately, it mattered little, from the point of view of criminal justice, that the government had condemned some of the reprisals which followed the death of Henriot, since, in any case, it would eventually have to assume responsibility for these incidents: Paul Touvier and his counterparts had acted under the supposed authority of the French government; this government, putting in place a "policy of ideological hegemony," had allowed Jews to be executed on the basis of "racial" criteria, whereas the "concerted plan" for extermination had been for the most part underway for two years and Vichy had lent its assistance to it. Finally, it had not been until August 6, 1944, that Philippe Pétain, chief of state, worried about the violent actions of the Milice, even though at the same time he granted the Milice a decisive role in collaborating with German police forces.[35] It was possible to defend the legal line of argument.

But this whole edifice of reasoning collapsed with the ruling for the dismissal of charges on April 13, 1992, and then the decision of the appeals court on November 27, 1992. From then on, how was it possible to prove the exact opposite, namely, that Paul Touvier had acted "at the instigation" of the Germans, *with the same witnesses and the same documents* (or rather the same lack of documented proof of this last point)? This highly unusual situation, although not alluded to explicitly, remained in the back of everyone's mind during the first sessions. The great majority of lawyers for the private parties, the witnesses (including the historians called to the stand) kept on hammering away with the themes that the Milice had been an instrument of collaboration, that the ties between Paul Touvier and Werner Knab had been very close, that Touvier's Deuxième Bureau had provided valuable information to the Sipo-SD of Lyons, a little unit of a few dozen men who, without the Milice, would not have been able to break up a number of Resistance groups as efficiently as it had. That was all well and good. But the trial dealt with the incident at Rillieux, not with the general history of the Milice, and even less with the Collaboration in general. It was thus necessary to avoid raising the sticky question of the autonomy of the Milice and act as if the content of the accused's declarations about the Rillieux incident, in spite of what Judge Getti might have concluded, were essentially truthful. In short, it was necessary to accept his lie at the price of highly unlikely contortions.

If what the accused said about Werner Knab's role was to be believed, why then refuse to believe him on the question of the "hundred hostages" reduced to seven? Why only believe a part of his story and thus separate the truth from the lies by fractional distillation, without having either the documents or the witnesses to do it? Completely disoriented, the lawyers for the private parties then sought to "spur" the witnesses on. On April 6, 1994, the former resister Louis Goudard, who was admirable when he related his experience, suddenly lost credibility when he affirmed, without the slightest proof and after having been incited before the session by a lawyer, that there had been a "contact by telephone" between Karl Oberg, Supreme Chief of the SS in France, and Laval, about the reprisals for the death of Henriot. Four years earlier, he had declared to Judge Getti: "For me, it is not possible for the Germans to have formulated such a demand."

This situation, at times amusing, at times pathetic, reached the height of its intensity during the session of April 1, 1994. That day, commissar Jacques Delarue took the witness stand. As a highly reputed historian on the subject and a former resister, he was a key witness for the prosecution. The report that he had filed in June 1970 in the State Security Court described Paul Touvier's doings in detail. About the incident at Rillieux, he had noted: "There exists no trace of any intervention of the Germans in this matter."[36]

Commissar Delarue was taken to task on this point by attorney Arno Klarsfeld, the son of Serge and Beate Klarsfeld.[37] Out of all his counterparts, only this young lawyer had maintained from the beginning that there had never been any instigation from the Germans, that Paul Touvier had acted alone, and that these facts nevertheless did not in any way prevent the prosecution from proving a crime against humanity.[38] Up until then, few people took him seriously. That day, he reversed the course of the trial in a certain way. Why, he asked the witness, had he changed his mind on such an important point? The answer: because of a "new" document . . . which Jacques Delarue took out of his briefcase and whose revelation had already been undertaken by several lawyers. This document concerned the testimony given by Joseph Darnand himself and recorded during the investigation of his trial in the High Court, on August 6, 1945. In this sworn testimony, the chief of the Milice declared that the Germans had supposedly demanded "about forty" hostages after the death of Philippe Henriot. This piece of information seemed new, since this was the first time that it was mentioned in court. The announcement made a big effect. Finally, here was the "decisive proof" of German instigation, even if this document (which in fact was well known by historians) had no direct link to the slaughter at Rillieux (even supposing that Joseph Darnand had told the truth).

Questioned by the prosecuting attorney, then by attorney Trémolet de Villers for the defense, Jacques Delarue explained that it was normal for historians to change their minds when new sources are discovered. That is when Klarsfeld recalled that, at the time of his testimony to the examining magistrate, Getti, in 1990, this document was already available to him and that he [Delarue] had nevertheless maintained before the judge that there had not, in his opinion, been any German intervention at Rillieux.[39] This had the effect of a bombshell that exploded the silence covering what everyone was thinking. Another incident was to ensue a few minutes later, when Klarsfeld attacked Jacques Delarue personally. This was a needless attack, which according to Klarsfeld was justified by the fact that he feared that the press would minimize the incident, a temptation that might indeed have been present from time to time in order to avoid playing into the hands of the defense.[40]

Pursuing this line of argument even further, attorney Klarsfeld brought up a document found in the investigation files which held no small interest. It was the report of a "dinner" held in Lyons, on June 28, 1944, the very day of the death of Philippe Henriot. Seated around the dinner table were, on one side, French collaborationist VIPs, and on the other side, German officials, including Werner Knab in person. Now, in this document which described the tenor of the discussions about the situation in France, at no time was the death of Philippe Henriot mentioned. "How is it that someone like Werner Knab, who, a few hours earlier, is supposed to have wanted to massacre a hundred Jews in reprisal for the death of Philippe Henriot, had that evening totally put the subject out of his mind?" declared Klarsfeld in his plea.[41]

An historian will not necessarily follow the lawyer in all of his interpretation; this would even make a good case study in the differences of textual analysis used respectively by each.[42] Still, if an historian had to explain the Rillieux incident outside of any legal context, taking into account existing documents and testimony, and taking into account what is known about the behavior of the Milice in 1944, that historian would certainly not conclude that there was any German instigation, and doubtless would not have spontaneously considered such an hypothesis, except for the purpose of questioning the word of Paul Touvier on this matter. If we remain within the framework of the trial, nothing would allow us to believe the former member of the Milice on this point either, since he constantly lied about all the rest, nor would anything lead us to dismiss the conclusions of Judge Getti. There was in other words a more than sizeable doubt on the question of German instigation, since there was not the slightest bit of evidence to prove it.

These inconsistencies and these revelations still did not prevent Paul Touvier from being convicted *on that basis*, with a total disregard for doubts as to the veracity of the facts. How could one not be unsettled by such a flagrant contradiction between, on the one hand, historical truth (or at least, historical likelihood), and, on the other hand, the inconsistencies of an accusation that kept changing with the circumstances, and what is more, a justice system that, believing itself to be serving memory, does a disservice to history?

Rillieux: Crimes against Humanity and the "Final Solution"

Paul Touvier deserves his fate and can even be thankful for having succeeded in escaping justice in 1946 and 1947, for if not, he would have left this world a long time ago. But the individual matters little here. It was too often repeated that this was a trial for history, for memory, for the teaching of young generations, so that it might no longer be necessary to question the essential facts of the matter and their symbolical meaning. Is the Rillieux crime, the avowed crime indisputably committed by Paul Touvier, a crime against humanity? This question may appear to be a sacrilege in more than one way, for no one can contest the authority of what has been judged and ruled on.[43] But the question merits asking.

The Versailles court answered in the affirmative. The fact remains that neither the demonstration of the prosecuting attorney nor that of the private parties was convincing. As for the defense, it did not succeed in demonstrating the contrary.

If the law is followed to the letter (the instigation of a "European country of the Axis"), the legal definition of crimes against humanity has not been established in this case, since the necessary and restrictive element is missing: Paul Touvier quite probably acted alone. But one would be just as narrowly legalistic to confine oneself to that view of things, even though this was a trial, and the respect of the law (in which case the accused must receive the benefit of doubt) is hardly the least of obligations.

If we follow the previous definition of crimes against humanity, that of 1985, and if we moreover follow the spirit of the laws of 1945 and of their application (which had as their primary objective to define a crime that was *exceptional* by its very nature and that was made particular and distinct from other crimes by being defined as beyond the statute of limitations), then two other questions are raised: did the murder of the seven Jews at Rillieux have a systematic nature? and did it fit into the framework of a "concerted plan"?

Two types of answers are possible here: that of the legal scholar and that of the historian. Since we are not legal experts, we can only express our doubts with respect to the demonstration that was put before the members of the jury in Versailles. On the other hand, however, the question can be posed quite differently from an historical perspective: did the Rillieux crime take place in the framework of the "Final Solution"?

It will doubtless be objected that we are thus changing the nature of the question; the notion of crimes against humanity does not apply only to the extermination of the Jews and can define other crimes of the same order. That is perfectly correct. But the opposite has turned out to be true most of the time. The association—not to say the equation—is made almost spontaneously in the minds of many people, including legal scholars and magistrates who have had to rule on these problems (except the final Court of Appeals in 1985). This is indeed one of the major characteristics of all the legal proceedings that have been initiated against French citizens: they all deal with crimes fitting in the context of the Nazi policy of extermination which, in France, only concerned the Jews.[44] It was indeed this type of trial that people wanted to have, pointing out the shortcomings of the purge. But the question is, in other words, can the Rillieux incident take on the symbolical function that people assigned to it for lack of having been able to try René Bousquet and to pronounce judgment on the crime of the massive Vél' d'Hiv' roundup?

In their final statements, the lawyers for the private parties constantly compared Klaus Barbie's crime at Izieu to Touvier's crime at Rillieux. But this comparison is far from being self-evident. At Izieu, in a house lost way out in the middle of the mountains, Klaus Barbie of the SS came on April 6, 1944, during the battle against the Resistance, to take hidden Jewish children; forty-four children and seven of their leaders were deported, most to Auschwitz. Only one adult survived and only one child managed to escape. One other was released because he was not Jewish. In its absolute barbarity, this act had for its sole and unique "justification" nothing other than a plan for systematic extermination targeting *all* Jews, wherever they might be, whenever they did not enjoy some rare diplomatic protection. The roundup at Izieu was not due to contingent motives. It constituted an action that had been premeditated long in advance and that was driven by an ideological determination to kill. There was no "terroristic" character about it (in contrast to the Nazis' executions of hostages) in that it was not intended to make an impression on public opinion. On the contrary, the Nazis maintained secrecy about the final destination of the deportation trains, namely the gas chamber. Izieu is thus a textbook example of the "Final Solution," which had the objective of eradicating an entire category of people from the surface of the earth.

The crime at Rillieux is of a different nature. Paul Touvier, a proven and particularly fanatical anti-Semite, did not carry out a systematic roundup. He arrested certain specific Jewish individuals (who had been picked out for that purpose long beforehand) with the sole aim of seeking vengeance for the killing of Philippe Henriot. Touvier preferred defenseless civilians who could not possibly fight back, rather than resisters; the latter were to be feared because of the likelihood that their comrades would immediately strike back in reprisal. Touvier did not round up women or children. And he had his victims killed on the spot, with their bodies left out in the open for everyone to see—not only did he kill the "enemies" of the Milice, but in addition he helped to terrorize the civilian population a little more. This was an objective inherent in the Milice's logic of "maintaining public order," in other words, fighting against the Resistance and, in a more general way, against all opponents of the National Revolution.

In that sense—and this is why the "lesson" of the Touvier trial is somewhat absurd—the Rillieux incident was a *French* crime, which fit in the context of infighting among the French themselves, since Touvier, the member of the Milice, had no need of help from the Germans nor of their "instigation" to act the way he did in this matter. The crime does not fit into the framework of the "Final Solution," for if such had been the case, the victims' family members who were Jewish would have been arrested too. This is what Judge Getti had well understood when he upheld against Touvier the charge of murder for the killing of Victor Basch and his wife, which was as much an anti-Semitic crime as taking revenge against the defenders of Dreyfus, of the Republic, and of democracy. That was the reason for the murders, committed at the same time, of the former government ministers Jean Zay and Georges Mandel, both Jewish or considered so, and who also symbolized what the Milice hated the most. Was it not the judgment of those crimes that the memory of the French nation (or at least some of its most prominent voices) demanded, just as it demanded that Vichy's complicity in the "Final Solution" be judged? The latter crime, however, stemmed from another logic, that of state collaboration, and took place in another period of time (1942), and was carried out by other figures (René Bousquet, Jean Leguay, and, accessorily, Maurice Papon).

Now, unless one considers the notions of "systematic" murder, of a "concerted plan," and of crimes committed in the name of a state (and not for the sake of an organization or a single individual) to be secondary—but to do so would be to risk dangerously emptying the very definition of crimes against humanity of its substance—it is by virtue of these elements that it is possible to voice doubts about the legal definition of the incident at Rillieux.

Paul Touvier was a murderer. But crimes against humanity are distinct from other crimes. They differ in a symbolic way, because the term defines an unusual act. They differ legally, for, at least in France, this is the only crime that is not subject to the statute of limitations nor to the rule that would require that the accused be tried in his own era by his peers. Perhaps that is where the crux of the problem lies, in having removed the statute of limitations solely for a crime that is particularly difficult to establish. If common law or war crimes had no statute of limitations either, then doubt and criticism would have been improper.

It remains possible, however, to raise several questions and objections with respect to this line of reasoning. They were, incidentally, articulated in the lawyers' closing statements. The most frequently expressed idea was the fact that the seven who fell victim at Rillieux were killed because they were Jews, therefore *because of what they were*, and not for what they might have done, to use the famous definition of André Frossard,[45] who, during the investigation of the Klaus Barbie case, expressed his opposition to any expansion of the definition of crimes against humanity designed to accommodate resisters. This definition, however, which has the great merit of being simple, is in itself nonetheless debatable. It does establish a condition that, granted, poses a mininum requirement, but remains far from being sufficient; otherwise, any racist crime that was premeditated could be defined as a crime against humanity. There are many other things that define crimes against humanity, beginning with the systematic, planned nature of the murder, as well as the fact that it is carried out on a large scale. What is more, the definition of 1945 did not limit itself to "ethnic" or "inborn" criteria, which are always those of the criminal: within the framework of the "Final Solution," a Jew was anyone whom the Nazis had declared to be so by virtue of laws just as murky as Vichy's Jewish Statutes, whatever the future victims might have thought about it. Accordingly, the Nuremberg laws included persecutions of civilians for religious or political motives: people are not born Communist, they become Communist, even if they do not necessarily become resisters who bear arms. Similarly, people can convert to a religion or renounce it. The difficulty, not to say the absurdity, of combining "racial" and religious criteria was even one of the pitfalls that both the Nazis and French legal experts under Vichy came across in defining the "Jew." That explains why racial criteria were not the only ones used by the London accords of 1945.

André Frossard's argument can also be answered by going back to the incident at Mâcon that was mentioned above. The Milice chief Clavier, who was responsible for the massacre committed on the very same day as the one at Rillieux and for the same contingent reasons (the assassination of Philippe Henriot), ended by being condemned to death and shot at the Liberation. Let's assume for a moment that he had escaped the law for decades, as had Paul Touvier. Then what would have happened, according to the law? Six of Clavier's victims were not Jews. Could he nevertheless be brought to justice in the criminal court in 1994 for crimes against humanity? Theoretically, no, or else it would be for only one of the six murders. While on the one hand the seven victims at Mâcon were indeed civilians, suspected by the Milice of being resisters, and not all proven combatants with the Resistance (although according to their logic of terrorists and fanatics, some members of the Milice had little use for such a distinction), and while they had indeed been shot, they nevertheless had not been subjected to "inhumane treatments" (such as torture or deportation), nor had they (except for one) been killed for simply having been born, and neither had there been any "German instigation" in the matter. The shootings at Mâcon would therefore today probably be legally defined as a war crime, as a crime of collaboration, or simply as a crime. In any case, any prosecution, and thus any trial, would be precluded by the statute of limitations. One could reply that it is exactly in order to make a distinction between the killing of Jews

who were "guilty" only by their birth certificate and the killing of opponents "guilty" of their actions or ideas, that André Frossard's definition is
so often invoked. In the Klaus Barbie case, it had the advantage of distinguishing between the Nazis' repression of resisters, which was much the
same as that undertaken by all dictatorships, and the persecution of the
Jews, which was specific to the Third Reich, by its very nature and by the
means used to carry it out. Frossard's definition focused attention on the
singularity of the "Final Solution." But what about the case of Paul Touvier? Can we imagine Joannès Clavier's coming to testify at the witness
stand for or against his former counterpart who is accused of the killings at
Rillieux, killings which, at the time, in the eyes of the Milice (and even of
everyone), had the same meaning and served the same ends as the killings
that Clavier himself had perpetrated at Mâcon? Can we, going further yet,
imagine Clavier's being tried for just one of the seven murders committed
on June 28, 1944, on the pretext that the six other victims, executed in the
same circumstances and for the same reasons, were not Jewish? Even if it
were obvious that the intention of Paul Touvier had been to execute *only*
Jews—he did spare the "non-Jewish" resister Louis Goudard from the firing squad at Rillieux—the situation would in any case have been absurd.
However that may be, such a situation would have illustrated the absurdity
of an a posteriori legal definition that establishes a radical distinction between killings that followed the same criminal logic of the Milice as a whole.
Or else it would mean that one particularly anti-Semitic member of the
Milice was being tried (which was indeed the case) and not the Milice, much
less Vichy . . .

   To show the complexity of this problem, let us add that one of the hostages executed, Léon (or Léo) Glaeser, could have been considered a resister, in view of his activities at the time. That is the argument put forward
by the former resister Adam Rayski, who pointed out to us that this aspect
of his personality was not mentioned during the trial at the request of certain lawyers for the private parties. Léon Glaeser had indeed been an active
member of certain Jewish rescue organizations, including the Comité de la
rue Amelot, and later one of the founders of the CRIF (the Representative
Council of the Israelites of France, which became, at the time of the Liberation, the Representative Council of the Jews of France, and then the Representative Council of the Jewish Institutions of France). This is an additional confusion created by this trial that, in one of the victims, saw only his
"Jewishness" to the detriment of his "resistance" activities. However, this
argument calls for two remarks. First, it is not certain that Paul Touvier included Léon Glaeser in the group of hostages because he knew about his
clandestine activities. Second, it should be specified that the designation
"resister" given to the members of Jewish rescue organizations is a relatively recent phenomenon, which occasioned fierce debates over the last

few years about the very definition of resistance activity and about the need
to include or not to include acts of "civil resistance"—which takes nothing
away from the (very real) efficacy and heroism of these men and women,
many of whom were arrested, deported, and killed. Whatever answer one
might give, one cannot leave aside the influence of an ex post facto interpretation of things, which now tends to see a "Jewish" commitment where,
at the time, there was a commitment motivated by patriotism or political
convictions, or which, on the contrary, uses the term "resister" to designate
both acts of direct opposition as well as attempts of rescue and survival,
which were more frequent and more numerous among those victims who
were targeted by the murderous anti-Semitism of the Nazis. There again
we have an example of anachronism.[46]

There is another, more frequently heard argument in support of the notion of crimes against humanity in the Rillieux incident: even though the
crime at Rillieux was a French crime, it fit into the framework of a "general
complicity" of the Milice with the SS. As a member of the Milice, Paul
Touvier was indeed the accomplice of a state (the Third Reich) and of an
organization (the Gestapo) which has been declared criminal by the London accords. Although taking exception to any notion of German intervention, attorney Arno Klarsfeld, along with a number of his colleagues, ultimately argued in favor of this idea, which made it possible to reintroduce
the question of Vichy—even though examining the Rillieux incident alone
considerably reduced the chances of treating the issue exhaustively. All in
all, however, that amounted to trying not the deeds that Paul Touvier was
accused of, but rather his capacity as a member of the Milice and his status
as a "collaborator." This was implicitly falling back into the reasoning of
the first trials that were held, and thus back into the context of the purge.
But that was not the goal that was aimed for; as would have much more
clearly been so in a Bousquet trial, the Touvier trial was indeed an implicit
criticism of this purge. (René Bousquet, contrary to Paul Touvier who was
tried in absentia, had been acquitted by the High Court in 1949.)

Similarly, attorney Henri Leclerc based his final statement to the court
on a line of reasoning carrying considerable clout: any crime committed
against a Jew by a civil servant, and therefore by a person acting in the capacity of a state official, fit into the framework of the "Final Solution" if
it had taken place during or after the summer of 1942, when the process of
total extermination was concretely underway; the criminal could not have
been unaware of this process. However, while Paul Touvier was indeed perfectly aware of the anti-Jewish policies that were carried out by the Nazis
and Vichy, in which he actively participated, nothing proves that he had
been informed about the way in which the extermination was carried out,
nor even that he had a clear idea of it. This is not to give Touvier an alibi,
but to avoid a frequently occurring anachronism which consists in the be-

lief that "everyone knew" or that a large number of people had "put together the pieces" of information (which were at times quite precise) that were circulating. Even if he had been informed, it would nevertheless remain extremely hard to prove; during the trial, it would have never been established, and it was not during the trial. Besides—and this is the most important point—French responsibility for crimes against humanity can, according to Henri Leclerc's line of reasoning, only be evaluated, legally speaking, outside of the context of the "Final Solution" established by the Nazis.

On this point, the historian will agree with the legal scholar, in that, as mentioned above, Vichy did not itself want to exterminate the Jews. Vichy was an accomplice to this crime for political reasons, those of state collaboration. But was this really the message that the activists for memory wanted to send to the public? The verdict of the court at Versailles in the final analysis convicted an accomplice of the Nazis, a collaborator, based on an interpretation of the facts that was wrong and on legal principles that were shaky, to say the least. The autonomy both of the French State and of the Milice, which people had sought to highlight for twenty years, was brought back into the discussion only at the last minute, thanks to a "maverick" lawyer. This is enough to call the exemplary stature of such trials into question. And, whatever the charges might be, the anomalies of the Touvier case raise serious questions as to the wisdom of demanding, right after the verdict was issued at Versailles, that Maurice Papon be brought to trial.

The Judge, the Witness, and the Historian

It was a highly unusual sight. Four professional historians, René Rémond, François Bédarida, Robert Paxton, and Michel Chanal, most of them internationally renowned, came to the witness stand at the Versailles trial. As did the other witnesses, they took an oath and swore to tell the whole truth. But what truth? Is it possible to articulate historical truth in a courtroom? If so, what is the status of such truth? Is it possible to consider things in the abstract, removing oneself from the context of the courtroom, from the pressure of a criminal trial, and, above all, from the moral and political issues surrounding such a case? This was a tremendous challenge, and the four historians met it squarely without compromising their professional ethics. We are therefore not concerned here with passing judgment on these individuals, but rather with raising questions about the historian's social role in such a matter, and more importantly, about the differences between legal discourse (that of law), judicial discourse (that of the criminal court), historians' discourse, and testimony.

On the surface, the historians were requested to come because of their "expertise," that is, because of their scholarly learning, which was based on rigorous methods. Their discourse by definition had strong legitimacy, since it expressed knowledge that was shared, verified, and sifted out by a process of constant critical review. This discourse established itself as a sort of guard rail in a trial dealing with events that took place many years ago and that were at times hard to establish clearly. But it sometimes happens that this knowledge is limited by lack of documents, by the subjective nature of interpretation, or by the impossibility of approaching what really happened in the past other than by groping at bits and pieces and by viewing it through the prism of the present day. All historians know this, even if they sometimes have to forget it in order to practice their profession: they cannot describe "what happened"; they can only, by means of traces available to them, reconstitute a plausible scenario meaningful for their contemporaries. From one isle of established truth to the next, they navigate over an ocean of uncertainties. But the courts have to find out "what happened," and if there is a doubt, the accused must receive the benefit of it. Hypotheses formulated by historians are not of the same nature and do not have the same consequences as the "inner conviction" of a prosecuting attorney or a jury.

It was possible to gauge the importance of this point when the prosecuting attorney, Hubert de Touzalin, based his charge on the interpretation of the incident at Rillieux: the matters of the "instigation," the "order," the "German intervention, which could have been insistent," were only an hypothesis, which was shaky in view of the documents and disputable on the level of history, for reasons spelled out previously. But coming from the lips of the prosecuting attorney, this hypothesis nevertheless turned into a conviction that he was keen on conveying to the jurors so that they might unhesitatingly convict the accused.

This radical difference between historical discourse and legal or judicial discourse was a theme constantly hammered on by the defense lawyer from the outset: "A trial in a criminal court is not a lecture at the Sorbonne." There is no refuting this observation. On the other hand, however, since the historians constituted an essential strong suit for the prosecution in this trial, attorney Trémolet de Villers was able to push this line of reasoning very far and to assert, for example: "History is nothing but an opinion," which provoked the wrath of François Bédarida: "Defense pleas and historical scholarship do not mix" (this occurred during the March 25 session). But if the history of historians is not compatible with the defense's strategy, can it find a home in the charge of the prosecution? Right from the start, we could gauge the difficulty of fitting truths that by necessity move and evolve with sources, perspectives, and epochs, into a rigid, normative framework, on which was hinged the fate of an individual. While denying that it was possible to bring a view that was the least bit objective or scientific to bear on the past—and this is the premise of every revisionism—the

defense lawyer nevertheless pointed out the limits of a trial that was supposed to have an "historical" vocation.

Indeed, the historians were not called upon as experts in the strictest
sense of the word. At the Versailles trial, only two licensed clinical psychi-
atrists were called to appear before the court in their official capacity. They
did not take an oath—and they were not supposed to.[47] The four university
professors did, however. They were witnesses *for the prosecution*, one of them
(René Rémond) having been called by the prosecuting attorney, the three
others by the private parties. Furthermore, how could such a situation have
been avoided? Given the case files, it was impossible for the historians to
consider Paul Touvier to be "presumed innocent" simply by the fact that
he had just been accused of a crime in the legal system. A former collaborator does not cease to be a collaborator once he has been indicted forty-five
years after the events happened! The historians gave their testimony during the first sessions, after the questioning of Paul Touvier, but before the
general review of the facts. They established the general setting: the history
of the Milice (provided by François Bédarida and Michel Chanal), the history of collaboration (provided by Robert Paxton), and the relations between Paul Touvier and the Catholic Church, presented by René Rémond,
who was called upon because he had presided over the commission on the
subject. (François Bédarida had also served on the commission.)

The meaning of the message delivered was clear: the Milice had been a
valuable and active auxiliary of the SS, "one of the occupying force's supplementary forces." It was fully in line with the regime and the government
that had created it. "Pétain provided the sanction, Laval handled the day to
day affairs, and the Milice ruled," summarized François Bédarida. There
could be no possible doubt on this point of general history. In addition,
these historians tried to avoid mentioning the incident at Rillieux directly.
Fully aware of the vexing contradictions between history and the law, they
sought to confine themselves to giving a global view of things without going beyond their field. But the lawyers for the private parties would not be
content with that: they incessantly asked the historians to give their assessment of what Paul Touvier had done, and this sometimes prevented them
from expressing themselves in their own way, or forced them to make awkward comparisons: "The Milice is to Vichy what the SS is to the Nazi state,"
one of the historians finally said. Pushed by a lawyer to say to what extent
the SS and the Milice worked in concert with each other, he was forgetting
that the SS existed within the logic of a one-party system that was the basis
and essential component of Hitler's state; this hardly corresponded to the
situation at Vichy, where the Milice was created subsequent to the formation of the regime and contrary to the principles of the traditional state.
Only the American Robert Paxton managed never to mention Paul Touvier's name, whereas the other three, and in particular the two members of

the commission on the Catholic Church's relations with Paul Touvier, were not able to avoid expressing an opinion on the individual, both on Touvier as an official, active member of the Milice and on the collaborator on the run.

Even more noteworthy is the fact that the historians particularly emphasized the importance of the Milice as an instrument of collaboration rather than as a polarizing force in the context of French infighting. Although they did not misrepresent the facts, the vision that they put forward was nevertheless influenced by the issues overshadowing the trial: they had to enlighten the court about the doings of the Germans' *accomplice*. That constitutes another difference from a course on history. In order to explain to students what the Milice was, both aspects really must be covered. Now that the role of the Milice as an accomplice to the Germans has been rather well assimilated, historians have in recent years been stressing the importance of the Milice as an instrument in France's internecine conflicts in order to deal with other issues and to excavate a little-known historical domain—that is to say, precisely, the historiographical issues of Vichy.

Once this general picture was sketched out, the examination of the facts was nevertheless separated from the historical summaries. The distance between the historians' history and the witnesses' (including the accused's) history thus appeared throughout the trial. The historians' history was gradually blotted out by the witnesses' history, which in turn quickly gave way to history as seen by the jurors. Moreover, the defense attorney and certain commentators expressed their frustration; in their view, the trial only began after the testimony of the last historian.[48] Now, this state of affairs is somewhat incoherent, as far as the historical method (at least the one applied to the study of contemporary history) is concerned. Historians elaborate their historical accounts *after* the witnesses have been heard and the facts have been examined. Their analysis involves constantly crosschecking the available sources, measuring the spoken word in comparison with the written document, and comparing individual testimony to what is recorded in raw archives.

The method followed within the confines of the courtroom is only vaguely related to such critical investigation. Throughout the entire trial, the presiding Judge Boulard constantly recalled that the rule of the "oral nature of all discussions" is mandatory in a criminal court. The jury must base its conviction on what has been said in the courtroom. It does not have direct accesss to the case file, unless the presiding judge, "by virtue of his discretionary power," finds it necessary to *read* such and such document aloud, which is far different from an individual reading silently and with the possibility of cross-checking or verifying such and such piece of information. Similarly, the jury must assume that "only the accused has the right to lie," since one can suppose that the sworn witnesses are telling the truth to the court. If this seems to be a rather rigid, or even abstract system, it never-theless weighed heavily upon the proceedings at Versailles. The facts under examination were not those of an ordinary crime. They were of an histori-cal order, and their meaning went far beyond the individual under accusa-tion. It was thus necessary to fit the analysis of a political crime not only into a rigid legal framework—the definition of the crime—but also into a frozen ritual which was not designed for such a purpose—that of the crimi-nal court. That is what accounts for the gaps, the contradictions, and the tensions between the four orders of discourse: that of the legal expert, that of the magistrate, that of the historian, and that of the witness, which at times were cut off from each other.

However, beyond providing a general picture, an historian's expertise would have been useful in solving certain concrete problems, dismantling one of Paul Touvier's lies, or correcting certain errors and misinterpreta-tions (and the courtroom debates were hardly lacking in them!). A trial dealing with things that happened fifty years ago is not of the same nature as a trial dealing with events that happened a few years ago. The historians could have provided some observations about the context and mindset of the time that would be essential in assessing a crime of that order. They could have helped the jury put aside widely held notions, clichés, and even errors that common knowledge carries with it, especially for younger peo-ple. They did so in giving their testimony, but they were never able to in-tervene during the rest of the trial, whenever an "historical" question was indeed raised during the hearings.

For example, on April 6, the court heard the testimony of Pierre Conte, whose mother had been arrested by the Milice at the end of July 1944 and taken to the Curial barracks, right in the middle of Chambéry. Madame Conte as well as another well-known personality of Chambéry, Madame Rozier, were set free on the orders of Paul Touvier, "for propaganda pur-poses," as the accused was to say. According to the witness, the two women had been handed over to the Germans. The Milice leader had thus suc-ceeded in having them released; this proved his influence over the occupy-ing forces, something that he constantly denied. However, Paul Touvier stated in the courtroom that he had taken the two women out of Milice bar-racks that were located at the same place as those of the Germans, with whom, he maintained, he had had no contact. But all that is untrue. Neither the Sipo-SD, nor the SS, nor the Milice were located in those barracks, which housed the troops of the German army.[49] Nevertheless, the discus-sion about this matter, which had suddenly become crucial, lasted a very long time, without anybody's being able to give an authoritative answer one way or the other. Was the question of crimes against humanity going to be stuck on this detail, as was the case for other very specific bits of information about certain places or individuals? A little historical research or simply a careful reading of the case file would have allowed them to take care of the problem.

If we wanted to emphasize the paradox even more, we could add that an historian could have—and should have—explained that, on the one hand, the Milice was not in the Curial barracks at Chambéry and therefore Paul Touvier did indeed have close contact with the German military authorities, and, on the other hand, that in the Rillieux incident, the absence of "German instigation" nevertheless appeared to have been established! We are dealing with two different things that may seem to be contradictory—especially in the heat of proceedings of a criminal court and for novices in the matter—but which clearly illustrate the ambivalence of the situation. Vichy and the collaborators, in order to exist as a regime or an autonomous force, and in order to establish themselves as the only French alternative to the Resistance, had to cooperate very closely with the enemy, while at the very same time trying to maintain their own identity and hatreds.

This example, although it is rather marginal, shows once more that judicial discourse's way of establishing the facts is of a different nature than historical discourse's approach. Historians have time and come to their conclusions only after they are certain that all existing evidence has been examined. They use both nuance and fine typological distinctions. They avail themselves of layers of knowledge deposited by generations of dissertations and books of all sorts. On the contrary, the justice system is pressed for time, particularly in the case of an investigation that has gone on for more than twenty years! Legal discourse is influenced by the force of conviction, the talent, and the intellectual liveliness of the magistrates and attorneys. It is not called upon to answer questions relevant to history; it rather has to convince a jury of one individual's guilt or innocence, sincerity or bad faith, all within the rigid framework of existing legal codes. Legal discourse is not a matter of dispassionate demonstration, but of oratory prowess; in the final analysis, it matters little whether an assertion is true or false, justified or unjustified, since it is the "intimate conviction" of the jury which will settle the question once and for all. Once the verdict has been rendered, no one, outside of a few specialists, is interested in the debates nor is concerned with rectifying mistakes, except in the case of obvious judicial error. This is a situation that cannot possibly be compared with a written work of history, which is constantly subject to the criticism of the readers, especially by the authors' peers. History is often revised; trials are rarely subject to revision. Unless history sees to it.

Not only did the historians not have the possibility of fulfilling their job as experts, but in addition, they were sometimes exploited, as are all witnesses in a criminal court trial. Such was the case of the work published by the commission of historians on the relations between Paul Touvier and the Catholic Church. This extremely well-documented piece of research was used as evidence against the accused, and was constantly brandished by the lawyers for the private parties, who had moreover requested, during the investigation, that the book be included in the case file. It thus constituted an official piece of evidence. During his testimony, René Rémond took issue with the fact that the work of the commission might have appeared to be a sort of "parallel investigation" and that accordingly historians might have shirked their duty to be reserved. This commission, created upon the initiative of Cardinal Albert Decourtray in order to shed light on the complicity that Paul Touvier had enjoyed within the Catholic Church, was in many respects something entirely unprecedented. It probed an institution that, while reputed to be jealous of its secrets and tight-lipped about its past, was suddenly making all its archives available. The commission was constituted in June 1989, at the very same time the actual investigation of the former member of the Milice was beginning. At Versailles, René Rémond reminded the court in no uncertain terms that this commission did not have the task of studying the incidents (including the one at Rillieux) that were at the time being investigated by Judge Getti: "The historian's role, when public opinion is confused and upset, is to reveal the truth without interfering with the work of justice." Indeed, the commission's field of investigation dealt for the most part with the period following the war.

Nevertheless, there were in fact points of "interference" between the judicial investigation and the historical probe, and they were inevitable. The work published by the commission devotes a lengthy chapter (and one of the most interesting) to Touvier the collaborator's mental environment and family. Now, this aspect of the case also occupied an important place in the Versailles trial. It was no accident that during the examination of the accused's personality, the presiding Judge Boulard constantly referred back to this work published by historians. In each case, he was immediately countered by the attorney for the defense, who at all times kept in front of him an extensively annotated copy of the same book that he himself would also use or castigate because of its "errors." Both the historians on the one hand and the judge and the *gendarmes* on the other, often studied the same documents, the same testimonies, and they constantly exchanged information, especially about the period during which Paul Touvier was a member of the Milice. This was no secret to anyone, and there is nothing reprehensible about it; when he was warmly thanked by the prosecuting attorney for having come to testify, René Rémond was keen on stating that he held "the greatest respect" for the justice system. On that score, the historians did indeed conduct themselves as would any citizen having the means—and the duty—to assist in revealing the truth. Moreover, it was Cardinal Decourtray himself who stressed this point in a letter addressed to the members of the commission on June 28, 1990, one year after the probe had begun. Of the three objectives given to the commission by the Cardinal, in addition to shedding light on the dealings of certain members of the clergy and contributing to the writing of a difficult page in French history, the first one that he articulated was totally unambiguous: "to cooperate with the justice system."[50]

"We have never been the private parties' historians," declared René Rémond in court, which is correct as far as he is concerned, since he was called to testify by the prosecuting attorney. On the other hand, however, the three others were indeed called by the private parties. There again, the historians had to deal with a pitfall of an ethical nature: how to testify for the prosecution while at the same time remaining impartial. Above all, how was it possible not to share the vast majority of their fellow citizens' desire to see the accused condemned, since history was doubtless the most damning piece of evidence against him. Once more, the links between the historical probe and the judicial investigation were inevitable.

It is also likely that the historians along with others shared the fear of seeing Paul Touvier slip through the cracks once again. In its book, the commission devotes a chapter to the Milice. In it one can read that the Milice had a "coherent ideological plan"; that it "systematically" used torture and (just ten lines farther down) that it sought to eliminate its opponents "in a systematic way"; that it was a "hegemonic party" and (two pages farther) that it had "stated hegemonic aims." All these terms have a rather self-evident or repetitive ring to them (even when they describe an indisputable reality), but, in January 1992, they all referred mimetically back to the definition of the Court of Criminal Appeals of 1985 . . . which had become obsolete in 1994.[51]

In final analysis, does the work published by the commission of historians have the same status as a traditional book of history? In many respects, no. In the first place, without the controversy over the protection that the former member of the Milice had received from religious circles, it is unlikely that the (private) archives of the archbishopric of Lyons would have been made available with such liberality. This is a classic case of a controversial event accelerating the process of historical investigation, after having slowed it down in the beginning, and before the matter ran once more the risk of being covered up.[52] As far as we know, for the time being, only the historians on the commission have had access to these documents, even though it is undeniable that the officials of the archbishopric wanted to make things transparent.

This book has drawn the fire of numerous criticisms, for the most part of a partisan nature. Two of them formulated by the defense, however, deserve to be examined, for they touch on the method used in the commission's published work. Out of all the large number of witnesses solicited by the historians, only Paul Touvier and those close to him were not questioned. There was probably no need to do so, in view of the mass of writings coming from this individual and his entourage. It was above all a more than delicate matter, given the context. But it is not certain that, if this had been the case of a doctoral dissertation, a doctoral committee made up of these same historians would not have criticized the doctoral candidate for not having used this primary source. Another reproach made was that the book made use of a mass of personal letters found in the archives of the archbishopric of Lyons without the consent of those who wrote them; this is a violation of the codes regulating private archives, in particular those of the Church. In general, historians respect the regulations in effect over public and private archives, even though absolute compliance with these rules is at times incompatible with the necessities of research. In the case of the probe into the relations of Paul Touvier and the Church, the historians justified themselves by declaring that their work had been condoned by Cardinal Decourtray; this benediction showed that the political stakes far outweighed the scholarly ones. Such difficulties appear when historical studies of the present time are carried out upon request by administrations, businesses, or private organizations. The problems always arise at the outset, when the researchers request the sponsors of the study to grant unrestricted access to their archives, and when the researchers demand from the sponsors the authorization to publish the results of their study without the slightest censorship. Now, these two conditions were met in the case of the commission headed by René Rémond, and this fact is especially remarkable since the project took on the dimensions of a matter of national interest, which is a rare occurrence.

The principle of truth did, therefore, win out over all other considerations. By virtue of its particular status, this published work, much more than the trial itself, made it possible to discover this very poorly known chapter of history. Furthermore, it has been widely distributed (with 12,000 copies sold) and doubtless has had an appreciable impact on public opinion. In addition to the fact that it is a highly detailed work, and although it focuses on one very specific incident, the book is probably one of the most interesting that can be found about the internal functioning of the French Catholic Church in the contemporary period.

But there is one question not taken up by the members of the commission headed by René Rémond, and which was indeed an important concern for the courts. During the session of March 24, 1994, the prosecuting attorney gave the following response to a question that the private parties had raised about the impunity that certain clergymen enjoyed in spite of the known assistance and protection that they had granted to Paul Touvier:

In view of the study ordered by Cardinal Decourtray, and in agreement with Cardinal Decourtray, I feel obliged to ask Professor René Rémond to account for this assistance. [. . .] Before initiating legal prosecution, one has to be able to demonstrate what Touvier told people, according to his version of the story and in his way of presenting things. There must be certainty about the intentional nature of his actions. No sufficient demonstration has yet been given on this score.

In listening to these words, it was impossible not to feel rather puzzled. In the view of the criminal court, had the commission's probe fulfilled the role of a judicial investigation or had it made it possible to avoid such a proceeding? Moreover, the probe had dealt with incidents much more recent than the ones under examination by the court at Versailles; those events were far from falling under the statute of limitations. The question was all the more pressing in that, the following day, right after the testimony given by René Rémond and François Bédarida, the court was to hear the testimony of Father Soltner, from the Abbaye de Solesme in the Department of the Sarthe, where Paul Touvier had on more than one occasion found refuge between 1981 and 1988, at a time when he was subject to an arrest warrant.[53] Father Soltner's testimony, during which he virulently attacked the two historians, should have removed the doubts expressed the day before by the prosecuting attorney. Indeed, Father Soltner left people dumbfounded in trying to show what, in his view, was the difference between "indictment" and "accusation" and in trying to justify the fact that he had never even considered encouraging his protégé to turn himself in to the law. When attorney Leclerc asked Father Soltner if he would protect someone who had murdered a judge or a priest (thus alluding to the Pope's recent declarations about the necessity of fighting against the Mafia), he refused to answer. The prosecuting attorney remained silent throughout this exchange, just as he had done for most of the time when this question was brought up. Had it been enough to discuss the compromising behavior of certain clergymen, if not of the Church altogether, in full public view? Was it desirable in this case to leave the matter under the veil of oblivion? The court could at least give a clear answer one way or another to this question, instead of seeking cover behind the historians' probe.

Beyond the satisfaction of seeing a criminal punished, the Touvier trial raised a number of questions. The doubts as to the legal definition of the crime were enough to make the verdict unsettling. It was almost impossible for justice to be rendered with serenity once public pressure, including that of the media, had made Paul Touvier into the stigma of an entire historical period of disgrace, or even into a sort of French Eichmann, which was a symbolic role far greater than his miserable self. It was difficult for historical truth to find its place among the imperious demands of memory, the sophistry of a legal code subjected to political issues, and the ritualized logic of criminal court proceedings.

These reservations may surprise or even shock some people. They nonetheless stem from moral or intellectual stands as much as from a question of generational perspective.

A few weeks after the trial, in a conversation with one of the authors of this book, Jacques Delarue acknowledged that he was probably wrong to change his mind about the question of the "German instigation" in the Rillieux incident, which had caused the stir described above. Fundamentally of good faith, he had feared, rightfully or not, seeing Paul Touvier acquitted and partly vindicated: "For someone of my generation, this was unacceptable."[54] Similarly, during a discussion over the trial, François Bédarida, after hearing one of the authors articulate positions much the same as those developed here in this book, and while expressing his disagreement with the interpretation offered, remarked that the doubts expressed reminded him of those that had crept to the surface at the time of the purge, even from voices that could not possibly be suspected of indulgence toward the collaborators on trial.[55] Thus it is a question of age: might those who lived through the ordeals of the time have been less sensitive to the symbolic, legal, and even historical nuances than those of younger generations? Certainly not, since we have on the contrary tried to show that this trial stemmed just as much from the demands of one generation, or in any case from a highly motivated fringe of that generation, which was asking the generation that had lived through the Occupation and the Liberation to account for its actions. Actually, it seems to us that the ideas defended in this book do not necessarily reflect the opinion of the majority of people, including those of all age groups.[56] Admittedly, the fact that we did not experience the tragedy of the Dark Years probably allows us to have a greater freedom of thought, not unrelated to the advantage of not having directly suffered from the war. But the question was rather of another order. Perhaps—and this is a lesson of this trial, or at least a hope—our generation, that which is now forty years old, has finally learned, from a distance of fifty years, what the debates were like when France was emerging from the Occupation. Our generation has probably become slightly more aware of the depth of the dilemma, in which, on one hand, the desire to convict at all cost an avowed criminal, had to be weighed against, on the other hand, the embarrassment of seeing the law and the courts somewhat misused, for the very sake of the cause that had to be defended—the respect for certain values, which were precisely those that had been flouted, at Rillieux and elsewhere, by Touvier, the member of the Milice. To all that must be added the fact that, in the case of the Touvier trial, liberties were taken not only with the law, but with history and memory as well—in other words, once again with values that in theory should have emerged stronger from the show put on in the Versailles courtroom. These are values that should be ours to an even greater degree than those of the generation that came before us; we do not have the excuse of having lived through an ordeal.

4

The Mitterrand Generation

On May 11, 1992, the *Bulletin officiel chronologique des armées*[1] published a ruling by the Minister of Defense dating from April 27 of the same year and "bearing a special declaration about one Resistance group." This ruling consisted only of one sentence: "The National Movement of Prisoners of War and Deportees (MNPGD)[2] has been given the status of a combat unit of the mainland French Resistance for the period extending from March 22, 1944, until the Liberation."[3] This movement had been created by the fusion of three Resistance organizations: the Resistance Movement of Prisoners of War and Deportees (MRPGD),[4] founded in March 1942, the National Gathering of Prisoners of War (RNPG),[5] created in February 1943, and the National Committee of Prisoners of War (CNPG),[6] which had been set up during the autumn of 1943. Almost fifty years after its creation, in March 1994, the MNPGD, whose most important leader during its clandestine period was François Mitterrand, was finally being recognized as a "combat unit" of the Resistance. This was the end of a long story.

A Belated Recognition

After the war, the "networks" and the "movements" comprising France's ongoing resistance to the Nazis went through complex accreditation procedures in order for their members to be able to enjoy honorary titles and pensions. The Ministry of Defense, after receiving the ruling of a national commission, had the authority to recognize these groups as having belonged to the "mainland French Resistance." Some of these groups were moreover allowed to obtain the highly sought-after title of "combat unit" of the Resistance, after a ruling by a special commission, which had been created in 1948 and which was headquartered at the national Office of War Veterans. In order to do that, they had to fulfill certain conditions, such as the existence of an autonomous military unit, with a leader having been

placed under the orders of the interallied command and having been provided with a budget and radio connections with de Gaulle's Free France or
Great Britain. The granting of the status of "combat unit," which therefore
was not a requirement for a clandestine organization to be recognized as
part of the Resistance, presented an obvious symbolic advantage. It also
made it possible to waive the rule governing the attribution of a title that
was highly prized after the war, that of a "combat volunteer of the Resistance" (CVR),[7] for the rule stipulated that this title could theoretically only
be awarded to persons having had at least three months of continuous resistance activity before June 6, 1944, which was not necessarily the case for all
resisters.[8]

Having reviewed the cases of hundreds of organizations, the special commission, which carried out its work for almost twenty years, ruled in favor
of only about a hundred of them. The Minister of Defense systematically
complied with these rulings. By virtue of the ruling of July 9, 1948, François Mitterrand's MNPGD had been granted the status of a "mainland
French Resistance movement" for the period extending from March 22,
1944, up until the Liberation. But in its session of March 7, 1951, the Special Commission suspended its ruling granting the MNPGD the status of a
"combat unit," because it had no documented historical synopsis of his activities. This suspension, which resulted in a refusal to grant the desired
status, can be explained by two reasons: first, it was difficult to distinguish
the actions that were specifically those of the MNPGD from the operations
that its members had carried out within the ranks of FFI,[9] with which they
had been integrated in 1944; second, it is likely that the members of the
special commission, who were for the most part resisters from the outset of
the Occupation, had examined the case of the MNPGD with a certain
amount of wariness, in view of the fact that the origins of the movement
were partly "Pétainists" and that it had been formed rather late in the Occupation (cf. below).

A few years after the Liberation, the procedures for accreditation and as-
signing status were supposedly brought to a close, even though several exceptions were subsequently allowed in order to compensate for the severity
of this measure, which had been intended to allow the official titles already
granted to retain their value and which had been motivated by the more
pragmatic concern of not weighing down the public budget with special
titles and pensions. According to the ruling of December 23, 1966, exceptional accreditation procedures were to be definitively suspended beginning on October 1, 1967, and not one status of "combat unit" was granted
until the 1980s.

In the autumn of 1981, not long after the Left's victory in the presidential election, the legal services of the Ministry of War Veterans and the
Ministry of Defense were given the task of exploring ways of, first, granting

to the RNPG, which counted François Mitterrand among its leaders and had been one of the three original components of the MNPGD, the status of "mainland French Resistance movement," and, second, of granting to the MNPGD the highly coveted status of "combat unit." This was a request that had been presented by Jacques Bénet, one of its leaders, on several occasions before the election of François Mitterrand, on April 3, 1980, and March 30, 1981, but was left unanswered. In view of the fact that the accreditation procedures had been closed and that it was particularly difficult, after forty years, to have the RNPG officially recognized as a Resistance organization when it had never requested such recognition, state officials considered several legal and administrative tricks . . . while at the same time cautiously concluding:

> None of the solutions considered seem appropriate at the present time. Indeed, all are only marginally legal and appear likely to provoke negative reactions among the ranks of former resisters. In addition, they would have the disadvantage of creating a precedent which other Resistance movements might try to cite in their favor.[10]

The case nevertheless continued to run its course. A few years later, on March 1, 1984, Prime Minister Pierre Mauroy signed a decree stipulating that "the Resistance movements not recognized as such or not accredited as combat units, shall, by virtue of a special declaration of the minister in charge of the Armed Forces, be able to be granted the status of Resistance networks or movements or of combat units."[11] The text specifies that the special declaration shall be drawn up after consultation with two commissions, one for "networks" and "movements" (The National Consultative Commission on the Resistance) and the other for "combat units" (the so-called Commission "on Article A 119," in reference to the Code of Military Pensions). On March 15, 1984, a ruling from the Minister of Defense, Charles Hernu, appointed the members of the latter commission.[12] Acting on an idea put forward by General Glavany, President of the Rhine and Danube Association, Minister Hernu placed one of the pillars of this association, Colonel Francis Masset, a former resister and member of the "Normandy March" regiment who had been decorated with the Cross of War medal and cited as a Commander of the Legion of Honor, at the head of the Commission "on Article A 119."[13]

Two years later, on February 17, 1986, after having examined the case, the Commission "on Article A 119" was called into session at the Invalides, with no formal agenda. Paul Quilès, Charles Hernu's successor at the Ministry of Defense, wanted to submit to the commission the cases of the RNPG, the CNPG, and the MNPGD, in addition to almost a hundred other requests. After deliberating on the matter, the commission decided to issue an unfavorable ruling on the accreditation of the RNPG and the CNPG as Resistance movements. It suspended its deliberations on the granting of the title "combat unit" to the MNPGD because the latter's dossier was incomplete.

That did not prevent Paul Quilès from signing, on March 5, 1986, a few days before legislative elections, three ministerial rulings. The first two granted respectively to the CNPG and the RNPG the status of "mainland French Resistance movements" and "combat units" for the period stretching from September 15, 1943, to March 21, 1944, and from June 1, 1943, to March 21, 1944. The third ruling, in its one and only article, granted to the MNPGD the status of a "combat unit" beginning on March 22, 1944.[14]

Now this represented a crass maneuver: the rulings made reference to the minutes of the meeting of the special "A 119 Commission" of February 17, 1986, while in fact the minutes had not yet been written up! The head of the commission had initialed it a few days after the session and it had found its way to the Defense Minister only on . . . March 17, twelve days after the publication of the rulings, which had been predated. These rulings were thus in violation of the procedures laid out by the Mauroy administration. Colonel Masset, the head of the commission, was flabbergasted. On March 26, 1986, he wrote a letter to the new Defense Minister, André Giraud, to make known his "stupefaction" and to request him, "for the sake of the genuine resisters and in the name of the members of the A 119 Commission, who were scorned and insulted by 'the Prince's deed' [. . .], kindly to intervene in order that those responsible for this abuse of authority be sanctioned and that the rulings concerning the three movements abusively recognized as combat units be canceled as soon as possible." Colonel Masset was politely informed that his anger was completely justified, but that, since the cohabitation,[15] which was something totally new, had its own imperatives, this matter, which was considered as belonging to the President's own domain, would not become a political bone of contention.[16] Colonel Masset did not accept this line of reasoning, which he felt to be contrary to the principles of "honor" and "rectitude." He did not back down and, in spite of the words of caution given by some of his fellow officers, filed suit with the Conseil d'État[17] on April 22, 1986, to have the rulings nullified.

The Conseil d'État did not appear to be very eager to respond. At the end of 1987, the case still had not designated an investigator and Colonel Masset had not even received an answer to his numerous letters of inquiry as to the status of his appeal. Almost five years went by in that manner. Colonel Masset finally had recourse to the services of a lawyer qualified to deal with the Conseil d'État; the lawyer investigated the matter, expressed his outrage, and managed to stir the august tribunal. On March 11, 1991, the Conseil d'État, choosing not to follow the example of the contorted reasoning of the Defense Ministry, nullified the three rulings.[18]

A year later, the Defense Ministry set out to try again. Meanwhile, the "A 119 Commission" changed heads, since Colonel Masset had resigned and, out of bitterness, abandoned all proceedings. The commission issued a new ruling, this time "blank," since the opposing votes and the abstentions equaled the votes favoring the granting of the requested titles. On the basis of that ruling, the Defense Ministry promulgated three new decrees which finally granted the long-awaited distinctions: the RNPG, the CNPG, and the MNPGD were given the status of "combat units of the mainland French Resistance."[19]

What is the meaning of this little bureaucratic soap opera? Was it necessary to wait until 1992 for the Resistance organizations to which the future President of the Republic belonged finally to be officially recognized as such, thanks to a few administrative stunts? It is important to understand the nuances here. In this undertaking, the first organization of François Mitterrand, the RNPG, as well as the CNPG, which before had not even been recognized as "mainland French Resistance movements," thus in 1992 snatched up the supreme honor of being a "combat unit," just as did the unified movement the MNPGD, which already carried the honorary distinction of being a "mainland French Resistance movement." Furthermore, another movement, the Resistance Movement of Prisoners of War and Deportees (MRPGD, not to be confused with the preceding movement), also obtained, in March 1987, the honorary title of "combat unit," without any dispute about the case.[20] These decisions were not without consequences for the members of these organizations and their descendants, both on the level of pensions and, more importantly, on the level of France's grateful recognition for what they accomplished—from that point of view, and in spite of the maneuvers described above, it remains undeniable that these movements had indeed been Resistance organizations, whatever may have been their ideological origins. The investigation, which occurred very long after the events took place, and which preceded the decision to grant to the MNPGD the status of a "combat unit," ended up revealing that about fifty of its members at the least had been arrested, of which twenty-eight were deported (seven never returned), and twelve interned in camps, while about ten perished in combats that took place during the Liberation of France. Whether or not it was the President himself who intervened, and whether or not it was certain government ministers who were trying to please him, the whole matter is nevertheless symptomatic of the Socialist party's ambiguous way of handling the aftermath of the Occupation—even if these facts went almost unnoticed at the very time when, in 1992, the disputes over memory were particularly intense, raging as they were over the incident of the "card file" and the controversial fifty-year commemoration of the massive Vél' d'Hiv' roundup.[21] These events with all their ups and downs all take place within the framework of the long controversy over François Mitterrand's past and over the way in which the President of the Republic had to face up to the memory of that era. On that subject, the matter, which is a crucial one for the recent issues of memory, is worth considering above and beyond both smug hagiographic commentaries and categorical partisan attacks.

"History's Forgotten Ones"

In order to understand this matter completely, we must return to the period of the Occupation. When France was defeated in June 1940, it was a debacle for French armed forces, as 1,850,000 soldiers were captured by the Germans. Between 1940 and 1941, 330,000 were eventually set free or repatriated for medical reasons, while 16,000 managed to escape. In all, almost one and a half million French prisoners of war were registered present in German prisoner of war camps and about 950,000 remained captive throughout the five consecutive years of the war from 1940 to 1945.[22] Their story remained unknown and unappreciated for a long time. They nonetheless constituted a large community of men who in many cases were young, active individuals whose absence weighed heavily on the country. Throughout the long years of captivity, they brushed shoulders with the enemy on a daily basis, but in a manner different from that of the French people living under the Occupation. They did not experience the inner torments that people in occupied France suffered, or if they did, it was only gradually and in a limited way. Even though they were patriotic, anti-German, and quite hostile to Collaboration, except for a minority, they still remained attached to a certain image of Marshall Pétain, both that of the victor of Verdun and of the military leader who had put an end to the fighting of May and June 1940. At first, not all understood the political meaning of the armistice, nor did they see that they were going to be a crucially important issue for the Vichy regime. Since it had managed to gain recognition from the Third Reich as the "protective power" of its own prisoners (a role traditionally granted to a nonbelligerent country), the Vichy government constantly justified a great number of its actions, and in particular the policy of state collaboration, by calling attention to the fate of the prisoners of war and to the possibility of getting them freed by making concessions to the occupying forces.

In spite of the situation of the prisoners' camps, some forms of collective resistance appeared very early. They first occurred in the camps themselves with the creation of escape networks, the making of false papers, psychological actions aimed at raising the captives' morale, secret listening to Allied radio, or even political work aimed at countering the propaganda of the "Pétain circles," which were spreading the message of the National Revolution. At the final phase of the war in Europe, when the Allied landing was approaching, and especially after the liberation of France, prisoner of war Resistance organizations encouraged acts of sabotage in factories (almost all prisoners were forced to work in German industries and farms and they were thus in contact with those who had been required to work for the Forced Labor Service, the STO[23]), created intelligence networks, and even, in some cases, prepared prisoners for the possibility of armed combat. These organizations were created in France by former prisoners who had escaped and who were using their connections in the prisoner of war camps. The impact of these resistance efforts was appreciable both militarily and politically, as demonstrated by the Germans' anxiety about these actions. But "history's forgotten ones," to use the expression coined by the historian Yves Durand, have not always found a place in the pantheon of the Resistance erected after the war.

The three main resistance organizations for prisoners of war were the MRPGD, the CNPG, and the RNPG: the slight differences between the acronyms cover deep ideological divisions which were to find their expression when the movements were combined within the National Movement of Prisoners of War and Deportees, the MNPGD. It is these first three organizations which have in recent years been involved in the questions of accreditation and status.

The Resistance Movement of Prisoners of War and Deportees was founded on March 15, 1942, from a nucleus of men who had come together in June 1941, in the Stalag XI B of Fallingbostel (near Hanover), by Charles Bonnet, André Ullmann, Philippe Dechartre, Pierre Le Moign', and Michel Cailliau, General de Gaulle's nephew. It was intended to be a "movement," after the example of the other great Resistance movements of the southern zone, and gave allegiance to de Gaulle.[24] The National Committee of Prisoners of War (CNPG) was created in October 1943 by Robert Paumier (Delarue), who had escaped from Stalag V B. This movement constituted the "prisoners' branch" of the National Front, the clandestine organization of the masses of the Communist party. But, thanks to the attention brought to it by the President of the Republic, the third organization, the MNPGD, is the best known.

From Vichy to the Resistance

The National Gathering of Prisoners of War was created in February 1943 by men who were working within the official entities of the Vichy state, and in particular at the General Commissariat for Returned War Prisoners and Families of War Prisoners, charged with helping prisoners.[25] Established by a law dating from October 14, 1941, this commissariat was until January 1943 directed by Maurice Pinot, who before the war had been a member of the cabinet of Claude-J. Gignoux, the president of the General Confederation of French Business Leaders.[26] He was the son of Robert Pinot, one of the founders of the Forges Committee. After Pinot was removed from his position by Pierre Laval in 1943, the commissariat was to take on a pro-Nazi orientation. But up until that time, the commissariat did not play a directly political role and was above all devoted to the reinsertion of repatriated prisoners: it created a "prisoner house" in each regional department and about 2,700 Mutual Assistance Centers on a local level, for the most part in the occupied zone.

In many ways, the commissariat was an entity that fit perfectly into the policy of the regime. Indeed, by their very number, the prisoners of war still absent provided a propaganda theme that was effective with the opinion of a group which was by definition receptive to Pétain's ideology. Marshall Pétain often spoke of them in his speeches, always associating them with his pet themes: suffering, redemption, solidarity. "Their return will make it possible to fill the great emptiness that we suffer from. Their spirit, strengthened by life in the camps, matured by long hours of reflection, will become the strongest unifying force of the National Revolution."[27]

At the same time, the great majority of those with Commissariat for Prisoners were quite hostile to the occupying forces and fought against the designs of the collaborationist movements. This hostility can be explained both by the origins of its leaders, who were almost all prisoners of war who had escaped or had been repatriated and thus harbored no good feelings toward their former captors, and by the commissariat's action, which was carried out first of all in the northern occupied zone and which included activities that had to be concealed from the Germans—for example, providing false papers and aid to escaped prisoners—even though these things were done within the framework of an official French administrative entity.

This apparent contradiction between fervor for Marshall Pétain and hostility toward the German occupier is only contradictory if we refuse to see the complexity of Vichy's policies and, more important, how various individuals and mindsets evolved over the course of the Occupation. From June 1940 to 1944, the regime simultaneously pursued a policy of collaboration with the German occupier and a policy aimed at reforming French society, the National Revolution. But this collaboration fostered, on the French side, the illusion that it was more or less possible to maintain a relative balance of power that would be beneficial to France's interests. That involved "resisting" pressure here and there, especially in the economic domain, which was the most important and vital; that is what Pétainists and neo-Pétainists, with a total disregard for overwhelming evidence and proof to the contrary, persist in calling "double dealing." It meant that there had to be cold refusals or on the contrary spontaneous offers, in other words, talks on the specific forms of this "Franco-German cooperation": this is the very principle of negotiation. It was the principle of state collaboration, in which ideological reasoning (that which advocated adhering to the Nazis' scheme of things) was a major factor for only a minority, while tactical reasoning (that concerned with the situation of occupied France) *and* strategical considerations (about the success of the National Revolution and France's place in a Europe dominated by Germany) were primary motivations, with some emphasizing domestic policy (as did Pétain) and others "European" policy (as did Laval). It was thus possible, especially between June 1940 and November 1942, to be a Pétainist while at the same time resolutely anti-German, even if this was far from being the case for all those who worked for Vichy. It was possible to believe or to pretend to believe that state collaboration and the National Revolution were two separate things, and that the latter could be of a piece with resisting the German occupier. On that score, in order to understand the resisters who began their journey within the institutions of Vichy, including those who later vowed allegiance to General Giraud before finally putting themselves under de Gaulle's authority, the date when the break was made—which indicates the direct causes for the break—is crucial. In some cases, the break came after April 1942 and Pierre Laval's return to power as "head of the government." For others it was after November 11, 1942, and the invasion of the southern free zone, or after February 1943 and Germany's defeat at the Battle of Stalingrad and the institution of the Forced Labor Service. At times it came later still. These dates provide some indications about the respective thresholds of tolerance and adhesion to the Vichy regime. It should be added that certain government employees were seen to be greater and greater security risks both by the Germans and by Pétain and Laval, and were fired. This was an unintentional favor for those who lost their jobs this way.

In any case, a good many administrative, economic, and social welfare tasks would have had to be carried out one way or another, with or without the presence of a legal government, as was the case in other occupied countries. And dealing with the prisoners of war would have been, and indeed was, part of all this work. What corrupted from within all activities conducted in an official context—whatever the innermost motivations of these individuals may have been—was the existence of a regime that, while on the one hand claimed to be rebuilding a house that was afire, on the other hand was collaborating with the arsonists. It is in this sense that the legacy of the Vichy regime is a cumbersome burden to carry; whoever wants to understand the case of the Commissariat for Prisoners of War, and along with it, that of the young François Mitterrand, must bear this in mind. The historian Christophe Lewin summarizes this state of things nicely:

> The attitude of the top officers of the commissariat was from the outset anti-German, thus anti-collaborationist. As for the Vichy regime, most of them gave it their support at first. However, the ambiguity of its relations with the occupying forces and its constant slide down the slope of collaboration increased their distrust and precipitated their departure from this line. Their action was above all one of civic and social service, carried out with an apolitical, wait-and-see attitude.[28]

In January 1943, Maurice Pinot was revoked by Pierre Laval, who could not tolerate Pinot's criticism about the "Relève." Most of Pinot's little team resigned. François Mitterrand, then twenty-six years old and head of the commissariat's information service for the southern zone, nevertheless held on to a position at the head of the Mutual Assistance Centers, which was one of the major accomplishments of Maurice Pinot's team; it was in this capacity that he was to receive the Francisque, to which we will return later. These centers were soon to constitute one of the fronts for his Resistance organization, which had within it a large network of contacts and clandestine bases of solidarity among the former prisoners who were led by Jean Védrine.

In March 1943, the all-new RNPG or "Pinot-Mitterrand group" obtained the support and financial backing of the Army Resistance Organization (ORA[29]), which had just been created from the Metropolitan Army Organization (OMA[30]) and which brought together soldiers who up until then had been faithful to Vichy but who had crossed over to the Resistance after November 1942.

In the spring of 1943, Eugène Claudius-Petit, second in command in the Franc-Tireur movement of the Resistance and one of the leaders of the United Resistance Movements (MUR[31]), met François Mitterrand in Lyons. The RNPG sought to be integrated into the unified organization of the mainland Resistance, which at the time was about to take a decisive step by creating the National Resistance Council on May 27, 1943, under the aegis of Jean Moulin. Eugène Claudius-Petit was dumbfounded by what the young Mitterrand supposedly said while they were slowly walking along the quais of the Saône River. While on the one hand wanting to join his embryonic organization with the Resistance, François Mitterrand held forth with a panegyric on Vichy's political and social reforms.[32] The resistance leader Claudius-Petit was wary and did not follow up on the meeting. A few weeks later, François Mitterrand would have better luck with another official of the MUR, Emmanuel d'Astier de La Vigerie, leader of the Libération-Sud movement. Actually, the key to the problem came at Algiers, with the French National Liberation Committee, which was created in June 1943. François Mitterrand, who was the most "political" of the permanent members of the RNPG, and doubtless already its real leader, charged himself with this mission.

It is well known that he was given a rather cool reception. The people on the French National Liberation Committee, beginning with de Gaulle, did not like for Resistance organizations to have a narrowly-defined social constituency, and the prisoners of war, who were among Vichy's pet alibis, were not exactly adulated by the general, who had from the beginning condemned the armistice and called for his compatriots to continue to fight against the Germans. "A movement for prisoners of war? And why not one for hairdressers?" de Gaulle supposedly quipped at his first meeting with François Mitterrand.[33] Actually, the Resistance movements wanted the different organizations for former prisoners to fuse into one according to the logic of the general unification that was underway. Henri Frenay, who was the founder of combat named to the CFLN[34] at Algiers and who served as commissioner for prisoners, deportees, and refugees, even recommended that the budding RNPG be integrated into the movement of Michel Cailliau and Philippe Dechartre.

On November 15, 1943, François Mitterrand took off for London thanks to the assistance of the ORA. In December, he was in Algiers, where General de Gaulle had taken over from Giraud for good on October 2. François Mitterrand was indeed counting on some connections he had in Giraud's entourage; he had visited Giraud immediately upon arriving in Algiers. "The source of support for François at Algiers was General Giraud. This was the mistake to be avoided! Especially at the time when de Gaulle had clearly gotten the upper hand. For the 'Who's Who' of Algiers, François was thus part of Giraud's clan," said later his older brother Jacques Mitterrand, who was then a lieutenant in a unit based in Morocco.[35] It was thanks to the intervention of Henri Frenay that he got an appointment with General de Gaulle. His meeting with de Gaulle on December 2, 1943, at the Glycines Villa went badly and did not last more than forty-five minutes. De Gaulle formulated his request more clearly: the organizations of prisoners had to fulfill the condition of joining forces under the aegis of the MRPGD in order to receive supplies and money. François Mitterrand refused to be placed under the leadership of the movement headed by Michel Cailliau, who was only one leader among others in this movement having little influence. At the same time, he was surprised to discover the existence of an organization of prisoners of a Communist bent which, indeed, had been created only two months before. He nevertheless accepted the principle of a fusion of the different prisoner of war organizations on the condition that "their qualified representatives be allowed to choose their leaders."[36]

Not judging it worthwhile, de Gaulle's special services in Algiers did not facilitate Mitterrand's return to France. He would, thanks to a friend who was a member of General Giraud's cabinet, have to get a seat on a military transport plane that was going to Morocco, from where he would manage to reach Great Britain in General Montgomery's plane. In London, he would again have to wait several weeks before being given the possibility of return to France, where he would not come ashore on the coast of the western end of Brittany until February 27, 1944.

It was then for the first time that he demonstrated his talents as a negotiator and organizational leader. Using what he had understood in Algiers and in London, he set out to play a determining role in the fusion demanded by de Gaulle and which henceforth seemed to him to be inevitable, in spite of the reticence he might have felt with respect to the other two movements. The undertaking was not a simple one. It consisted of unifying three Resistance movements: first, a Gaullist movement created well before the two others but of limited influence; second, a branch of the Communist National Front whose activities were marginal; and finally, an organization reputed to be loyal to Pétain and Giraud, whose role would be a decisive one because of the work carried out in 1942 and 1943 by the former officers of Vichy's Commissariat for Prisoners. In addition to the controversy after the war over the Pétainist origins of the RNPG, another quarrel was to be stirred up by Henri Frenay, who accused François Mitterrand and his "cold ambition" of having "skirted and adulterated" the CFLN's directives and of having taken the Communists into the fold against his advice. This accusation is characteristic of Frenay, the former Resistance hero, who, long after the war, got it into his head that the Communists had thoroughly infiltrated the ranks of the mainland Resistance, including Jean Moulin. But this accusation will not hold up to scrutiny; not only is it in complete contradiction with the policy of integrating the Communists that was followed at the same time and at all levels by the CFLN, it is also disproved by documents and personal testimony.[37]

On March 12, 1944 (and not on the 22nd, as is specified in the recent accreditation decrees), under the aegis of a representative of the National Council of the Resistance, Antoine Avinin, the leaders of the three movements met clandestinely in Paris and founded the MNPGD; François Mitterrand was one of the four members of the national steering committee. Afterwards, the MNPGD was to be at the origin of the only federation of former prisoners, the National Federation of Prisoners of War (FNPG[38]): at the founding convention in April 1945, François Mitterrand became one of three of its vice presidents. The FNPG counted more than a million members in 1946. There would still be more than a half a million of them in 1959; the political importance of this group is easy to understand.

The "victory" of the RNPG over the other two movements left deep, lasting bitterness, especially with certain former leaders of the MRPGD, who have often been called upon by those critical of François Mitterrand's past. In reality, beyond the question of personalities, this victory can be accounted for by the better correspondence of views between this movement and most prisoners of war. The RNPG was in tune ideologically with its milieu. It was full of fervor for Marshall Pétain at the outset and maintained good relations with the Army Resistance Organization. It also had contacts with other organizations favorable to Marshall Pétain who had become dissident, such as the leaders of the Uriage School or the Compagnons of France. The RNPG was termed a "Giraudist" movement. The path that it had followed did not fit in very well with the epic vision of General de Gaulle, who cast an everpresent shadow on the subsequent representations of the Resistance. It did not correspond to a schmaltzy picture of things, but it nevertheless belonged to that story.

The Small Portion of Truth

Before September 1994, when an enormous controversy over his past broke out, François Mitterrand had alluded to this period of his life several times, but rarely in a way that was spontaneous or thorough enough to ward off attacks. He often did this by way of metaphors or by leaving things to those writers who were favorably disposed toward him. Perhaps he felt that there were certain truths that the World War II generation—which was his own —had trouble conveying to later generations. Perhaps, as did so many other French in all stations, he thought that he would be able to maintain, if not secrecy, at least a great discretion about certain things.

In his brief revelations about this era, François Mitterrand at times had recourse to shorthand. In one of his few autobiographical writings, after having spoken of his experience as a prisoner of war and of his return to France in December 1941, he writes: "Once back in France, I became a resister, without going through any inner torment. I later realized that in the camps we had not approached the issue in the same way as they did in Paris. As seen from Germany, Pétain and de Gaulle were not the embodiments of two contradictory strategies."[39] Then he skips from the end of the year 1941 to December 1943 and his meeting with General de Gaulle, without the slightest mention of his presence at Vichy, where he had gone in early 1942, shortly after his return to France, and where he would, thanks to good connections with the regime through his family, fill a position in the Commissariat for Prisoners. A year and a half had disappeared, as if put in parentheses. It was a time in which, according to one of his hagiographers,

> he chose not to choose and surveyed the ground before planting his feet on it
> [. . .] He did not throw himself into the Resistance: it came to him by way of

his superior in the administrative hierarchy who, unlike Mitterrand, was sure of his ideas; Mitterrand first joined the Resistance without knowing it, by making fake papers for former prisoners. Then, in early 1943, he committed himself completely to clandestine life and very quickly carried considerable responsibilities. The solidity of his resolution came from its gradual process of maturation.[40]

Perhaps the author might have managed to recall that, during the years in question, history often moved faster than the slow incremental advances of conscience.

Was it thus impossible to assume responsibility for the fact that, at his modest rank, Mitterrand had been one of those Vichy officials that the Resistance sought to win over, finally succeeding on a large scale from 1943 on, when it had become clear that the war had changed its course? In the early 1970s, at the time when he aspired to the highest office of the nation, reminders of this sort were doubtless not easy to give, nor were people ready to hear them. But as was the case with a large number of political personalities who had to answer for their past conduct before the public, secrecy and understatements probably cost him more in the long run than an early confession would have.

These years did indeed leave material traces, such as, for example, the often-referred-to article published in December 1942 in *France: Revue de l'État nouveau*. This Pétainist journal with its cover bearing a Francisque[41] was created in June 1942 by Gabriel Jeantet, a youth leader in Pétain's civilian cabinet who was also a former member of the Cagoule.[42] It defined itself as the "journal of the elite of the National Revolution," charged with presenting every month "some of the most important problems of the revolutionary doctrine."[43] François Mitterrand provided a very short, melancholy text about his experience as a prisoner of war for this journal; this often-cited text, "Pèlerinage en Thuringe,"[44] recounts his departure into captivity.[45] People have tried to uncover the "Vichy" mindset in this piece, especially because of what François Mitterrand wrote in the final paragraph:

By feeding Europe with its ambitions of brotherhood, by imposing its eagerness for war, by spreading bloodshed outside of its borders and for borders impossible to defend, France had exhausted itself; and I kept thinking that, as inheritors of one hundred and fifty years of errors, we ourselves were hardly responsible for what had happened. I was angry with this triumphal history that had unavoidably preceded a whole generation's slow journey in cattle-cars. I discerned the logic of events and wondered if it were right that our wretched state should be the wages of poorly understood glories, or more exactly, if it were right that our demise should be imputed to us, because, while we had abandoned our weapons, all the rest had previously been taken away from us. I thought of the harsh judgments that would sanction our debacle: people will blame the sagging regime, the worthless men, the institutions that had been emptied of all substance, and they will be right. Will people blame the glorious mistakes? There in the middle of Germany, in that encounter of France's splendor with France's wretchedness, I saw two sections of the same cyclical chain which were destined to link together.

In quoting a part of this passage, Catherine Nay explains laconically that the "one hundred and fifty years of errors" stigmatized "every political regime since the Revolution of 1789." According to her, the author took "virtually no precautions in placing himself in the counter-revolutionary line of thought."[46] This is a hasty interpretation, to say the least, since the article mentions in particular the places in Thuringe that Mitterrand went through on the train of prisoners—Eisenach, Erfurt, Gotha, Weimar—all of which recall to the learned young man the military campaigns conducted by the revolutionaries and by Napoleon. Coming closer to the stalag, it was the defeated soldier who was talking, stigmatizing not the principles of republican democracy, but the victorious revolution carried beyond borders, that is to say, not 1789 but indeed 1792 (which moreover adds up to "one hundred and fifty years").[47] In other words, rather than seeing an overtly Pétainist text here, one can interpret it as a pacifist piece written after the military disaster, and as the reflection of a prisoner balking at having to bear the shame of the defeat for the sake of past victories. Granted, the article was written a year after his return to France when he was working for Vichy in an official capacity, though not at a high rank. The allusions made to the responsibilities for the defeat ("all the rest had previously been taken away from us" and again to "the sagging regime," which refers to the Third Republic) are real. But one can hardly argue that these examples are in themselves sufficient to make the piece a political one. Furthermore, much more vicious attacks on the Third Republic can be found in the clandestine press. The following year, at a time when he was already with the Resistance, François Mitterrand wrote another, lesser-known text in the same vein, in which he related, this time, his return from the stalags and his moving rediscovery of the colors and fragrances of his native land, "my almost forgotten France."[48]

On the other hand, however, the proximity of his article with those of other rather notorious contributors to this issue of *France* is more embarrassing; this is the point that the detractors of François Mitterrand have not failed to make.[49] His piece was published along with a "Watchword Addressed to Ground, Sea, and Air Forces" by Philippe Pétain dating from November 28, 1942, saluting the "self-denial" of French soldiers facing the "ordeal" of the invasion of the free zone and the scuttling of the fleet at the port of Toulon.[50] Mitterrand's article appears side-by-side with articles by

Paul Creyssel, Vichy Director of Propaganda for the southern zone, about the Communist plot against France; and with another by Louis de Gérin-Ricard about papal Rome's "Jewish Statutes": "Few historical examples give us a better sense of the Semitic peril than the manner in which Rome had to treat the Jews over the course of the centuries [. . .] they lived there, trafficking in everything, from magic to medicine, 'favoring prostitution, gambling, smuggling, pederasty,' in the words of one of Pope Clement the VIII's own bulls."[51] Dr. Alexis Carrel, in a brief article, vaunts his foundation and his plan for "Androtechnie."[52]

Strangely enough, while François Mitterrand's adversaries have sought to exploit fully this journal's rather unseemly table of contents, no one has mentioned the most ignominious article to be found there: that of Noël de Tissot, secretary general—and a doctrinaire one—of the Legionary Guard (SOL[53]). This article is a hateful reaction to the "invasion of North Africa [which] should have put an end to our internal quarrels and rally the Country around its Leader in the same united outpouring of indignation and in a unanimous desire for revenge."[54] The virulence of this article foreshadows the favorite themes of the Milice, which was to be created the following month out of the SOL and of which he was to be a leader:

The Jews on the French Riviera are smugly waiting for their American friends to bring them flavored cigarettes that the black market cannot provide in sufficient quantities to satisfy their desires. Sitting back in their easy chairs, the Gaullist members of the bourgeoisie greet the death of our sailors with an odious smile.[55]

Later in the same article, this author writes:

For two years, from their microphones in London and New York, in the cellars where their clandestine newspapers are hiding, in tufted sitting rooms where, between two dances, they offer champagne toasts to de Gaulle, the Jews, the Masons, the Gaullists, and the Communists, have continually waged their sly battle. United in the same villainy, they have joined hands in order better to strangle you [. . .] They are waiting for the time to betray, ready to stab France, as long as they can eat and be "free," that is, free to live basely in the soft, comfortable mud of Anglo-Saxon materialism and Jewish prosperity. If France does not want to die from being stuck in that mud, the last French people worthy of the name must declare a merciless war on all those who, within and without the country, are getting ready to open the flood gates: Jews, Masons, Communists . . . always the same and all Gaullist.[56]

The table of contents of this political and intellectual journal does indeed reflect the Vichy of the period after November 1942: doctrinaire fanatics still keep company with fervent supporters of Marshall Pétain about to break with the regime, while scientists, intellectuals, and other writers continue to believe in the normal course of things.[57]

Finally, there had been the Francisque: an inexhaustible source of delight for his adversaries and a source of continual contortions for his faithful followers.

François Mitterrand's activities within the official entities in charge of attending to prisoners of war won him the privilege, one he shared with at least 2,626 other French citizens, of being honored with the Gallic Francisque, a medal that had been created in May 1941 by Philippe Pétain to reward "services rendered to the French State."[58] Recipients of this award had to have fulfilled at least two of the three following requirements: "a) before the war, to have participated in a social action for the nation that was in keeping with the principles of the National Revolution, b) to have demonstrated, since the armistice, an active interest in Marshall Pétain and his work, c) to have brilliant records of military or civil service."[59] These awardees were introduced by two sponsors. For François Mitterrand, this would be Gabriel Jeantet and Simon Arbellot, who was a member of the Action Française[60] and a press secretary for the Ministry of Information. Upon receiving the award, the recipients were supposed to take the following ritual oath: "I offer myself up to Marshall Pétain just as he offered himself up for France.[61] I pledge to serve his teachings and to remain faithful to him and to his work."[62]

At first the Francisque had been distributed rather liberally, according to Henri du Moulin de Labarthète, the former head of Pétain's civilian cabinet: "We gave it to everybody, and first of all to 'pals,' to Pétain's entourage, to roommates, to bellhops or elevator attendants, to dishwashers, and soon to girlfriends. 'You like the Marshall, don't you?'—'Hell, yeah!'—'Here you go, have the Francisque!'"[63] But after the publication, in July 1942, of the statutes that spelled out more clearly the mechanics of attributing this award one year after it had been created, the honor was given after the applications had been subjected to a much more rigorous examination. Meanwhile, the National Revolution had changed character and the Vichy dictatorships had very clearly become more hard-line. In addition, those who had received the Francisque could be stripped of the honor; from the end of the year 1942 up until the beginning of 1944, seven out of twenty-three recipients of the Francisque had their medal taken away from them because of their "dissidence." Finally, a few returned their decoration.[64]

François Mitterrand's Francisque bears the number 2202. It had thus been among the last ones attributed. It had been awarded to him during the year 1943 (the exact date remains unclear) at the time when he was already involved in Resistance activity and perhaps, while he was in Algiers. This decoration had for a long time been a taboo subject; any mention of it was chalked up to the viciousness of the extreme Right, as François Mitterrand had never taken the risk either of denying it or of offering a clear explanation. Pierre Viansson-Ponté had already summed things up in 1976:

> What did you do? You first faintly muttered a sort of denial, in pointing out that while this medal had perhaps been awarded to you, you had never received it since it was never pinned on you. Then, without denying or confirming the fact, you dismissed the scandal with muddled declarations as if you did indeed have something to hide, as if you were concealing some shameful secret.[65]

Since then, it has no longer been possible to brush things aside contemptuously because Vichy's closets have been thrown wide open. François Mitterrand thus felt obliged to account for his actions. He did so extensively in the context of a biography published in 1986 and for the first time in public, in the video version of this biography that was broadcast over TF1[66] on January 21, 1987. "I wound up being a recipient of the Francisque as were many other important members of the Resistance, for example, my friend the future Marshall de Lattre de Tassigny. When it was awarded to me in 1943, I was in England. It was very useful when I returned, as a good alibi."[67]

The President's explanation unfortunately carries with it a major error and an incorrect statement. It was in theory a smart choice to mention Marshall de Lattre de Tassigny as someone who shared the same (mis)fortune: the legalistic superior officer had remained loyal to Vichy until November 11, 1942. He was then arrested by Vichy and convicted on charges of insubordination. In September 1943, he escaped, reaching first London and then Algiers in December. At the head of France's First Army, he would later become one of the heroes of the liberation of mainland France from the Germans. But the problem is that, in spite of his initial allegiance to Vichy, the future Marshall was never decorated with the Francisque. Furthermore, contrary to what François Mitterrand states, the distinction of having been a fervent supporter of Marshall Pétain does not seem to have ever been given to any "*other* important member of the Resistance."

When she heard what the President of the Republic had said, Marshall de Lattre's widow, who keeps a particularly watchful eye over her deceased husband's memory, was outraged, and, in a letter sent to the Presidential Palace, demanded an immediate rectification. This was a rather serious incident, but as often was the case in moments of difficulty, François Mitterrand found a way to get off the hook without the matter taking on too great an importance. Wishing above all to avoid making a denial on television, he personally apologized to Madame de Lattre, explaining that one "could never check up on the facts enough," he pledged that he would find an occasion for correcting the mistake himself in public. Two months later, on March 31, 1987, he chose to do so in sufficiently discrete circumstances, during a trip to Besançon to visit the Museum of the Resistance and Deportation. There, he declared that it was not a matter of insulting the memory of a great soldier, but of showing how some authentic resisters had to "hide their colors" in order to throw the enemy off track.[68] And he specified that Marshall Jean de Lattre de Tassigny was never decorated with Pétain's medal. Since the press had little to say about this trip, the rectification went by unnoticed.

What are we to make of all this? Did François Mitterrand wish to receive the Francisque? Did he request it in order to cover himself? Was it awarded to him without his having expressed the least desire? On that score, the testimony is contradictory. Simon Arbellot declared after the war that he had sponsored this young fervent supporter of Marshall Pétain in order to protect his clandestine activities: "He had asked us, both myself and Gabriel Jeantet, who was a leader of youth movements, to apply for a Francisque on his behalf. He was unanimously accepted for the award in the Council of the Order of the Francisque, with the full backing of Admiral Platon."[69] Such testimony, given by a former Pétainist in a journal (*Écrits de Paris*) for those who maintained a fond memory of the Collaboration, and at the time when François Mitterrand was in the limelight (since the text was written in 1965[70]), must be taken with caution, which does not mean that it is false.

But that is doubtless not where the real problem lies. For a lack of better evidence, it is possible to question the real meaning of the controversy. The Francisque was not necessarily the clearest mark of commitment to Vichy nor was it always a collaborator's pedigree, as François Mitterrand's adversaries pretend to believe: it was often a sign of gratitude awarded to faithful, fervent supporters of Marshall Pétain, in other words, to those who believed above all in the Marshall himself before adopting Vichy's political agenda (although the two were not incompatible—far from it). This was especially the case after Pierre Laval's return to power in April 1942. Nor was the Francisque an ideal cover for Resistance activity: there were many others of the same sort that were much more effective, beginning with a position within the machinery of government. Moreover, while the medal was awarded to François Mitterrand during the year 1943, the precise chronology of the application is not known. When was it filed? By whom? Even Pierre Péan remains unclear on this essential point. Now, supposing that the dossier took several months to make its way through, it nevertheless remains that the period of time involved was precisely that of François Mitterrand's break with the regime. It is true that Mitterrand's successive declarations contributed in no small way to fueling the controversy. But these polemics must be put into proper perspective: the Francisque constituted a symbol, both literally and figuratively. It was the mark of professional service rendered in the framework of a regime; whatever his innermost motivations may have been, François Mitterrand in effect played a minor role in it. The Francisque was awarded at a time when things were changing, when the Marshall's fervent supporters and even faithful ideologues were crossing over into dissidence and into the Resistance, no more no less.

The Recurring Quandaries

The case of the young Mitterrand is one of a trajectory that was quite common at the time. The official epic of the Resistance has disqualified this narrative and reduced it to the status of an embarrassing secret. Thousands of French people have not found their place in this theatrical production which for a long time pitted a France that resisted (supposedly the majority) against a France that followed Pétain (supposedly a minority). They experienced another history in which it was possible to be a fervent supporter of the Marshall without being an ideologue of the National Revolution, one in which it was possible to be a convinced backer of the National Revolution before becoming a resister, one in which it was sometimes possible to remain a fervent supporter of the Marshall or of the National Revolution after having entered the Resistance. These were all common situations that existed alongside the itineraries of the minority of those who were from the outset hostile to both Hitler and Pétain and who entered into dissidence and resisted right from the start. A large number of resisters came on board in 1943. It is possible to recall examples (admittedly, these are the exception) of those who, like Maurice Couve de Murville, who joined the Resistance after having served in the important capacity at Vichy's Ministry of Finance up until 1943; that in no way prevented him from later being one of General de Gaulle's Prime Ministers. Similarly, François Valentin, director of the French Legion of War Veterans (which was the spearhead of the National Revolution), crossed over into dissidence on August 30, 1943.

The meaning of the year 1943 in the history of the Resistance has moreover been the subject of an implicit allusion made by the President during the ceremonies celebrating the fiftieth anniversary of the creation of the Medal of Resistance on October 13, 1993:

> Remember that what brings us together today and always is the determination that we saw as indispensable at a particular time in our history: the determination to rally around the same flag all those who had refused servitude

wherever they may have been. [. . .] This medal bears witness to a decisive moment in the history of the liberation of our country.

This was in October 1993: in other words, a few weeks before the anniversary of his departure for London and Algiers on November 15, 1943. "A particular time in our history . . .": did he mean the war in general or more precisely the year 1943, which was the year of the unification of the various movements of the mainland Resistance and the time when many crossed over into the ranks of the Resistance, as he had done? "Wherever they may have been . . .": here, the message is clear and refers to resisters of every stripe, those outside the country as well as those on the mainland, those who had resisted before 1943 as well as those who joined later.

This historical reality of a multifaceted, at times belated Resistance, still remains difficult to accept, both for those who decided after the fact that it was only possible to belong to one single camp once and for all, and for those who, on the contrary, want to wipe some of the hesitations of the early days of the Occupation out of their memory. These reactions are understandable to the extent that, on the level of values, they stand for a rejection of any ideology even slightly resembling Pétainism. That, however, goes for today. Yesterday, it was another story, and it behooves us to measure the complexity of that story before we either reinvent it or pass categorical and unjust judgments on it.

Some of the former President's hagiographers have thus attempted to twist the facts. Some have claimed that François Mitterrand created the MNPGD "in 1942" on the basis of "an idea that had taken root in captivity."[71] One even wrote: "Being in intellectual dissidence against the established powers, François Mitterrand immediately espoused de Gaulle's cause."[72]

As an individual, François Mitterrand has also been accused of "suffering memory lapses" and proving himself "unable to exercise self-criticism."[73] That's likely so. But when all is said and done, is not that blaming him for all the shortcomings of an entire generation? For his story is first of all that of a whole branch of the Resistance and of a good portion of the French people as well. Some people have kept on looking for the skeleton that was hiding in some secret trunk in the presidential palace of the Élysée. A few have even discovered some little and not so little secrets.[74] But will that explain to us the ambivalences of a man who belonged as much to his past as to our present? Will we be more enlightened about Mitterrand's generation, which lived through the war and still bears the mark of the era's ambiguities?

The story of Vichy's Commissariat for Prisoners of War, within which François Mitterrand earned his first stripes as a fighter, is quite significant:

[This is] a unique example of an administration's claiming to represent faithfully the interest of its clients. Beginning at Vichy, it crossed over massively to the Resistance and wound up at the head of the same social group after the Liberation. From this standpoint, the personal itinerary of François Mitterrand is typical: he was in turn an escaped prisoner, an officer in the Commissariat, principal leader of the RNPG, head of the MNPGD, Secretary General of the Ministry of Prisoners, Deportees, and Refugees at the time of the Liberation, Vice President of the FNPG in 1945, Minister of War Veterans in 1946. Is this idealism, opportunism, or fidelity? As with Pinot and many others, there is probably a little bit of all three at the same time.[75]

The American historian Robert Paxton, so often cited, has expressed a similar idea:

> The personal story of François Mitterrand during the war makes him a rather typical, representative Frenchman. Many French people sincerely believed, in the beginning, that Pétain would be able to do better, many believed that they could hold technical posts at Vichy for a year or two. But the National Revolution and the gradual escalation of Collaboration made the situation impossible: a good number of them distanced themselves from the regime or changed sides. Moreover, the tragedy of Vichy is that it recruited some men of good will who took time to realize that instead of forming a sacred union as in 1914, the regime began by a policy of exclusion. This is an essential point.[76]

These ambivalences, ambiguities, and murky itineraries could not, once peace had been reestablished, withstand the radiant light of General Charles de Gaulle's heroic legacy. A good many men and women who had crossed over from being enthusiastic backers of Pétain's National Revolution to worried admirers of the Marshall himself then had to keep their memories to themselves and make their experience of the war years a highly personal matter, which in time became a taboo subject. In addition, there have also been, in the history of the Resistance, conflicts about legitimacy between the "exterior" Resistance (that of de Gaulle's Free France) and the "interior" Resistance (the Resistance movements and parties within mainland France). Many of those who crossed over from Pétainism to the Resistance did not give their allegiance to General de Gaulle; such was the case of the young Mitterrand. The former President is moreover the one who has the most persistently attacked de Gaulle's capture of the Resistance legacy. In 1969, Mitterrand wrote:

> The story of the skillful elimination of the mainland Resistance by the Resistance of London and Algiers remains to be written. It will reveal how the head of the Free French managed to confiscate the accumulated wealth of sacrifices, suffering, and dignity gathered by the unknown people who served

as soldiers of the night. The Gaullist dictionary, like its Stalinist counterpart, has marked out the pages that told the real story of the struggle against the enemy and has identified favors done for General de Gaulle with services rendered to France; those services rendered to France without having contributed to the glory of General de Gaulle have been considered negligible, if not suspect. Thus it is that after having eliminated all competition, Gaullism succeeded in making patriotism, once monopolized, into a base of flourishing business that has reaped heavy profits for a long time.[77]

In the early nineties Mitterrand had a similar line of discourse, though without the rancor:

I have always defended the idea, which is more widely accepted today, that the Resistance had been twofold; the mainland Resistance and the exterior Resistance coexisted. And there was a secret struggle between them. General de Gaulle feared that the Resistance might produce men who subsequently would have come to embody the plight of the whole country and thus would lead it astray. I think that many things were done in order to behead this mainland Resistance. Most of the great leaders of the Resistance who went to Algiers did not come back: Frenay, d'Astier de La Vigerie, and ten others. I myself, who was not a great leader, had a hard time returning. I really had to desire it and make the decision alone. There were additional factors: the distribution of arms, parachute drops, financial means . . . And finally, there was the fact that command posts were set up by the exterior Resistance: in no way do I minimize its merits on the level of efficacy and morality, but its reflexes were those of power. Once one accepts this explanation, as I do—and I am one of the few people who do—one sees things differently. That's why I have a position which is divergent from that of the majority of the French people about the role of General de Gaulle. I recognize his work and his great deeds. But . . .[78]

This presentation of the facts is quite a clever one. Nevertheless, if François Mitterrand is speaking here in the name of the "mainland Resistance," it can be supposed without malice that he is also implicitly referring to the mindset of those who began the Occupation on the side of Vichy before entering into clandestinity. General de Gaulle and his entourage had always been wary of these men and women, save for a few illustrious exceptions.

From that viewpoint, it is instructive to see how the former President explicitly analyzed the Vichy regime:

This regime was created in conditions that were unacceptable in and of themselves. And then, Marshall Pétain, who was eighty-four years old, was not fit to fulfill his duties. Moreover, his background incited him to be, let's say, reactionary. He was attempting once more to undertake a task that Mac-Mahon had not been able to carry out, that of restoring the rule of morality. This project was derived from the most common and stupidest ideas that had been circulating behind the scenes of the Republic for a century. Dictated by racism and xenophobia, this undertaking was touted as an embodiment of a France based on French values, whatever that means. National values do exist. But they are not necessarily those. Actually, the Vichy regime boasted allegiance to national values in keeping with a history that had been made over. And then, Vichy officials put themselves in submission to the occupying power. Since it was the Nazis who occupied France, they obviously committed many mistakes. However, it is not really possible to consider them as Nazis.[79]

More generally speaking, the case of François Mitterrand and the opinion that he formed about handling the aftermath of Vichy bring us back to another obvious point: the President was a man of his generation, which was that of the defeat, the Occupation, Vichy, but also of the Resistance, the Liberation, and in addition that of the purge, the dilemmas of the postwar years, and of reconstruction. In order to understand that, one has to consider the entire era of crisis as a whole; we cannot project our present-day categories into the past, nor can we forget sequences of events that people experienced as a continuum, in spite of radical, successive departures. The divisions of the Occupation had also gone on inside of people's own minds, while, for their part, individuals attempted to get through the ordeal as intact as possible. These cleavages of a half a century ago probably explain—even if they do not justify—the former President's positions on these very sensitive issues. Furthermore, it should be pointed out that François Mitterrand had to fulfill his duties as chief of state at a time when the obsession with the memory of Vichy had reached its greatest intensity. The flowers that he had placed on Pétain's tomb were the expression of a certain fidelity to the spirit of the war veterans, even though the gesture is unacceptable, since it signifies the refusal to see that the marks of shame have wiped out the memories of heroism. Mitterrand's gesture may also have been—but this is just an hypothesis—the sign of fidelity to a man that he believed in, and even certain feelings that he shared with millions of other French citizens. That did not prevent him from being at the same time aware of other demands, those of the victims of Vichy and its most criminal chapter—the complicity in the extermination of the Jews—even though he refused to consider this most vindictive awakening of memory.[80]

Of course, with respect to the specific case of François Mitterrand, one would have to be naïve to believe that certain statements or acts stem only from moral concerns; that is particularly true of his role in the delaying of the legal proceedings against René Bousquet, to whom he was highly indulgent and with whom he had long maintained close ties.[81] But that is not the most important point, for the feelings that Mitterrand, the chief of state, expressed about this subject are those of a large number of French people who have not all kept company with René Bousquet.

General de Gaulle had given France the gift of an "invented honor." François Mitterrand struggled to cope with the dilemmas that arose over the era. Who turned out to be closer to the truth of the past?

Final Episode [82]

It is true that the controversy over François Mitterrand's past, which had been latent for almost fifty years and recurrent since his becoming President of the Republic in 1981, was in September 1994 taking a dramatic turn and plunging the entire country into feverish confusion. There are several reasons that explain why this outbreak was particularly acute. First of all, this affair was the direct result of the publication of the book by Pierre Péan (*Une jeunesse française*), which marked a real advance in our knowledge of this character. As the fruit of a meticulous investigation, this book took its sustenance from a good source, beginning with the willful and well-spoken testimony of its very subject: one might even wonder which one of these two protagonists chose the other, and to what extent François Mitterrand might have decided that Pierre Péan's project was a good opportunity to make a clean breast of things and get a jump on the scandal that had every chance of breaking out sooner or later, given the number of "sleuths" who were hot on the trail. This takes nothing away from the merit of *Une jeunesse française*—on the contrary—since the author's gamble essentially paid off: the book supplied no small amount of previously unknown information, which managed to appear as shattering revelations for most of the general public.

What is more, the flap broke out only a few months before the end of the second seven-year term of office that was to conclude the political career of François Mitterrand. Both on the Left and on the Right, the rights of succession were open, with some campaigning for his presidential office, and others thinking of the inevitable changing of the guard between generations. The weapon of history thus offered itself not only to dyed-in-the-wool opponents, but also to all sorts of inheritors. And that weapon lent itself to a simpler and more formidable use than that of political discussion. You could not find a better example of the way substitutions are played out than the one offered by the controversies about Vichy that occur in French political life: the expected debate over the end results of Mitterrand's fourteen years in office was totally swept aside by the row over the presence of François Mitterrand at Vichy and his dangerous liaisons with René Bousquet. Added to all that was the fact that François Mitterrand himself, far from snuffing out the scandal, took the initiative of giving a long televised interview on September 12, 1994, with Jean-Pierre Elkabbach, who was then president of the public television channels. Breaking with the traditional presidential reserve about two particular subjects, Mitterrand intended to make his own case to the public on his illness (which was stirring up rumors and expectations) as well as on his past. Far from calming things down, the discrepancy between the expectations of a confused public opinion and the President's ambiguous statements about the Vichy regime and the lessons that he drew from it, on the contrary, unsettled people's consciences even more.

When we step back to put things in perspective, it is worthwhile to take a quick look at the subject of the dispute. In his book, Pierre Péan answers several queries that had remained murky for a half a century. Yes indeed, before the war, François Mitterrand was circulating in a Catholic milieu imbued with nationalism and xenophobia. And yes, after his return from captivity in December 1941, he sought and found a job at Vichy: earlier than was thought (toward the middle of January, 1942) and providing services more compromising than those involving the prisoner of war office that he was subsequently to work in. Namely, he worked for the French Legion of War Veterans. Yes, he progressively and belatedly broke away from Vichy during 1943, without, however, cutting off all ties to the regime. This accounts for his preference—which was known and declared—for General Giraud rather than General de Gaulle within the Resistance and for the episode of the Francisque that Pierre Péan does not completely elucidate. Yes, he had known René Bousquet and had continued his friendship with him up until recently (at least until 1986), when he was already President of the Republic and at a time when the activities of the former Secretary General of the Police were widely and publicly known, especially after the indictment of Jean Leguay, Bousquet's former assistant, for crimes against humanity, in 1979.[83]

Pierre Péan, who conducted his study with impartiality, also puts a rightful end to certain legends that had been spread particularly since the Liberation by the extreme right-wing press, which had for a long time made François Mitterrand into one of its favorite targets and had already "revealed" a certain number of facts. But these facts could not really be regarded as reliable information, in view of the lack of tangible proof and of the obvious partiality of these publications. No, François Mitterrand had been neither a member nor a close follower of the Action Française. He had even, like a large number of Catholics, approved of its condemnation by the Church in December 1926. No, he had not been a member of the Cagoule, even though some of his close friends were part of it. No, he had not belonged to the Croix-de-Feu, even though his youthful leanings made him lean in the direction of Colonel La Rocque.[84]

Very briefly summarized, those are the main new facts brought to the case, and they are far from being negligible. Reading *Une jeunesse française*, we get the portrait of a young Mitterrand immersed in a right-wing Catholic milieu, more excited by literature than politics in the 1930s. The war and especially captivity left durable marks on him: the only three important texts that he wrote during the Occupation—including only two that were actually published at the time—deal with his captivity and the lessons he drew from it.[85] He was already displaying a personal ambition that led him into the paths of power, even though the portrait sketched by Pierre Péan shows us a young man just as preoccupied by the frustrations of his love life as by politics. In this light, the photo taken at an audience that Pétain had granted to the leaders of the Center for the Mutual Assistance of Prisoners of War of the Allier Department on October 15, 1942, was not one of the most interesting contributions of Péan's book: although this shot,[86] which is featured on the cover, is indisputably a real find, it does not in itself have any particular historical meaning, since at the time Pétain visited hundreds of government employees and officials of all sorts. The orginality of Pierre Péan's book lies much more in the fact that he describes a François Mitterrand who was clearly much closer to the values of the Vichy regime than was thought up until the publication of his book, with Mitterrand appearing more "Pétainist" than "Maréchalist," to use the traditional distinction:[87] Pierre Laval's return to power in April 1942, which was at the time perceived as a hardening of the policy of state collaboration, had not posed any problems for his conscience, as he would indicate in a letter to a friend on April 22, 1942.[88] This fact is noteworthy in that this event had, for many of the Maréchalists of the first wave, constituted a major motive for breaking with the regime, just as, later, the invasion of the southern free zone would be in November 1942.

Pierre Péan thus cleared away the fog that still surrounded the young Mitterrand's itinerary. He resituated the facts within a precise chronology, shedding light on a few pivotal periods: his return from captivity, his very gradual movement toward resistance. As far as we are concerned, this is the main merit of the book, provided that we do not lose sight of the fact that this is one of several possible portraits of the young Mitterrand. Granted, it is based on firsthand sources, but it has one sizable drawback: it is completely beholden to a teleological perspective that takes interest in Mitterrand's younger days in view of what will later become of the political leader. Indeed, these youthful years and this part of François Mitterrand's career are reduced to their political and ideological dimensions, even though the author clearly shows that those were not the only preoccupations of his protagonist in those times. The experience of the stalags, the fear of losing his fiancée at that time, and an unbridled ambition clearly outweighed any ideological presuppositions. François Mitterrand's evolution thus takes its

source as much from the Vichy episode as from his subsequent rallying to
the Resistance. His political consciousness was forged in those years, with
the passage from Vichy over into dissidence constituting a defining moment. One only has to look at Pierre Péan's excessive use of personal correspondence or the very rare public texts written by the young Mitterrand:
certainly, this is valuable information which allows us namely to have an
idea of his mindset at the time. But it is above all a source of counterexam-
ples that indicate that, for lack of convincing evidence, the author found it
hard to depict Mitterrand as a politician driven by ideological motivations.

But it is on this level, however, that Pierre Péan's book deserves to be
discussed, for it is one of the causes of the ensuing controversy. For all its
indisputable merits, *Une jeunesse française* is only a partial biography, which
is entirely centered on this delicate period *because of the subsequent political
stakes that it constituted*. Nothing, or at least very little, is said about the rest
of his career, about the way in which a convinced, unhesitating Pétainist
who little by little crossed over into the Resistance gradually transformed
himself into a leader of the Left, even though this period obviously played a
crucial role in the development of his political maturity. The link between
the various facets of this character, who is hardly lacking in them, has not
been established. It is left to the free assessment of the reader, whose attention is almost entirely drawn to the Occupation years. Most commentators,
moreover, have narrowed the perspective even more by focusing solely on
his stint at Vichy, thus forgetting what followed, particularly his Resistance
activity, on the unfair pretext that the "new facts" and "current issues" lay
there.

The nationwide outcry of indignation stirred up by these revelations
only takes on its full meaning because we know that this was not some
anonymous character, but the future President of the Republic and the first
President of the Fifth Republic from the Left. That is the reason why the
itinerary, relatively commonplace, of an ambitious young Catholic man,
and of a lower-ranking functionary in the Vichy regime (and there were
many such employees), became, in the writings of some commentators (including historians who were nevertheless aware of the pitfalls of anachronism and the teleological perspective) a troubling symptom of French political life. Some even went so far as to give an interpretation that was, to say
the least, imprudent and cocky: they saw François Mitterrand's presence at
the head of state as an implicit rehabilitation of the Vichy mindset.[89]

In the considerable excitement aroused by this affair, a good number of
more or less sincere commentators, political leaders, journalists, and historians "forgot" or pretended to be unaware that the most important facts,
namely that François Mitterrand had worked deep within the Vichy regime,
that he had been decorated with the Francisque, and that he had published
texts imbued with fashionable *maréchalisme* before joining forces with the

Resistance, had been largely known, even if he had tried to disguise them or cover them in a thick fog: they had been at the heart of the very last political quarrels in May 1981, just before the second round of the presidential election. But in the context of that time, with the expectation of a change of political majority that was euphoric for some and dreadful for others, the question did not have any impact, except on a few old barons of Gaullism, such as Alain de Boissieu, who after the election of Mitterrand on May 10, 1981, resigned from his position as Grand Chancellor of the National Order of the Legion of Honor in order not to have to pin this prestigious decoration on the chest of a man "who had worked for Vichy," and who had been one of General de Gaulle's chief adversaries.[90]

Also "forgotten" was the fact that General de Gaulle had, in 1943, just barely prevailed over his rival, General Giraud, who at the time was supported by President Roosevelt, and the fact that this political victory signaled the total defeat of the ideas of the "National Revolution" to which an entire current of the Resistance (symbolized by loyalty to Giraud) explicitly adhered even while fighting against Germany. François Mitterrand was nothing less than one member of this movement, which did not prevent him from being an authentic resister. Just as François Mitterrand's backers had, before this affair, refused to see anything in this itinerary but the case of a resister who had momentarily wandered astray at Vichy, so did the Pétainist episode of his life, after the outbreak of this controversy, constitute for some people the proof of an irreparable infamy. Men such as Maurice Couve de Murville, a future Prime Minister for General de Gaulle, and General de Lattre de Tassigny, a great hero of the liberation of France, went through the same evolution during that era. Nevertheless, as Serge Klarsfeld—who then could hardly be suspected of being favorably inclined to François Mitterrand—said publicly in 1994, the resister who returned from Algiers clandestinely in 1944 probably did not risk much if he had been arrested by Vichy's regular police, where he had retained certain connections, but he did run the risk of death if he had been arrested by the Milice or the Germans. Why then should François Mitterrand be refused what was granted to a large number of Pétainists who changed sides, taking particular risks? Out of concern for moral rigor that is a particularly facile one to the extent that it remains ignorant of the dilemmas faced by the protagonists of that time? It is certainly easier to have a clear view of the future once the battle is over. There is no doubt that the most virulent critics of François Mitterrand in 1994 would have probably done better in 1944 than the followers of de Gaulle in Algiers who had agreed, albeit with difficulty and a bit of rancor, to work with men who had come from Vichy.

Also "forgotten" was the fact that, before September 1994, the Vichy episode had been swept under the rug or downplayed not only by the President but also by an entire current of the best informed people within the circle of power. "For fifty years, the press was content with the official biography without looking any further," one read in an editorial of *Le Monde* of September 9, 1994: this was a generous self-criticism granted to the entire gamut of the French press in step with its most prestigious representative.[91] However, scarcely two years earlier, following a long investigation by *L'Express* which revealed that François Mitterrand had been having flowers placed on Pétain's tomb every year since 1986 and which was then recalling the President of the Republic's "Vichyite-resister" past, *Le Monde* had published a full-page attack on the weekly newsmagazine, taking it to task for bringing up "the vilest of old rumors that are trafficked about the past of the President of the Republic." And the author of the article added: "Perhaps François Mitterrand is now paying the political price for the modest reserve that he has always maintained about this period of his life. Every time that people try to lead him back over this historical terrain, he lets it be understood that, as someone at peace with his conscience, he does not grant anyone the right to demand any justification whatsoever from him about his Francisque or his writings of the time, which he himself has made public in his collections of writings." Which means that in 1992 a certain number of things were already known and publicly disseminated, even though they were termed "vile rumors." The same article ended with the following remark: "Once he became President of the Republic, Mr. Mitterrand wanted to make a complete break with this past, just as he did when, against the wishes of certain leaders of the Socialist party, he granted amnesty to the former generals who tried to lead a putsch in French Algeria. While this conception of the President of the Republic's role is perhaps subject to debate, it certainly does not deserve the unhealthy reopening of a phony trial which, in any case, history has already put away on the shelf of political aberrations."[92]

How does what was a "phony trial" in 1992 become, in 1994, an urgent duty to remember? How is what was "subject to debate" in 1992 regarded two years later as a guilty desire to "trivialize Vichy"? The answer, beyond the case mentioned here, does indeed lie in the variable perspective from which certain people approach the past: the real issues are always formulated in the present. For in this instance, memory is just an alibi. It would be naïve to think that *Le Monde* devoted so much energy to the Mitterrand affair in the fall of 1994, when the media's obsession with Vichy reached an unequaled peak, just to defend a "duty to remember," which can be seen to fluctuate in response to political circumstances. The answer obviously lies elsewhere, when one takes the trouble to remember that the presidential election was approaching and that Édouard Balladur's candidacy was finding favor with some of those (including the editorial staff of *Le Monde*) who had become disillusioned with Mitterrandism: from then on, these people were constantly setting themselves apart from the President and making their jilted love forgotten.

What takes the cake in this whole affair is that the principle person in question greatly contributed to sowing the seeds of doubt in people's minds. And he did so in a way that deserves its own explanation. Far from clarifying things, his television appearance on September 12, 1994, seemed to prove the point of those who were remembering only the Pétainist of 1942–1943, and forgetting the resister of 1943–1944 and even more the President of 1994.

Without analyzing the President's televised statements in detail, we can go back over a few of the main ideas here. In the first place, François Mitterrand played on the charisma that he thought he still could use to sway public opinion. He tried to lay out his truth as a truth that was historical, universal, and *comprehensible* for the greatest number of people. However, he did not speak with the detachment that his age and presidential function should have conferred upon him. Instead, he spoke with the words of that time, with strangely loaded memories, and with the same blindness to the real nature of Vichy that he doubtless displayed during the Occupation: in spite of all that we now know about the regime's ideology, its choices, and its objectives, Mitterrand characterized it as "a motley crew." Oddly, Mitterrand seemed to be speaking to an audience he perhaps thought would instantly understand the era's ambiguities, its hesitations, it small and large acts of cowardice, and its about-faces: in other words, his own experience.

Hence his error and his omission, which were grave and carried heavy consequences, about the French anti-Semitic legislation: "You say to me: 'the anti-Jewish laws'; although it does not mend or excuse anything, this was actually a matter of legislation against foreign Jews that I know nothing about." The statement is completely wrong, since Vichy's legislation also targeted *French* Jews. This one single sentence illustrates the position that he found himself in, for in uttering a totally inaccurate statement, he implicitly showed what his priorities of that time were: they were those of a number of the regime's civil servants who were doubtless not particularly anti-Semitic but in no way felt that this was a major "problem" in comparison with other preoccupations. Here we have precisely the whole issue of the time lag of anachronism: his error remains *a truth*. While no one can now believe that he "knew nothing," the fact remains that at that time, he probably didn't give the slightest importance to the matter of anti-Semitic persecutions, which has nowadays become central and impossible to ignore.

But instead of gaining citizens' favor and understanding, he aroused their indignation, for public opinion was hardly prepared to hear about the "complexity" of that era from the lips of its President: people were expecting not a course on historical criticism, but the respect of the symbolic aspect of his office. This shortcoming is flagrant in two other aspects of his televised appearance. First, he said nothing about his resistance activity; this would at least have allowed people to understand how he crossed over from one side to the other. And this seems to have been a deliberate choice: he felt that his resistance activity—which was real and emphasized in Pierre Péan's book—spoke for him and constituted an implicit form of redemption of his previous conduct, and that he therefore did not have to have recourse to the subject.[93] Second, in speaking about his friendship with René Bousquet and moreover admitting that he had delayed judicial proceedings directed against the former Secretary General of the Police, he seemed to be confusing his private life (in which he arguably had the right to maintain his friendship with anyone he pleased) with his public life. Not only could he hardly justify maintaining such a relationship, he could moreover not possibly disregard the fact that talking about it so complacently was going to arouse quite virulent reactions. Now, what shocked a good portion of public opinion (and rightly so), was precisely Mitterrand's reaffirmation of his friendship with Bousquet more than the Vichy episode; at least for the generation that had lived through that era, this part of his itinerary could at the limit be understood and even accepted in view of his subsequent evolution.

It is in this sense that François Mitterrand confined himself within the perspective opened up by Pierre Péan. Limited in that book (which moreover had no other explicit purpose) to his youthful years, reduced down to his stint at Vichy in the controversy that ensued, Mitterrand's image shrank and deteriorated singularly as soon as he himself used this angle of observation to explain his past. Is it not strange that during the entire broadcast lasting almost two hours—and this would be one of the last televised appearances of his second term of office—the President did not bring up his political achievements one single time? In the whole line of great political leaders who went through the ordeal of the Occupation, with so few of them coming out of it unscathed, François Mitterrand ended up being one of the last to suffer the effects of the "Vichy syndrome" after having tried, to no avail, to bring them under control.

5

The Resisters,

Our Guilty Conscience

On February 3, 1993, the television series *La Marche du siècle*[1] devoted a new program to World War II entitled: "Spies Above All Suspicion. Frenchmen Serving Moscow. Who Were They?" The evening promised to be a lively one which would attract a large television audience. The primary guest was Thierry Wolton, the star of the day. In a book that had just been published, *Le Grand Recrutement*,[2] the author, a self-proclaimed "historical investigative journalist," suggested that the leader of the Resistance, Jean Moulin, who was General de Gaulle's representative in occupied France, had been a spy working for Moscow, and that the real truth had come out of the archives of the KGB.[3] Nothing less. Daniel Cordier, who had been Jean Moulin's personal secretary during the period of his clandestine activity and who, more importantly, had become the biographer who had dug up and sifted through the most important documentary holdings ever put together on the subject of Jean Moulin, was the only one there to give an immediate response to Thierry Wolton's allegations. As he had been invited to the television studio at the last minute, he hardly managed to get a word in. This calumny was thus made into a "major event": the screening of such a program contributed in no small way to echoing astounding assertions, by means of the "hypothesis" put forth in this manner and even more by the sources and method used. In response to the outcry provoked by this edition of *La Marche du siècle*, the producers finally had to make up for their crass mistake and come back to the topic. Another program screened on May 19, 1993, gave occasion to a much higher quality discussion with Daniel Cordier (who this time was in a position to express his ideas comfortably) and a good number of great figures of the Resistance, not to mention the usual flock of secondary school students who had been invited there once again to fulfill their "duty to remember": this practice has become the most common alibi used by television in order to present programs with a veneer of pedagogical value.[4]

Thus in the space of a few months, the same program (which is one of the best of this sort of show) praised to the highest heaven a courageous investigator who claimed to make a spectacular revision of the "official" history of the Resistance, and then engaged in the celebration of that same Resistance in a manner that has become ritual. It is worthwhile to note this ambivalence of the media, because it is nothing but the symptom of a much deeper problem. For several years now, the memory of the Resistance has been bounced around between, on the one hand, head-on attacks, and on the other hand, the old tendency of commemorative speeches. It is hard for the Resistance to enter into history.

This difficulty in passing from the epic narrative to an historical narrative has brought about a loss of direction in the memory of the French nation. Since the memory of the Resistance remains a political issue, the vulnerability that it has recently developed has caused it to draw fire on a regular basis, with such attacks being carried out on the pretext of the need to transform myth into history. That is the way in which ideological and partisan revisions have been carried out for the last few years. Moreover, this occurrence cannot but remind us of how, in spite of basic differences, in the 1970s, all sorts of rereadings of the history of the war had made room for the deniers, who took advantage of the situation to tout their fanatical claim of denying the existence of the Genocide. This ideological revisionism has grave consequences not only because it flouts fundamental values, but equally—and this is the essential point—because it tends to raise doubts about the possibility of writing history objectively.

In addition, the memory of the Resistance has suffered a bit from a polarization of the nation's memory, which has resulted from an intense focus on the most hideous aspect of the Dark Years: Vichy and anti-Semitism. Because people have for years now dwelled on the dark side of this history, they have, out of masochism, indifference, or ignorance, ended up turning their backs on the bright side.

The Bright Side

One sign among others of this relative disaffection is that the history of the Resistance has for the last few years been rather neglected in favor of numerous studies of the Vichy regime and the Genocide, although the number of such studies is not always synonymous with quality or rigor. Scholars have concentrated their work on subjects which, just fifteen years ago, constituted so many blank pages waiting to be written and gaps to be filled. It was not only a scholarly imperative which drove their efforts at that time but equally a social demand that had to be met: if not, people would have kept on pointing the finger at the French and their refusal to examine their past.

But this state of affairs can also be explained by the very nature of the events in question. Since history is a pursuit that seeks to demythify things, it was easier, as far as France's internal strife was concerned, to take on the subject of Vichy than that of the Resistance. Controversies on the one hand and, on the other, the fact that certain members of the Resistance were tempted to preserve an idyllic image of their struggle, probably hampered scholarly inquiries for a time. This is especially clear since there are few historical fields in which the majority of those writing the historical accounts are those who were former protagonists in the events and not professional historians, as the historian Pierre Laborie has pointed out.[5] Even though its star has faded a bit, the memory of the Resistance in France remains a civic religion which is observed in all local communities and in all schools. But myth and cult sometimes signify a refusal of History and can lead to harmful effects. Conversely, the decline of the "résistancialiste" myth, including both the Gaullist and Communist versions, has brought about excesses and occultations: such rewritings, carried out for the sake of "the duty to remember," are sometimes (but not always) entirely fanciful.[6]

Historical scholarship is thus only beginning—or rather beginning over again, since the Resistance had been the focus of everyone's attention in the 1960s, albeit in another frame of mind. A new generation of historians has begun to produce precise, well-documented scholarly works on the subject.[7] The first break with the historical tradition, however, came from one who was a protagonist of that history.

Daniel Cordier and his monumental biography of Jean Moulin provided the basis for a new political history of the Resistance, perhaps the first global history of the "Resistance of leaders," which is an historical nexus crucial to the understanding of contemporary France.[8] Based on archival sources that had been previously unavailable for the most part, the book raised a number of questions. Most important, however, it brought new elements of proof and certainty; with respect to their past, citizens need truths, even though these truths may constantly need to be reviewed. Over the last fifty years, the Resistance has been subject to several narratives, and even fads, but has never occasioned an historical synthesis of a scholarly nature, in spite of the contributions of the Comité d'Histoire de la Deuxième Guerre Mondiale[9] (which in 1978 and 1979 was made part of the Institut d'Histoire du Temps Présent[10]). The very definition of the concept of "resistance" still remains uncertain, as shown by the work of the sociologist Jacques Semelin, who is the first in France to have called attention to the various forms of civil resistance, that of ordinary people and common society outside of political parties, intelligence networks, and resistance movements, and thus outside of the heroic legends.[11]

Since the publication of Daniel Cordier's book, the personal accounts published in the past and those that continue to come out have lost a good deal of their preeminence. While they may remain important and moving, and retain their intrinsic truth that the historian must take into account as such, many of them must now be approached with caution if one really is keen on having a verifiable knowledge of the facts.[12] The precision of Daniel Cordier's documentation exposed their contradictions, their errors, their omissions (voluntary or otherwise), and their tendency sometimes to present a saccharine version of the facts.

There is nothing surprising about this observation: history cannot be written simply by relying on witnesses. The respect for the right to remember (for this is a right as much as a duty . . .) does not mean that we must accept what these voices from the past say to us as gospel truth. And these remarks are simply reminders that well-meaning reporters and activists sometimes forget when they hold out their microphones to these great witnesses who nevertheless refuse all critical analysis of what they say, and even all attempts to put things into proper perspective.[13] Granted, this is no easy task, since these witnesses, or at least some of them, enjoy the stature of heroes. They keep a jealous watch over their narratives and at times hamper historical research, which is hardly charitable in its treatment of sacred history.[14]

The Resistance is not just one episode among others in French history. It is, and still remains, a sacred story, thus often simplified and spruced up. It was thanks to this founding narrative that France's national identity, which after the tempest of the Occupation had been splintered, was able to mend itself. And so it only made sense, and perhaps it was necessary, for the break to come from one who had taken part in the ordeal. Daniel Cordier, however, is a protagonist who resisted the temptation to write an autobiography. Contrary to what a good number of his companions did after the war, he had wanted to turn the page and devote himself to his passion as a collector of modern art, which would become his profession. It was much later, in the middle of the 1970s, when he had broken his ties with his past, that the declarations of Henri Frenay, the founder of the Resistance movement "Combat," who accused Jean Moulin of having been a "cryptocommunist" during the war, finally prompted him to react. Subsequently, his work would prove to be all the more credible in that he mistrusted his memory and discovered highly important personal archives to which he had previously given little attention. He thus refused to let himself be held up as a witness by the historians and to add another stone to the heap of memoirs that he had shown to be inaccurate. He intended to do the work of an historian, and that is what he indeed accomplished, at times by being more "positivistic" than the most traditional of historians: the documents, all the documents, and nothing but the documents.[15]

And so it was a former member of the Resistance who drove the final nail into the coffin of the commemorative narrative. Whereas for years, most historians (including the coauthor of this book) thought that the Resistance, given its clandestine character, was a history relatively poor in archival remains, Daniel Cordier found, dug up, and published an enormous mass of highly important, previously unknown documents. Most of these documents shed new light on the Resistance. Thanks to Cordier, we have a better understanding of the complex ties between London and Algiers, on the one hand, and the mainland Resistance movements on the other. We have a better understanding of the importance of Jean Moulin, a figure who was a bit forgotten after the war and who was lifted up as a hero of the first order by France's national memory with the aid of de Gaulle's Fifth Republic when, on that day of December 1964, his ashes were transferred to the Panthéon accompanied by the eulogy of André Malraux. Now a symbol, the man with the scarf, whose name has been given to dozens of lycées in France, had remained one of the "unknown" with respect to history; this gap has now been filled.

Although he is an historian, Daniel Cordier nevertheless remains the resister that he was. In spite of having pored over the archives and being extremely wary of witnesses, he continues to be a committed protagonist of this epic saga. That takes nothing away from his objectivity and rigor. As is the case with any scholar, however, he speaks and writes with his own sensitivity, which, for him, has been strongly marked by the weight of the past. This dimension, which is obviously lacking in a university scholar born after the war, gives to the work of Daniel Cordier, as it does to other works of the same kind, a particular quality. This quality stems from a "top-down" vision of the Resistance, the Gaullist vision—that of wartime Gaullism, not that of the postwar. It is dependent on this view of things not only because that is its main focus, but also because Cordier himself experienced the events from this vantage point. Having had a front seat at the reunification of the Resistance movements and the formation of the Secret Army—which was the most important step of 1942 and 1943—he has kept the "institutional" view of things which was that of Jean Moulin. Hence his difficulty in accounting for the rebellious, intuitive, and at times disorderly character that was the trademark of the leaders of the Resistance before de Gaulle enlisted them in "his" great army of the night. There again we find the gap between the "exterior" and the "mainland" Resistance that François Mitterrand liked to emphasize. Above all, we recognize a crucial point in this story, whose disputed memory accounts for the recurring quarrels over the memory of Jean Moulin, whether it be the accusation of "crypto-communism" thrown at him by Henri Frenay or the mystery surrounding his arrest by Klaus Barbie at Caluire on June 21, 1943.[16] Coming into contact while moving between several Resistance circles that were both quite close and quite different, it was impossible for Jean Moulin to be General de Gaulle's disciple without colliding with the ambitions and sensitivities of the leaders of these movements—not to speak of the clandestine apparatus of the Communists. These leaders were suddenly thrown into history without in any way having been prepared for the task. Fighting as they were within France, they did not all have the same planetary vision of the conflict nor the same acute political sensitivity as General de Gaulle who, as far as he was concerned, had quickly assumed the role of a statesman. Was it possible for Jean Moulin to avoid the at times fierce confrontation with men and women who, while they graciously accepted General de Gaulle's leadership, at the same time defended their independence? All they were doing, after all, was demanding their own specific legitimacy, in that, often, their initial resistance had not been in obedience to General de Gaulle's prophetic call of June 18, 1940, but rather had been prompted by a spontaneous reaction of the same nature. When all was said and done, they fell in step behind General de Gaulle, whom subsequent events proved right: in the heat of the battle, however, no one could predict the future.

At first Daniel Cordier's work was not discussed. It was attacked. His approach to the subject clashed squarely with the official narrative in that it analyzed in an almost diabolically meticulous manner the origins of certain movements, the sharp internal conflicts within the Resistance, and the stand-off between de Gaulle and the leaders of the mainland Resistance. The end product is something that does not correspond with the idealized storybook images of a Resistance that supposedly had clearly arisen as early as 1940 and then, crystallized by de Gaulle, had entered into a fierce struggle against Pétain and his policies. "Why should we refuse to realize that the beginnings of the Resistance were sometimes, among other things, within mainland France, a reflection of the predominant ambivalences of a public opinion that was totally disoriented? It is only a short step from venerating the past to making it up," writes Pierre Laborie.[17] Many former members of the Resistance, imprisoned within the Gaullist postwar narrative, refuse to undertake this reexamination and deny the diversity of the Resistance for the sake of a mythical unity.

This is something analogous to the incomprehension created by the wartime itinerary of somebody like François Mitterrand, who exemplifies the ambivalences alluded to by Pierre Laborie. Some members of the Resistance—and not the least among them—got involved more out of patriotic convictions (in opposition to the Germans, the invaders) than anti-fascist sentiments. Some believed that Vichy was double-dealing with the Germans; they shared Vichy's nationalistic ideology and ignored the reality of state collaboration. Up until 1942, and sometimes much later, these mem-

bers of the Resistance founded their hopes on the person of Marshall Pétain. In other words, a comprehensive history of the Resistance must take
into account the very early refusals that appeared outside of Gaullist ranks.
It must take into account—before coming to any value judgment—the political ambivalences of some of the first resisters, who believed that Pétain
and de Gaulle were secretly (or objectively) allied with one another. And it
must take into account the belated resistance of men who had first worked
within the Vichy regime.

The refusal to admit this diversity after the fact caused a scandal. The
object of the controversy? A few pages devoted to Henri Frenay. In November 1940, he who was to become one of the principal leaders of the Resistance in the southern zone drew up a text entitled "Manifesto of the
Movement for National Liberation" in which he expressed the feeling that
"the National Revolution will come after the Liberation of the Nation,
which is aimed at kicking the Krauts out of France."[18] In this text, Frenay
affirms his allegiance to Pétain and ends his call with this sentence: "May
Marshall Pétain have a long enough life to support us with his towering authority and his incomparable prestige." The text explicitly fits itself into
Pétainist thematics: "All those who shall serve in our ranks, like those who
are already with us, shall be authentic French. Jews shall serve in our ranks
if they have indeed fought in one of the two wars." This piece was written
after the meeting of Pétain and Hitler at Montoire on October 24, 1940,
which is mentioned in the text: Henri Frenay asserted that the policy (of
collaboration) followed by Marshall Pétain and the one that he himself was
advocating "are easily reconciled." This manifesto was made after the publication of the first "Jewish Statute" in the *Journal officiel* on October 18,
1940. At the same time, Henri Frenay the officer declared: *"It is therefore to
England that we turn, for that is whom we want to help"* (Frenay's emphasis), in
spite of the fact that the memories of Mers el-Kebir and Dakar were still
quite recent.[19]

Daniel Cordier's mention of this "Manifesto" was not entirely innocent,
since his vocation as a biographer sprung from his outrage at listening to
Henri Frenay's attacks against Jean Moulin in the 1970s. The fact remains,
however, that this text is an interesting one for understanding the complexity of the first years of the Resistance, even though it does not by itself sum
up these years and though one should not retrospectively give it too much
importance just because of present-day controversies. The text is indeed
anti-German but pro-Pétain, anglophile but condoning the politics of the
Montoire meeting, fiercely anti-Communist and beholden toward the ideology of anti-Semitic discrimination.

This was quite a bombshell. Some individuals mounted an attack as in
1940. This is "the scheme put together by a second-class member of the
Resistance," declared one former member of the Resistance after the publi-

cation of the first two volumes; he was forgetting that Daniel Cordier had been decorated as a "Companion of the Liberation."[20] Others claimed that it was in fact a forgery. Still others said that the text had not been written by Henri Frenay, who supposedly had never been pro-Pétainist—even though Frenay himself had expressed his feelings about Pétain in his memoirs in 1973.[21] What a barrage of words in an attempt to deny the evidence! And what a spectacle to give to these younger generations that people are constantly trying to educate about the war! True, this text did not fit very well with the idyllic image of things. Just as was the case for so many other texts, such as the first *Cahier*[22] of the Organisation Civile et Militaire (OCM),[23] which was the Resistance movement created in the northern zone and which put out an underground newspaper in June 1942 with an anti-Semitic article that aroused bitter, heated controversy among members of the Resistance at that time. True, Frenay's manifesto posed a problem for those who wanted to maintain a "pious history." But this point was already moot, since at that time, very few people still believed in the storybook images of the Resistance, outside of the few guardians of the temple who attempted to play memory off against history.

These reactions in the face of a reexcavated (and not revealed) truth doubtless encouraged other offensives which were aimed at undermining the very legitimacy of the struggle against the Nazi forces occupying France.

The Great Lie

The "Moulin Affair," or rather the "Wolton Affair" of 1993, was not, and doubtless will not be, either the first or the last of its kind. The difference from the preceding incidents stemmed from two things: first, the author was neither a firsthand witness nor a former member of the Resistance, and he claimed to have discovered the secret in the "Soviet archives," which supposedly gave indisputable proof of the egregious offense. Having written works about spy rings, Thierry Wolton felt authorized to offer a new type of privilege as an exclusive first to his readers: "investigative historical journalism."

> While historical investigation is something France is rather unaccustomed to, it is at any rate the only thing that is suitable when one is interested in the role of intelligence services. With this method, one understands that history is not to be understood only in terms of nations tearing away at each other, of self-seeking states confronting each other, and of great men transcending the circumstances. When light is shone into shady areas, one discovers that often all it takes to change the course of events is a handful of determined individuals playing their roles in secret.

> As is always the case when one takes a peek behind the scenes, these observations are upsetting.[24]

To say the least. Never mind the fact that the author seems in this passage to have called upon his schoolday memories to give a lesson to a discipline that he knows virtually nothing about.[25] It is really the very genre—secret history—which is a lucrative type of literature that leaves the door open to all sorts of manipulation. This is a history that supposedly only the cleverest sleuths, armed with patience and cunning, are capable of reconstituting with the aid of certain venal or political complicities, in these shady circles of people who supposedly held the fate of the planet in their hands . . .

But "historical investigation" is nothing but a deceptive formula. It does not stand for anything, except for justifying a method which consists of uttering accusations without proof about the reliability of "secret sources." Neither historians nor journalists enjoy such license. Nevertheless, this permissiveness has gained credit in the eyes of certain specialists on the subject (and not the least among them), who have done more than a little to help make this approach legitimate.

The whole book is based on one central hypothesis: in the 1930s in France, in the same manner in which they had succeeded in Great Britain, Soviet intelligence services recruited "agents" not only in Communist circles but also within the group of "young hotheads" of the Radical Party, a group that was led in particular by the government Minister of the Air Force under the Popular Front, Pierre Cot, whose chief of staff was Jean Moulin. These progressive members of the Radical Party supposedly constituted an ideal pool for recruitment because of their commitment to anti-fascism. That is the way in which Thierry Wolton recounts the life and career of a lynchpin in this undertaking, the spy Henri Robinson, called "Harry," someone previously unknown. Wolton points to the existence of a Soviet network in France, whose role was doubtless appreciable—this point is a credit to the author. If the book had confined itself to revelations about the Soviet penetration in France, it would have amounted only to a success admired by a limited circle of specialists, and not a best seller. The accusation made against Jean Moulin, which was always an insinuation that was never clearly articulated, gives the book an entirely different dimension. This is what the general public will remember from it when the refutations finally come back. *Le Grand Recrutement* actually says very little about Jean Moulin: only about forty pages out of four hundred are devoted to him. He is only there to serve as an attraction, especially on the book's cover. Even if that was perhaps not the original goal, the mere fact of having found Jean Moulin's name in documents coming from Soviet archives obviously made the author's head spin: he undoubtedly believed he had hold of the great secret of the century.

And so, according to Thierry Wolton, Jean Moulin—or rather, a few of his followers, such as Maurice Panier and Pierre Meunier, who had been on Pierre Cot's team and who, in 1945, would be chief of staff for Maurice Thorez[26]—supposedly transmitted information to Henri Robinson during the war. What was the proof? The "archives of the KGB," which for several years has been a providential gold mine for all those who, with just one book, claim to rewrite the entire history of our century.

The pages that Thierry Wolton devotes to Jean Moulin are a compilation of knickknacks combining a few real facts with hypotheses and insinuations. Three major sources were solicited for this purpose. The first is an interrogation of Léopold Trepper, former leader of a Communist intelligence network known by the name of Orchestre Rouge,[27] who was detained in the USSR after the war and interrogated in 1946 by Soviet counterespionage services. In this document—which was "provided" to the author, who had not himself discovered it—Léopold Trepper cites the name of Jean Moulin: "Was he recruited as an intelligence agent by Harry? It would be difficult for me to say for sure, but I know that they were often meeting and that Harry was getting information from him."[28] The second source, which is also new, is made up of the "Robinson papers," especially the secret messages sent to Moscow by agent Harry between July 24, 1940, and June 24, 1941: during the time, that is, from the signing of the nonaggression pact between Germany and the Soviet Union on August 23, 1939, and the German offensive against Russia on June 22, 1941, the USSR was objectively allied with the Third Reich. Some of agent Harry's messages carry information dating from the fall of 1940 about the Eure-et-Loire administrative district for which Jean Moulin was then prefect. They never mention Moulin's name, but show that Maurice Panier had been one of the agents in Robinson's network. These archives of Soviet origin had supposedly been provided to him by "a Western secret service agency."[29] Finally, the third "source"—we must use quotation marks here—is made up of information about the itinerary of Maurice Panier, a "source" whose existence has to be postulated by the reader, since the author does not say one word either about his background nor about his existence. This information is dispensed in the book as if it were in the public domain, and that is perhaps the worst manipulation there can be on the subject. Rumor has it that we have a "testimony" (an "interrogation," a "confession"?) obtained after the war by the DST.[30] The historian Stéphane Courtois, one of the best scholars of Communism, declared about this subject: "The difficulty stems from the fact that, if he respects the rules of investigative journalism, Thierry Wolton cannot name the (French) sources from which he got Panier's testimony. It would moreover be desirable that, in matters of such importance, the quite understandable secrecy with which French intelligence services maintain their archives be waived."[31] Very well. But until then, do people have the right to write anything whatsoever? On that score, it could be pointed out that this kind of book continually claims to unveil the most cynical methods and lies of secret intelligence services while at the same time considering their documents as containing gospel truth, sworn on the head of a KGB secret agent!

The declarations trumpeted out about the "secret sources" actually conceal a good deal of bluff. Just on the subject of Wolton's book, it is strictly incomprehensible how the author found, analyzed, and checked out his sources—this was the point forcefully made by Daniel Cordier.[32] In the first place, four fifths of the references cited in the notes of *Le Grand Recrutement* are to already published works (and not the most reliable among them). Second, among the so-called Soviet archival sources, most come from the holdings of "Western" (French) secret intelligence services; only the interrogation of Léopold Trepper and the "Robinson papers" are indeed documents of Soviet *origin*. Make of that what you will! The important point here is that no one can check on either the supposedly "decisive" papers nor on the whole set of the documents used. On the other hand, however, everyone can easily observe that Thierry Wolton was more than abusively heavy-handed in his interpretation of his "mysterious" documents, including many that might, moreover, using the same method, or rather the same lack of scrupulousness, lead to different conclusions altogether.

Just what are the conclusions that Thierry Wolton draws from these scattered, unverifiable pieces of evidence, none of which provides any real proof? That there are "serious and concordant indications" of the possibility that Jean Moulin may have been a Soviet agent, declared Wolton to a weekly newsmagazine.[33] In his book, Wolton uses a myriad of circumlocutions to say the same thing, while not really saying it, giving himself the aura of someone who remains cautious, someone that you cannot fool anymore.

The method of the "historical investigator" has been taken apart by several of these historians that Wolton despises (except for those who helped him in Moscow or in Paris) and to whom he refuses the right of criticizing his theories: since the real players of the century are spies—preferably Soviet —the only really valid history is that which he is in charge of promoting. Historians are "much too busy with so-called official history," writes Wolton in his own defense in an article entitled "Memory Against History."[34] The title, moreover, illustrates beautifully how this kind of undertaking seeks cover by claiming to remove taboos that allegedly lock up an official memory, which is itself allegedly maintained by similarly official historians. Who, in point of fact, terms this history "official"? Former KGB agents?

The said historians responded by invoking the rules of their trade and not "by invoking the values and the memory of the Resistance," as Stéphane Courtois pretended to believe.[35] Nor did they respond for political reasons, as Courtois also claims: "I was surprised to see that many who had not even read the book reacted to it in a really hysterical way. Undoubtedly the political turnabout that we are currently experiencing—both on the international level (with the collapse of the Soviet regime) and on the national level (with the historical failure of the Left)—has a good deal to do with this."[36] This argument curiously resembles the political method elsewhere despised: to refuse to acknowledge a "truth" that is nothing but a lie, or at any rate an allegation that is strictly unfounded and even historically absurd, is not to become an accomplice of Stalinism nor is it giving way to "hysterical" or "archaic" reflexes; it is defending a principle of intellectual honesty that should be incumbent upon all historians and journalists, whether they be on the Left, on the Right, in the Center, or nowhere.

Displaying his proof, Daniel Cordier has demonstrated the inanity of Thierry Wolton's arguments: Cordier's book showed that on the contrary, Jean Moulin had been one who had the most effectively limited Communist ambitions within the Resistance.[37] Pierre Vidal-Naquet has underscored the ignorance of the historical context demonstrated by Thierry Wolton, ignorance that led Wolton to make absurd assertions, such as the one about an (imaginary) meeting between Joachim von Ribbentrop and Molotov, the two signatories of the nonaggression pact between Germany and the Soviet Union in June 1943, a few months after the battle of Stalingrad![38] François Bédarida has shown how Thierry Wolton takes his readers for fools in claiming, for example, that it was Jean Moulin the prefect who allegedly informed "Harry," then stationed in Paris, about a military secret of the utmost importance, namely that Chartres had been bombed by the English on September 10, 1940, and that the cathedral had been spared.[39] Finally, Jean-Pierre Azéma has taken apart Wolton's method, which consists of talking about only those of Jean Moulin's collaborators who were of Communist persuasion while leaving out all the others, who nevertheless held essential command posts within the mainland Resistance. The honorable "investigator" also invented another concept, which is typical of the mindset of those circles on which he claims to be an expert: guilt by association.[40]

The Target in the Pantheon[41]

The reason we are dwelling so much on this book is that it once again opened up one of these chronic phony debates that keep the media busy, avid as they are for these scoops which, under the guise of "demythification," are nothing but hoaxes. Above all, however, Wolton's *Le Grand Re-*

crutement reopened controversy over Jean Moulin. For the last few years, most of the attacks aimed at the memory of the Resistance have been concentrated on him, on the meaning of his action, and on his combat.

Wolton's theory garnered endorsements that are hardly negligible. It was the springboard of one of the most serious attempts at ideological revision of the history of World War II in the last few years. The surprise of Stéphane Courtois, who was amazed by the "hysterical" reactions aroused by Thierry Wolton's calumnies, we can counter with the surprise of having seen the appearance of a previously concealed bitter resentment against Jean Moulin, who was prima facie the most universally admired figure of historical Gaullism.

Thierry Wolton's claims received the considerable support of such prominent university scholars as Annie Kriegel[42] and even François Furet.[43] About Jean Moulin, Furet writes: "The fact that he was a Communist—if indeed he was one—would not keep him from being a Resistance hero. The times were like that. Now it is up to historians to unravel all the secrets, giving people the benefit of the doubt as to their patriotism."[44] That was a hastily pronounced verdict, which, without even bothering to check on the accusation, immediately granted extenuating circumstances. Given the stature of the author, this position caused great sadness and stupefaction. The carelessness of such statements—that would be enough to flunk any history student or any university professor of lesser renown—allows us to measure the extent of the devastation caused by the media, whose approximations can skew the reasoning of France's best intellectuals. Thierry Wolton also received the support of the journal *Commentaire*. Calling his book an "important" one, the editors of this high level journal wrote with mordant irony: "A few ultrasensitive, righteous souls were outraged for the sake of the anti-fascist cult over which they have made themselves the exclusive guardians (perhaps so that their own past as a fellow traveler with the Communists might be forgotten?) and have condemned the book as if it profaned the Holy Sacrament."[45]

Actually, these statements are evidence of a partisan use of history, which is being done at the expense of critical reflection. The intellectuals cited are often themselves ex-Stalinists (which makes *Commentaire*'s irony rather silly), and their motivations in this controversy seem clear. Communism was the central event of their life, so much so that they have an irrepressible tendency to read the past in light of that matrix. By claiming that Jean Moulin and wartime Gaullism were lackeys to Stalinism and by waving the book of an ex-Maoist (Wolton), they are able to bring both Moulin and de Gaulle down to the same level as their own youthful error which keeps on tormenting them. There is such a thing as pretentious guilt: that which will not admit that there are others who are not guilty and which must at all cost try to seek forgiveness by having others share in sin.

Whatever the existential reasons for this campaign may be, the crassness of its means should be underlined. This campaign displayed a simplistic anachronism (as if to show that no one, not even a great historian, is immune to such an error), one which relativizes the fight against Nazism and retrospectively reduces it to a simple tainted alliance with Communism. In the name of condemning Stalinist crimes after the fact—and belatedly— they now put on trial the way people acted during the prewar and Occupation years. The commitment to anti-fascism, which is something complex that was born of a variety of motivations, is from that perspective nothing more than a *means* often used with cynicism by the Communist International and Soviet spy networks. Certainly, everything about these networks must be revealed without any self-censorship, but this has become their *one and only task*, as if fascism and Nazism had not been things that—thankfully!—some people tried to fight. That had already been used as one of the main arguments by the Nazis and by the Vichy regime in their fight against the Resistance, whose members were called "terrorists on Moscow's payroll" in propaganda. The tactical alliance between the three great powers in the anti-Nazi coalition is thus discounted. And in the final analysis that amounts to accusing all the members of the Resistance of having served the Communist cause once they were fighting—and not without rivalries and conflicts that were at times very harsh—alongside active members of the Communist party. It amounts to accusing the very principle of a unified Resistance (and therefore General de Gaulle and Jean Moulin) of having been conducive to the aims of the USSR, to which we owe in part (and what a part!) the defeat of the Third Reich, although that takes nothing away from the criminal nature of the Stalinist regime. It has been forgotten along the way that all the players involved in those times were not necessarily duped or blind. In an article published in 1979 by the very same journal, *Commentaire*, Raymond Aron reflected on the perception of Stalinism that he had had when he was in London during the war: "Constrained to exercise a certain self-censorship, we did not treat the Soviet Union with as much liberty as we did Nazi Germany."[46]

All those who supported Thierry Wolton have therefore implicitly approved of the terrible accusation formulated in the very first lines of his book: "With hindsight, we better gauge to what extent the French who chose Moscow in order to fight Berlin committed, at the best, a tragic political error, and at worst, an act of treason."[47] Should they then have chosen Berlin in order to fight Moscow?

This ideological offensive is aimed, beyond Jean Moulin, at General de Gaulle's leadership and those who followed it during the war, which was an exceptional time, both in an objective and subjective sense of the term. That is what makes this controversy emblematic of the presence of the past and of the political uses to which it is constantly subjected.

The accusation that Jean Moulin could serve both de Gaulle's and Stalin's causes because they were not in conflict with each other in fact originated during the war itself among certain members of the Resistance who were defectors from Pétainism. It is only the latest episode of an old quarrel, and the controversy surrounding the "Manifesto" of Henri Frenay was just another example. It goes all the way back to the confrontation between General de Gaulle and General Giraud in 1943; this is a rivalry whose memory has been made especially lively at the present because we have witnessed the rebirth of a reactionary Right while the Gaullist tradition has been fading away. The issue was indeed a major one, for each one of the two tendencies proposed an alternative to Vichy: de Gaulle's cause was wholly based upon the refusal of the armistice and the reaffirmation of democratic values (although this was done after a slight moment of hesitation), while Giraud's movement was, after the turning point of November 1942, claiming to lead both a concerted fight against the invader and a national revolution modeled on Pétain's. Not only France's role in the war, but even more so its political orientation during and after the war, depended on the victory of one or the other side.

The failure of Giraud's movement between June and October 1943 created frustrations still quite present—as we saw in the preceding chapter—for this defeat left once and for all the way clear for General de Gaulle, and it was to mark the whole history of France after 1945. That is what accounts for present-day accusations claiming that de Gaulle was nothing but a puppet manipulated by the Soviets, and that he supposedly granted his support to the USSR because the English and the Americans gave him theirs only grudgingly (which is true, especially in the case of the Americans, since the United States supported the alternative offered by Giraud up until its final failure). In this partisan rereading of history, Jean Moulin presented an ideal profile for the part of the liaison agent "sent by Moscow."[48] But these observations are ignoring an observed fact, which is backed up by a great many historians and even more by archives (and not only those of the "KGB"): namely, that the Gaullist strategy, which consisted of taking the Communists into the fold in order to keep better control over them, did in fact allow France to avoid situations comparable to those which occurred—in other national contexts—in Greece or in Yugoslavia.[49] This had been exactly one of the main tasks of Jean Moulin; the accusations made against him after fifty years are therefore pointless.

An Acknowledgment of Debt

This current anti-Gaullist front brings together those who long for a return to Pétainism, those who are champions of free enterprise while strongly attached to the NATO alliance, and those who are former Stalinists: in other words, all those who have always been bothered by Gaullism and who could not bear to compete with it. Paradoxically, this front feeds on obsessively keeping alive our Vichy past, which is of origins that, in other contexts, these people condemn, but which in this case indisputably provides them an opening: "It only made sense that by constantly viewing our past as a garbage sack full of base and cowardly deeds, people end up striking those who opposed these actions," writes Paul Thibaud.[50] Speaking of today, he adds:

> What has been most censured in our national memory of the war years is not Vichy, the National Revolution, the Milice, all of which are used as punching balls, it is rather Gaullism, that is to say, the recovery that we enjoyed and in which we have trouble believing. The bothersome thing about that episode is that it makes us feel just how much we are indebted. Perhaps one could even claim that a good deal of France's history since the war can be explained by the difficulty the French people have had in taking responsibility for this debt that was contracted in 1940.[51]

Memory has thus turned away from the Resistance somewhat. If it has proved itself fickle toward great figures on the pretext that it no longer wanted any of the mythologies of the past, it has proved itself even more unjust toward the early Resistance, which had been kept in the dark by the Gaullist epic. Today, it is being rediscovered little by little, just as we are rediscovering to what extent "the" Resistance was not something homogeneous.

These initial forms of resistance still appear mysterious, in that they confronted an indescribable despair: the certainty that the Third Reich was going to extend its domination over Europe throughout many decades. "When everything seemed lost, committing oneself to Resistance was nothing less than an act of faith, a bet in which there was nothing to gain."[52] At that time, the act of resistance meant a commitment made out of principle, undertaken for the sake of values and not for a practical outcome sought out of common sense, as would often be the case in 1943 and 1944. Such resistance action was heroic, isolated, and above all, resulted from a whole series of individual actions often transcending traditional collective commitments. Crossing over into resistance often meant breaking with one's family and friends, at any rate making a person run considerable risks; the first Resistance organizations in the occupied zone were decimated by Nazi repression. To enter into resistance was to enter into a world where no one knew the rules, except for Communist activists, who were already trained in clandestine activity. Even in London,[53] very few people came on board in the beginning, as the leader of the Free French often said and repeated. He was expecting diplomats and officers, and he wound up above all with mere soldiers, a few intellectuals, and political activists who had broken away from their party, not to mention those anonymous individuals who have in some cases become legendary figures. General de Gaulle had been one of the very few members of the upper classes to have refused the conditions of the armistice, which the politicians in general had in their majority accepted. He was also one of the very few people who, from beginning to end, had had a planetary view of the conflict. For that reason, he had for a long time been alone, having to fight constantly just to exist and to get his point of view finally and belatedly accepted. Daniel Cordier's book has helped to reevaluate once again (if it were necessary) the lucidity and the political intelligence that were those of the one who created the Free French and of Jean Moulin, who was the ally and servant of that strategy.

The revolt of those who resisted at the very beginning, for the most part young people, also originated from this breaking of social ties, from this vacuum created by the collapse of France, social ties that Vichy would try to rebuild around the "mystical body" of Marshall Pétain. The usual social and political channels had been put in a state of upheaval: "When institutions no longer function, when it is impossible for the common people to express itself, history nevertheless does not stop and the heavy responsibility for political values falls directly upon the shoulders of individuals. Individual personalities, who are always present but are usually held in balance by the rule of law, appear to make the law and to rule directly by their own will."[54]

Thus various movements and networks rubbed elbows with each other, as later, in prisons and camps, did aristocrats, upper-class people, and workers: French Jews and foreign Jews, Spaniards, anti-Nazi Germans, Armenians, and others, some of whom saw in the Resistance the sacred duty of the nation's elite while others saw the form that the international proletarian movement should ultimately take on. While they did not all stand up against Pétain in the beginning, the first resisters were in agreement in stating by their actions, even if desperate and to no avail, that the "reconstruction" of France advocated by Vichy was not to happen until the top priority —driving out the occupying forces—had been reached. The context of clandestine activity shook up social hierarchies and removed young people, women, foreigners, and those without diplomas from the subjection in which they had been held in the rigid society that France had been in 1940. The nucleus of a new group of leaders was formed in the state of social weightlessness; those who survived are even today full of nostalgia about this time. This nostalgia, being a matter of feeling, is especially strong since, for some, it is mixed with the regret of not having had the chance, or not having managed, to create the "great party of the Resistance" that they had dreamed of during their clandestine life. On that score, the highly individualistic nature of resistance action perhaps explains why, at the time of the Liberation, a political agenda that would have truly reflected the values of the Resistance failed to materialize. This logic of individualism had been too quickly swept away by traditional partisan issues and the logic of party politics; it is easier to rise above one's habits in wartime than in peacetime.

France's complex thus resides just as much in its difficulty in assuming the responsibility for Vichy as in the difficulty of admitting that the Resistance, the national myth, not only had been the accomplishment of a small number of people, but even more so of outstanding *individuals*. The failure was that of the state; social, political, and economic leaders; and of the nation's institutions. They bore the main responsibility for it, before the work of General de Gaulle and of his delegate Jean Moulin began reviving this very state. In 1940, not one single social group, not one political party, not one collective unit called for resistance. The first refusal of the armistice and resignation was expressed through spontaneous, individual appeals (such as the "Manifesto" of Henri Frenay, whose "National Liberation Movement" was comprised of only a handful of individuals at the time). That is why it is still hard, even today, for most political parties, the Catholic Church, the universities, and professional associations to articulate their memory of this era *as groups*. Since none came out of this ordeal unscathed, none can escape from the feeling of guilt, except by celebrating the memory of a few exceptional men and women, whose names adorn commemorative plaques in public places, but who, in final analysis, were acting only of their own accord at that time.

The other side of the "Vichy syndrome" is thus this difficulty in acknowledging our debt toward the first resisters, beginning with the most illustrious of them all; this is what Paul Thibaud has called the "Gaullian syndrome." This debt is particularly hard to assume since, in the beginning, it was General de Gaulle *himself* who made a point of writing it off and constructing the myth of a France united against the invader out of his own eloquence and genius. The French, who in their majority had experienced the war in a state of material hardship and as onlookers made more or less sorrowful by their nation's downfall, had no other choice but to accept this honor that had been saved by a few individuals and that, after the fact, General de Gaulle was generously offering to them:

> If a Savior is an authentic hero, a political genius and an artist of history like de Gaulle, his glory shines over everyone and allows them to believe that it is really theirs, and not only his (and Lord knows if de Gaulle, who one day said to one of his collaborators that after June 1940 he had always acted "as if," succeeded in taking advantage of this tendency of the French to believe that they are great through him or because of him, in order to incite them really to achieve this greatness).[55]

The rejection of this myth in the 1970s caused people to forget the nation's debt to General de Gaulle, who was accused by the youngest of having hijacked memory; as a result, they could see only the red ink left by Marshall Pétain and thus discovered that the deficit was staggering. Since then, people have been constantly demanding that the nation balance its accounts and clear up the Vichy deficit. At the same time, they have underestimated the original debt contracted toward the resisters.

The discomfort that the Occupation period still arouses continues to feed off this same original failure, the failure of a myth that claimed to cover and redeem a collective sin, in other words, a secular form of "indulgence."[56] But the absence of indulgence for the war generation that those generations (including our own) born after the war have displayed cannot and must not cause people to forget that the time of total dereliction into which the nation had sunk was redeemed by the glory of a few rebels. Admittedly, these heroes did not make up the courageous avant-garde of French social, political, and economic leaders, but rather their guilty conscience—a guilty conscience that we have inherited . . . for having rejected de Gaulle's indulgence.

6

So What Is the Teacher Up To?

In February 1993, a few months after the controversy over the fiftieth anniversary of the Vél' d'Hiv' roundup, the French Jewish Students' Union (UEJF)[1] organized a "Tour of France for Memory" to the sites of the former French internment camps. This initiative, which took on quite an original appearance, had a goal: "to initiate real changes in education." To that end, the UEJF commissioned a study by a communications services company about "the treatment of the Holocaust in history textbooks." In this study, the chapters covering the entire period from 1939 to 1945 in eight of the most widely used textbooks were analyzed. The conclusions reached by this study were stern and even alarming: the coverage of this historical period was limited and teachers were devoting a particularly small amount of time to this historical series of events, which had been put into the history curriculum for the eleventh grade classes since the school year of 1988–1989,[2] but which is no longer tested on the baccalaureate exam.

The tone of the report is set right from the very beginning: "If we went along with the removal of this time in history from the exam that tests knowledge acquired at the lycée, we would be accepting the idea that, in order to be a citizen today, it is not necessary to understand in what sense the Second World War marks something utterly different in this century. That would be relegating the Holocaust to the status of a peripheral event. It would be trivializing that which constitutes the atrocity specific to that war, out of which—by comparison, by redefinition, by reaction—our present-day political commitments have come."[3] Good grief! Since the French Revolution has not been covered on the baccalaureate exam for a long time, have its values thus disappeared from our nation's culture? In a preliminary remark, the report announced: "It is our finding that the history of the Holocaust remains difficult to express and that the discourse in the textbooks too often still bears the mark of these difficulties."[4] With such hypotheses as points of departure, the conclusion was predictable: "The teaching of the Second World War and the Holocaust is problematical, often even ambiguous, at times contradictory and inaccurate, for example, in dealing with numbers."[5] So what in the world is going on in our lycées?

The History Text, A Scapegoat

If such statements were isolated and inconsequential, the study would deserve a shrug of the shoulders at best. But such is not the case. This survey, solemnly turned in to the Minister of National Education and to the influential Association of History and Geography Teachers, reflects almost to the point of caricature the reproaches ritually made about schools, so much so that it cannot be ignored. Certainly, the request made by the UEJF was legitimate per se. The teaching of history is a matter that concerns a common heritage not restricted to the specialists. There is no reason why it should escape criticism, quite the contrary. The observations formulated and the objections pursued by this survey nevertheless constitute a major symptom of the shortcomings and even the risks of a certain current discourse about the history of the last war and the manner of teaching the history of the war.

In face of such a radical judgment, we can, to begin with, ask a number of questions about the very relevance of the indicator that was chosen: the study of school books. The 1993 survey is not the first nor the last of its type. Debates over teaching this period of history have taken place repeatedly for over ten years. They have periodically occasioned updates and often caused controversies. Most of the time they have focused on history texts, doubtless because these texts can be approached in an immediate and concrete way: all, with just a thin layer of historical learning (acquired, incidentally, in these same middle and high schools that are so berated), are able to exercise their critical talent against them. Certainly it is proper to ask questions about these widely distributed books, since their quality and content can have significant repercussions on the judgment of young people. These queries, however, must be properly focused. The method currently used does indeed have major drawbacks. A textbook stems first of all from a curriculum, which is set out by the national Ministry of Education in close collaboration with various committees of university professors and teachers. Although the textbook by definition complies with the directives, it is nonetheless a singular work realized by authors each having their own sensibility, and marketed by private publishing houses. Each book thus has its differences and its particularities, each one takes a certain viewpoint and makes choices in its treatment, presentation, and selection of the facts; this is a principle of freedom dear to our academic tradition. Still more important is the fact that no textbook has ever reflected the actual subject matter taught in a program of instruction, given by teachers who are also individuals in their own right: most often, they use the text as a guide and tool, not as a bible. Finally, the program of study in all its forms in no way predetermines its real impact on students: its immediate outcome is quite difficult to assess, as is the long-term effect. These are just a few precautions that should be recalled every time people start taking aim at textbooks.

Another preliminary question deserves to be raised: how have both textbooks and programs of instruction evolved over the last few years? This is a point about which the study carried out for the UEJF says nothing. It was in the year 1961–1962 that World War II first appeared as a topic in the lycées, at the end of the eleventh grade, following decisions that had been made a few years earlier but which had not been acted on until then.[6] Beginning in the school year 1965–1966, the period from 1914 to 1945 was placed in the first half of the program of instruction for the final year of the lycée, the other half being devoted to the study of contemporary "civilizations," in the vein of Fernand Braudel. The reform of the 1982–1983 school year introduced a new formula: the contemporary world from 1939 to the present would be studied in the final year of the lycée. Accordingly, World War II was not only placed at the beginning of the year and designated as part of the preparation for the baccalaureate exam, it was also integrated into a new historical sequence which had the "second Twentieth Century" begin not in 1945 (as before) but in 1939. Since the year 1988–1989, the curriculum has again been modified: the time sequence spanning the years from 1890 to 1945 is taught in the eleventh grade, with the war thus being covered at the end of the school year, and the period stretching from 1945 to the present is covered in the final year. It was moreover in the mid-1970s that, thanks to the Haby reform (named after a Minister of Education), the war was put into the new history curriculum for the ninth grade (covering the period from 1914 until the present). It thus took fifteen years from the end of the war for the era to be studied in school, but almost forty years— and the reform of the 1982–1983 school year—for it to become a bona fide subject in the program of instruction.

The beginning of the 1980s marked not only a change of this program, but more important, a fundamental qualitative break, which was unanimously saluted. Until then, the attention devoted to World War II on the level of the lycée was minimal, with some major aspects not even mentioned. Without going back over all of this hefty dossier, let us recall, for example, how the Vichy regime was presented in a textbook representative of those used in the lycée before 1982:

> German laws concerning the Jews were put into effect in the occupied zone, with all of their sinister effects: searches by the Gestapo, arrests, deportations to Germany, concentration camps, horrible atrocities, etc. As for the Vichy government, it set out to shape a "new France" in the zone where its author-

ity was directly exerted [. . .] Three successive phases, it would seem, marked
[the] development [of collaboration] from July 1940 to July 1944. First of all
Pétain, backed by most of the ministers of his government, managed to
thwart the maneuvers of Laval, who was in favor of complete collaboration.
As offensive as it may have been in many respects, the meeting between Marshall Pétain and Hitler at *Montoire* [emphasized in the text] in October 1940,
was nevertheless concluded with evasive statements. The conclusion of this
conflict[7] came about brusquely on December 13: Laval was "fired." During a
second phase, economic and, to a certain extent, even military collaboration,
widened under the influence of Admiral Darlan.[8] In the final phase, the Germans imposed Laval's return to power in April 1942, and from then on collaboration was constantly intensified: it proved to be particularly scandalous
once the "clique" of "Parisian collaborators"—Doriot, Déat, Darnand, Brinon, etc.—imposed its ideas and methods.[9]

Up until recently, most textbooks spread false or extremely vague information about Vichy's anti-Jewish policies: "Little by little, the difficulties
linked to the Nazi regime and the war—undernourishment, anti-Semitic
persecutions, great sums of money levied for the costs of occupation, arrests of patriots, executions of hostages—created increasing irritation."
Similarly: "The dignitaries of the Freemasons and the Jews—under pressure exerted by the Nazis—were subject to a census, and later excluded
from holding employment in the public sector. The Nazi authorities carried out mass arrests of Jews in the occupied zone: 4,000 children from two
to twelve years old arrived in the span of two weeks at Drancy.[10] While the
government remained silent, Pastor Boegner and the Cardinals and Bish-
ops of France protested vigorously."[11]

A few rare textbooks were closer to the historical truth: "Vichy enacted
by itself anti-Semitic legislation of a racial character. On October 3, 1940,
the 'Jews of French nationality' were subject to a statute. They were excluded from the army and from employment in the public sector. A *numerus clausus* limited their number in universities to 3% and in the profes-
sions of law and medicine to 2%. Prefects had the power of interning them;
as of the spring of 1941, 40,000 Jews were behind barbed wire fences."[12]

We will not insult our readers' intelligence (nor that of those who were
lycée students at the time, nor anyone else's) by setting the facts straight for
them, since we take it for granted that the native character of the Vichy
regime, its state anti-Semitism, its choice of a strategy of collaboration,
which was already made in the summer of 1940, and its active complicity
with the Nazis in repressing Resistance forces and persecuting the Jews are
now part of a body of knowledge that has been acquired and is widely
shared, thanks in particular to the progress made in our schools over the
last ten years.

Indeed, current textbooks for the eleventh year highlight the history of World War II. They thus comply with directives mandated in 1987, right before the new reform entered into application:

> Directly caused by the totalitarian states, the war closes the first part of the twentieth century and sketches out the contours of the contemporary world. A detailed study of the war is indispensable in view of the program of study for the final year of the lycée [covering the period from 1945 to the present]. A rigorous selection of the facts and precise problematics will make it possible not to get lost in the plethora of events. The war must be analyzed as something revealing: the defeat of 1940 reveals, in mid-century, the state of affairs in France; the genocide reveals the true nature of Nazism.[13]

Currently, textbooks devote between 6 and 15 percent of their contents to this event. In order to appreciate the significance of this portion, let us recall that the program of instruction deals, in addition to the time stretching from 1939 to 1945, with a period that includes the history of the main great powers (including Japan), the end of the nineteenth century and the birth of the twentieth century, World War I, the advent of the Soviet Union and Communism, international relations between the two wars, the worldwide economic crisis, Nazism, fascism, Stalinism, and France in the 1930s. All these overviews are necessary even if one intended to deal just with World War II . . .

Monitoring the current health of middle schools and lycées required that we go beyond the well-traveled roads and not limit ourselves to laudable official intentions, nor only to textbooks, as meritorious as they might be. We therefore questioned men and women directly involved, that is to say some sixty active teachers, asking them about their teaching practice, their difficulties, their expectations, and their overall assessment of this program of instruction (see questionnaire in box). This is in no way a "poll," but a deliberately empirical survey, from which we hoped to obtain a qualitative advantage because of its individualized nature and not because of abstract average percentages. The enthusiasm with which most of the teachers we contacted responded shows that the subject still poses certain problems, but perhaps not for the reasons suggested in the study commissioned by the UEJF.

The Teaching of World War II in Middle Schools and Lycées

Our survey was conducted between November 1993 and February 1994 by sending a written questionnaire to some sixty middle school and lycée teachers. We deliberately avoided the usual channels (of associations and unions), for we were looking for individual, spontaneous, and informal responses to a questionnaire that was intentionally succinct (with only a dozen questions). Half of the responses come from regional correspondents of the Institut d'Histoire du Temps Présent (IHTP)[14] who, as researchers, periodically work on these issues (they are identified in the text as "respondents"). They constitute a special group which is particularly crucial and interesting for the study, since they all have an excellent knowledge of the era and have reflected on it for a long time and have often been among the first in their schools to point out shortcomings and problems in the teaching of World War II. The other half is made up of some of their colleagues to whom they conveyed the questionnaire or of teachers who were directly contacted by us. Slightly less than half of the sample teach only ninth grade classes and a slight majority teach eleventh grade or the final year of the lycée. The great majority teach in schools in the provinces, covering some forty regional departments randomly scattered over the entire territory of mainland France. Big cities, including greater Paris, are for once largely underrepresented. The average age is about forty, which translates into about fifteen years of experience, but all generations are present, from beginning to retired teachers. Finally, the sample is for the most part predominantly masculine. The list of teachers who responded is given in the "Acknowledgments" section at the beginning of this book.

Questionnaire Sent to a Cross Section of Teachers
(November 1993)

Name:
Age (optional):
Teaching Location (regional department):
Level(s) Taught In Recent Years:

1) Do you feel that this curriculum has changed in nature over the last ten years, with respect either to the contents of textbooks and programs of instruction or to the reaction of teachers in general, students, and parents?

2) Would you say, for example, that this period is covered better than before or not? What about at the qualitative level? What about the quantitative level, in other words its place in the program of instruction and within the curriculum?

3) Do the recurring complaints about the "meager" amount of attention given to this period in the secondary school curriculum seem warranted in your opinion?

4) Do you yourself devote a substantial amount of attention to this subject when you have the task of teaching it or are you caught up in the pace of the syllabus and the exams? Does this period provide opportunities for activities outside of the classroom or joint activities with other teachers more readily than other periods of history?

5) What textbooks do you prefer to use, and what do you think of the way in which they deal with this period? Do certain taboos, silences, and unexplored subjects still exist, or are there on the contrary some topics that are given too much attention? In short, do you think that the treatment of the facts is balanced—if not "objective"—in view of your own knowledge of the period as an historian?

6) What are the expectations of students on these issues? Do you find their curiosity, on the one hand, and their ignorance or persistent clichés, on the other, greater, the same, or less than for other periods of contemporary history?

7) Does the continual presence of this era (trials, commemorations, scandals) in the news, particularly on TV, have an effect on your teaching or on the reaction of students and their parents? If yes, what?

8) What do you think of certain ministerial directives of a topical nature (systematic broadcast of certains films such as *Night and Fog*, ad hoc lessons . . .) in face of a current event linked to the memory of the Occupation: the Barbie trial, the dismissal of charges against Paul Touvier, the death of René Bousquet? Does the Ministry of National Education seem to you to be in step with what you feel would be suitable in order to make school students sensitive to these issues?

9) What do you think of the National Resistance and Deportation academic contest? Do your students participate in it?

10) In your region, have subjects touching on the war often appeared on the baccalaureate exam in recent years? With what results? (Were they too difficult, too hot to handle, poorly prepared, or on the contrary in step with the content of the program of instruction?)

11) You yourself are a specialist on these questions and thus you certainly give more attention to the importance given to World War II in the curriculum. Do you have the impression that your colleagues might respond to this questionnaire in the same way? (If the occasion arises, you may of course convey it to them.)

12) Miscellaneous comments.

Five questions dealt more or less with the developments of the last few years, as most of our respondents had been either witnesses or directly involved in them. Has the teaching of World War II changed in nature over the last ten years? There were 38 out of 58 who unhesitatingly answered "yes," with the opposite opinion being rare, and with a mixed assessment given by a minority. Almost all observed that the teaching of this period deals less with the military aspects—some were sorry that this was the case, because the subject is of great interest to young male students—than with the political and ideological aspects of the war. All observed considerable progress in dealing with the history of Vichy, Collaboration, the persecution of the Jews by the French State, and the Genocide in general. What did they think of present-day textbooks? The vast majority had a good opinion of them: those published by Hachette, Belin, and Hatier—which were part of the cross section used in the study commissioned by the UEJF—were the most often cited. A majority of teachers answered "no" to the question about the persistence of "taboos" or "silences": "Over the last few years, we have seen a net increase in the amount of attention given to Vichy's responsibility for anti-Semitic measures," notes Geneviève Gauf-fillet, from a middle school in the Seine-et-Marne region. "We seem to have come a long way since the time when, for having used Paxton's recently published book [*Vichy France: Old Guard and New Order*, translated into French in 1973], an inspector general advised me to be 'careful,'" remembers Gérard Boeldieu, who teaches in a lycée of the Sarthe region. He remarks moreover that the period extending from 1939 to 1945 has become "central" and "impossible to get around."

Several respondents, however, pointed out omissions. There were a large number who regretted the over-hasty treatment of the purge. This omission fits into the framework of the general tendency that we have already pointed out in this book. Other teachers regretted the meager amount of attention given to the French Empire during the war (which was of crucial strategical importance for both Vichy and de Gaulle's Free France movement), to economic questions, to the role of the Catholic Church, and to other theaters of operations (the war in the Pacific, for example). While Vichy's internment camps, which have been at the heart of recent issues of memory, are very widely covered in textbooks, few texts mention the camps created in 1939 by the Third Republic in order to "take in" Spanish republicans and other "undesirable aliens," in particular German and Austrian anti-fascist refugees. The demands of teachers thus no longer bear on the necessity of filling in the lapses of memory that existed twenty years ago, but rather on the desire not to create any others, to refine the presentation of the facts, and to bring out the complexity of the period. These teachers are very consciously part of an intellectual current that has attempted not only to bring this history out of oblivion and to combat all sorts of ideological "revisionisms," but also—and this is at times forgotten —to counter a Manichean view of things and strident oversimplifications. Moreover, these demands are possible today because the "hard-core" elements of this history now enjoy substantial coverage in textbooks, which are judged to be quite objective and balanced by most responses.

Test Fetishism

Is this era better covered or not? Almost all the responses show the same tendency: yes, the coverage of this era—in textbooks, in the curriculum, and thus its impact on students—has clearly improved on the qualitative level since the 1960s and 1970s. It nevertheless experienced a relative decline from a quantitative viewpoint since the last reform, compared to the school years 1982–1983 and 1988–1989. The fact that the coverage of this era was moved to the end of the year for eleventh grade classes and that it was removed from the final year reduced the amount of time that teachers and students devoted to it. That is the only point on which the responses to our questionnaire agree with the study commissioned by the UEJF, without, however, falling into the alarmist discourse cited above.[15]

Having made this observation, we should, however, given our teachers' responses, point out nuances on several points. First of all, those expressing disappointment were almost exclusively lycée teachers. Middle school teachers hardly ever criticized the amount of attention given to the war in their curriculum, and for a very good reason: it is already overloaded. Second, some teachers rightly reminded us that, during their entire academic career, middle and high school students deal with the subject three times, at least theoretically: in the ninth grade, in the eleventh grade (at the end of the year, within the cycle of the years extending from 1890 to 1945), and in the final year, since the program of instruction begins with a global assessment of the year 1945. Contrary to what is widely claimed to be the case by many (including the study commissioned by the UEJF), part of the subject does indeed appear on the baccalaureate exam and has been tested in recent years. In this respect, the notion of "global assessment" should generally be understood rather loosely and should, for example, include the issue of the human cost, and accordingly, the nature and the consequences of the Genocide.

Similarly, not everyone agrees as to what extent the exam stimulates learning about the subject: this is a point that the study commissioned by the UEJF takes for granted, echoing the repeated complaints made by associations of former resisters and deportees. Roger Falcon, who teaches in a lycée in the Haute-Garonne regional department, asserts on the contrary that, in the eleventh grade, with the World War II era placed on the syllabus toward the end of the school year, there is "a greater leeway given to students and teachers," since there is no exam coming up (except for the French test[16]) and therefore less tension than in the final year. He adds,

however, that many teachers "sacrifice the end of the syllabus," a tendency
that has been aggravated by the reduction of the program of instruction for
history and geography from four hours to three hours a week in certain
curricula.[17] Jeannie Bauvois points out that the complaint about the "disap-
pearance" of the war from the baccalaureate exam and its placement at the
end of the eleventh-grade curriculum is based on a series of erroneous, but
widely held, assumptions, namely: "Teachers do not get to the end of their
syllabus; this matter is not a priority for them; one only retains well what
one has to learn for an exam."[18] Now, as for the last assertion, and whatever
the period studied may be, the history questions included in the programs
of instruction for the baccalaureate exam often are covered only in a factual
manner in order to provide candidates with the bare minimum that will
save them from disaster. To prove the point, all one has to do is to cite
some of the test questions given between 1987 and 1989, when the war was
still on the syllabus for the bac: "The World in 1939," "The World at War
from 1942 to 1943," "The World in 1945," "Resistance and Resisters in
Europe (1939–1945)," "The French Resistance," and so on, for the essay
questions. As for the textual commentary questions, they most often dealt
with excerpts of speeches or declarations by political figures (Pétain, Laval,
Churchill, and the like). These are all topics which are by definition not
conducive to deep reflection, which is not the purpose of an exam such as
the baccalaureate.[19] In the eleventh grade, however, in spite of the small
amount of time allotted, teachers have the time to make the students reflect
on the underlying issues instead of just cramming their heads with dates
and statistics that will be forgotten just as quickly as they have been learned.
The debate is thus far from being settled.

A more judicious assessment of the relative importance of the baccalaureate exam should moreover take other elements into consideration. First,
only one out of three students actually studies history in the final year of the
lycée, since not all sections offer this subject as a choice in the curriculum.
The problem thus concerns only a minority of lycée students, and criticism
should therefore deal not with the presence of World War II on the baccalaureate exam, but instead with the total absence of history from the curriculum of the majority of those students about to get their baccalaureate
degree. Second, these issues have already been tested, since they appear on
the exam given at the completion of the ninth grade, which marks the end
of compulsory schooling.[20] Finally, the exams given at the end of the ninth
year and the final year are not always a guarantee of rigorous pedagogy. If a
subject does not necessarily have to appear on a subsequent exam in order
to be learned, it is true, however, that a subject covered in the context of a
test often marks those who take it. Thus the titles of certain test questions
sometimes deserve as much attention as the content of textbooks or programs of instruction, as witnessed by several recent incidents.

The New Ponthus Incident

Jean-Pierre Ponthus teaches French in Valognes, in the regional department of the Manche. He made a name for himself in 1984 by leading a drive to rename his school, which bears the name of the former mayor of the town, Henri Cornat. Under the Occupation, Cornat, who had been appointed mayor by Vichy after elected city councils had been suspended and replaced by appointed "special delegations," distinguished himself more by his fervent activism for Pétain than by his Resistance activities. These facts had been conveniently forgotten by local people of power and influence who at the time only wanted to remember the courageous attitude of the mayor during the bombardments. That had not prevented him from being suspended when France was liberated. This incident was the opportunity for the lycée teacher to put into practice what was asked in official calls to "the duty to remember." This turned out to be unfortunate for him. In his impassioned commitment, he made a mistake: at the municipal library, he wrote notes in the margins of a book about Cherbourg during the Occupation which also obfuscated the true character of the former mayor. He was taken to court, accused of being "demented" and subjected to psychiatric studies. The incident remained momentarily at that stage.

This showed, among other things, just what difficulties teachers run into locally, especially in small towns in the provinces, where sensitivity to memories of the Occupation remains much higher than in big cities, as we have already pointed out in the chapter devoted to archives. On the local level, collaborators and resisters, Pétainists and Gaullists do not represent abstract universal categories, but concrete memories and faces that everybody can name. Teaching history in these circumstances, as a number of our interlocutors reminded us, is just as tricky as finishing the syllabus on time.

Jean-Pierre Ponthus repeated his transgression a few years later. In 1988, at the June session of the ninth grade exam, in the regional district of Caen, two famous texts which are often compared to each other were placed on the history test: General de Gaulle's call of June 18 and Marshall Pétain's message of June 20, 1940. The presentation of these texts, however, left a few things to desire. In the text of the call, a huge typographical error adulterated the meaning of one of the most famous sentences: "*Even though* it may happen [instead of: *Whatever* may come—emphasis added],[21] the flame of French Resistance must not and will not die out." It was obvious that the faulty wording made no sense. What was more serious, since the texts were not presented in their entirety, was that the cuts made in the body of de Gaulle's text were indicated (but not always) by ellipses without either the parentheses or brackets required. The reader would thus logically have to attribute them to de Gaulle himself. In Pétain's text, nothing indicated that some passages had been whisked away. The cuts made there, however, were not innocuous. In de Gaulle's call of June 18, two essential passages had disappeared: that in which he declared that the conflict, far from being limited to France's own territory, was "a world war" and that in which he urged the French, both military personnel and civilians, to join him in London . . . Nevertheless, students taking the test were asked to explain how de Gaulle saw the future at that time! In Pétain's text, there were also key passages that had been deleted, passages in which he revealed his own interpretation of the defeat: "too few children, too few arms, too few allies," "the spirit of hedonism prevailed over the spirit of sacrifice," and so forth. However, that did not prevent those who composed the test from asking: "What causes does Pétain find for the defeat?"

Outraged by this careless and sloppy presentation, which was hardly a credit to the institution of learning, Jean-Pierre Ponthus filed a motion in the administrative court of Caen to have the exam nullified. He received the support of Pierre Vidal-Naquet and Stéphane Khémis, editor-in-chief of the magazine *L'Histoire*. The latter found what had happened to be "damning" and blamed "the training of primary and secondary school teachers."[22] The historian Dominique Veillon, who is a scholar of the Occupation, likewise protested indignantly such a way of presenting texts: "Pétain appears in this text as a possible recourse (or even a shield) just as effective as de Gaulle. He is draped in a coat of respectability. The way in which de Gaulle's call of June 18 is presented is equally subject to criticism. It is dishonest to have deleted the beginning of the paragraph, in which General de Gaulle clearly indicated that in his view the war was a world war. These two 'documents' thus bear meanings which are distorted and the opposite of what was really being said."[23]

Before the administrative tribunal, the superintendent nevertheless judged that "the clumsy error made in the presentation of the quoted passages [. . .] does not appear to be such that it would skew the thinking of those taking the test." In defense of the Ministry of National Education, he cited the fact that a whole group of teachers, beginning with the regional pedagogical inspector, had not noticed the mistakes! These errors had indeed escaped the attention of the members of the commission charged with developing test questions and checking on their accuracy. "They were not pointed out either by the graders, nor the students, nor the students' parents." The meaning of the texts had thus not "been adulterated even for knowledgeable adults."[24] In other words, once "knowledgeable" adults approve of obvious mistakes, these mistakes become negligible!

Jean-Pierre Ponthus argued on the contrary that this was damaging to respect for the students and the coherency of the curriculum, be it history or grammar. As a French teacher, he recalled that the students who took the test in question had throughout the same year studied the very meaning of ellipsis: there had been pedagogical directives stressing the point. During the same administration of the ninth grade exam, the French test moreover included a text with an ellipsis in brackets. The ninth grade curriculum also teaches students to distinguish between "although" and "whatever."[25] Coincidence would have it that the French textbook used by the students in Valognes had as an example General de Gaulle's famous phrase which was to appear in a defective form on the test. Jean-Pierre Ponthus concluded that this was enough to "skew thinking and confuse" young students and that the public education system was not fulfilling its role.[26]

Hardly anxious to continue the debate in this area, the regional superintendent Pierre Lostis requested in October 1989 that the Ministry of National Education put an end to "the unacceptable situation created by this teacher"[27] as soon as possible. The request was not granted by the Ministry. On May 7, 1991, the Administrative Tribunal of Caen rejected Jean-Pierre Ponthus's request for the annullment for technical reasons (he should have contested the test committee's decision for all of the exams). The Conseil d'État was to confirm this ruling on July 23, 1993.

This is a textbook example of how the transmission of knowledge that occurs in schools involves a complex chain in which multiple players intervene. The whole process is subjected to social and political pressures, to local situations varying greatly from one region to the next, and to the influence of various personal and institutional factors. An in-depth study would doubtless show just how frequent this type of malfunction is. In the long run, it would probably stem less from the problematical nature of the history and memory of the war than from certain inflexibilities of France's school system. This is at any rate what has come out of our own investigation, even at a relatively limited level.

An Overcharged Period of History

We have tried to give an accurate assessment of two other clichés pointed out by Jeannie Bauvois, in addition to the one dealing with the sacrosanct examination: the allegation that teachers do not finish their syllabus and that, for them, the period of World War II is not a priority. While on the one hand a large number of teachers polled in our survey mentioned the acrobatics they had to do in order to get to the point of beginning the study of the war at the end of the eleventh grade in spite of a hectic schedule, clearly all of them consciously give it prime importance: they spend from at least five to ten hours of class time, and even more in some cases, on this subject. Moreover, the most determined to teach the subject are not always those serving as correspondents of the IHTP (which comprise half of those surveyed), who, since they are a priori highly motivated, are not representative in this area.

On the subject of how much time is allotted to the war in the curriculum, another and probably more decisive point deserves to be made. No other era besides the history of World War II has been the subject of such special attention outside of the formal hours of classroom instruction. The war often appears in the context of the "educative action projects," known as "10%." Some of these projects have recently even given rise to remarkable first-hand work, such as the study carried out by Maryvonne Braunschweig and her students in the middle school of Avon (a town in the Seineet-Marne regional department where the story told by Louis Malle in his 1987 film *Au Revoir, Les Enfants* took place).[28]

Added to that are the usual enjoinders made by ministers of National Education (both from the Left and from the Right), eager to display their faithfulness to the duty to remember. Periodically, on the occasion of an anniversary commemoration or a large-scale scandal (such as the profanation of the Jewish cemetery in Carpentras in 1990, or the dismissal of charges against Touvier in 1992), a multitude of memoranda request that teachers sensitize their students to these issues. In general, the cabinets of government ministers do not have much imagination: they ask lycées and middle schools to screen without delay *Night and Fog*, the film by Alain Resnais, which is admirable but dated (made in 1955) and often poorly suited to the facts that are to be explained or recalled. But it has become almost a conditioned reflex to have recourse to this brief documentary.[29]

What do the teachers think of these directives? All responded to the question at length. A clear majority stated that they had reservations about the very idea of such directives and about such hierarchical commands: "They should let us do our work not with directives but with our conscience and away from all the media commotion; only in this way will it be possible to conduct serious study," responded Michel Chaumet, a correspondent from the Deux-Sèvres regional district, who, like many of his colleagues, thought that in such circumstances the Ministry of National Education was not at all in tune with the teachers. While all do not condemn these initiatives, which nevertheless encroach on their freedom of action (Rémy Gaudillier, a respondent from the Jura, stated that he felt wary of teaching on order), many criticized their artificiality, which is too closely linked to the fleeting, fast-changing developments of current events and even tainted with ideology. The main difficulty for the teachers is not that of explaining every three months who are Paul Touvier and René Bousquet, but that of teaching the whole historical era of Vichy and the Collaboration in its historical logic and continuity. As for the morally edifying nature of Alain Resnais's film—which perhaps was not worthy of such heavy-handed use—the two following reactions are worth contemplating: "For twenty years, I showed *Night and Fog* to students who had been made sensitive by what had happened to people; for the first time, this year [1993–1994], I will not screen it, because the students watch this documentary like a film of Stallone; now that violence has been made commonplace by movies, from now on, I will choose written testimony" (from Madame Jeannet, a teacher in the Saône-et-Loire regional department). Gilbert Beaubatie, a respondent from the Corrèze regional department (he teaches in Tulle), describes "in just what state of mind" he had to deal with his class after one of his colleagues in French, who was complying with sudden directives that had come from the Ministry of National Education, had screened Resnais's film for them during the preceding period, without the slightest preparation.

Finally, let us recall that the National Resistance and Deportation Contest, created in 1964, always mobilizes many lycées and middle schools which have their best students participate, even if the contest seems a bit outmoded these days. Every year, a ministerial commission, which includes representatives from various associations of resisters and deportees, defines a general theme, which is then examined at the level of the regional districts by commissions composed of both resisters and teachers. Each regional department thus defines different subjects, both for students in the eleventh and final grades, as well as for the students in the ninth grade and in the vocational schools. This latter group moreover has the opportunity to deal with the subject either individually or collectively. For example, in the Saône-et-Loire regional department, in 1972, the contest mobilized 57 schools and 542 contestants. In 1990, it interested only 32 schools and 423 students, most of them in the ninth grade.[30]

The major interest of this contest is first of all memorial. It allows young students, whose parents were for the most part born after 1945, to meet protagonists of the war years, who for years have constantly toured schools to give personal testimony and to explain the difficulties of resistance or the horror of deportation. This contest is moreover followed with particular interest by lycées and middle schools located in "sites that have been martyred," in the words of Jeanne Gillot-Voisin, who explained that the cities or towns the hardest hit by repression during the Occupation are those in which one observes the best results in the contest. The interest is equally pedagogical in that, for the contest, teachers and students study original sources, testimony, archives, and press articles from the era.

Questioned about their interest in this contest, our teachers responded in a varied manner. The respondents with the IHTP were particularly in favor of it, since they are often in charge of organizing or grading it in their regional districts. On the whole, the contest maintains a positive rating among teachers: "It is the chance to engage in research with documents about a topic that is still sensitive today for families in rural areas, who still

approach it through oral tradition and rumor!" notes Jean-Paul Thibaudeau, from the middle school in Éguzon (in the Indre regional department). Many stress that it is a chance to introduce young students to the ag-
onies and ecstasies of historical research . . . even when they scarcely have
the time to engage in it themselves. The lack of time and the high level of
work required indeed discourage most teachers, inasmuch as that in the
end, they are the ones who do most of the work and compose texts that
sometimes become "veritable deluxe master's theses" intended to impress
the panel of judges favorably, remarked Jean-Pierre Besse, a respondent
from the Oise regional department.

Does this thirty-year-old ritual, which has scarcely changed in terms of
format or type of topics assigned, appeal to the younger generation? Jean-
Louis Laubry, twenty-nine, from the middle school in Issoudun, expressed
a major disagreement with the very principle of a contest of this sort: "Resistance and Deportation are subjects that are essential to the education of
the future citizens who are now ninth grade students, and these topics are
given special attention during the [school] year." But he added: "Middle
school principals often make it into an issue of prestige for their school
(with articles and photos in the regional or local newspaper)." Is it then a
superfluous initiative or a necessary tradition? An issue of local pride or of
remembering martyrs? Marc Bergère, thirty, a respondent from the Maine-
et-Loire regional department, gave this response: "The contest offers a restrictive view of the era, and looking exclusively at the Resistance can lead
to a tendency close to 'resistancialism.'[31] Nevertheless, while the teacher in
me is wary, the contest does have certain virtues: I happen to be on the regional department's panel of judges and my students often participate in
the contest. Indeed, it is a chance to call on witnesses, to demonstrate the
complexity of the era, to testify to the difficulty of committing oneself to
resist, and to reflect on what can be decisive for making such a choice in
such an exceptional period of history."

Finally, it can be pointed out that for a short time now there has been a
new prize, the "Annie and Charles Corrin Prize for the Teaching of the
History of the Shoah," which was created by the United Jewish Social
Fund, and sponsored by the Ministry of National Education. Awarding two
prizes annually, it rewards works by teachers or students, educative action
projects, pedagogical efforts to spread historical information, and initiatives by associations. Here again, the study of this historical period is
clearly encouraged and supported outside of the classroom itself.

Civic History, Critical History

Are then the complaints about schools justified, when all is said and done?
A majority of our respondents answered no, and vehemently so: "These

complaints seem to me to be rather out of date, improper, and even mali-
cious, in other words unjustified," wrote Gilbert Beaubatie. Alain Monchablon, a respondent from the Val-de-Marne regional department, spoke of
"ritual indignation." Some twenty teachers did nevertheless answer affirmatively, most often while at the same time expressing a sort of guilty feeling. Were they doing enough? Would it be better if this subject were
moved back to the beginning of the syllabus for the final year? But in that
case, wondered some teachers, how would it be possible to teach properly a
chronological sequence—that of our "present time"—which by definition
grows ever longer and must include the most recent and the most burning
topics in history, which concern other equally urgent issues?[32]

In reality, as long as it bears on the question of whether there is "too
much" or "too little" attention given to this era within the history curriculum, the current debate does not make much sense. The real question lies
elsewhere: for what reasons should it now be granted special attention,
given that it is henceforth no more or less adequately taught than other eras
and that it has even become the object of individual and institutional em-
phases that are rather unique in their domain: the teachers' motivations,
ministerial directives, and the National Resistance and Deportation Contest? The question may seem to be a sacrilege and very politically incorrect,
but it deserves to be posed clearly:

> Although I cannot prove it, I personally have the feeling that this part of the
> curriculum is a sort of an island, an aerolite with respect to the rest of the cur-
> riculum: relatively isolated from previous historical developments (ideally,
> we should situate the beginning on January 30, 1933), and isolated from the
> aftermath of the war by the historical break of the Cold War, it forces us into
> a sudden reemphasis on moral and civic instruction, and within this island
> there is another island, the extermination of the European Jews. How is it
> possible to historicize without becoming a Nolte?

So writes Alain Monchablon, perfectly capturing the whole problem in a
nutshell. The allusion to Ernst Nolte, a conservative revisionist with whom
the great quarrel of German historians broke out in 1986, is not just a simple provocation. It refers to one of the major issues of this dispute, which
has been more heated in Germany than in France, namely the "historicization" (from the German *Historisierung*) of the Nazi era and World War II,
in other words the possibility of writing history with the detachment, rigor,
and critical perspective inherent in all scholarly analysis without lapsing
into relativization or implicit rehabilitation. We have been dealing with
this problem throughout this very book. If it comes up in teaching, it is because, on a higher scholarly level, historians have been posing themselves
the question for several years. The recent transformation of the historiog-

raphy of Vichy and the Occupation, which has progressed in the direction of digging up the truth, has inevitably been accompanied by a similar process touching on untouchable subjects, such as the history of the Resistance or of the Genocide. It is easier to undertake a quest for truth when one is attacking the executioners than when one is taking an in-depth look at the history of heroes or victims; the recent "Aubrac Affair," in 1997, is a good example of this problem. It is easier to remain within the comfort of an activist discourse—everyone or just about everyone agrees on identifying Nazism as an absolute evil—than it is to sensitize students to the tremendous complexity of such an era. This, however, does not work the same way in school as it does in university colloquia: a teacher cannot simply be content to state that "it is more complicated than people think." The teacher has to explain.

The difficulty is not just a matter of sensitivity and tact. The subject raises questions of an ethical nature. Does not the necessity of presenting history with critical distance, in non-Manichean manner, and set in the context of a long historical continuum run the risk of making tragic events lose their symbolic value and their "irreducible" richness and depth? Is not this a manner of chipping away at our moral values, that were painfully and incompletely rebuilt after Auschwitz? Teachers are on the firing line here. On the one hand, they can only relay the evolution, the difficulties, and even the hesitations and errors of an historiography that is constantly changing and set within its own time: and it is this historiography that has a heavy influence on the content of history texts and classes. On the other hand, teachers are charged with a heavy responsibility toward adolescents of various different sensitivities, cultural backgrounds, and social milieux. These young people are especially interested once this part of the curriculum is begun, but for most of them, World War II is often just as far removed as is the time of Louis XIV or that of Napoleon. This is a point that comes up over and over again in our survey. At the slightest misstep, the teacher risks running into a disaster. For example, several teachers pointed out to us the difficulties they had in dealing with students expressing negationist views, in general less out of personal conviction than out of a desire to stand out and be "nonconformists," as they say in the coded jargon of the extreme Right. Should teachers go back over Faurisson's arguments in order better to take them apart? Should the issue of the Genocide, admittedly a central one, then be given excessive attention, with the risk of making students miss the overall coherence of the period being studied? Generally speaking, the moral "efficacy" of a class on the Genocide is pretty much agreed upon. Adolescents often have trouble grasping the meaning and deeper usefulness of the study of history. They approach history from their present experience. "Children have been made very sensitive to problems dealing with xenophobia, racism, and anti-Semitism, to the point of transposing their present perception of the issues into the historical period under study, and that weakens their ability to pay attention to other aspects of the subject, as well as their ability to analyze," observes Jean-Henri Calmon, a respondent from the Vienne regional department. In other words, not only is the issue inherently a delicate one, but also it is a source of confusion if students do not understand the dividing line between the "lessons of history" and anachronism. But how can they if adults, who are nevertheless "better informed," constantly use this past for their own ends and stumble into the pitfall of anachronism before their eyes?

In this regard, it is worthwhile to return briefly to the survey commissioned by the UEJF, since it is the textbook example of such a tendency. While pointing out the historical specificity of World War II, the report rules out the possibility of viewing the subject with critical distance. The author of the report even constantly criticizes the massive use of written and iconographic raw documents in history textbooks (which make up half of their present content).[33] And she does not hesitate to drive home a few of her heartfelt epistemological truths: "What characterizes these events is precisely the fact that they are not subject to dispute: beyond historical truth, there is about them an ideological truth in response to the ideology that brought them about."[34] Farther down, she adds: "Again, there is a danger in opening the debate on this subject, in failing to make it clear that socially there is a way of thinking concerning the Genocide and that this discussion necessarily becomes ideological."[35] One might think that this continual reference to a fixed body of knowledge, to a "definitive" history of the subject, which would describe this "social way of thinking" the event—which, moreover, the author of the report is hard put to spell out—concerns only the history of the Genocide. Throughout its seventy-seven pages, the report actually advocates approaching the *entire* history of the war uniquely from this angle, in pointing to the fact that "social discourse even now still tends to regard the Second World War as specific and different in that it is attributable largely to the coming to power of one man (Hitler) and to his demented racism (anti-Semitism)."[36] Having built up a head of steam, the author does not stop there: she goes on to venture a look at other aspects of the period. Two textbooks suffer from the weakness of presenting contradictory texts from the era under the titles: "Armistice or Surrender?" and "For or against Collaboration?" This is a serious mistake according to the author: for in her view, "this is giving lycée students the job of judging and deciding how these issues should be thought through."[37] And by the way, how about the teacher? If we are to believe the report, teachers seem to be nothing but helpless spectators. It is almost as if we could imagine them tallying up the score between groups of students, suddenly disguised as either Reynaud, Pétain, or Weygand and fighting it out tooth and nail in the back of the class, as did the real protagonists in the château of Cangey![38]

Yes, we feel like saying to this communications specialist, the French are nowadays all (except for a tiny minority) in favor of the Resistance instead of Collaboration and, if it were explained to them, all would doubtless choose (military) surrender over (political) armistice: they are not crazy, since they know what happened afterward! However, all these moving words can take nothing away from the fact that these questions were actually "debated." Indeed, these debates were crucial and painful, and were actually the most important for the French at that time, much more than the question of anti-Semitism. This is precisely the most important task facing all historians, both in research and in teaching: to recreate the atmosphere of those times and to make it understandable to minds that are steeped in an entirely different mental universe. You could not find a better example of the gap between moral debate and historical debate. You could not find a better illustration of our present dilemma: should this period of history be used in place of a civics course or should it be used as a chance to introduce critical thinking?

> More than the study of institutions as such, the work done on the Second World War seems to me indispensable to educating students in civics. It is a special moment in which they perceive rather clearly the impact of choosing and the personal dimension of political commitment, which are inseparable from the notion of citizenship, especially for them, who are not interested (or so little interested) in politics and who never view social change as something that can stem from a political decision stemming from a collective choice to which they can contribute as individuals.

So writes Jean-Louis Laubry. This remark is particularly interesting inasmuch as it was made by a very young teacher. However, one of the most important findings of our survey was that this period of history provides the chance to view the education of students in civics not only in terms of moral values, but also in terms of reflection on their own social environment.

One of the questions asked in our survey dealt with the impact of current events, scandals, judicial investigations, and stormy commemorations. What effect does the incessant reactivation of memory have on classes, student reactions, and possibly on parent reactions? What role does television play? What about its "pedagogical virtues," touted by certain programs? "Young people are impervious to current events: one image takes the place of another, having the effect of a kaleidoscope with no assimilation," writes Nadia Michel, a respondent from the Seine-Saint-Denis regional department. Students, especially lower class students, do not watch the celebrated "educational programs" of the type such as *La Marche du siècle*. "No more than 5 percent [of ninth-grade students] are interested in the news on television. Fewer still read the (local) newspaper. The only ones who have any interest in political events are often just interested in *The Clowns in the News* (*Guiguols de l'info*, a very popular TV show similar to *Spitting Images*). What is more, the constant presence of this historical period in the news has no effect on either the students' or the parents' reaction," observes Jean-Louis Laubry. Parents are furthermore the ones most obviously missing from this survey: apparently for lack of sufficient contact with them, teachers often do not know what reaction they have with respect to these problems. Finally, and this is perhaps the most serious problem, the presence of the past in the news, as perceived by students, leads—and this is not surprising—to the formation of new clichés, and thus makes it necessary for the teacher to go back over the subject or to study it in greater detail.

Nevertheless, given the attention it receives in the media and the debates that it still stirs up, the World War II period makes it possible to give depth and richness to history in a concrete way: "Current events have as their primary virtue that of giving a justification for the class (it's important, since it is talked about on TV), and of making it possible to study not in a vacuum but on the basis of knowledge that is already there, and about which it is possible to have discussion go over in detail," writes Bruno Carlier, a young middle-school teacher in the Seine-et-Marne regional department. For the World War II era more than for other periods in history, media coverage of current events makes it possible to use a wider range of material (videos, newspapers, personal testimonies); more than is true for other periods, it offers the possibility of using critical thinking about myths and clichés; more than for other periods, it provides material for reflection on the relation between the past and the present, not in the sense of the "lessons of history," of making the past serve the present, but in the opposite sense, that is, of understanding the past thanks to the present, through a dialectic rich in information.

In other words, whereas ten years ago the war constituted a "black hole" in school, today it makes it possible to teach future citizens the material reality of a political or social "fact," to make them grasp the uncertain nature of raw information (texts or images) and, as a result, to develop students' faculty of judgment, which is the antithesis of foolish calls for official or activist history. Paradoxically, the teaching of the history of this era one way or another leads us back to the primary mission of history in school, which is neither to enlighten students nor to pound them over the head with morals—the French are attached to secular education in every sense of the term—but to give them some keys to understanding the world in which they live.

What are the actual results? It is difficult to tell. Recent surveys conducted on a national level about the interest of young people in these issues and about their knowledge nevertheless provide a few indications. In June 1990 and in September 1992, the SCP company, the one that the UEJF was to ask for the study of textbooks, conducted two almost identical surveys that were commissioned by the Ministry of War Veterans and the Teaching League within the framework of a colloquium held at the Sorbonne about "The Echos of Memory."[39] Questioned about their interest in the history of World War II, in 1990, 58 percent of them were "very much" or "fairly" interested, and in 1992, 71 percent of the group of 15- to 19-year-olds and 67 percent of the 20- to 24-year-olds were either "very much" or "fairly" interested: there was a clear progression. If one evaluates the proportion of "correct answers" to specific historical questions, one observes a contrast between the two surveys, varying according to the questions. In 1990, 38 percent of university and lycée students got the right answer to the question about the number of elected representatives to the parliament having refused to vote for giving full constitutional power to Pétain on July 10, 1940 (there were eighty). In 1992, no more than 17 percent of those between ages 15 and 24 gave the correct answer. In 1990, 63 percent named the French police (and not the SS or the Wehrmacht) as those responsible for carrying out the massive Vél' d'Hiv' roundup (it should be noted that the question itself contained a major error, since it mentioned "more than 12,000 French Jews that were arrested" whereas it was actually foreign Jews). In 1992, between 70 and 74 percent gave the correct answer (the error had been corrected). This should doubtless be attributed to coverage of current events: in 1990, the fiftieth anniversary of the year 1940, the matter of the parliamentary representatives had been brought up on several occasions; in 1992, it was the massive Vél' d'Hiv' roundup that was at the center of the debate over commemorations. Nevertheless, these responses, even though they are not entirely satisfactory, give us a measure of the ground covered. Let us recall, for example, that a survey conducted in 1976 showed that 53 percent of French people who were questioned did not know who had been the head of state between 1940 and 1944, and that another survey, in 1980, revealed that half of those questioned thought that it was Germany that had declared war on France.[40] Teachers have not done such a bad job since then . . .

7

The Future of an Obsession

Jean-Marie Cavada (journalist): "Why is there a duty to remember?" That is
what testers [for the baccalaureate exam on June 11, 1993] asked young
people who, for their part, only wanted to know. Paul Ricoeur, as a philosopher and one of the greatest minds of this century, how would you
yourself have responded to this question?

Paul Ricoeur (philosopher): Let me say first of all that it is the conclusion that
you are asking us for, because I suppose that this duty proceeds first from
the understanding of what memory is, and what the relation between
memory and history is. Now I will go straight to the moral conclusion—
but I hope that after that we will go back to the construction of memory
and history . . . It is certainly a debt. We have a debt with respect to the
dead, and that is what gives us a long memory and an identity that lasts.
And then maybe also we have a need to deliver ourselves from the guilt of
the past by leveling out and clarifying our memory, and so there is a thera-
peutic value to it. And then perhaps also we must deliver the past from
that which has simply lapsed and gone by, that can no longer be changed,
and to retrieve the unfulfilled promises of the past, and thus that in the
past which is also a project for the future.

It was with this verbal exchange that the television program *La Marche du
siècle* of June 30, 1993, devoted to the "duty to remember" began, before
the program sank back down to the level of the worst clichés about the
"taboos" and "forbidden archives" of Vichy. In several penetrating sentences, Paul Ricoeur had summed it all up. The duty to remember is nothing but an empty shell if it does not proceed from knowledge. It is nothing
but a test question or a pompous moral lesson if it is not connected to a respect for the truth. That is the fundamental conclusion of our study. As we
have attempted to show, the untempered exercise of this fashionable en-
joinder, proclaimed everywhere and most often by voices poorly qualified
to give moral lessons on the subject, can lead to all sorts of excesses.

The Irreparable

For several years the obsession with Vichy has marked the triumph of anachronism. There is nothing surprising about this. History is perpetually subjected to rewriting by succeeding generations, and the gaze that people cast upon the past flows from the present. This is a commonplace. But when anachronism becomes a permanent exercise and a refuge used to escape the complexity of human beings and events, and even more so, when it is used as an ideological weapon, then it is worthwhile to drive home a few well-worn truths.

The vice of anachronism seems all the more unacceptable in that knowledge of the era has changed considerably thanks to French and foreign advances in historiography. Twenty years ago, we knew less. Today, we know better. However—and this is another paradox—the more knowledge kept progressing, the more people kept talking about taboos; as more and more light was shed on misunderstood or unknown aspects of the era, the more we saw a proliferation of discourses totally cut off from historical credibility. No one is supposed to be ignorant of history under the pretext of imposing a duty to remember: some people prescribe this clearsightedness for us without practicing it themselves.

Anachronistic is certainly the term that describes a certain ideological reading of the Resistance and of the history of the members of the Resistance that castigates anti-fascist political commitments, in spite of their diversity and various motivations. And all under the cover of an "anti-Stalinism" which is particularly suspect, since those who are trumpeting its cause today were yesterday its best defenders. The term anachronistic also applies to a simplistic view of things which in one sweeping movement brushes aside both precocious and belated resistance; both the anonymous resisters of 1940, who are often forgotten, and those, who are sometimes more famous, of 1943, constantly condemned in the name of the facile morality of those who know how the story came out. This anachronism reaches a climax when people end up mixing up in the same opprobrium both the "resistancialist" myth of the postwar years and the reality of actual resistance activity: this is a process that is just as antithetical to the truth as were the Gaullist or Communist legends which sought to rewrite the history of the entire French people under the Occupation following the pattern of the minority that had saved the nation's honor.

Equally anachronistic is the temptation of "judeocentrism," which seeks to reread the entire history of the Occupation throught the prism of anti-Semitism. While in our eyes, the anti-Jewish policy is a major aspect of the Occupation, it was at the time of the Occupation only one among many others, since the Jews were victims just like others who had been persecuted or condemned. The fact that this may shock our conscience is one thing, but the notion that it should lead us to remake history is another; the anachronism here consists of confusing the morality of posterity with the reality of the past. This is often what causes the most misunderstanding among those who lived through the war and who were not directly affected by this problem. They are all the more ill at ease in that they are being asked to be accountable to boot.

There we see what has been the most salient and the most constant occurrence since the seals of silence have exploded, if we can judge by the events underlined in this book:

—the "Jewish card file" affair, or how the policy governing public archives is supposedly totally subject to the intention of hiding state anti-Semitism, which some people tell us did not stop with the fall of the Vichy regime;
—the memory of the massive Vél' d'Hiv' roundup, or how, because it was necessary to commemorate an episode of the past that had formerly been covered up, people wound up with a policy of national commemoration that was absurd: at Izieu, where a Nazi, and solely Nazi, crime against humanity had been perpetrated, Vichy was officially declared to be an accomplice; at the site of the Vél' d'Hiv', where its complicity was overwhelming, the crime was committed only "under" its authority. Furthermore, in official memory, anti-Semitism has become central: whereas deportation is commemorated twice—on Deportation Day in April, which is devoted to the memory of all deportees, including both resisters and those deported for "racial" reasons, and the new day commemorating racial and anti-Semitic persecution on July 16—no commemoration of the same order is specifically dedicated to the Resistance, which is celebrated only through its martyrs or through the May 8 celebration recalling the fall of Nazism. We should add that while the memory of June 18, which is not a national day, is often celebrated in grand style, no celebration of the same order is devoted to the mainland Resistance. This arrangement is especially surprising, since the Resistance remains an object of civic worship, particularly in schools;
—the Touvier trial, or how to rewrite the history of the Milice: the armed branch of police collaboration between Vichy and the occupying forces had been first of all charged with fighting against the Resistance; at the time, the members of the Milice did not make any distinction between their enemies, be they "Jews," "Communists," "Gaullists," or other (we use quotation marks here to recall that it was the criminals who defined their future victims in that manner).

To these issues of memory, which are of national importance, one could add the debates that have been open for ten years about the "Jewish Resistance," or how, in certain cases, people transform something, which at the time was a patriotic or anti-fascist political commitment made by men and women who did not want to make themselves stand out from the rest of their companions in the fight as Jews, into a strictly community-based, "differentialist" commitment; this is a retroactive reading of events that has been completely driven by present-day political stances.

A similar occurrence can be seen in the manner in which people today perceive the memory of the Genocide as it was kept alive immediately after the war. When the petitioners of the Vél' d'Hiv' 42 Committee claim that the condemnation of Vichy's anti-Semitic crimes is a "demand made by the victims," or when certain people demand the destruction of the "Jewish card file" in the name of remembering these very same victims, they are forgetting, or are unaware, or are refusing to see that the said victims, or rather the survivors, had not, during the purge trials, demanded that a special case be made of the anti-Jewish policies and had on the contrary desired that, for the sake of memory, all traces of the crime be preserved. That is doubtless the most enlightening example of contradictory readings of the very same occurrence which have been made in the name of the same values, but which, separated by fifty years, lead in radically different directions.

The objective that has been pursued since the 1970s has been to make the nation take into account these anti-Semitic crimes and their specificity: in other words, the necessary distinction, which is justified on an historical level, between crimes perpetrated by National Socialism and since condemned by humanity and by history, and those committed by a regime, government employees, and French collaborators, crimes whose reality had faded from memory or had not been made to stand out after the war. However, the continuous exercise of the duty to remember has led to strange results for anyone willing to respect the meaning of words and symbols.

The Touvier trial? A Nazi *collaborator*, not a member of the French Milice, was convicted. He was convicted by virtue of a convoluted legal definition, which depended on a narrow interpretation of the Nuremberg statutes, whereas these strictures should have actually been transcended in order to apply the statutes to French crimes and no longer only to Nazi crimes. This was done in the framework of something that will doubtless be remembered as one of the last trials of the purge more than the first trial of a French citizen for a crime against humanity—in spite of the verdict that was pronounced, which is of little importance as far as considering the case as a great history "lesson."

The massive Vél' d'Hiv' roundup? Since 1993, the event has become the official symbol of the anti-Semitic aspect of Vichy. But this great mass arrest of July 1942, as well as all those that followed in both the northern and southern zones, had been less the consequence of state anti-Semitism than of state collaboration. The role played by Bousquet, Leguay, and their cronies can be explained not by any anti-Jewish fanaticism, but by the politics of a regime ready to pay the price in blood, that of others, and its intention of defending a certain conception of "national sovereignty." This policy did not necessarily result from the anti-Jewish laws that had been promulgated two years before by Vichy. This is in fact what was supposed to be integrated into the memory of our nation: the degree of autonomy with respect to the occupying forces. Certainly, these laws were subsequently conducive to the application of the "Final Solution," a crime that was premeditated and organized by the Nazis. *French* statutes, card files, and exclusion laws facilitated the massive arrests of 1942 and 1943. But the gist of these laws, which were promulgated between July 1940 and the summer of 1941, was not to lay the groundwork for an extermination—at that time, this project had not yet been drawn up either in Vichy policy, nor even in that of the Third Reich. These French laws were the expression of a principle of political and social exclusion inscribed in the heart of a certain French tradition and which still today remains alive.

Granted, one may reply, but so what? The consequence of all this is that traditional French anti-Semitism, that of the police and bureaucracy, which was that of Vichy in 1940, henceforth runs the risk of being overshadowed by one dramatic event, the great massive roundup of 1942, which is an episode that is too momentous, too exceptional, and too closely tied to the context of the German occupation—it was the SS that demanded contingents of deportees—to serve as an example a half a century later. This massive roundup cannot be dissociated from the crime of the Nazis. However, one can attempt to distinguish Vichy's principle of exclusion from the policies of the occupying forces without separating the two, even if this principle was only able to reveal itself in all its horror in the context of the defeat.

If we want to draw lessons from this history, we can put it more bluntly: a discriminatory "statute" against such and such category of people is, in the France of the 1990s, a much more plausible (and troubling) scenario than the threat of a concentrationary process sending tens of thousands of people to a methodical death. Rampant xenophobia, the obsessive keeping of files on people, and the rejection of the Other can perfectly well exist in times of peace; indeed, they continue to belong to our political traditions. In this respect, the symbolic value of the memory of the massive Vél' d'Hiv' roundup is not very helpful to us, to the extent that we believe in these lessons of history.

"Judeocentrism" has another perverse effect: the upsurge of memories that also demand their right to be recognized and to be different. This is an occurrence that has stood out over the last few years. The memory of our nation indeed remains incapable of giving a unified historical account. For on the one hand, there was a common destiny which linked together almost all the French people and all the foreigners who had taken refuge on French soil. This was a population that experienced the same ordeal: the ordeal of the war, the defeat, a dictatorship, and the enemy occupation. But on the other hand, there were radical differences in the situations to which various groups were subjected: the Jews and the non-Jews; the inhabitants of the free zone (who, up until November 1942, experienced the dictatorship of Vichy but not Nazi terror) and those of the occupied zone, not to mention the people living in the zones that had been declared forbidden, reserved, and annexed, and which had been cut off from the rest of the country; the two million prisoners of war, half of whom remained in captivity for five years; the hundreds of thousands of forced laborers, who experienced the Dante-like twilight of Nazi Germany; the victims of racial, religious, or political persecution, the victims of repression, those who fell victim to the war and the bombings, and finally, those sometimes innocent victims of the summarily conducted purge—women who were shorn and humiliated, families who were massacred and who disappeared in the context of the cathartic violence (which was brief and relatively contained) that accompanied the return of good times.

It used to be that the memory of the "racial" deportation had been relegated to the background, behind the memory of the martyrs of the Resistance or of soldiers who had fallen in the battles for the Liberation. This was moreover the case for other categories: prisoners of war, members of the armed forces killed in the battles of 1940, those formerly known as the "work deportees," and so on. Today, the opposite is taking place. In addition, the full and entire recognition of the memory of the Genocide, and even more so, the excesses to which it has led some people, have encouraged new demands: similar statuses are requested for Gypsies or homosexuals, people speak of the "extermination" of the mentally ill and of German prisoners of war. Everyone wants his own "genocide." Not without a more than abusive interpretation of historical reality,[1] and not without the development of veritable retrospective fantasies, especially in the case of the mentally ill or of German war prisoners, who were quite real mass victims of the war and of its hardships, but not of a deliberate and criminal policy.

When all is said and done, these anachronisms give us the sense that, in the general confusion resulting from them, we are seeing a break in historical continuity. In common discourse, this continuity seems to be fragmented and blown apart, thus dissociating what is the period of the Occupation strictly speaking (June 1940 through summer/fall 1944) from the years that precede it: the crisis of Munich, the pact between Germany and the Soviet Union, the phony war, the extent of the defeat and the terrible dilemmas that it created (whether or not to continue the war, and the choice between armistice and military surrender). All of these things are at

the origin of both the Vichy regime and de Gaulle's Free French movement. In such a perspective, "Vichy" seems to pop up out of nowhere, outside of time and the Nazi occupation, and entirely stemming from the
depths of the French soul, from the "French ideology."[2] Similarly, some
people claim that as early as August 1944, we lapsed into a state of total oblivion and amnesia: the ten-year purge period, with its ten thousand deaths
and hundred thousand some-odd convictions and sanctions of all sorts, is
thus forgotten and swept away with one stroke of the pen.

If these aberrations were simply due to a distorted view of things, they
would be of no great consequence. But in the name of this anachronistic
view of the past, people think they can *influence* it. Thus it was that people
wanted to replay the scene of the Liberation by demanding an official acknowledgment of Vichy's crimes and by asserting that the Vichy regime
had never been tried and that it was time to do so with Bousquet and then,
for lack of anything better, with Touvier and more recently with Papon.
Let's get on with it, they said, and added that this was indeed an unexpected
chance to compensate for the shortcomings and omissions of the purge. A
new generation, or at least a few particularly active individuals, constantly
tried to remake the history of the "Vichy syndrome," claiming that they
could now better handle the aftermath of the war than their elders had previously done. This is an empty illusion which fell back into the Liberation
dilemmas that had been revived and which ran into that which is irreparable in history: on the level of assessment, how can one distinguish clearly,
among Vichy's deeds, between that which is attributable to collaboration
with the enemy, that which stemmed from the constraints of the defeat,
and that which came out of an indigenous ideological project? And as far as
getting rid of the aftereffects of the war, how can we find the ideal balance
between respect for the law and the need to punish the guilty? How can we
reconcile the duty to remember with the right to forget, which, in spite of
everything, does constitute a right inscribed in our legal principles (and
which moreover is inherent in any construction of memory, both individual and collective)?

One Generation Puts Another on Trial

The way in which the memory of the war has been handled recently has not
had only negative effects, far from it. But the contradictions, paradoxes, and
stutterings of this memory are too flagrant for us not to see that they constitute a veritable social phenomenon whose causes deserve to be examined.

The first reason, as we have already stressed repeatedly, has to do with
the depth of silence marking the 1950s and 1960s, which was too pronounced for us to avoid the backswing of the pendulum that has taken us

too far in the opposite direction; no one has managed to escape this turn of things, not even historians. Annie Kriegel, who has constantly criticized the French school of history about Vichy on the basis of her own (reactionary) view of things, has pointed out on several occasions that French historians have been more concerned with the accomplice than with the main criminal, more with Vichy than with the Third Reich. Those same historians retorted that it was urgent and necessary to study Vichy. And this reply retains all its validity except for the fact that, once again, we risk falling back into the anachronism and forgetting, while we look at bookstore windows and at the overabundance of publications about Vichy, in what situation they were hardly fifteen years ago. Nevertheless, there is not, and doubtless there will never be a French school of history on Nazism on the same level as there is in the United States, in Israel, and obviously in Germany. And the reason for that is, in particular, a polarization of scholars and of the social demand for the history of Vichy, a polarization which is now no longer a crisis, even if there is no reason for research to stop—there are kilometers of shelves of files which have not been studied and await researchers.

The second explanation has to do with the notion that crimes against humanity are exempt from the statute of limitations. While this notion corresponds with a humanist idea which is recent in France, and which has been inscribed in tradition after Auschwitz, it nevertheless contains hidden pitfalls once it comes to trying individuals long after the fact, in a different context, and with a view of things that is by definition anachronistic (in the literal sense of the word). The notions of the statute of limitations and amnesty are not principles of our legal code for nothing. It is true that this legal code seemed to be unable (in the past as well as nowadays) of dealing with a tragedy such as the Genocide, and it was thus reasonable to bring about changes in certain traditions. But as we have said, such a debate should have been taken out of its ideological ruts.

But there is another aspect of the exemption from the statute of limitations that has created a strong tension in our memory: the discrimination that is made between crimes against humanity on the one hand and war crimes, collaboration crimes, and just plain crimes on the other. This concept, which has been at the bottom of the main issues of memory for twenty years, and which gave the justice system a decisive role, was in fact only the legal expression of a much more essential question—that of the singularity of the Genocide.

This notion is inherent, explicitly or implicitly, in every discussion about the war in Germany, in France, and elsewhere, whatever the topic in question may be. It has decisively influenced most of the occurrences described in this book. Now, the problem has often stemmed from the confusion between, on the one hand, the historical *definition* of the event, which is in step with memory and regards the event as being indeed "singular," and, on the other hand, the repeated *use* of this notion of "singularity" in present day discourses.

The survivors and all those who have tried to understand this tragedy have said so, demonstrated it, and hammer it in: the will of a state to exterminate an entire category of human beings solely on the basis of the fact that they existed, or rather, on the basis of a definition of their essence—those that the Nazis, their accomplices, and their counterparts designated in "statutes" as "Jews," sometimes by religious criteria, sometimes by "racial" criteria, and without taking their identity or their own choices into account—and the will thus to exterminate them wherever they might be, systematically and industrially, because of a principle found at the heart of its ideology, is something unique in the history of humanity. And even if the Jews were not the only victims of the criminal undertaking of the Third Reich, and even if the genocide carried out against the Jews was neither the first nor the last genocide in history, the event is singular with respect to the past. Who can claim that it is singular with respect to the future?

Having said that, it is nevertheless the case that viewing this event *exclusively* from the angle of its singularity in the long run causes major contradictions, not to mention weariness of this theme, or the revolt of groups of people who thus feel forgotten (as we have seen above).

Let us consider for an instant the reflex that consists of stating, with an air of grave solemnity, that this event is "uncommunicable" or "unthinkable," and then going on to devote feature articles several pages long or broadcasts of several hours: what a river of words in order to express the "inexpressible"! The syndrome of silence and the terror of the unspeakable have also struck many survivors of the extermination camps after their repatriation and in the postwar years.[3] But what properly belonged only to them —and which deserves our complete respect—in a certain period of their history, over time has turned into a media slogan, while most of the last surviving deportees on the contrary only desire one thing: to testify, even when communicating that experience involves a suffering and a tension almost without equal. Moreover, many would have liked to testify as early as 1945, and some voices did make themselves heard, overcoming the embarrassment and refusals of the rest of the population. But the present-day knee-jerk slogan has little to do with the suffering of the past. It takes away from the victims that which is rightfully theirs, and this is done over and over again in the name of the duty to remember, if not because of less noble preoccupations. This is certainly a more serious and unbearable dispossession than the one that historians are often accused of, namely, that of depriving survivors of their memory by claiming to write their history.

The most serious problem is elsewhere. By constantly emphasizing the *singularity* of the Genocide, all its possibilities as an *exemplary* event are removed. By constantly seeing only that which makes it unique, we wind up depriving ourselves of the lesson of universality that we claim to draw from it. As we observed with the question of crimes against humanity, and again with the problems raised in the classroom by such a subject, students, like most adults, imagine the past on the basis of their current representations of things and they approach the problem of racism from their own daily experience of it. This is what many teachers have said to us again and again. However, in regarding the event solely as "something completely apart"—to borrow the words of one of these teachers, the historian Alain Monchablon—we run the risk of bringing about the opposite effect. Instead of dispensing civic education about memory, we wind up distancing our audience from this event, which becomes so terrifying (which was indeed the case) that it risks remaining permanently "unique" in many people's minds. And in that way we run the risk of never stimulating our audience to do a comparison, with what is "always possible," in other words, with the universal values that the discourse about the memory of the Genocide is supposed to defend. This is a particularly high risk in France and other places where this memory has become a veritable cult, with its temples and high priests, its rites and its anathemas: let us recall Claude Lanzmann's virulent reaction against Steven Spielberg and his film *Schindler's List*; Lanzmann denied Spielberg any right to produce a fictional film on the subject, as if the Genocide had not given rise to a large number of creative works (beginning with his own monument, *Shoah*), and as if it should be forbidden to represent it, according to a new version of the Second Commandment.

There again we have a major source of tension between memory and history: while scholarly works abound and as we continue to get a better grasp of the legal, political, technical, and psychological mechanisms of the "Final Solution," discourses refusing any possibility of a rational, reflective, historical, or even "aesthetic" approach to this singular event proliferate.[4] This almost enters into the realm of mystery, or even of mysticism. But this singular event is not diabolical, it is human and strictly human.

This reflection leads straight to a third explanation of the tensions pointed out in this book, and it also pertains to the transmission of lived experience from one generation to another. If the memory of the Genocide and, therefore, the issue of Vichy's anti-Semitism are currently so potent, it is because in this area—and in spite of the commonly held idea of an "intransmissibility"—there has been a real transmission, even if it is only partial. Resisters, deportees ("racial" deportees as well as the others), and prisoners of war or veterans all have their associations or clubs. They are led by those who experienced the ordeal, at times with the assistance of younger people. However, the memory of the Genocide has presently found special support within associations in which most of the members do not speak strictly for themselves and are not directly victims of this tragedy, but rather their descendants: The Union of French Jewish Students or, even more characteristically, Serge Klarsfeld's association, the Sons and Daughters of the Jews Deported from France, and still others. These are the associations that have led the battle for years. It is through them that the transmission of memory has been carried out. However, nothing comparable exists for the Resistance: there are no associations of sons and daughters of members of the Resistance who were deported. And for a good reason: former members of the Resistance get together to celebrate the memory of what they did, while former deportees and their children get together to remember what wounded their identity as Jews. Heroism is not handed down, but a wound resulting from an attack on one's identity is.

Finally, there is one last explanation, which is again of a generational nature, and which deals this time less with a highly active minority, identifiable as such, than with an ambiant, more political "discourse" carried here and there by belated activists for the cause of memory. These people seem to have converted themselves over from a prophetic political activism into an inquisitory and retroactive political activism. For lack of exerting a real force against today's "fascism," be it real or fantasized, they resolutely lead the attack against the fascism of the past. They demand a "gesture" from the President, they petition, they denounce the intrinsically "Vichy-like" state for keeping the "secrets of the archives" locked up, they carry out purges of memory, and they remove street names without authorization . . .[5]

These most recent representatives of the "ideology of suspicion" reveal to us, on a deeper level, the sign of an impotence that prevails over many aspects of the obsession with Vichy. Daniel Lindenberg has rightly spoken of a new "anti-fascist, anti-colonialist, anti-racist catechism [which] could never be sufficient."[6] As for Paul Thibaud, he is much crueler:

> Why is our era so relentlessly determined to dig evil out of the archives? People say that it is in order to keep the horrors thus identified from happening again: I believe on the contrary that people are in fact cultivating a new sort of apathy, the apathy of a generation which, having donned the advantageous garments of anti-Nazism and anti-Communism, finds itself to be the bearer of "a good moral conscience without any purpose" (Maurice Agulhon), which it does not know how to use other than for purging the past of its progenitors.[7]

This generation—which is ours—seems so lost and helpless, at least in comparison with political involvement in its century, that some of those who belong to it try to purge the past. But in addition, they want to smooth it out and take away its richness and opacity, in other words all ambiguity, probably for fear of facing up to their own. They cannot stand historical discourse about the World War II era. They accuse history of having hooked up again with "scientism" or "neopositivism": "In claiming to have evacuated all ideological dogmatism, all political controversy from the sphere of research, neopositivist history, which is now triumphant without having achieved that illusory objectivity, nevertheless runs the risk of taking the life out of historical discourse and in the end making worse the crisis of national identity, which is inseparable from the social and political crises that are rocking our democracy."[8] Good grief! For having made it possible for the history of Vichy to repose on a minimum of scholarly standards, the historians get accused of undermining the morale of the nation! This is the desire to legitimate once again a "Communist," or a "rightist," or any other history of the Resistance, or perhaps a "sixties generation" history of the Occupation, and therefore, in the end, a "Pétainist" history of Vichy, all in the name of indispensable national cohesion . . .[9]

At times these same people accuse historians of being nothing but the spokesmen of an "official history." This invective moreover emanates both from circles of former leftists and from those who would like to hark back to Vichy as well. It is also hurled forward by some activists for memory who are exasperated by not being taken seriously, and by negationists, for whom it is a livelihood. This strange collection of bedfellows ought to make us reflect on the matter. For the fans of retroactive activism, the term "official history" encompasses professional historians all lumped together (as if they made up just one and the same drove . . .), to which they oppose "admirable" self-taught people, just as the "little" people used to be pitted against the "big," or as the proletarians were put up against the bourgeois. Along with archivists, these historians are supposedly part of the "great conspiracy of silence." In the extreme right-wing press, historians who assert that Pétain collaborated with Germany are termed "official" historians; they are countered with the claim that there is a "nonconformist history," in other words, the one written by the activists for the National Front or the Nouvelle Droite.[10] Finally there are the negationists, who obviously refuse this term, and who are self-proclaimed members of a "revisionist school" supposedly in competition with an "exterminationist school," namely that of official historians, who peddle the "great Jewish lie" of the Genocide.

Wherever it comes from, the current condemnation of an "official history" displays the same symptoms: a detective story view of history (with "conspiracies"), the refusal of the past and of its diversity, and finally, the pronounced taste for simplistic and reassuring categories ("ideological" ones). This produces the opposition between the view of the "winners" and of the "losers" (those who were purged); or else between the "bad" resisters (those who dealt with Moscow) and the "good ones" (the followers of Giraud[11]); or else an intrinsically anti-Semitic and Pétainist France against which a minority of exclusively "Jewish" or foreign resisters arose, and so forth. When all is said and done, it is not so much the historian that is being attacked as it is the wall of facts, which this inability to admit the complexity of the past runs up against.

These attacks underscore the extent to which professional historians have found themselves in the line of fire in these last few years.[12] In these matters, social demand has taken on unusual forms: courtroom testimony, in criminal courts (which is thus given under oath, and at times in favor of the prosecution, as was the case in the Touvier trial), or the creation of ad hoc commissions by the hierarchy of the Catholic Church or the Ministry of Culture, not to mention the proliferation of public research contracts, scholarly consultants for museums and exhibits,[13] and so on. True, the response to this multifaceted demand has not gone without problems. The difficulty of maintaining critical distance, of resisting pressure from those making the demand, or even of simply giving a reasoned answer and even a plain answer is a very real one. Moreover, historians are not above the weaknesses of their fellow citizens: a good number of aberrations that we have denounced in this book also came from historians. And we are not about to oppose summarily the "right" discourse of the historian with the "wrong" discourse of activists or the media: there are very bad historians and quite good journalistic writers, terrible TV reporters and excellent self-taught individuals, shoddy books from university scholars and remarkable TV documentaries. As for the activists, the sincerity of their convictions is not the best gauge of the reliability of what they say. That is not the problem; the joint effort of a journalist and an historian in writing this book was nothing if not an attempt to get beyond this kind of competition, which is pointless as long as each person respects the division of labor. The difficulty comes instead from the need to respond to a civic duty: fulfilling the requirement of certitude, proof, and truth. Granted, historians as well as journalists know that this truth is elusive and subject to review, and that it depends on a multitude of factors, and that the modes of representation (including collective memory) are historical *facts*, studied as such. They know that the gaze of the observer (the historian or someone else) as well as the nature of the sources that they use to study the past (personal testimony, written traces, and so on) carry with them a major, sometimes decisive degree of subjectivity: History is made, and written, by and for beings of flesh and blood and speech. This is a filter that is inevitable in any approach to the past or present. But that does not mean that all points of view and all perspectives should be deemed legitimate and equivalent, nor does it deny any possibility of the existence of "reality" within these representations. Such "relativism" is loaded with dangers, for it ends up postulating that there is no possibility of a common history, be it national or other, but only competing and differentiated representations of the past, based on ideological, ethnic, geographical, social, or gender-based criteria. No historian worthy of the name, even if one of the most relentlessly opposed to "positivism," can remain indifferent in the face of doubt about the possibility of writing a history that contains a minimum of irreducible truth and unity that is thus instilled. In point of fact: to whom did people turn when the sect of negationists popped up? What request was directed to historians, if not the following: tell us, tell them, tell public opinion that the gas chambers did exist?

Should the duty to remember be shelved back away in school lockers? Not at all, but let us bring an end to the silly ritual that consists of being indignant every six months because a new scoop reveals that some French people collaborated or that Vichy was an accomplice to the "Final Solution": this is known, it is said, it is taught, and it is commemorated. What is important now is no longer to denounce nor to unveil secrets, but to understand and, even more, to accept—not to resign ourselves, but rather to admit that this past, and perhaps even more the way in which it was handled after the war by the generation that had gone through it, is over. Granted, this is not an easy thing to do—it is not an easy thing to write either. This is particularly difficult in that what is insufferable about "Vichy" is not so much collaboration or organized political crime, but rather that which was at the very foundation of Pétainist ideology and which, at one time, enjoyed the support of the majority of people: the desire to get an entire people out of the war and to put the course of history in parentheses.

This temptation is not just a thing of the past; it is a constant temptation, and not just for the French. All one has to do, between documentaries on the Allied landing in Normandy and the Liberation of Paris, is to ask ourselves a few questions about the meaning of these faraway images from Rwanda or Bosnia and imagine what future generations will say to us. They will not speak to us about Munich or Vichy, but about Kigali and Sarajevo.

That is what makes the memory of the Occupation so unbearable and so obsessional: it is the permanent reflection not of "our" crimes, which were always committed by a minority, but of our indifference and of the difficulty in breaking with them, as did the first resisters. About that era, it has been said over and over again that "a people that does not remember the past is condemned to repeat it." But the generation of the war years has lived in the prison of an incomplete and impossible period of mourning. It had decided, after the crisis, to live again, to turn the page and to disregard, as much as it could, its real or alleged guilt. For many years, it had accepted the advantageous myth offered to it by de Gaulle, who had saved the honor of France with his first call to resistance on June 18, 1940. But it had not been wary of the return of memory. The succeeding generation thought, after the death of this holy man, that it was the right time to reopen the loaded files of the Dark Years. In this sense, exploding the taboos was a necessary and healthy thing to do, and tribute must be paid to those who lit the wick or threw the stones. But today, does the duty to remember give the right to put the war generation constantly on trial? This question is especially pressing in view of the fact that, for our own generation, the obsession with the past, with that past, is just a substitute for the urgent demands of the present, or still worse, a refusal of the future.

Appendix A
A Chronology of the Remembrance
of World War II, 1990–1997

This chronology is a sequel to the one published in Henry Rousso's *Vichy Syndrome*, pp. 309–17. It is an indicative and selective listing, with some items concerning countries other than France.

The period stretching from August 1994 to July 1997 (when the American edition began production) has been accounted for in this edition.

1990

January 28. *Le Monde* discloses the scandal surrounding Bernard Notin, a lecturer at the Université Jean-Moulin (Lyon-III) who published, in August 1989, an article in the scholarly journal *Économies et Sociétés* containing negationist statements. On July 18, 1990, he is fordidden from teaching for a period of one year.

February 9. In West Germany, a few months after the fall of the Berlin Wall on November 9, 1989, Hans Modrow, the head of the government, acknowledges, after forty years of silence, "the collective responsibility of the German people for the past." He expresses his "remorse for the terrible crimes committed toward the Jews by the Germans" and announces reparations for the victims of racial persecutions. On October 3, 1990, Germany is reunified.

February 13. The examining magistrate in Lyons decides that the investigation of the case of Paul Touvier (the former member of the Milice was arrested and indicted for crimes against humanity on May 24, 1989) will be conducted exclusively in Paris and ruled in favor of handing the case over to Judge Jean-Pierre Getti. At the time, however, the question of the venue of the trial (Lyons or Paris) was not decided.

February 14. The defamation suit filed by Robert Faurisson against George Wellers, who accused him of being a "falsifier of the history of the Jews during the Nazi era," is dismissed.

April. The government of Mikhail Gorbachev acknowledges the responsibility of the USSR in the massacre of 14,600 Polish officers, soldiers, and policemen at Katyn and elsewhere in April 1940. It appoints a military commission charged with investigating the responsibilities of the NKVD, Stalin's police. The following year, this commission was to find two former members of this police who had participated in the massacres.

April 27. The weekly newsmagazine *L'Express* publishes a cover story on the French camps at Pithiviers and Beaune-la-Rolande (in the Loiret department), where Jews arrested during the massive Vél' d'Hiv' roundup were interned: there were men, women, and more than 3,500 children whose final destination was to be Auschwitz.

May 7–8. For the commemoration of May 8, the public television network FR 3 schedules "The Longest Night: May 7 1940–May 8 1945"; this consists of twenty-four consecutive hours of programs about World War II, covering all aspects of the conflict.

May 10. Discovery of the profanation of the Jewish sections of the cemetery of Carpentras: thirty-four tombs had been violated. Accusations are hurled at Jean-Marie Le Pen and the National Front, even though the preliminary results of the investigation do not make it possible to establish the involvement of extreme Right activists. That was finally the case, as demonstrated in 1997.

May 13. Jewish associations stage a demonstration in front of the Parisian residence of René Bousquet, former Secretary General of the Police for the Vichy government in 1942 and 1943.

May 14. Gigantic demonstrations take place in Paris (with for the first time the participation of the President of the Republic) and in the provinces, after the profanation at Carpentras. The "Carpentras affair" crystalizes a number of issues of memory: negationism, which was more and more active on the university level, the Bousquet affair, and the resurfacing of the memory of Pithiviers and Beaune-la-Rolande.

May 16. New charges of crimes against humanity are filed against Maurice Papon, former Secretary General of the Prefecture of the Gironde: these charges concern his activities during the years 1943 and 1944.

June. After the incident at Carpentras, Jean-Marie Le Pen is tacitly boycotted by the media. Several cities in France forbid meetings of the National Front during the summer.

June 17. Colloquium sponsored by the Institut d'Histoire du Temps Présent (CNRS) on "The Vichy Regime and the French People": for the first time in twenty years, it provides an historiographical assessment of the studies conducted on this era (the proceedings would be published in 1992 by Fayard).

June 20. Commemoration by the entire National Assembly of the de Gaulle call of June 18, 1940. Conjointly, the Left tries to offer a tribute to the eighty members of Parliament who, on July 10, 1940, refused to vote for the granting of full powers to Pétain. This effort sparks a controversy.

June 21. The weekly newsmagazine *Le Nouvel Observateur* publishes a cover story about "The French People Who Were Accomplices to the Genocide." Maurice Papon, who was cited among these accomplices, sued the magazine for defamation. He was to win his lawsuit.

June 30. The National Assembly passes a bill introduced by the Communists: this bill punishes "those who dispute . . . the existence of one or several crimes against humanity" such as these crimes have been defined by the statutes of the international military tribunal of Nuremberg. (This is the law of July 13, 1990, commonly referred to as the "Gayssot law.")

September. Publication of *L'Histoire de Vichy* (Perrin), by François-Georges Dreyfus. This rekindles debate over the possibility of a "revisionist" history of Vichy.

October 1. Colloquium organized at the Senate, by Serge Klarsfeld and the Association of Sons and Daughters of the Jews Deported from France and the Center for Contemporary Jewish Documentation, about Vichy's "Jewish Statutes."

October 22. The Bousquet case comes up again in the High Court. Georges Kiejman, Delegate Justice Minister, makes a controversial declaration to the daily newspaper *Libération* about the necessity of maintaining "civil peace."

November 11. The President of the Republic has flowers placed on the tomb of Philippe Pétain on the Ile d'Yeu.

November 19. The Court of Criminal Appeals of Paris declares itself competent to prosecute the Bousquet case. In its ruling, René Bousquet is designated as having the "status of being indicted." Bousquet files an appeal three days later.

1991

January 31. The Final Court of Criminal Appeals rejects the motion to appeal filed by René Bousquet against the ruling of November 19, 1990. The last legal obstacle to indictment is removed.

March 28. A search warrant is served at the cosmetics firm L'Oréal by Judge Jean-Pierre Getti. A few weeks later, on May 6, the weekly newsmagazine *Le Point* publishes an article on the activities of one of the executives of this cosmetics firm, Jacques Corrèze, during the Occupation. Corrèze had been a member of the Cagoule, following in the wake of the founder of the business, Eugène Schueller, and had been convicted at the time of the Liberation. The scandal lasts up until the death of Jacques Corrèze, on June 26, 1991, a few weeks after the publication of documents about his role in the expropriation of Jewish shop owners in 1941. Along the way, this incident brought to light the postwar ties between Eugène Schueller and François Mitterrand; this information resurfaces periodically and had caused a virulent altercation at the National Assembly in February 1984.

April 3. The indictment of René Bousquet for crimes against humanity, which was carried out on March 1, is made public.

April 18. Robert Faurisson is convicted of violating the "Gayssot law." He has to pay the sizable sum of several hundred thousand francs.

May 1. The House of Commons modifies British legislation in order to allow the prosecution of Nazi war criminals who took refuge in Great Britain.

June 6. Judge Jean-Pierre Getti submits his report on the charges leveled against René Bousquet to the Criminal Court.

July. The trial of Josef Schwammberger begins at Stuttgart. The former Nazi is responsible for the death of 3,000 Polish Jews. He was extradited from Argentina in May 1990.

July 11. Ruling of the Criminal Court of Paris granting the liberation of Paul Touvier, since detention was supposedly not necessary now that the investigation was almost concluded. He is placed under court surveillance.

July 19. Controversy over the plan to construct a supermarket on the site of the former Nazi concentration camp of Ravensbrück.

July 19. Judge Jean-Pierre Getti sends out an international warrant for the arrest of the former Nazi leader Aloïs Brunner, who, among other things, had been in charge of the staging camp of Drancy in 1943 and 1944, and who is known to have taken refuge in Syria. A similar warrant had already been sent out by Judge Claude Grellier in 1988.

July 22. Adoption of the new penal code, which includes in its innovations a definition of crimes against humanity distinguishing "genocide" from "other crimes against humanity" (according to Articles 211-1 and 212-1). These crimes are not subject to the statute of limitations and are punishable by life in prison without parole.

October 23. Maurice Papon holds a press conference, during which he announces that he has written a letter to the President of the Republic requesting that he either be tried or that charges against him be dismissed, since eight years have gone by since the beginning of legal proceedings against him.

November 11. The President of the Republic has flowers placed on the tomb of Philippe Pétain on the Ile d'Yeu.

November 13. Serge Klarsfeld announces in the daily newspaper *Le Monde* that he has just found "the card file of the census of Jews in the Paris regions taken in 1940" in the archives of the Office of the Secretary of State for War Veterans.

December. On the occasion of the fiftieth anniversary of Pearl Harbor, the Japanese Socialists criticized the government of Kiichi Miyazawa for his refusal to acknowledge the crimes committed in what was then called the "sphere of coprosperity of Greater Oriental Asia." The controversy highlights the ambiguous nature of Japanese society's memory of the war, in which the trauma of Hiroshima still weighs heavily.

1992

January 6. The report of the commission of historians presided over by René Rémond on "Paul Touvier and the Catholic Church" is made public, in Lyons, at the seat of the Archbishop and in the presence of Cardinal Decourtray. It is published (by Fayard) a few days later.

February 10. Putting an end to a controversy dating from the Liberation period, a ruling by the Court of Criminal Appeals forbids those who were requisitioned in the context of the Forced Labor Service (STO—Service du Travail Obligatoire) to call themselves "work deportees."

February 19. In the United States, the House of Representatives gives the status of national historic site to Manzanar (in California), where one of the main internment camps for "Japanese-Americans" (American citizens of Japanese ancestry) had been built. In 1988, the Senate had approved reparations for them, by virtue of the "racial prejudice" to which they had been subjected from 1942 to 1944.

April 19. The Court of Criminal Appeals of Paris rules in favor of dismissing the charges against Paul Touvier and thus prompts a considerable outcry. A motion to appeal this ruling is filed on the same day by Pierre Truche, the general prosecutor for the Paris Court of Appeals.

May 11. François Mitterrand's National Movement of Prisoners of War and Deportees (MNPGD) as well as two other Resistance organizations are declared "combat units of the mainland French Resistance."

May 17. Ceremonies at Pithiviers and Beaune-la-Rolande in memory of the victims of the massive Vél' d'Hiv' roundup, in the presence of two members of the government.

May 18. Josef Schwammberger is condemned to life in prison without parole by the tribunal of Stuttgart.

May 27. Certain magazines, such as *L'Événement du jeudi*, *VSD*, and others, publish and broaden the allegations made by Kurt Schaechter about the supposedly secret archives of the camps of the southern zone.

June 17. The Vél' d'Hiv' 42 Committee circulates a petition for François Mitterrand to acknowledge officially that "the French State of Vichy is responsible for persecutions and crimes against the Jews of France."

July 6. The press divulges new indictments against Maurice Papon and René Bousquet, which were issued on June 19 and June 22 in Bordeaux, in the context of the prosecutions of the Papon case. This is an indirect consequence of the outcry caused by the dismissal of charges against Paul Touvier even among a large number of magistrates.

July 6. After months of hemming and hawing, Japan officially acknowledges that it forced tens of thousands of Korean women into virtual sexual slavery when they were sent to the camps of the imperial army during the war.

July 16. Fiftieth anniversary of the massive Vél' d'Hiv' roundup in front of the stone marker in the fifteenth arrondissement in Paris, the site of the former covered stadium. François Mitterrand, booed by part of the crowd, attends the speeches, including the one given by Robert Badinter, president of the Constitutional Council, who speaks as a private citizen.

July 21. Serge Klarsfeld announces that a source close to the President of the Republic has told him that François Mitterrand has decided not to have flowers placed on Pétain's tomb anymore; this information is denied by the Élysée on the following day. Attorney Arno Klarsfeld, the son of Serge and Beate Klarsfeld, will reveal in June 1994, in an interview given to *Information juive*, that this was a false declaration intended to "give a golden opportunity to Mitterrand so that he could get out of the situation gracefully by confirming [it]." The young attorney, who had since distinguished himself in the Touvier trial, added: "He was not graceful and persisted."

October 15. Inauguration in Lyons, by Mayor Michel Noir, of the Center for the History of the Resistance and Deportation.

November 10. A bill is introduced in the Senate by Charles Lederman for the Communist senators "concerning the acknowledgment of crimes against humanity committed by the Vichy regime."

November 11. The President of the Republic has flowers placed on the tomb of Philippe Pétain on the Ile d'Yeu. This time the ritual provokes a considerable outcry. Shortly after, just before a trip to Israel, François Mitterrand announces a commemorative "gesture" concerning the responsibility of Vichy with respect to the Jews.

November 27. The Final Criminal Appeals Court partially overturns the ruling for dismissal of charges against Paul Touvier issued in April, pointing out that the Criminal Appeals Court of Paris technically contradicted itself by retaining against Touvier only the charges of "complicity in a crime against humanity" in the execution of seven Jewish persons at Rillieux on June 29, 1944.

December 30. The commission of specialists presided over by René Rémond, which was to establish the exact nature of the "Jewish card file" found by Serge Klarsfeld in the archives of the Office of the Secretary of State for War Veterans, denies that this is the huge card file of October 1940, which was destroyed in 1948 and 1949. This information rekindles the controversy.

1993

January 6. The *Times* brings up the recent opening of archives about the occupation of the island of Guernsey by the Nazis . . . or Collaboration British style.

February 3. Decree creating a "national day commemorating the racist and anti-Semitic persecutions carried out under the de facto authority of the so-called 'government of the French State' (1940–1944)." This day will be observed every year on July 16 (the anniversary of the massive Vél' d'Hiv' roundup of 1942) if it is a Sunday, or if not, the following Sunday.

February 4. Louis Mexandeau, Secretary of State for War Veterans, inaugurates a monument located in the Père-Lachaise cemetery in Paris and dedicated to 3,500 deportees from France (almost all Jewish) who died at Auschwitz III (Buna-Monowitz), where a total of 30,000 persons perished.

February 6. "Jean Moulin agent soviétique" appears as the cover story of *Figaro-Magazine*. Beginning of the controversy over the book *Le Grand Recrutement* by Thierry Wolton (published by Grasset).

March. Claude Chabrol's *L'Oeil de Vichy*, produced in collaboration with the historians Jean-Pierre Azéma and Robert Paxton and made from French and German cinema newsreel images, is shown in movie theaters.

March 11. Maurice Papon files a statement of case for his defense requesting the dismissal of charges after ten years of fruitless legal proceedings.

April 25. On the occasion of Deportation Day, some associations of homosexuals, supported by the Greens and the Socialist party, ask as they do each year to participate officially. They are met with a firm refusal from the Union of Associations of Deportees, and in particular from former resisters.

May. Jean Marboeuf's film *Pétain*, adapted from the biography by Marc

Ferro, with Jacques Dufilho in the role of the Marshall and Jean Yanne in the role of Pierre Laval, is shown in movie theaters. This is one of the very first times that a general historical reconstitution of the Vichy regime has been produced.

June 2. The Final Criminal Appeals Court of Versailles sends Paul Touvier to be tried in the Criminal Circuit Court of the Yvelines regional department.

June 8. The Communist members of the National Assembly introduce a bill "about the preservation of street names referring to resistance to Nazism."

June 8. René Bousquet is assassinated at his Parisian residence by Christian Didier, who calls the press before being arrested. Didier had already attempted to kill Klaus Barbie in 1987.

July 9. The press reveals that the fifteen Polish nuns who were occupying the Carmelite convent of Auschwitz since 1984 left the site.

July 16. First official commemoration of Vichy's "racist and anti-Semitic persecutions," presided over by Prime Minister Édouard Balladur, in front of the stone monument in the fifteenth arrondissement in Paris.

July 30. In Israel, the Supreme Court acquits John Demjanuk on the benefit of doubt, since proof that he is indeed the "butcher of Treblinka" was not established. There then begins a controversy over the necessity of a new trial for the crimes that he supposedly committed as a guard in the extermination camp of Sobibor, in March 1943. He will be authorized to leave Israel on the following September 19.

August 5. Announcement of the liberation of one of the last Nazi criminals imprisoned in Germany, Kurt Hubert Franz, assistant to the commander at Treblinka, condemned to life in prison at his trial in Düsseldorf in 1965.

August 20. "I personally believe that this war was a war of aggression and an unjust war," declares the new Prime Minister of Japan, Morihiro Hosokawa, just a few days before the anniversary of the Japanese surrender; this official stance is the first of its kind. It fits into the context of a controversy surrounding the plan for an historical museum scheduled to be inaugurated in 1995.

September 22. British Prime Minister John Major, on an official visit to Japan, asks that "the situation of English prisoners be taken into account." He thus reiterates the position of the Association of Survivors of Japanese Labor Camps (which has 12,000 members), which is demanding 250 million dollars for forced labor done during World War II for Japanese companies such as Nissan and Mitsubishi.

November 3. The Court of Criminal Appeals confirms once and for all that the Touvier trial will indeed take place in the Criminal Circuit Court of the Yvelines, thus ruling against the plea of the prosecuting attorney Pierre Truche and the private parties, who wanted the trial to take place in Lyons.

November 8. The Élysée announces the end of the practice of placing flowers on the tomb of Pétain. The commemoration of World War I will henceforth take place in certain symbolic places (at Verdun, for example) and no longer, as custom would have it, at the tombs of great military leaders.

1994

February. Steven Spielberg's film *Schindler's List* is shown at theaters in France. France is one of the rare countries in which a heated controversy broke out over whether or not it was possible to produce a fictional film about the Genocide. This was particularly due to the radical stance taken by Claude Lanzmann, the director of *Shoah*, who takes exception to what Spielberg did.

March 1. The new Penal Code takes effect, bringing with it the new definition of crimes against humanity. During the Touvier trial, the defense will to no avail mention the possibility of applying some of its provisions, by virtue of the rule stating that if these provisions are "more favorable toward the accused," the accused must receive the benefit of them.

March 15. While celebrating the fiftieth anniversary of the plan for the National Council of the Resistance, François Mitterrand declared: "This plan and this institution have been too long forgotten! [. . .] For an episode of history begins with the National Council of the Resistance and we have not concluded it."

March 17. Opening of the Touvier trial in Versailles.

April 10. François Mitterrand participates in the ceremonies of the fiftieth anniversary of the fighting of Glières. In February and March 1944, about 500 members of the French underground were attacked by Vichy's forces of order, including the Milice's special unit of La Franc-Garde, then by the Wehrmacht and the Luftwaffe, who finally get the better of them: about 150 to 200 resisters and civilians were killed in combat, shot, or died under torture or in deportation.

April 20. Paul Touvier is condemned to life in prison without parole for crimes against humanity. He files an appeal. As soon as the verdict is announced, certain associations demand the opening of a trial of Maurice Papon.

April 24. On the occasion of Deportation Day, François Mitterrand inaugurates the memorial museum at Izieu (in the Ain regional department), erected to preserve the memory of the roundup orchestrated by Klaus Barbie. The stone marker located on the site reads as follows: "Here, on April 6, 1944, the Gestapo arrested and deported forty-four children and seven adults because they were born Jewish. Fifty were exterminated at Auschwitz II and Reval. The French Republic pays tribute to the victims of racist and anti-Semitic persecutions and crimes against humanity committed with the complicity of the Vichy government, the so-called 'government of the French State' (1940–1944). Let us never forget."

May 9. Upon the request of the Italian government presided over by Silvio Berlusconi—which, for the first time since the end of the war, includes four members of the (neo-fascist) National Alliance—Argentina has the former SS Captain Erich Priebke arrested in view of a possible extradition. Priebke is accused of having participated in the massacre of the Ardeatine caves in Rome on March 24, 1944. This massacre claimed 335 civilian victims, including seventy Jews.

May 18. The commemorative plaque for the seven victims of Paul Touvier in the cemetery of Rillieux-la-Pape is destroyed by unknown intruders.

May 24. The Court of Appeals of Versailles rejects the request for the release of Paul Touvier that was made on May 11.

June 5–6. Grandiose ceremonies for the fiftieth anniversary of the D-Day Landing. The chiefs of state and sovereigns of the countries that took part in the fighting in Normandy attend. The German Chancellor was not invited; this chills relations between France and Germany and stirs up the beginning of a controversy.

June 10. François Mitterrand and Édouard Balladur participate in the fiftieth anniversary commemoration of the massacre of Oradour-sur-Glane. On June 10, 1944, 642 people (almost the entire population of the village) were wiped out by the Waffen SS division "Das Reich," which included Alsatians who had been forced to enroll. Thirteen of them were tried and convicted in Bordeaux in January 1953. One week later, the Parliament passed an amnesty law in their favor. Up until 1965, the members of Parliament who had voted for this law—including François Mitterrand—were deemed to be personae non gratae on the grounds of the village. After the war, a new village was built next to the ruins of the martyred village, which was kept as it was. Until very recently, Oradour observed an exceptionally austere period of mourning: it was only in 1993 that a bureau of tourism was created (almost 350,000 people visit the site every year). On June 10, 1994, the model of a future Center for the Memory of the Martyred Village of Oradour was presented to the public.

June 20. In Orléans, François Mitterrand presides over the ceremonies in memory of the former minister Jean Zay, who was assassinated by the Milice on June 20, 1944. "Jean Zay," the chief of state was to say, "in the Ministry of National Education was an outstanding example of the work of the Popular Front of which I continue to be proud. I was just over twenty years old at the time and I remember things that show that this difficult era appears now, fifty years later, as one of the times when people imagined, created, and built a large part of what France is today."

June 26. As is his habit every year, François Mitterrand attends ceremonies celebrating the memory of the thirty victims killed by the retreating German army on June 26, 1944, in Dun-les-Places (in the regional department of Nièvre).

July 7. The cemetery at Rillieux-la-Pape is profaned a second time.

July 17. François Mitterrand inaugurates—without addressing the audience and along with his Prime Minister, Édouard Balladur, and the mayor of Paris, Jacques Chirac—a monument in memory of the victims of the massive Vél' d'Hiv' roundup. This monument was placed at the sight of the former indoor stadium. Beneath the bronze statue, which represents seven people, is the following inscription: "The French Republic pays tribute to the victims of the racist and anti-Semitic persecutions and crimes against humanity committed under the de facto authority of the so-called 'government of the French State' (1940–1944). Let us never forget."

July 21. François Mitterrand being hospitalized, Édouard Balladur alone inaugurates the Memorial of the Vercors plateau at the La Chau pass. This memorial celebrates the most famous memory of the French underground at the place where, on July 21, 1944, 15,000 German soldiers attacked 4,000 resisters who were isolated and without logistical support. The fighting and the savage repression carried out by the Nazis and the members of the French Milice claimed almost 840 victims, including more than 200 civilians.

August 14–15. Ceremonies celebrated the landing in Provence on August 15, 1944, and the liberation of the South of France. In attendance are the President, the Prime Minister, as well as several African heads of state, in memory of the 180,000 men of the colonial troops who participated in this combat.

August 25. Ceremonies celebrating the liberation of Paris, with the President and the mayor of Paris, Jacques Chirac, in attendance.

September 1. The publication of the book *Une jeunesse française. François Mitterrand, 1934–1947* (Fayard), by Pierre Péan, as well as the appearance of several other books, rekindles the controversy over the President of the Republic's past, just a few months before the end of his second seven-year term of office.

September 12. François Mitterrand offers explanations about his sickness and about the revelations concerning his activities under the Occupation in a long interview given to Jean-Pierre Elkabbach on the TV channel France 2. The broadcast, which was a first in every respect, fuels an already heated debate because of the ambiguous statements that the President made about Vichy and because of his admission that he had kept his friendship with René Bousquet.

October. Serge Klarsfeld publishes *Le Mémorial des enfants juifs déportés de France* (Memorial of the Jewish Children Deported from France) (Paris, FFDJF) in which, over the nearly 1,600 pages of the book, he provides a list of the names of the 11,000 children who fell victim to the Nazis and Vichy. At the same time, some newspapers, including *Le Monde*, once again stir up the controversy over the so-called "forbidden archives of Vichy."

October. Steven Spielberg announces the creation of a "Foundation for Audiovisual History," charged with gathering filmed testimony from "150,000" survivors of the Genocide throughout the world before the year 2000. The publicity given to this initiative seems to be unaware that similar initiatives are already underway, led by nonprofit institutions and associations in the United States (at Yale University), in France (Foundation for the Memory of the Deportation), and elsewhere in Europe.

1995

February 12. The newspaper *Le Monde* attempts to stir up the "Oréal affair" once again by publishing "revelations" about the "Vichyite" past of André Bettencourt, president of the holding company that controls the cosmetics company, and a longtime friend of François Mitterrand. For several weeks, this "affair" garners media attention until the American Anti-Defamation League announces that it will not issue a call to boycott Oréal products in the United States. This decision runs counter to the desires of the Frydman brothers, who are engaged in serious financial disputes with a branch of the firm. *Le Monde*'s initiative was not widely followed by the rest of the press.

May 6–7. Grandiose ceremonies in London in celebration of the surrender of the Third Reich. Some fifty heads of state, scheduled to visit subsequently Paris, Berlin, and Moscow, are in attendance.

May 7. Jacques Chirac is elected President of the Republic with 52.64 percent of the vote. He will assume office on the following 17th of May.

May 8. After the ceremonies in Paris commemorating the fiftieth anniversary of Germany's surrender, the President of the Republic still in office, François Mitterrand, delivers a speech in Berlin in which he pays tribute to the "courage" of the soldiers of the Wehrmacht, touching off a new controversy. This declaration is made at the very moment when the debate over the responsibility of the German army in the persecution of the Jews and the atrocities committed in the territories occupied by the Nazis is being stirred up again. The debate contradicts the notion made popular after the war, that there was a "difference" between the behavior of the regular army and that of the Nazi organizations (SS, Waffen SS, Gestapo, and so on).

May 8. Kaspar Villiger, President of Switzerland, acknowledges "a certain error of the past," in particular the "J" stamp that Swiss authorities had asked Nazi Germany to put on the passports of German Jews, so that Switzerland could turn them away more efficiently: "such an aberration is ultimately inexcusable."

May 9. Ceremonies in Moscow in celebration of the victory over Nazism. François Mitterrand and German Chancellor Helmut Kohl do not attend the military parade in order to protest against the war in Chechnya and the "violations of human rights."

May 16. First staging of *Violences à Vichy*, a play by Bernard Chartreux, directed by Jean-Pierre Vincent in the Théatre des Amandiers at Nanterre. This is a remake and updating of a show that created quite a stir when it came out in March 1980.

June 1. The Final Court of Criminal Appeals, presided over by Christian Le Gunehec, rejects the appeal filed by Paul Touvier, thus confirming that the former member of the Milice, who remains imprisoned, did indeed commit a crime against humanity.

July 16. The President of the Republic, Jacques Chirac, delivers a speech in front of the monument dedicated to the Jews who fell victim to the massive Vél' d'Hiv' roundup of July 16 and 17, 1942. This speech is given on the national day that since 1993 has commemorated Vichy's racist and anti-Semitic persecutions. In his speech, President Chirac acknowledges the "responsibility of the French State" and even speaks of "collective sin." These words, a sharp break with his predecessors' tradition, are greeted with satisfaction by the great majority of the public.

July 17. Following revelations made by Serge Klarsfeld on July 15 in the newspaper *Libération* about the absence of compensation for property confiscated from the Jews interned at Drancy, and following the declarations made the previous day by Jacques Chirac about the legal responsibility of the "State," there is a new controversy over the supposed lack of any form of compensation made by the Republic to the Jews who had been dispossessed by the "Aryanization" measures enacted by the Nazis and Vichy. This controversy was quieted in rather short order. It had not sufficiently taken into account the compensation (doubtless partial) paid during the 1950s after painstaking investigations. The controversy will arise again in 1996 and 1997.

July 26. Subsequent to revelations made by the international press, the Association of Swiss Banks announces that it has set up with the "mediator of the banks" (who arbitrates disputes with clients) a "central office" charged with helping the descendants of the victims of Nazism in their search for funds not claimed since the end of the war and still held by Swiss banks. This marks the beginning of one of the major controversies over the legacy of World War II.

August 6. The fiftieth anniversary of Hiroshima takes place amid a climate of controversy both in the United States, where there is a debate over the strategic presuppositions involved in the use of the first atomic bombs, and in Japan, where the commemoration masks a series of silences about the responsibilities of Japan during World War II. The announcement made shortly afterward by the French government of the resumption of nuclear tests in the Pacific helps give the event a current dimension.

November 2. The Argentine Supreme Court issues a favorable ruling on Italy's request for the extradition of Erich Priebke, responsible for the massacre of the Ardeatine caves in Rome in 1944. This is the second time that Argentina has agreed to extradite a former Nazi, after the extradition of Josef Schwammberger in 1990. It is the first time that Italy will experience a crimes against humanity trial.

November 6–13. Trial of Christian Didier who killed René Bousquet on June 8, 1993, with several shots from a revolver. His lawyers plead for acquittal. The Criminal Circuit Court of Paris sentences him to ten years in prison.

November 30. The Swiss courts rehabilitate Paul Grüninger, a police officer from the canton of Saint-Gall, who had been dismissed in 1940 and convicted of "violating prescription of service and falsification of documents" after having allowed 3,000 Jews illegally to gain refuge in Switzerland from 1938 to 1940. From 1968 until 1994, Swiss authorities had rejected all requests made for the sake of this former police officer, who died in 1972.

December 19. After twelve years of legal proceedings, the District Attorney's Office of Bordeaux produces its indictment of Maurice Papon, former Secretary General of the Prefecture of the Gironde from 1942 to 1944. Papon was a former Gaullist member of Parliament and former government minister under the presidency of Valéry Giscard d'Estaing. The District Attorney's Office finds that Maurice Papon is to be tried by the Criminal Court for "crimes against humanity according the definition of complicity in criminal arrests and detentions," and with respect to Jews who were rounded up in the Bordeaux region in 1942 and 1944.

1996

January 8. Death of François Mitterrand.

January 27. Germany decrees January 27, the day marking the liberation of Auschwitz, to be the "Day in Memory of the Victims of National Socialism." This decision, long in coming, was taken at the initiative of President Roman Herzog.

February 27. The Socialists in the National Assembly introduce a bill concerning "the conditions for compensating victims of the 'Vichy' regime."

April. Beginning of a controversy in the international press following the publication of the book by Daniel J. Goldhagen, a young political scientist at Harvard, *Hitler's Willing Executioners: Ordinary Germans and the Holocaust,* published by A. Knopf (New York, 1996). It was published in France by Le Seuil in January 1997.

April 19. Abbé Pierre—highly popular in France for his crusade to help homeless people—gives his support to a book denying the Holocaust by Roger Garaudy: *Les mythes fondateurs de l'État d'Israël,* published by La Vieille Taupe (an "ultra-left" publishing house that publishes the works of the Holocaust denier Robert Faurisson).

May 8. Beginning of the trial of Erich Priebke in Italy by the Military Tribunal of Rome. Being eighty-two years old, he was incarcerated at Forte Boccea. At the time of this first trial, he benefited from "extenuating circumstances," but the verdict was to be thrown out and Priebke maintained in detention. He was to be retried and ultimately convicted and sentenced to five years in prison on July 22, 1997.

July 3. The commission on the "Jewish Card File," presided over by René Rémond, submits its report to the Prime Minister. It was published at the same time by the Plon publishing house.

July 17. Death of Paul Touvier, at the Fresnes prison in Paris.

September. Rekindling of the controversy over Switzerland's attitude during World War II, and in particular over the "Nazi gold" deposited in Swiss banks, and over the "Jewish holdings" that were not restituted.

September 18. The Court of Criminal Appeals of Bordeaux sends the case of Maurice Papon to the Criminal Circuit Court of the Gironde department for "complicity in criminal sequestration." Four indictments concerning the Jews deported by the trains of January 12, 1942, August 26, 1942, October 23, 1942, and January 12, 1944. The text of the ruling, unanimously saluted by the press, nevertheless raised numerous questions as to the historical validity of certain assertions.

October 8. The newspaper *L'Humanité* (8 October 1996), followed by *Le Monde* (11 October 1996) kindles the "Lacroix-Riz affair," from the name of the historian who claimed to have the "proof" that French firms had supposedly manufactured Zyklon B. This piece of information—unfounded—circulated throughout the international press.

October 12. The French government announces that the documents constituting the so-called "Jewish card file" will not be placed in the French National Archives, even though these are public documents. They will be placed in the Centre de Documentation Juive Contemporaine, in an "enclave" of the French National Archives.

October 27. Beginning of the controversy over the private real estate holdings of the city of Paris: it was alleged that certain buildings belonging to Jews whose property was confiscated during the German Occupation had not been restituted to their rightful owners and that in other cases property holders had not been compensated for their losses. This would turn out to be largely untrue.

November. Controversy over the book by the historian Karel Bartosek, *Les Aveux des archives* (published by Le Seuil), that is critical of Arthur and Louise London, as well as Raymond Aubrac, legendary figures of the Resistance, for their attitude within the apparatus of the Communist International during the 1950s.

1997

January 21. After Switzerland, Sweden is in turn accused of having held "Nazi gold."

January 23. The Court of Criminal Appeals rejects the appeal presented by Maurice Papon, whose case had been sent before a circuit court on September 18, 1996. The opening of the trial is scheduled for the beginning of October 1997.

January 26. Prime Minister Alain Juppé announces to the Council Representing the Jewish Institutions of France (CRIF) the creation of a commission charged with shedding light on the "Jewish property" confiscated by Vichy. This decision takes place in the context of the controversies over the Nazi gold in Switzerland, over works of art allegedly held by the French National Museums, and over Parisian buildings.

February 26. Screening of the film *Lucie Aubrac* directed by Claude Berri. The publication of the book by Gérard Chauvy (*Aubrac, Lyon 1943*) about Mr. and Mrs. Aubrac is delayed by the publishing house Albin Michel, which seems to have come under pressure. The book is finally published on April 2.

July 9. The daily newspaper *Libération* publishes a special series of articles about the "Aubrac Affair." It contains the complete text of the encounter that the former resister Raymond Aubrac and his wife, Lucie Aubrac, requested with seven historians and the former resister Daniel Cordier, who was also Jean Moulin's secretary. This document stirred up a controversy both over the attitude of the Aubracs during the war as well as the vocation of historians.

July 20. During ceremonies commemorating the Vél' d'Hiv' roundup, the new Socialist Prime Minister, Lionel Jospin, reaffirms the responsibility of the Vichy government in the application of the Final Solution in France, just as President Jacques Chirac had done two years before. The Prime Minister announces a modification of the law governing the access to archives and the creation of a Holocaust Museum ("Musée de la Shoah") in Paris.

Notes

Throughout the Notes section, translator's notes are set within square brackets.

FOREWORD (PP. ix–xiii)

1. Henry Rousso, *The Vichy Syndrome: History and Memory in France since 1944* (Cambridge, Mass.: Harvard University Press, 1991).

2. *Sans oublier les enfants* (Paris: Grasset, 1991).

3. A particular *bête noire* of the authors is Sonia Combe, *Archives interdites: les peurs françaises face à l'Histoire contemporaine* (Paris: Albin Michel, 1994), and her accusation—surely excessive—that only a few "official historians" (such as Rousso) have access to the French archives.

4. Guy Braibant, *Les Archives en France, Rapport au Premier ministre* (Paris: La Documentation française, 1996), pp. 59–62 acknowledges these difficulties. See also *Le Monde*, 22 June 1966, p. 7.

5. Jean Planchais, "La mode Vichy," *Le Monde des livres*, 9 September 1994, p. ix.

6. Charles S. Maier, *The Unmasterable Past: History, Holocaust, and German National Identity* (Cambridge, Mass.: Harvard University Press, 1988).

7. John Charmley, *Churchill and the End of Glory* (London: Hodder and Stoughton, 1993), thinks Churchill's refusal of a compromise peace with Hitler doomed Britain to loss of empire and world power. Clive Ponting, *1940: Myth and Reality* (New York: HarperCollins, 1990) and Len Deighton, *Blood, Tears, and Folly* (London: Hamish Hamilton, 1993) see mainly mismanagement.

8. The German Democratic Republic (East Germany) took the position that, having adopted Socialism, it bore no relationship to the previous Germany that had spawned Nazism.

9. The *Institut für Zeitgeschichte* in Munich had no equivalent in France until the 1980s, when the *Comité d'histoire de la deuxième guerre mondiale*, which had studied almost exclusively the Resistance, was broadened into the present *Institut d'histoire du temps présent*, whose mission includes work of very high quality on Vichy. Henry Rousso is its director today.

10. Maier, *The Unmasterable Past*, provides the most searching account.

11. *Hitler's Willing Executioners: Ordinary Germans and the Holocaust* (New York: Alfred Knopf, 1996).

12. Ernst Nolte, "Die Vergangenheit die nicht vergehen will," *Frankfurter Allgemeine Zeitung*, 6 June 1986. See Maier, pp. 29, 180.

INTRODUCTION (PP. 1–15)

1. [*Translator's note*: The German occupation of France, extending from the signing of the Armistice on June 25, 1940, to the Liberation of Paris on August 25, 1944, is commonly referred to in France as "les années noires," literally, "the black years."]

2. See the recently translated 1991 book by Israeli journalist Tom Segev, *Le Septième Million* (Paris: Éditions Liana Levi, 1993), which caused a stir in his country. The author analyzes both the long-term history of the memory of the Genocide in Israel, with its taboos and heroic myths, and the gradual awakening to the indifference that the Zionist authorities in Palestine displayed throughout the war toward their fellow Jews who were being persecuted.

3. [*Translator's note*: This work was translated into English by Arthur Goldhammer and published as *The Vichy Syndrome: History and Memory in France since 1944* (Cambridge and London: Harvard University Press, 1991). Future references to the book will use the English title.]

4. Henry Rousso, *Le Syndrome de Vichy, 1944–198* . . . (Paris: Le Seuil, 1987), in the collection "XXe siècle," headed by Michel Winock; second edition revised and updated: *Le Syndrome de Vichy de 1944 à nos jours* (Paris: Le Seuil, 1990), in the collection "Points-Histoire."

5. [*Translator's note*: All the items in quotation marks allude to the French Revolution. 1789 marked the beginning of the end for the Ancien Régime, with the storming of the Bastille in July and the abolition of aristocratic privileges in August. 1793 marked the extreme radicalization resulting in the Reign of Terror. The Jacobins were a group of radical republican revolutionaries advocating a strong, highly-centralized democratic regime, while the "vendéens" were the people of the Vendée region who, after originally supporting the Revolution, vigorously opposed the military draft decreed by the Revolutionary government in 1793. The "vendéens" led an insurrection which was mercilessly crushed by Republican troops who devastated the region and decimated the population.]

6. [*Translator's note*: Marshall Philippe Pétain, widely revered as an heroic military leader ("le Vainqueur de Verdun," or "the Victor of the Battle of Verdun") before the Occupation, was chief executive of the Vichy regime from its creation in July 1940 until its total dislocation in the wake of the Allied liberation of France in late 1944.]

7. [*Translator's note*: Henry Rousso conducts historical research for the CNRS (Centre National de Recherche Scientifique) at the IHTP (Institut d'Histoire du Temps Présent) in Paris.]

8. [*Translator's note*: Éric Conan writes for the weekly newsmagazine *L'Express*.]

9. [*Translator's note*: The Ile d'Yeu is a small island off France's mid-Atlantic coast near the Vendée region. It was there that Marshall Pétain was sent in 1945, after General de Gaulle had his death penalty commuted to life in prison. He was buried there after his death in 1951.]

10. Since the publication of this work, many books about the memory of the war have been published, including several that challenge or convincingly flesh out some of its original hypotheses. See the bibliography at the end of this book.

11. This was the theme used for the headlines of many newspapers after the assassination of René Bousquet in June 1993. This cliché is all the more surprising in that historical research of the last few years has focused heavily on the subject. Cf. Henri Amouroux, *La Grande Histoire des Français après l'Occupation*, vol. 9: *Les Règlements de comptes, septembre 1944–janvier 1945* (Paris: Robert Laffont, 1991); Philippe Buton and Jean-Marie Guillon, directors, *Les Pouvoirs en France à la Libération* (Paris: Belin, 1994); Klaus-Dietmar Henke and Hans Woller, directors, *Politische Säuberung in Europa: die Abrechung mit Faschismus und Kollaboration nach dem Zweiten Weltkrieg* (Munich: DTV, 1991); Herbert R. Lottman, *L'Épuration. 1943–1953* (Paris: Fayard, 1986); François Rouquet, *L'Épuration dans l'administration française: agents de l'État et collaboration ordinaire* (Paris: Éditions du CNRS, 1993); Henry Rousso, "L'Épuration en France. Une histoire inachevée," *Vingtième Siècle Revue d'histoire* 33 (January–March 1992): pp. 78–105.

12. [*Translator's note*: the term "collaborationniste" in French is used to designate the hard-line intellectuals and politicians in Paris who generally favored a one-party French state and pro-Nazi domestic and foreign policy. The term "collaborateur" designates the more opportunistic cooperation with the Nazis motivated not so much by ideology as by desire for receiving some benefit in return.]

13. About this aspect of the purge, which up until very recently had not been studied, in spite of the current importance of the subject, see: Katy Hazan, "La politique antijuive de Vichy dans les procès de l'épuration," in "L'Après-guerre" special issue of *Archive juives, Revue d'histoire des Juifs de France*, no. 28/1, 1995, pp. 38–51; and Henry Rousso, "Une justice impossible. L'épuration et la politique antijuive de Vichy," *Annales* 3 (May–June 1993): pp. 745–70.

14. [*Translator's note*: In desperate need of replenishing its workforce increasingly depleted by military demands as the war progressed in 1942, the Germans pressed Vichy to supply laborers for its farms and factories. In February 1943, Pétain's Prime Minister Pierre Laval instituted the "Service du travail obligatoire," the Forced Labor Service, which required all French males born between January 1, 1920, and December 31, 1922, to report for work in Germany. This highly unpopular measure caused many to take refuge in the "maquis" (underbrush) and thus to join the "Maquis" (French underground). See Jean-Pierre Azéma, *De Munich à la Libération* (Paris: Le Seuil, 1979), pp. 210–12.]

15. [*Translator's note*: In the French constitution, the "Haut Court (High Court) de Justice" has the supreme jurisdiction of judging political officials in office. It is composed of members of Parliament and of senators, and, in 1945, was presided over by a magistrate. At the time of the Liberation, it was incumbent on this High Court to try the officials of the Vichy government indicted for high treason or intelligence with the enemy. Pétain and Laval, among others, were tried and convicted by this court. The translator thanks Henry Rousso for providing this information.]

16. The figures given here differ from those in *The Vichy Syndrome*, which used the toll commonly accepted by all historians until very recently, and which is found in most of the works cited in note 11 above. This toll has since been reevaluated at a higher figure (cf. "L'épuration, une histoire inachevée," an article cited above, and, on the subject of the administrative purge, François Rouquet, *L'Épuration dans l'administration*). The figures given here are thus the most recent.

17. There are, however, some cases in which the pertinent facts were there,

such as in the trial of René Bousquet in 1949, when the High Court, it seems, deliberately neglected charges relating to the policy of anti-Jewish persecutions, which
nevertheless could be found in rather complete form in the record of the court investigation. See "Le dossier Bousquet," *Libération*, supplementary dossier to issue
number 3776 of July 13, 1993, in addition to the works of Serge Klarsfeld and the
article cited above, "Une justice impossible." This dossier has been published in
Richard J. Golsan, editor, *Memory, the Holocaust, and French Justice: The Bousquet and
Touvier Affairs* (Hanover and London: The University Press of New England, 1996
[translations by Lucy Golsan and Richard J. Golsan]).

    18. [*Translator's note*: De Gaulle issued his first call from London over British
radio on June 18, 1944, the day after Marshall Pétain had announced over French
radio that France had to lay down its arms. As Under Secretary in the Ministry of
War, de Gaulle was little known outside the top ranks of military and government
officials, and thus remained somewhat isolated in London during the beginning of
his campaign to rally the French around him and continue the fight against Nazi
Germany.]

    19. [*Translator's note*: Overlooking the northeastern part of Paris near Suresnes,
the Mont Valérien is the site of a fort where, according to recent works, some 1,000
hostages and resisters were executed by the Germans. In 1960, de Gaulle inagu-
rated the "Mémorial national de la France combattante," which is now one of the
shrines of the Resistance. Ouradour-sur-Glane is a small village in the départment
of Haute-Vienne (near Limoges) which was the site of one of the most infamous
Nazi atrocities of the summer of 1944. Some 640 villagers and refugees, including
240 women and children, were either shot or burned to death by the SS Division
"Das Reich" on June 10, 1944. The Vélodrome d'Hiver was a covered stadium
which was used by French authorities to detain thousands of men, women, and children in highly overcrowded and unsanitary conditions during their massive roundup
of some 12,000 to 14,000 foreign Jews on July 16 and 17 during the operation dubbed
"Vent Printanier," Spring Wind. The vast majority of those detained were to be deported to their deaths at Auschwitz. Located not far from Lyons, Izieu was the site
where Jewish children were hidden. Some forty of them were arrested and deported
to Auschwitz by order of Klaus Barbie.]

    20. [*Translator's note*: After returning to power in 1958 at the height of the Alge-
rian war, which with the rebellion of a part of the military was threatening to become a civil war on the French mainland, de Gaulle ushered in a series of constitutional reforms which created the institutions of the Fifth Republic that continue to
govern French political life at present.]

    21. [*Translator's note*: This is basically a notion describing the Gaullist vision of
resistance according to which the French had been united in heroic struggle against
a common enemy, the Nazi oppressor. Vichy, Collaboration, and the violent clashes
of the Milice with the Resistance, not to mention the fate of the Jews, are simply left
out of this vision of things. See Henry Rousso, *The Vichy Syndrome*.]

    22. It is not certain that this scheme of things will be able to continue long in the
future, and leave out the two great economic and political powers that yesterday's
losers, Germany and Japan, have now become. But that's another story, although
not unrelated to the future evolution of our representation of World War II, on an
international level this time.

23. [*Translator's note*: Immediately after receiving full constitutional and legislative powers in July 1940, Marshall Pétain, along with his ministers, initiated a broad series of measures aimed at instituting a more authoritarian, hierarchical, agrarian, and traditional social and political order. While reactionary in every sense of the word, these measures were nevertheless called the "Révolution Nationale."]

24. [*Translator's note*: The Milice was formally created in January 1943 as a special Vichy police force charged with fighting the Resistance. It was also a kind of fascist and pro-Nazi organization that became known for carrying out particularly violent acts of repression.]

25. [*Translator's note*: May 1968 was a period of social unrest marked by student demonstrations and violent clashes with the police, and by a series of strikes which paralyzed transports and communications and threatened to bring down the government.]

26. [*Translator's note*: The "sections spéciales" were special courts constituted by Vichy to try to punish Communists and resisters after the assassination of a German officer in the Paris metro in August 1941. See Azéma, *De Munich*, p. 207.]

27. [*Translator's note*: The "Front National" is the party of Jean-Marie Le Pen which focuses mainly on anti-immigration themes and what it considers to be France's traditional European heritage.]

28. [*Translator's note*: In 1969 Marcel Ophuls made his documentary, *The Sorrow and the Pity*, which, along with Robert Paxton's *Vichy France: Old Guard and New Order, 1940–1944* in 1972, fundamentally changed the dominant view of Vichy by stressing the extent of state collaboration and Vichy's responsibility for the fate of Jews deported from its territory.]

29. *Bibliographie annuelle de l'histoire de France* (Paris: Éditions du CNRS), volumes for 1988 and 1992, which provide summary tables. This tool, extremely valuable to historians, is admittedly an imperfect one when it comes to this kind of tallying: an article or book does not always fit into one single neatly-defined category (in this case, that of "World War II"), the statistics provided are not always well explicated (certain calculations have been redone in this area), and the *Bibliographie* combs through all the journals that might be concerned with the subject. This is the case, for example, with the journal published by the Centre de Documentation Juive Contemporaine, *Le Monde juif*, which is almost entirely devoted to the history of Jews during World War II. However, when it comes to measuring an evolution, the drawbacks of using this source as an indicator are not prohibitive, in that they remain constant from one year to the next. Moreover, if a finer measure were possible, the raw figures and percentages should be revised upwards. For just the works (excluding fiction) dealing with World War II published between 1945 and 1984, one can also consult *Les Échos de la mémoire. Tabous et enseignement de la Seconde Guerre mondiale*, a collection of essays edited by Georges Kantin and Gilles Manceron (Paris: *Le Monde*-Éditions, 1991): pp. 206–207.

30. See *Il y a cinquante ans la Libération*, a brochure which was provided to the press by *France Télévision* in early 1994, and which announced all such programs to be broadcast up until spring of 1995.

31. [*Translator's note*: *The Burns of History*.]

32. [*Translator's note*: "Our Century on the Move." There will be numerous references to the television program throughout the book, particularly in chapter 5.]

33. Paris: Grasset, 1993. See chapter 5.

34. [*Translator's note*: Those having tried to help save Jews from the Holocaust are honored by the Yad Vashem in Israel as "Righteous among the nations," or "Justes parmi les nations" in French. Thus I have chosen to translate "juste" as "righteous" in this context.]

35. See chapter 2. Part, but only a part, of the mistakes were corrected by those invited to speak on the program, including Chantal Bonazzi, general curator of the National Archives, and the historians Pierre Nora and Denis Peschanski. The presence of the philosopher Paul Ricoeur and of France's chief prosecutor Pierre Truche on the panel also helped keep the program in line somewhat.

36. Cf. Max Lafont, *L'Extermination douce. La mort de 40,000 malades mentaux dans les hôpitaux psychiatriques en France, sous le régime de Vichy* (Le Cellier: Éditions de l'AREFFPI, 1987). Dr. Escoffier-Lambiotte had reviewed this book (in *Le Monde*, 10 June 1987) without the least critical analysis of its sources and method, and without pointing out the hasty generalizations made by the author, who confused the context of the Occupation with Vichy's policies. (Actually, these policies never involved the slightest intention of "exterminating" the mentally ill.) The revelation of this piece of "information" caused a veritable scandal, to the point that some people continue to believe that the matter involves one of Vichy's hidden crimes. For a second opinion from historical scholars, see Olivier Bonnet and Claude Quétel, "La surmortalité asilaire en France pendant l'Occupation," *Nervure. Journal clinique et biologique*, vol. 4, no. 2 (March 1991): pp. 22–32. The authors show that this high rate of mortality (almost twice that of the figures given by Max Lafont) resulted from insufficient food rations and the local management of certain hospitals (involving in particular illicit trading in supplies by the personnel), problems which were reported by certain doctors as early as 1941.

37. Cf. the inflammatory pamphlet by Lucien Bonnafé and Patrick Tort, *L'Homme, cet inconnu? Alexis Carrel, Jean-Marie Le Pen et les chambres à gaz* (Paris: Éditions Syllepse, 1992), in which the technique of confusing the theories of the Nazis with those of Alexis Carrel results in far-fetched notions that no "anti-fascism" can justify. The total lack of respect for truth and historical accuracy is always a singular favor offered to all sorts of revisionists in this domain.

38. Cf. Alain Drouard, *Une Inconnue des sciences sociales, la Fondation Alexis Carrel* (Paris: Éditions de la Maison des sciences de l'homme, 1992). Even if Alain Drouard sometimes overlooks the ideological dimension of Alexis Carrel's work, his well-documented book shows how the author of *L'Homme, cet inconnu* played only a marginal political role under Vichy: his foundation, which was created by the regime, was devoted to the relationship between the various human sciences, and in particular to the links between medicine and the social sciences. It is from this foundation that the first French polling institute, the IFOP, and the National Institute for Demographic Studies (INED), will come after the war. This researcher for the CNRS (Centre National de Recherche Scientifique, the National Center for Scientific Research), has recently been the target of an intrigue which tends to present his work as a "rehabilitation" of Carrel's ideas. On the subject of eugenics in France, see the studies done by Pierre-André Taguieff, especially: "L'eugénisme, objet de phobie biologique. Lectures françaises récentes," in the dossier "La bioéthique en panne?" *Esprit*, November 1989: pp. 99–115; or "Sur l'eugénisme: du fantasme au

débat," in *Pouvoirs*, special number entitled "Bioéthique," no. 56, 1991: pp. 23–64. Pierre-André Taguieff, who is also with the CNRS, has likewise been the victim of a loud campaign denouncing his publications on the pretext that they "trivialize extreme right-wing ideas," to use the terms of a defamatory article published in *Le Monde* (13 July 1993), under the signature of Roger-Pol Droit. The article was a "commentary" on a "Call to Vigilance," published in the same edition of the paper, dealing with the risks of "legitimizing" the ideas of the extreme Right, and signed by university professors and intellectuals. Other researchers signed a petition defending their colleague—to whom we owe the best of recent publications on the "New Right" (which was the title of his latest book published in 1994 by the Éditions Descartes). Above all, these colleagues defended the possibility of studying delicate subjects with the necessary objectivity and rigor, without getting targeted by an archaic ideology of suspicion (this was the tenor of their letter published in *Le Monde*, 27 July 1993).

39. In 1989, a Canadian writer, James Bacque, also made up a "genocide," in claiming that the Americans and the French had knowingly let hundreds of thousands of German prisoners of war die of hunger between 1944 and 1945 (*Other Losses* [Toronto: Stoddart Publishing Co. Ltd.]). A counter-investigation, demonstrating that the idea of premeditated mass murder (even though the number of deaths among German prisoners was indeed massive) was totally incoherent and that the use of documents had been skewed, was conducted for the newspaper *Libération* by the journalist Sélim Nassib and Henry Rousso: "En quête des camps de la mort pour soldats du Reich" [Searching for death camps made for the Reich's soldiers], 4 December 1989. That did not keep the author from being invited to the TV show *Apostrophes* on April 27, 1990, after his book had been translated in 1990 by the Éditions Sands, under the title *Morts pour raisons diverses*. This TV appearance gave the book a large audience even though its main ideas had been torn to pieces by American and German specialists.

1. VÉL' D'HIV' (PP. 16–45)

1. [*Translator's note*: The term "French State" is another name for the Vichy regime. Upon receiving full legislative and constitutional powers from the last legislative session of the Parliament of the Third Republic assembled at Vichy in July 1940, Marshall Pétain did away with democratic institutions and referred to himself as "Chef de l'État Français," Head of the French State.]

2. That is essentially what Henry Rousso said during his appearance on June 10, 1992, on the TV program *La Marche du siècle* devoted to the Vél' d'Hiv' roundup, when he reiterated the idea of a political gesture suited to easing tensions.

3. *Le Monde*, 17 June 1992, with an editorial by Laurent Greilsamer ("L'amnésie et la faute") whose tone was more measured and clearly less of protest. The petition was drawn up by Gérard Chomienne, Betty Dugowson, Michèle Grinberg, Juliette Kahane, Claude Katz, Jean-Pierre Le Dantec, Michel Muller, Robert Pépin, Éveline Rochant, Anna Senik, and Talila Taguieff. Among other historians, Henry Rousso helped write this text, but he took exception to its definitive version for reasons explained in this chapter. Like the majority of historians specializing in the Occupation, he did not sign the document.

4. *Libération*, 11 July 1992.

5. *L'Express*, 10 July 1992.

6. [*Translator's note*: The Palais de l'Élysée in Paris is the presidential residence. Accordingly, "l'Élysée" functions metonymically to designate the French President and his team, just as "the White House" refers to the President of the United States.]

7. [*Translator's note*: Completed in 1932, the Douaumont ossuary is situated at one of the famous sites of the Battle of Verdun, and holds the remains of some 300,000 soldiers who fell in battle there.]

8. [*Translator's note*: French President from 1974 to 1981.]

9. [*Translator's note*: The "Commissariat général aux questions juives" was a government agency created by Vichy on March 29, 1941, to oversee Jewish affairs. It concerned itself with such matters as defining who was or was not Jewish, the application of Vichy's racial laws, and the expropriation of Jewish property. Darquier de Pellepoix was the second commissioner, appointed by Laval on May 6, 1942. See Susan Zuccotti, *The French, the Holocaust, and the Jews* (New York: Basic Books, 1993), pp. 60, 97.]

10. [*Translator's note*: The institutions of republican democracy in France have taken various forms under different constitutions in vogue in various historical periods. These sets of institutions are thus referred to as the "First," "Second," "Third," "Fourth," and "Fifth" Republics.]

11. *Le Monde*, 16 July 1992.

12. This is a quotation of virtually the whole text which appeared in *Le Monde*, 16 July 1992.

13. [*Translator's note*: Paris is divided into twenty administrative sections called "arrondissements."]

14. Cf. the complete text of the speech in *Le Monde*, 18 July 1992.

15. Jean Daniel, *Le Nouvel Observateur*, 23 July 1992.

16. *Le Monde*, 19–20 July 1992.

17. Ibid.

18. On this point, cf. Henry Rousso, "La Seconde Guerre mondiale dans la mémoire des droites françaises," in *Histoire des droites en France*, under the direction of Jean-François Sirinelli, vol. 2: *Cultures* (Paris: Gallimard, 1992).

19. This is the facetiously naïve title of an essay by the historian Denis Peschanski published in the book he himself edited: *Vichy 1940–1944. Archives de guerre d'Angelo Tasca* (Paris and Milan: Éditions du CNRS/Feltrinelli, 1986), pp. 3–49.

20. Dominique Rousseau, "Vichy a-t-il existé?", *Le Monde des débats* (November 1992).

21. *Journal officiel de la République française* (Alger) (10 August 1944): p. 688. The GPRF [provisory government] was constituted on June 2, 1944, a few days before the Allied landing in Normandy.

22. *Journal officiel de la France libre* (Brazzaville), 1 (20 January 1941): p. 3.

23. [*Translator's note*: It was on this date that the National Assembly and the Senate, meeting in a special joint session, voted full constitutional and legislative powers to Marshall Pétain.]

24. Dominique Rousseau, "Vichy a-t-il existé."

25. Olivier Duhamel, *Les Démocraties. Régimes, histoires, exigences* (Paris: Le Seuil, 1993), p. 281.

26. Cf. René Cassin, "Un coup d'État. La soi-disant Constitution de Vichy," *La France libre*, Londres, vol. 1, no. 2 (16 December 1940) and no. 3 (January 1941).

27. This was the one and only bill on the constitution published in the *Journal officiel, Débats parlementaires*, 11 July 1940.

28. [*Translator's note*: The elections of May 3, 1936, had brought the Popular Front, headed by Léon Blum, into power.]

29. The best recent analysis of the vote of July 10 has been given by Jean Sagnes. See "Le refus républicain: les quatre-vingts parlementaires qui dirent 'non' à Vichy le 10 juillet 1940," *Revue d'histoire moderne et contemporaine*, 38 (October–December 1991): pp. 555–89; and (in collaboration with Jean Marielle) "Pour la République. Le vote des quatre-vingts à Vichy, le 10 juillet 1940," Comité en l'honneur des quatre-vingts parlementaires du 10 juillet 1940, Centre national de documentation pédagogique, 1993.

30. [*Translator's note*: The Légion de Volontaires Français contre le Bolchevisme (LVF) was a group of French volunteers who enrolled in a special German military unit which was to join the regular German forces in Hitler's campaign against the Soviet Union.]

31. Jean-Pierre Chevènement, "La République n'est pas coupable," *Le Monde*, 18 December 1992.

32. Paul Thibaud, "La Républic et ses héros. Le gaullisme pendant et après la guerre," *Esprit*, special issue, "Que reste-t-il de la Résistance?" January 1994: p. 64. In November 1940, Cardinal Gerlier, Primate of the Gauls, greeted the Marshall at Lyons in these terms: "Pétain is France, and France, today, is Pétain!"

33. *Agence France-Presse*, 11 November 1992. This was a purely polemical warning, since the visit to this memorial (created by Serge Klarsfeld at Roglit, in Israel) was not on the President's schedule.

34. *Agence France-Presse*, 13 November 1992.

35. *Présent*, 13 November 1992.

36. [*Translator's note*: The "Francisque" was the battle axe of the Franks. The Vichy regime made it into a symbol of the French State's return to supposedly indigenous values. As will be seen in chapter 4 of this book, it was also a medal in the shape of such a battle axe that Vichy dispensed as its highest honor.]

37. *Agence France-Presse*, 13 November 1992.

38. *Le Monde*, 17 November 1992. [*Translator's note*: François Mitterrand had the habit of climbing the rock of Solutré in the company of a few friends or close collaborators every year at Pentecost, which is a holiday in France. This supposedly private ritual was regularly given wide coverage in the press and media, on the lookout for presidential pronouncements.]

39. Cf. excerpts published in *Le Monde*, 15–16 November 1992.

40. "La République, Vichy et les Juifs," *L'Histoire* 165 (April 1993): p. 83.

41. Text published in *Le Monde*, 28 November 1992.

42. Emphasis ours. This interview was granted by François Mitterrand, President of the Republic to the newspaper *Yedioth Aharonoth* (Tel Aviv), 20 November 1992. (Provided by the press service of the President of the Republic.)

43. Article quoted in *Le Monde*, 28 November 1992.

44. The reform consisted notably of changing the site. From 1954 to 1985, the ceremony had taken place solely at the Mont Valérien (a symbol of the deportation

of resisters), whereas since 1985 (excepting the years of cohabitation [*Translator's note*: between the Socialist President Mitterrand and the opposition party majority] in 1986 and 1987) it has taken place in two places, the Memorial [*Translator's note*: Mémorial de la Déportation, behind the Notre Dame cathedral] on the Ile de la Cité and the Memorial of the Unknown Jewish Martyr [*Translator's note*: just a few hundred yards away, in the "Marais" section of Paris]: "The affiliation of the two memorials makes it possible to underscore both the overall historical reality of deportation and the tragic specificity of the Shoah within this historical reality" (Serge Barcellini, *La Journée des héros et victimes de la déportation 1945–1992, outil et miroir d'une mémoire de la déportation* [Paris: Secrétariat d'État aux Anciens Combattants, 1992]).

45. Théo Klein, *Oublier Vichy?* (Paris: Éditions Critérion, 1992).

46. Sabine Zlatin, *Mémoires de la "Dame d'Izieu,"* with a preface by François Mitterrand (Paris: Gallimard, 1992), p. iii.

47. *Présent*, 5 February 1993.

48. *Le Monde*, 5 February 1993.

49. It is he who since March 1988 has presided over the association that has bought back the Izieu boarding house in order to make it a place of memory and pedagogy, an idea which originally came from Serge Klarsfeld. This association has brought together many volunteers around Sabine Zlatin, including the lawyer Roland Rappaport who pleaded for the prosecution in the Barbie trial. The establishment of the memorial museum was monitored in particular by a scholarly council composed of former resisters, deportees, and personalities as well as numerous historians, including Anne Grynberg, who was charged with designing the historical itinerary. This is the council that raised the problem of the inscription on the stone marker at Izieu.

50. On the history of the commemorations of World War II, see: Gérard Namer, *Batailles pour la mémoire. La commémoration en France de 1945 à nos jours* (Paris: Papyrus, 1983); Institut d'histoire du temps présent, *La Mémoire des Français. Quarante ans de commémorations de la Seconde Guerre mondiale* (Paris: Éditions du CNRS, 1986); Serge Barcellini, "Réflexion autouor de deux journées nationales," in the proceedings of the international colloquium "Histoire et mémoire des crimes et génocides nazis," Bruxelles, November 1992; *Bulletin trimestriel de la Fondation Auschwitz*, special issues, Acts II, 38–39 (October–December 1993): pp. 25–43.

51. In fact, as early as 1945, the associations of former resisters had chosen May 8, which thus made it possible to associate prisoners of war, the men forced to labor in Germany under the Service du Travail Obligatoire, the veterans of the Rhine and Danube unit, of the Second Armored Division, and so forth, with each other. As the years went by, the Resistance dimension faded away in favor of commemorating the defeat of Nazism and European peace.

52. This paragraph comes from the afterword to the second French edition (Gallimard, 1996). Between the publication of the first edition in September 1994 and the second in January 1996, Jacques Chirac was elected President of the Republic in May 1995 and François Mitterrand died in January 1996.

53. This is the official transcription, distributed to the press by the press office of the President of the Republic.

54. *Le Monde*, 20 July 1995.

55. "L'humiliation sans précédent," *Présent*, 18 July 1995.

56. [*Translator's note*: Michel Rocard has for many years been one of the most prominent and popular public figures in the Socialist party. He served as Prime Minister under François Mitterrand from 1988 to 1991.]

57. See Michel Rocard, "Les mots justes de Jacques Chirac," *Le Monde*, 19 July 1995.

58. Serge Klarsfeld, "Le silence de Jospin," *Libération*, 21 July 1995.

59. Lionel Jospin, "La tache sombre de l'histoire," *Libération*, 25 July 1995.

60. [*Translator's note*: I have chosen to translate "faute collective" as "collective sin," since in this context the word "faute" signifies both a mistake and a moral offense.]

61. Marie-France Garaud and Pierre Juillet, "Non, Vichy n'était pas la France," *Le Monde*, 22 July 1995.

62. Blandine Kriegel, "Vichy, la République et la France," *Le Monde*, 8 September 1995. See also her forum in *L'Histoire*, no. 193, November 1995: "Pardon et crime d'État."

2. THE ARCHIVES (PP. 46–73)

1. The existence of "Jewish files" thought to be hidden was an idea first tossed forward by the weekly satirical newspaper *Le Canard enchaîné* on March 6, 1980. The paper announced that these files were held by the gendarmerie. Following an investigation, the National Commission on Computerized Information and Liberty (CNIL) specified in December 1981 that most of these files had probably been destroyed after the war, but that others, such as the one made in October 1940, "might" still exist. According to the commission, however, neither proof of their existence nor of their destruction could be established with certainty. Senator Henri Cavaillet, member of the commission, revealed at the same time the tenor of a letter sent by Christian de La Malène, an RPR [*Translator's note*: Jacques Chirac's Gaullist "Rassemblement pour la République" party] member of Parliament, to Parisian voters "of Jewish confession," which seemed to prove that files on various confessions were used in electoral campaigns. These two reports, which were unrelated except for the fact that they both emanated from the same commission, were presented in the same article in *Le Monde* on December 17, 1981. In several instances, the resurfacing of a or the Vichy "Jewish card file[s]" and the disclosure of the existence of electoral files of a confessional nature appeared concomitantly, casting a shadow of suspicion as to a possible link (although this was absurd) between the two news stories.

2. [*Translator's note*: Mexandeau is an "agrégé d'histoire," meaning he succeeded in a long, rigorous, highly competitive state examination (the "agrégation") which opens the door to the most important teaching positions in the lycée system.]

3. Published at the author's expense in 1978 after two years of painstaking research, this *Mémorial* tabulates the list of names for the seventy-nine trainloads of Jews deported from France. The research was based for the most part on the onionskin paper copies (sometimes almost illegible) that were located in the archives of the Union Générale des Israélites de France (UGIF) [*Translator's note*: the umbrella

organization regrouping all Jewish community groups that was founded upon Vichy's order] and which were recovered after the war by the Centre de Documentation Juive Contemporaine (CDJC). The lists were drawn up during the Occupation at the moment when the trains were formed, particularly at the moment of departure from Drancy. Now, the card files of the French administration of that time, which included more extensive information than just these lists, would have greatly facilitated his work. Cf. Serge Klarsfeld's declarations to the newsmagazine *L'Express*, 21 November 1991.

4. Testimony provided by Serge Klarsfeld to Éric Conan.

5. *Le Monde*, 13 November 1991.

6. Declaration made to Éric Conan.

7. Cf. *Le Monde*, 14 November 1991.

8. Report given by Christian Gal, inspector general, André Delvaux, and Basile Pozel, assistant inspectors general, November 29, 1991, p. 8.

9. Ibid., p. 18. Claude Lévy and Paul Tillard found this out the hard way when, in writing their work *La Grande Rafle du Vél' d'Hiv'* (Paris: Robert Laffont, 1967), they were refused access to the archives of the Ministry of War Veterans, where they thought they would find the list of the victims of the roundup. The ministry's response to them was: "The data which are found on these documents may only be used for administrative purposes, and do not constitute the historical documentation that you are looking for" (letter of September 20, 1966, quoted on p. 14 in the 1992 edition, published before the disclosure of the mistake about the card file "discovered" in 1991).

10. Ibid., p. 20.

11. Ibid., p. 24

12. Ibid., p. 25.

13. *Le Monde*, 17 December 1991.

14. Ibid. The substance of the prefects are given in the article.

15. Cf. *Libération*, 14 November 1991.

16. Speaking on the radio program "Grand O" on station O'FM-*La Croix*, 14 November 1991.

17. Adam Rayski, "Contribution à l'histoire du 'Fichier des Juifs,'" *Les Nouveaux Cahiers*, no. 48, Spring 1992): p. 52. He cites documents from the Ministries of the Interior and of War Veterans. The author is the former national leader of the Jewish section of the Resistance group Main-d'Oeuvre Immigrée (MOI), affiliated with the French Communist Party.

18. [*Translator's note*: The National Commission on Computer Science and Liberty.]

19. Created in 1943, in very midst of persecution, by Isaac Schneersohn, a French Jew of Russian origin, the CDJC [Centre de Documentation Juive Contemporaine] gathered a huge number of documents concerning the fate of the Jews from France under the Occupation. After the war, a team (Léon Poliakov, Henri Hertz, Joseph Billig, George Wellers, and others), which included numerous volunteers, brought together official documents and individual testimony in the center, and succeeded in saving a considerable number of archival holdings from destruction. These holdings would prove to be instrumental especially during the Nuremberg trials, as well as during the trials of Adolf Eichmann and Klaus Barbie. The CDJC is considered

to be one of the main centers of documentation on the Genocide. Up until the 1970s, it had been one of the only places where researchers could have free access to key archives of the Vichy regime. It is located in the same building as the Mémorial du Martyr Juif Inconnu [Memorial to the Unknown Jewish Martyr] in Paris.

20. Cf. *Le Monde*, 26 February 1992.

21. This was the objection expressed by Adam Rayski, in the article previously cited.

22. In particular from documents held in the possession of the Center for Contemporary Jewish Documentation and cited by Serge Klarsfeld in *Vichy-Auschwitz. Le rôle de Vichy dans la Solution finale de la question juive en France. 1942* (Paris: Fayard, 1983), p. 20. Whatever errors Serge Klarsfeld might have committed in the card file affair, it is still largely thanks to him that today we have a more than abundant dossier on anti-Jewish persecution in France. In July 1993, Serge Klarsfeld published the most complete and most detailed compendium ever written on the subject: *Le Calendrier de la persécution des Juifs en France 1940–1944*, published by The Sons and Daughters of the Jews Deported from France and the Beate Klarsfeld Foundation (38, rue La Boétie, 75008 Paris), 1,263 pages long.

23. According to the testimony given by René Rémond to Éric Conan. When the error was made public, the right-wing press did indeed make hay: "While waiting for further developments in this matter, we are entitled to snicker, aren't we?" *National Hebdo*, 7–13 January 1993.

24. According to the testimony of René Rémond given to Éric Conan.

25. Annette Kahn, *Le Fichier*, preface by Serge Klarsfeld (Paris: Robert Laffont, 1993).

26. In an interview given to *L'Histoire* 163 (February 1993): p. 60.

27. Excerpts of these various declarations can be found in *Le Monde*, 31 December 1992, and in the newsmagazine *L'Express*, 31 December 1992.

28. "Fichier des juifs: l'erreur inavouée," *L'Express*, 31 December 1992.

29. Official communiqué of December 30, 1992.

30. [*Translator's note*: French Jews most often referred to themselves as "Israelites" in the 1940s.]

31. Most of this information can be found in the letter of December 28, 1992, that René Rémond sent to Minister of Culture Jack Lang. This letter was termed a "pre-report."

32. [*Translator's note*: The term "Shoah," signifying "total destruction," without any connotation of religious sacrifice, is preferred to "Holocauste" in French.]

33. *Libération*, 12 January 1993.

34. *Libération*, 8 January 1993, p. 4. This is the title of the article. Cf. note 44.

35. Scheduled to be turned in "a few weeks" after December 1992, the final report was actually submitted in July 1996. It was published at the same time as *Le "Fichier Juif." Rapport de la commission présidée par René Rémond au Premier ministre* (Paris: Plon, 1996). It provides an exhaustive study of all the card files put together by Vichy in view of listing, locating, and arresting the Jews of France. Even before this report was completed, and even though the commission strongly recommended that these documents of public origin be turned over to the French National Archives, the President of the Republic himself, Jacques Chirac, had decided that they would be placed in the Centre de Documentation Juive Contemporaine

(which is a private, and not a public, center), in a special room called an "enclave" of the French National Archives. Although the struggle for the preservation of memory demanded that Vichy's anti-Semitic persecutions be reintegrated into the nation's history as one of its darkest pages, this decision reinforced the idea that the history of the Jews was separated from that of the French nation, a notion completely at odds with all the traditions of the Republic.

36. Cf. Schaechter's letter of June 21, 1990, addressed to Serge Klarsfeld, a document which can be found among others in the packets sent to reporters and historians.

37. These declarations can be found in the numerous letters that Kurt Schaechter sent to the press in 1992. The timetable for making these documents public that he alludes to is purely imaginary (cf. below).

38. See Alan Ring's interview with Kurt Schaechter in the *New York Times*, 7 April 1993. Adam Rayski, the former resister, was to deny the allegations of this article in a letter sent to the daily American newspaper and published on 18 April 1993.

39. [*Translator's note*: The "Société *n*ationale de *c*hemin de *f*er," or the national rail company.]

40. [*Translator's note*: "Vendredi, Samedi, Dimanche," or "Friday, Saturday, Sunday."]

41. Cf. among others the following articles which appeared in weekly newsmagazines: "Les archives interdites des camps français," *L'Événement du jeudi*, 7 May 1992 and "Château avec vue sur la mort. En 1942, René Bousquet invente, pour rançonner les Juifs, un camps d'internement payant," *VSD*, 28 May 1992. The response of historians Anne Grynberg and Denis Peschanski was publicized in a press release through the Agence France Press on May 29, 1992. Anne Grynberg is the author of a work which is the basic reference of the subject, totally ignored by the newspapers who set this hoax into motion: *Les Camps de la honte. Les internés juifs des camps français (1939–1944)* (Paris: La Découverte, 1991). In it she mentions the Château du Doux case in a note (on p. 285). As to the magnitude of recent publications devoted to the question of the French camps, cf. Jean-Claude Farcy and Henry Rousso, "Justice, répression et persécution en France de la fin des années 1930 au début des années 1950. Essai bibliographique," *Les Cahiers de l'IHTP* 24 (June 1993): p. 166 ("Justice" series). This nonexhaustive bibliography numbers almost 150 works on the French camps as such.

42. "N'en déplaise aux historiens, l'Histoire n'est pas leur propriété," *L'Événement du jeudi*, 11 June 1992.

43. "Vichy, zone interdite," *VSD*, 4 June 1992. It should be noted that in the weekly newsmagazine *VSD*, the author of the scoop was Philippe Palat, a reporter who had been convicted by the court in 1991 for having published in the magazine *Passages* an interview with Pierre Sergent (a leader of the National Front, since deceased) of an anti-Semitic and xenophobic nature, which Palat subsequently admitted was completely made up.

44. Sonia Combe, in an op-ed column published in *Libération*, 19 March 1993, under the title "Libérez les archives." This scholar of oral history in Eastern Europe undertook a veritable campaign against the French National Archives and "official historians," most notably in radio program broadcast on May 8, 1993, on *France-Culture*. This program seemingly took it for granted that there was a "plot" by

archivists to prevent the "true" historians from doing their job. Curiously, outside of the archivists interviewed and the inevitable psychoanalyst on call, not one real historical scholar of the Vichy period was invited to participate, except for the German scholar Rita Thalmann and the writer Maurice Rajsfus, both authors of works (based on archives) about the Occupation. The search for the truth doubtless required that the accomplices to the conspiracy of silence be left out of the picture . . . This theme was also dealt with by the television program *La Marche du siècle* on June 30, 1993, which we refer to several times in this book.

45. Chantal Bonazzi, "La vérité sur les archives," *La Lettre des archivistes* 16 (May–June 1993): pp. 5–6. Sonia Combe reiterated her remarks in an article recently published in a special issue of the journal *Autrement* (April 1994), *Oublier nos crimes. L'amnésie nationale, une spécificité française?* edited by Dimitri Nicolaïdis: "L'archive du crime," pp. 139–47. The opportunity given to an incompetent author, who had never worked on the subject nor on the archives of that period, to write just about anything is without any possible doubt something very specific to France, as evidenced by the polemical essay *Archives interdites* [Forbidden Files] (Paris: Albin Michel, 1994), which came out after the first edition of our book had been published.

46. [*Translator's note*: The French acronym stands for "le *C*entre d'*a*ccueil et de *r*echerches des *A*rchives *n*ationales."]

47. Michel Duchein, "Législation et structures administratives des Archives de France, 1970–1988," *La Gazette des archives* 141 (second trimester 1988): pp. 7–17. The author, inspector general of the French Archives, played an important role in the reform of 1979.

48. [*Translator's note*: French acronym for "*I*nstitut *n*ational pour la *s*tatistique sur l'*e*mploi et l'*é*conomie," or the "National Institute for Statistics on Employment and the Economy."]

49. In 1987, the CNIL had discovered that the INSEE was using codes noting racial origins in its files on persons of foreign birth (cf. *Le Monde*, 15 November 1991). These codes had been established from 1941 to 1944, since Vichy, after the abolition of the Crémieux decree of 1870 [*Translator's note*: which had granted French citizenship to Algerian Jews], had distinguished between "French citizens," "natives of Algeria and all colonies, except Jews," "native Jews," "foreigners," and so on. These codes were at the time developed by the National Statistical Service, the forerunner of the INSEE, which elaborated the data processing system of punchcards used for the present Social Security numbers. On the subject of the risks that existed in the Occupation years that these punchcards might be used by the Germans, cf. Alfred Sauvy, "Heurs et malheurs de la statistique pendant la guerre (1939–1945)," *Revue d'histoire de la Deuxième Guerre mondiale* 57 (January 1965): pp. 53–62, as well as Michel Volle, *Histoire de la statistique industrielle* (Paris: Economica, 1982).

50. Memorandum of October 6, 1969, from the National Archives to the Ministry of War Veterans, p. 17, and in the appendix I.F of the report of the General Inspection of the Ministry of War Veterans, November 29, 1991, of the document previously cited.

51. The personnel file of a civil servant born in 1900, hired in 1920, retired in 1965, and deceased in 1980 is thus theoretically (except for the granting of special permission) not accessible until 2020, or forty years after his death.

52. *Journal officiel. Débats parlementaires, Sénat*, 25 May 1978, p. 1002.

53. [*Translator's note*: The "Renseignements généraux" (literally, "General Information") is an intelligence service which conducts security checks and monitors and collects data on sensitive matters and potentially dangerous individuals on French territory.]

54. [*Translator's note*: Mehdi Ben Barka was a Moroccan political activist opposed to Hassan II who, in October 1965, was kidnapped in Paris, then tortured and killed by Moroccan agents. While the complete truth about this affair was never discovered, it is widely believed that those carrying out the crime were aided by the complicity of some elements of the Paris police as well as some government administrations.]

55. [*Translator's note*: The *Rainbow Warrior* was a boat belonging to the organization Greenpeace, which was sunk by French secret agents.]

56. The National Archives in collaboration with the Institut d'Histoire du Temps Présent [the Institute of Contemporary History] published in the fall of 1994 *La Seconde Guerre mondiale. Guide des sources conservées en France, 1939–1945* (Paris: Archives nationales, 1994), listing the major public and private archival holdings of handwritten, printed, audio, photographic, and audiovisual materials now existing. No doubt a few sad souls will see in this undertaking only one more sign of collusion between archivists and "official historians." The rest, the majority, will, throughout the almost 1,500 pages of this work, discover the rich resources provided to interested scholars.

57. Rita Thalmann worked intensively on these documents for her book *La Mise au pas. Idéologie et stratégie sécuritaire dans la France occupée* (Paris: Fayard, 1991). These holdings are subject to the system of requests for special permission, but the latter are almost always systematically granted to researchers, since these archives depend directly on the National Archives and thus by definition are not under the jurisdiction of any government ministry. There is indeed, due to the presence of sensitive documents concerning individuals, a good deal of administrative red tape that wastes time. And it is certainly true that this set-up does not make much sense in view of the fact that the Nazi archives in Germany are completely open. But why let people believe that these holdings are in fact more or less inaccessible, as Rita Thalmann suggested during the television program *La Marche du siècle* devoted to the "duty to remember," on June 30, 1993?

58. Jean Favier, "Les Archives de France n'ont rien à cacher," *Libération*, 21 May 1993.

59. According to an interview of February 24, 1994, with Henry Rousso.

60. The contemporary section of the French National Archives received a total of 461 requests for special permission in 1992, and 698 in 1993 (from 80 to 90 percent concerned the Occupation era), which works out respectively to 2,300 and 3,400 boxes per year, or an increase of 50 percent between these two dates. These figures were kindly provided to us by Madame Bonazzi, and based on her annual activity report. The ratio of series refused to series granted is hard to evaluate, since it has to be calculated for each individual request. It rarely exceeds 5 to 10 percent and largely depends on the type of documents requested: on a request concerning the archives of the Ministry of the Interior, the ratio would be quite high; on a request concerning just the archives of the Ministry of Justice, it would be low, or even nil. But since all researchers request at the same time special permission to consult sev-

eral archival sources governed by very different sets of rules, it is difficult to figure the precise ratio.

61. Jean Favier, "Les Archives de France n'ont rien à cacher."

62. [*Translator's note*: This was the time of massive student protests which degenerated into riots that were brutally quelled by the police. During the same time, a general strike paralyzed the country and threatened to topple President Charles de Gaulle and Prime Minister Georges Pompidou.]

63. In order to prevent any misuse of this vivid example, let us specify that it is *completely* imaginary. On the reality of archival holdings concerning May 1968, see the remarkable work carried out under the direction of the BDIC and the association Mémoires de 68: *Mémoires de 68: guide des sources d'une histoire à faire*, prefaced by Michelle Perrot (Paris: Éditions Verdier, 1993).

64. Alain Brossat, "Libération fête folle," special issue of *Autrement* 30 (April 1994): p. 64. Not only does this author articulate a series of counterfactual statements on the question of consultation by special permission (about which he obviously knows nothing), but he also contradicts himself by asserting on the one hand that the supposed plot of archivists ("the systematic and concerted nonapplication . . .") maintains state secrets, and, on the other hand, that these secrets are flouted every day! This same author, in a recent book devoted to the phenomenon of the women shorn at the time of the Liberation—a book, incidentally, which is interesting, even though one finds the same overbearing tone in it—shows just how much attention he, as a researcher, devoted to the archives, since he did not consult practically any of them in dealing with his subject (*Les Tondues. Un carnaval moche* [Paris: Manya, 1992]).

65. That did not prevent the Socialists from introducing, on June 21, 1987, a bill (number 910) in the National Assembly, tending to "favor the historical use of public archives concerning the Second World War." This proposition requested moreover that there be created a "National Center for the History of the Second World War" which would inventory "all archives" concerning the period. The honorable representatives seemed to be unaware of the fact that such a center had been created as early as 1944 by General de Gaulle, under the name of the Commission Historique de l'Occupation et de la Libération de la France, which in 1951 was incorporated into the Comité d'Histoire de la Deuxième Guerre Mondiale, which was in turn integrated, in 1978, into the Institut d'Histoire du Temps Présent, an autonomous entity of the CNRS, which incidentally, by virtue of a law passed a year later, deposited all the archives that it had collected into the holdings of the National Archives. Still another oversight in the name of memory . . .

66. See Richard J. Golsan, editor, *Memory, the Holocaust, and French Justice*.

67. Guy Braibant, *Les Archives en France. Rapport au Premier ministre* (Paris: La Documentation Française, 1996).

3. The Touvier Trial (pp. 74–123)

1. Cf. Alain Bancaud and Henry Rousso, "L'épuration des magistrats à la Libération," special issue "L'épuration de la magistrature de la Révolution à la Libération: 150 ans d'histoire judiciaire," *Histoire de la justice* 6 (1994): pp. 117–44.

2. [*Translator's note*: That is, the Touvier trial.]

3. According to the testimony of attorney Jacques Trémolet de Villers, while the trial was in session.

4. Alain Griotteray, "Une 'justice' médiatique," *Le Figaro*, 16 April 1992.

5. [*Translator's note*: Simone Veil survived deportation to Auschwitz and has become one of the most prominent and highly respected political leaders in France, having served as Minister of Public Health under Valéry Giscard d'Estaing and in the European parliament in the 1980s.]

6. This is an excerpt of an interview given to the daily newspaper *Le Figaro*, 25 March 1994, just after the beginning of the Touvier trial. Two days earlier, Simone Veil, in her capacity as Minister of Social Affairs and former deportee, had inaugurated a monument to the victims of the Bergen-Belsen camp in the Père-Lachaise cemetery.

7. *Libération*, 22 October 1990.

8. When questioned on this point, Georges Kiejman declared that he regretted this sentence, in which he felt he had "verbally careened off course." He explained that, without being the spokesman for the President's thought on the subject, he shared the latter's viewpoint on the Bousquet case. He added that he had never intervened in the proceedings—the public prosecutor's office was not one of his responsibilities—and blamed the cabinet of the Minister of Justice of the time (Henri Nallet) or inner circles of the prosecutor's office for any possible pressures having delayed the case. From Kiejman's viewpoint, a real, but muted debate was going on among the magistrates in question and the political officials: this explains, more than any particular personal interventions, the delays and diversionary tactics in the Bousquet case. (According to an interview with Henry Rousso on December 4, 1993. The authors thank Mr. Kiejman for his testimony.)

9. [*Translator's note*: The "Commune" refers to the leftist-led Parisian insurrection of common people, who in March 1871 revolted against the docility of the Versailles government in the face of the Prussians and also against the harsh living conditions to which they were being subjected. The insurrection was crushed by troops from Versailles in late May 1871: some 20,000 "Communards" were subsequently massacred.]

10. Olivier Wieviorka, *Nous entrerons dans la carrière. De la Résistance à l'exercice du pouvoir. Claude Bourdet, Jacques Chaban-Delmas, Michel Debré, André Dewavrin, Pierre Hervé, Daniel Mayer, Pierre Messmer, François Mitterrand, Christian Pineau, René Pleven, Gaston Plissonnier, Maurice Schumann, Georges Séguy, Pierre-Henri Teitgen* (Paris: Le Seuil, 1994), pp. 349–50. When questioned about the book's publication date, the author declared to us that it had been decided on long before by the publishing house and was only coincidentally related to the Touvier trial.

11. [*Translator's note*: In late April 1961, a small group of high-ranking officers attempted a coup d'état by siezing power in Algiers. However, they were not massively followed by the rest of the military, and surrendered according to General de Gaulle's demands a few days later.]

12. Ibid., p. 351.

13. Vladimir Jankélévitch, *L'Imprescriptible. Pardonner? Dans l'honneur et la dignité* (Paris: Le Seuil, 1986), p. 47. Written between 1948 and 1971, and in particular subsequent to the debates of 1964 and 1965 over the possibility of applying a statute

of limitations to Nazi crimes, these essays remain the most powerful arguments ever written against the idea of pardons and statutes of limitations.

14. This question was raised in July 1992, at the time of the stormy commemoration of the Vél' d'Hiv' roundup of 1942. Cf. chapter 1.

15. Both of the authors of this book attended the Versailles trial in its entirety, one in his capacity as a reporter (for the weekly newsmagazine *L'Express*), the other in his role of historian (for the daily newspaper *Libération*, in which Sorj Chalandon covered the day-by-day accounts). A good number of passages in this chapter expand the articles and reports that the authors wrote at the outcome of the sessions. The articles by Henry Rousso have been published in Richard J. Golsan, ed., *Memory, the Holocaust, and French Justice*.

16. The quotations given here of what was said during the proceedings come from notes taken by the authors. In France, no transcription of the hearings is made and it is forbidden to record the discussions. However, the trial of Paul Touvier, like those of Klaus Barbie and Maurice Papon, was filmed in its entirety. But the film will not be made available for thirty years.

17. This excerpt was quoted by Laurent Greilsamer in *Le Monde*, 19 March 1994.

18. Olivier Wieviorka, *Nous entrerons*, p. 318.

19. Ibid., p. 410.

20. [*Translator's note*: Philippe Henriot was a brilliant orator and a prominent leader of the Milice who had become Vichy's Secretary of State for Information and Propaganda. Known as the most powerful purveyor of pro-Vichy, anti-Resistance propaganda, he was assassinated by the Parisian Resistance on June 28, 1944.]

21. Paul Touvier's line of argument has been summarized in quite a large number of texts: it is not possible to cite them all here. The main sources for the Touvier affair are first of all the legal documents. From that extremely voluminous dossier, it is important to remember the following documents: Judge Getti's order to transfer the case to the criminal court and the final charge of the substitute prosecutor Valdès-Boulouque (prosecution department of the High Court of Paris, October 7, 1991); the ruling for the dismissal of charges of the First Court of Criminal Appeals of Paris (April 13, 1992); the ruling of the Final Court of Criminal Appeals overturning the previous ruling (November 27, 1992); the ruling of the Court of Criminal Appeals of Versailles, bringing Paul Touvier to stand charges before the Criminal Court of the Yvelines department (June 2, 1993); the ruling of the Court of Criminal Appeals rejecting the defense motion to review the case and confirming the previous ruling (of October 21, 1993); the ruling of the same court rejecting the request made by the private parties (which had been supported by Attorney General Pierre Truche) to hold the trial in the Criminal Circuit Court of the Rhône department, as well as the defense statement written by attorney Jacques Trémolet de Villers (December 1991) and the statements of the private parties. For books published on the Touvier affair, see the Bibliography.

22. This text exists in a large number of publications. See for example W. Michael Reisman and Chris T. Antoniou, editors, *The Laws of War. A Comprehensive Collection of Primary Documents on International Laws Governing Armed Conflict* (New York: Vintage Books, 1994).

23. The London accords were signed between the bombing of Hiroshima on August 6 and the bombing of Nagasaki on August 9. It was prior to Japan's surren-

der, which came about on September 2, 1945. The crimes committed during the war by the Japanese would fall under the jurisdiction of another tribunal, which would hold its sessions in Tokyo. As for the massacre of almost 14,600 Polish officers, intellectuals, and political officials at Katyn and elsewhere, which was perpetrated by the Soviets, the responsibility for the crime was at that time attributed to the Nazis: the crime would be mentioned in the indictment at Nuremberg, but would disappear from the final judgment. This was an omission that weighed heavily on the credibility of the trial. On this point, see the memoirs of the former general prosecutor, the American Telford Taylor, which have been recently published: *The Anatomy of the Nuremberg Trials. A Personal Memoir* (New York: Alfred Knopf, 1992, and Boston: Back Bay Books, 1994).

24. Cf. Pierre Mertens, *L'Imprescriptibilité des crimes de guerre et contre l'humanité. Étude de droit international et de droit pénal comparé*, Centre de droit international de l'Institut de sociologie de l'Université libre de Bruxelles, no. 6 (Bruxelles: Éditions de l'Université libre de Bruxelles, 1974).

25. According to the United Nations agreement of November 26, 1968, and the European agreement of January 25, 1974. Cf. Pierre Truche, "La notion de crime contre l'humanité. Bilan et propositions," *Esprit* 11, special issue, "Que faire de Vichy?" (May 1992): pp. 83–84.

26. See in particular André Frossard, *Le Crime contre l'humanité* (Paris: Éditions Robert Laffont, 1987), and Alain Finkielkraut, *La Mémoire vaine. Du crime contre l'humanité* (Paris: Gallimard, 1989).

27. Cf. chapter 1.

28. Pierre Truche, "Le crime contre l'humanité," lecture given at the Institut d'Histoire du Temps Présent (CNRS) on December 7, 1992.

29. [*Translator's note*: The "bataille d'Alger" refers to the 1957 confrontation in Algeria, when an implacable wave of terrorist bombings committed by Algerian nationalists fighting for independence from France was fought by an equally implacable crackdown by the French military, which used systematic torture in combating terror.]

30. [*Translator's note*: Allied forces successfully landed in North Africa on November 8, 1942, in a landmark undertaking known as "Operation Torch." This event marked a major turnabout the military situation, and paved the way for the liberation of North Africa, Sicily, Italy, and Corsica from German control. The armistice between France and Germany dates of course from June 22, 1940.]

31. Final indictment of the assistant public prosecutor Valdès-Boulouque, Public Prosecutor's Department of the High Court of Paris, October 7, 1991, pp. 264–65.

32. On the history of the Milice, the main sources used by the whole group of those present were the work of Jacques Delperrié de Bayac, *Histoire de la Milice. 1918–1945* (Paris: Fayard, 1969) (republished in 1994 at the time of the trial), which was constantly cited for historical detail surrounding the deeds; that of René Rémond et al., *Paul Touvier et l'Église* (Paris: Fayard, 1992) (cf. below); the works of Jean-Pierre Azéma, in particular his article "La Milice," *Vingtième Siècle. Revue d'histoire* 28 (October–December 1990): pp. 83–105; and finally, the works of the historian Michel Chanal, cited as a witness at the Versailles trial: "La Collaboration dans l'Isère 1940–1944," *Cahiers d'histoire. Lyon, Grenoble, Clermont, Saint-Étienne,*

Chambéry, vol. 22 (1977): pp. 377–403, and "La Milice française dans l'Isère (février 1943-août 1944)," *Revue d'histoire de la Deuxième Guerre mondiale et des conflits contemporains* 127 (July 1982): pp. 1–42. See also the most recent book on the subject: Pierre Giolitto, *Histoire de la Milice* (Paris: Perrin, 1997).

33. The seven victims of Clavier were: André Bouquet, a captain who had been demobilized; Jean Bouvet, a professor at the École Normale, who was known for his political activism for the Socialist party during the time of the Popular Front government; Effime Dick, a Jewish craftsman, who was of Russian origin and a naturalized French citizen, and whose name was added to the list because Clavier's assistant, the Milice Chief Terrel, insisted that the list include some "Israelites"; Raymond Papet, a member of the cabinet of the prefect of the Saône-et-Loire; Robert Sourieau, a young man killed in place of his father, with whom the Milice Chief Clavel had a personal dispute; and finally, Guy Josserand and M. Rigollet, two young students at the Cluny school of arts and crafts, who had had the misfortune of crossing the path of the killers of the Milice. See Jeanne Gillot-Voisin, *Les Répressions allemandes dans le département de Saône-et-Loire, 1940–1944. Problématiques nouvelles et histoire comparative* (Ph.D. diss., Université de Bourgogne, 1992), p. 335ff. We thank her for having pointed out the significance of this episode, and we thank Maurice Bouvet, the son of one of the hostages of Mâcon, who sent us valuable information about this tragedy, which was obliquely referred to during the Touvier trial.

34. The documents of the district attorney's office of Lyons that relate this episode can be found in the case file (the authors thank attorney Arno Klarsfeld, who made them available). On this incident, see also Delperrié de Bayac, *Histoire*, p. 504 of the new edition.

35. According to the letter of Philippe Pétain to Pierre Laval, dated August 6, 1944, ibid., pp. 522–27. Pierre Laval handed this letter over to Joseph Darnand, who responded to Marshall Pétain: "For four years, I have received your compliments and congratulations. You encouraged me. And today, because the Americans are at the gates of Paris, you start to tell me that I am going to be the stain on the History of France? One could have started earlier."

36. This report, dated June 10, 1970, was published in its entirety by Laurent Greilsamer and Daniel Schneidermann, in *Un certain Monsieur Paul. L'affaire Touvier* (Paris: Fayard, 1989), pp. 249–66 (pp. 254–55 in the augmented edition published in 1994).

37. [*Translator's note*: Serge and Beate Klarsfeld have won considerable respect and esteem for their role in tracking down and prosecuting Nazi criminals. It was for example largely thanks to their efforts that Klaus Barbie's presence in Bolivia was publicly revealed in the early 1980s and that he was subsequently extradited to France, prosecuted, and convicted for crimes against humanity.]

38. That is what he had unambiguously stated in an interview given to the daily newspaper *Libération*, 9 March 1994, before the start of the trial, which cost him the most severe criticisms from the ranks of the private parties.

39. This declaration by Joseph Darnand, presented as a scoop by certain lawyers, had thus already been in the case file from the beginning, since the testimony made by Commissar Delarue to Judge Getti was there. Jacques Delarue said he based his 1994 opinion on the fact that, a few days after the Rillieux incident, on

July 7, 1944, Georges Mandel, who had been a prestigious figure of the Third Republic and a fierce opponent of Philippe Pétain, was killed by members of the Milice, and that, in this matter, German intervention was manifest, since he had been repatriated to France from Germany just a few days prior (according to the testimony given to Henry Rousso in June 1994). Nevertheless, Mandel does not, in spite of the declarations made by certain chiefs of the Milice, seem to have been handed over in order to avenge Philippe Henriot's killing, but rather in reprisal to the death penalty that the GPRF [Gouvernement Provisoire de la République Française—The Provisory Government of the French Republic] in Algiers gave collaborationist leaders arrested after the retreat of the Germans from Tunisia. In fact, Mandel was probably handed over by Hitler's order so that he might be executed officially and that Vichy would be a bit more compromised in this time of incertitude and frequently changing loyalties. Cf. Jacques Delperrié de Bayac, *Histoire*, p. 505ff.

40. According to the testimony provided by attorney Klarsfeld, which was taken after the court session by the authors.

41. This plea was published in Arno Klarsfeld, *Touvier, un crime français* (Paris: Fayard, 1994), p. 71.

42. The document in question, taken from the Knab case file (the case was investigated in absentia in the military tribunal of Lyons, and Werner Knab supposedly died in February 1945), is signed by Dr. Haitinger, who was one of the officials of the German economic organization in Lyons. It is addressed to Dr. Struve, at the German Embassy in Vichy, and dated July 3, 1944. The "dinner" in question was in fact a "meal," with no precise indication of the time of day. It remains more than probable that the assassination of Philippe Henriot was known to the participants, even if this meal might have taken place at noon (the radio announced the news around 12:30 P.M., and Werner Knab, as Chief of the Sipo-SD of Lyons, was probably notified in the early hours of the morning after the killing). The document relates an attempt by VIPs from Lyons who had come "to make themselves available to the German offices in this critical time" and who were in fact demanding key positions in case of "serious disturbances." This was a common practice among collaborationists, who were then under the pressure of fierce rivalries (among these VIPs could be found representatives of the Parti Populaire Français of Jacques Doriot), and who were trying to take the place of civil servants named by Vichy. The French present at the meal spoke explicitly of raids and assassinations, and of the necessity of stepping up the fight against the Resistance, and so forth. However—and this is an essential point—there is not one word in the report about what was said by the Germans present at the meal, who were moreover, except for Werner Knab, economic officials. Indeed, the document ends with this sentence: "It should be noted that the preceding report is simply an account of French declarations and contains no commentary on our part." In other words, nothing allows us to conclude here that Werner Knab did not speak of Philippe Henriot, since we know nothing about anything he said at the meal. It nevertheless remains true that the absence of any explicit mention of the death of the Secretary of State for Information and Propaganda is at the very least curious. (We thank Arno Klarsfeld for making this document available to us, in both the original German and in the translation given by the professional translator P. Bonnefous.)

43. [*Translator's note*: It is illegal to dispute publicly an official court verdict in France.]

44. We are speaking here of the extermination project, and not of the deportation of resisters or other categories of people. This project also hit the Gypsies, homosexuals, and others, but according to different criteria. In France, the homosexuals targeted were from the administrative districts of the Moselle and the Alsace, which had been de facto annexed by the Third Reich, and which were thus subjected to German legislation beyond all control of French law. But neither the homosexuals nor the Gypsies were included in the contingents demanded of Vichy by the Nazis beginning in the summer of 1942 and concerning only the Jews. That is one of the reasons for the now ritual controversy between the associations of former deportees and certain homosexual associations which occurs at the time of the ceremonies for Deportation Day. The question of Gypsies in France, of which 3,000 were interned by Vichy, has just been the subject of a very detailed study carried out under the direction of l'Institut d'Histoire du Temps Présent (of the Centre National de Recherche Scientifique): Denis Peschanski, with the collaboration of Marie-Claire Hubert and Emmanuel Philippon, *Les Tsiganes en France, 1939–1946* (Paris: CNRS Éditions, 1994).

45. [*Translator's note*: André Frossard is a renowned author of several books and a regular columnist for the daily newspaper *Le Figaro*. In his book inspired by the Barbie trial, *Le crime contre l'humanité* (Paris: Éditions Robert Laffont, 1987), Frossard asserts: "Le crime contre l'humanité, c'est tuer quelqu'un sous pretexte qu'il est né" (The crime against humanity is to kill people just because they have been born), p. 96.]

46. On Léon Glaeser, cf. *La Lettre des résistants et déportés juifs* 12 (June–July 1993), and 15–16 (April–May 1994). On the CRIF and rescue organizations, cf. Lucien Lazare, *La Résistance juive en France* (Paris: Stock, 1987) and Adam Rayski, *Le Choix des juifs sous Vichy. Entre soumission et résistance* (Paris: La Découverte, 1992). For a rigorous synthesis of the history of the Jews during the Occupation, cf. Renée Poznanski, *Etre juif en France pendant la Seconde Guerre mondiale* (Paris: Hachette, 1994).

47. This provided a moment of considerable entertainment. One of the so-called experts, in probing the accused's mindset, explained his "surprise" when he had realized that Paul Touvier still considered General de Gaulle to be a "terrorist" leader. That was a very telling statement about the absurdity of this procedure, which consisted in asking this expert to determine if Touvier the member of the Milice was of sound mind on the 28th and 29th of June 1944. . . . Very hard put to answer, the expert was content just to evaluate Touvier's "opinions." His surprise became stupefaction, since he had obviously never heard a former collaborator speak. Is anti-Semitism a chronic, pathological disorder? What a question for judicial psychiatry . . .

48. See for example the newspaper article by Dominique Jamet, "Dans le vif du sujet," *Le Quotidien de Paris*, 30 March 1994.

49. According to the testimony provided to Éric Conan by Marcel Kervran in a letter dated April 14, 1994. Mr. Kervran, a former resister, had been arrested on July 2, 1944, by the German military police and transferred to the Curial barracks. He was questioned on this matter by Judge Getti during the investigation. His in-

terrogation—and the solution to the problem—were thus to be found in the case file.

50. Rémond et al., *Paul Touvier et l'Église*, pp. 15–16.

51. Ibid., pp. 66, 67, and 69.

52. On this point, cf. the controversy over the "Jewish card file" in chapter 2.

53. Rémond et al., *Paul Touvier et l'Église*, pp. 306–307. See also Father Soltner's response: "Paul Touvier and the Monasteries," *Lettre aux amis de Solesmes*, no. 1, 1992, a document kindly made available to us by François Bédarida. Father Soltner is one of those who disputed the propriety of using private correspondence.

54. In statements made to Henry Rousso, after a lecture about the trial given at the IHTP [Institut d'Histoire du Temps Présent].

55. Ibid.

56. It should be noted, however, that this trial did not mobilize our "great intellectuals," as did the trial of Klaus Barbie. Granted, the case was more complex and lent itself less to grandiose speeches about the duty to remember. Similarly, it is striking to observe that, with the exception of a few, who had been caught up in the matter in one way or another, historians remained rather quiet throughout the trial. As for the reporters, both French and foreign, their ranks in the press box very quickly became sparse. The secretary general of the courthouse, after having mounted a guard worthy of Cerberus for a few days, saying that there was a crowd of reporters that he would not be able to contain, finally opened the press box to some lycée students standing in line at the entrance. For these students, at least, the show turned out to be a new and rewarding experience.

4. THE MITTERRAND GENERATION (PP. 124–55)

1. [*Translator's note*: The "Official Chronicle of the Armed Forces."]

2. [*Translator's note*: The acronym for "Mouvement national des prisonniers de guerre et déportés."]

3. *Bulletin officiel chronologique/PP*, Service historique de l'armée de terre, 11 May 1992, no. 20. Ruling of April 27, 1992, signed by Defense Minister Pierre Joxe.

4. [*Translator's note*: Acronym for "Mouvement de résistance des prisonniers de guerre et des déportés."]

5. [*Translator's note*: Acronym for "Rassemblement national des prisonniers de guerre."]

6. [*Translator's note*: Acronym for "Comité national des prisonniers de guerre."]

7. [*Translator's note*: Acronym for "combattant volontaire de la Résistance."]

8. According to the rulings of May 4, 1948, and December 23, 1949, and Article A 119 of the Code of Military Pensions.

9. [*Translator's note*: Acronym for "Forces Françaises de l'Intérieur." Henry Rousso specifies that this was "the homefront army under the orders of de Gaulle's provisional government, which united most of the armed resistance forces in 1944."]

10. Memorandum from the Office of General Correspondence and Discipline of the Ministry of National Defense, November 12, 1981, p. 6.

11. Decree number 84-150 dating from March 1, 1984, *Bulletin officiel chronologique*, p. 1347.

12. Ruling dating from March 15, 1984, *Bulletin officiel chronologique*, p. 1873.

13. General Glavany is the father of Jean Glavany, who was then cabinet head of the President of the Republic. Most of the items of this case file come either from the direct testimony of retired Colonel Francis Masset, whom we thank, or from the proceedings of the suit that he filed with the Conseil d'État (see below).

14. Rulings dating from March 5, 1986, *Bulletin officiel chronologique/PP*, Main office of the Army, Historical Services Division, March 17, 1986, number 12, pp. 1337–39.

15. [*Translator's note*: The legislative elections of March 1986 replaced the former Socialist majority in the Parliament with a conservative majority. This obliged the President of the Republic, François Mitterrand, to name his political adversary, the conservative leader Jacques Chirac, as Prime Minister. This marked the first time in the Fifth Republic that a President of the Republic had to work with a legislative majority and Prime Minister of rival parties. The new situation was thus dubbed "cohabitation."]

16. According to the testimony provided to Éric Conan by Colonel Masset.

17. [*Translator's note*: The "Conseil d'État" is a sort of administrative supreme court, ruling on the legality and constitutionality of administrative decisions and legislation.]

18. The Conseil d'État ruling on the dispute, case number 77 876, from the sessions of February 25 and March 11, 1991.

19. Decrees dating from March 31, 1992 (for the RNPG and the CNPG) and decree of April 27, 1992 (for the MNPGD), *Bulletin officiel chronologique/PP*, Service historique de l'armée de terre, 13 April 1992, number 16, and 11 May 1992, number 20. The periods of accreditation are the same as those set by the rulings of March 5, 1986.

20. Cf. Michel Cailliau, known as "Charette," *Histoire du "MRPGD" ou d'un vrai mouvement de résistance (1941–1945)* (Paris: MRPGD, 1987), pp. 286–87. According to the author, who was one of the founders of the movement, several members of the MRPGD had already been individually awarded the honor of the Volunteer Fighter of the Resistance card as early as 1945 and 1946. This recent testimony is in fact an attack on the rival Resistance organization the RNPG, and even more on François Mitterrand. The publication of this book is doubtless not unrelated to the whole matter of the disputed rulings of March 1986, as is the honorary status belatedly granted to the MRPGD.

21. Very few newspapers took notice of this matter, which was the subject of a forum in the daily *Le Figaro*, 29 April 1988, written by Paul Rivière, "Compagnon de la Libération" [*Translator's note*: an honorary title granted to those who rendered outstanding service to the cause of General Charles de Gaulle's Free France], and of the open letter of 6 April 1989 by André Jarrot, a representative in the Parliament, to Defense Minister Jean-Pierre Chevènement (who responded by saying that the matter was at the time under litigation at the Conseil d'État).

22. These are the figures cited by Christophe Lewin in his book, *Le Retour des prisonniers de guerre français. Naissance et développement de la FNPG 1944–1952* (Paris: Publications de la Sorbonne, 1986), p. 284. In addition to the numerous personal accounts of this captivity, the ground-breaking works of Yves Durand can be cited. They include: *La Captivité. Histoire des prisonniers de guerre français 1939–1945* (Pa-

ris: Fédération nationale des combattants prisonniers de guerre et combattants
d'Algérie, Tunisie, Maroc, 1981), and "Les Associations des anciens prisonniers de
guerre," in *Mémoire de la Seconde Guerre mondiale, Actes du colloque de Metz, 6–8 octobre 1983*, ed. Alfred Wahl (Metz: Centre de recherche histoire et civilisation de
l'université de Metz, 1984), pp. 41–53.

23. [*Translator's note*: Acronym for "le service du travail obligatoire."]

24. In addition to the historical works already cited, the personal account of
Cailliau, *Histoire du MRPGD*, can also be consulted about the history of the
MRPGD. There is a certain ambiguity as to the meaning of the word "deportee"
used in the acronym of this first movement, and also in that of the unified movement, since the term refers in particular to the "work deportees," that is, those who
were required to go work in Germany under the Forced Labor Service (STO): it
was not until February 10, 1992, that the highest Court of Appeals settled a long
controversy by henceforth forbidding those who had been in the STO to call themselves "deportees." The MRPGD had been created before Vichy promulgated the
laws on the use and later the requisition of manual laborers (on September 4, 1942,
and February 16, 1943), but as early as 1942, some French workers had been subject
to requisition measures and had gone more or less voluntarily to Germany, or, after
June 1942, had been sent there under the auspices of the "Relève" [*Translator's note*:
The French verb "relever" designates what happens when one crew or "shift" re-
lieves another at work.] (The "Relève" was the bargaining tool concocted by Laval,
which was to provide for the return of one prisoner of war in exchange for the sending of three trained workers.) The prisoners of war, who were also forced to work,
often experienced situations similar to those of these workers; that explains why
certain Resistance organizations also concerned themselves with their plight. Moreover, in view of the activity of the MRPGD as of the activities of the other movements of the same type, it is clear that the term "deportees" applies first of all to
those who were sent to Germany under the STO. They were requisitioned on a
massive scale beginning in 1943: 650,000 workers (to which about 40,000 "volunteers" must be added) were affected, including about 45,000 women. The term "deportee" also refers, but rather peripherally, to certain resisters who were deported.
It was by the actions of other organizations, and in particular the Communist Resistance, that certain people were able to undertake action within concentration camps,
where contact with the outside was very rare. (Such was not the case in the stalags,
which were subject to a much less terrifying set of rules.) Finally, contrary to what
Michel Cailliau (p. 19) would suggest, the term "deportee" did not, at least not during the war, designate "racial" deportees sent to the extermination camps (that is, in
the case of France, almost exclusively the Jews). On the history of the word "deportee," after the war, see Annette Wieviorka, *Déportation et génocide. Entre la mémoire
et l'oubli* (Paris: Plon, 1992).

25. In addition to the work published by Christophe Lewin about the RNPG and
upon which we have based our information here, see the personal account of one of
its founders: Jacques Bénet, *Historique de la création et des activités du Rassemblement
national des prisonniers de guerre* (Paris: J. Bénet, 1983). See also *Dossiers PG-Rapatriés
1940–1945*, a two-volume collection of notes and testimony edited by Jean Védrine
(Asnières: Jean Védrine, 1981). As a personal friend of President Mitterrand, Jean
Védrine was, like the President, an escaped prisoner of war, and later a high-ranking

official within Vichy's General Commissariat for Prisoners of War. He was a member of the leaders of the MNPGD, and later Secretary General of the National Federation of Prisoners of War in 1945, having also been one of its founders. His son Hubert served François Mitterrand in several capacities at the Élysée. These records are the main source used by all the historians cited as well as by all of François Mitterrand's biographers. All are thus beholden to its great wealth of information, but also to its lacunae and to the fact that they are basically personal accounts, which poses a problem of method to which we will return in the following chapter.

26. [*Translator's note*: In French, "Confédération générale du patronat français." The "patronat" is made of all those who are in command of a factory or a large business.]

27. Quoted from a message of the Chief of the French State on August 12, 1942, the one known as the "ill winds" speech. See the exhaustive analysis of rare precision by Jean-Claude Barbas in his critical edition of Philippe Pétain, *Discours aux Français. 17 June 1940–20 August 1944* (Paris: Albin Michel, 1989).

28. Lewin, *Le Retour*, p. 36.

29. [*Translator's note*: French acronym for "Organisation de résistance de l'armée," a resistance organization formed within the French army.]

30. [*Translator's note*: Acronym for "Organisation métropolitaine de l'armée."]

31. [*Translator's note*: Acronym for "Mouvements unis de résistance."]

32. Cf. Franz-Olivier Giesbert, *François Mitterrand ou la tentation de l'Histoire* (Paris: Le Seuil, 1977), pp. 45–46. Giesbert cites testimony from Eugène Claudius-Petit. The latter, in an interview given to Éric Conan, specified that the meeting did not take place "toward the end of 1942," as Franz-Olivier Giesbert had said, but indeed in the spring of 1943: this is a difference of a few months which is not at all negligible historically, especially since the creation of the RNPG dates from February 1943.

33. This anecdote is taken from a personal account given by Maurice Pinot after the war, and can be found in Védrine, *Dossiers*. It is quoted by Lewin, *Le Retour*, p. 37.

34. [*Translator's note*: Acronym for "Comité Français de Libération Nationale."]

35. Statement quoted by Giesbert, *Mitterrand*, p. 60.

36. Cf. Lewin, *Le Retour*, pp. 44–45. The only source for this interview is the testimony of François Mitterrand, in particular that which is found in Védrine, *Dossiers*, and which was written by Jean Védrine. Christophe Lewin also cites an important document taken from Védrine's archives: it is a letter from Henri Frenay himself to Maurice Pinot dated December 27, 1943, which gives an account of the "detailed instructions" given to François Mitterrand, and shows that the joining of the three movements had indeed been demanded by General de Gaulle (letter quoted on p. 45). François Mitterrand had given several versions of the end of his face-to-face meeting with de Gaulle in Algiers. In 1969, while General de Gaulle was still alive, he related: "He coldly dismissed me" (*Ma part de vérité* [Paris: Fayard, 1969], p. 21). In 1971, after the death of de Gaulle, he wrote: "I responded that, as useful as this discipline might have been, the Resistance had its own laws that could not be reduced to the simple carrying out of orders coming from the outside, and that, as far as the networks in question were concerned, his instructions remained inapplicable. The meeting was over" (*La Paille et le Grain* [Paris: Flammarion, 1975]).

37. See Henri Frenay, *La Nuit finira* (Paris: Robert Laffont, 1973), pp. 399–400,

and the refutation by historian Lewin, *Le Retour*, pp. 44–45, which he was able to make thanks particularly to the letter cited in the preceding note.

38. [*Translator's note*: Acronym for "Fédération nationale des prisonniers de guerre."]

39. François Mitterrand, "Fragments d'autobiographie pour une explication politique," in *Ma part de vérité*, p. 20.

40. Jean-Marie Borzeix, *Mitterrand lui-même* (Paris: Stock, 1973).

41. [*Translator's note*: The Francisque was a double-headed battle axe used by the Gauls; its image was adopted as the symbol of the Vichy government.]

42. [*Translator's note*: The "Cagoule," a term meaning a "hood" such as the ones used by criminals wishing to avoid being identified during, for example, a bank heist, was a clandestine group on the extreme Right which conspired to overthrow the Third Republic in the late 1930s. After committing several violent crimes, its leaders were arrested and the group was disbanded.]

43. *France. Revue de l'État nouveau* 5 (December 1942): p. 801.

44. [*Translator's note*: "Pilgrimage to Thuringe."]

45. François Mitterrand, "Pèlerinage en Thuringe. Notes d'un Prisonnier de guerre," ibid., pp. 693–97. The article was reproduced in its entirety in François Mitterrand, *Politique. Textes et discours* (Paris: Fayard, 1977 and 1981, and in the Marabout paperback edition of 1984), pp. 21–25, even though it is referred to in a way that is obscure to the uninitiated reader: the text is designated with its date as if it had been taken from the journal *France*. This truncated title could also be that of a clandestine journal . . . In his previously cited biography of François Mitterrand, Franz-Olivier Giesbert, who obviously has a few problems with dates, places the publication of this text in "December 1941." This error of a whole year has not been corrected in the paperback edition of 1990.

46. Catherine Nay, *Le Noir et le rouge ou l'histoire d'une ambition* (Paris: Grasset, 1984, and Le Livre de Poche, 1987), pp. 140–41 of the latter edition. This is also the interpretation that the historian Claire Andrieu gave of this text during the controversy surrounding Mitterrand's past in the autumn of 1994: "Questions d'une historienne," *Le Monde*, 15 September 1994.

47. [*Translator's note*: The year 1789 marks of course the end of the Ancien Régime, with the storming of the Bastille on July 14, and, more important, the abolition of aristocratic privileges on August 4. The year 1792 marks end of the monarchy, with the storming of the Tuileries and the arrest of the King on August 10, and the beginning of the war against hostile European powers with the victory at Valmy on September 20.]

48. François Mitterand (sic), "Sur la route qui mène en France," *Métier de chef* 23 (April 1943): pp. 190–95. Giesbert, *Mitterrand*, cites excerpts of this piece, but without giving any references. He sees in this very short article, even less political than the previous one, "a leitmotif to Vichy theology": supposedly, any allusion to native soil or country during this era was only an ode to Marshall Pétain. However, we must point out that the journal *Métier de chef* was that of the "Compagnons de France," a fiercely Pétainist youth movement founded by Henry Dhavernas on July 25, 1940, and which would gradually become dissident in 1943. In the issue cited, in spite of a few articles of political tenor about the "revolution," there is hardly any mention made of Marshall Pétain.

49. Cf. Edwy Plenel, *La Part d'ombre* (Paris: Stock, 1992), pp. 413–14, and Nay, *Le Noir et le rouge*, pp. 140–42.

50. [*Translator's note*: After the Allies had successfully landed in North Africa on November 8, 1942, quickly establishing control over Algeria and Morocco, the Germans made a mockery of the demarcation line they had established between the northern zone of France occupied by their troops and the southern zone left under control of Vichy: they invaded the unoccupied zone on November 11, 1942, quickly rushing down to secure strategic points along the Mediterranean coast. However, when they tried to lay their hands on the French fleet stationed at Toulon, the French naval officers scuttled their ships.]

51. L. de Gérin-Ricard, "La condition des Juifs à Rome sous la papauté," *France*, p. 698.

52. Alexis Carrel, "La science de l'Homme," *France*, pp. 682–87. This piece deals with a "new" science that he was calling for, which was to combine all forms of studying human beings, including medicine, psychology, sociology, and so forth. As we have said, this person is certainly not very pleasant. But was it really necessary to say that he wrote the kinds of pieces implied by Catherine Nay? "Less than two years after suffering the most utter defeat in its history, France stated its will not only to revive, but also to develop optimally hereditary qualities that are still intact even though dormant in its population. We must take on the problem of modeling the personality by chemical, physical, and psychological factors in the environment!" This is the complete excerpt quoted by Catherine Nay from Alexis Carrel's article. Now what we have here is really a manipulation of the text: the first sentence of her excerpt is in fact the *conclusion* of Dr. Carrel's article, while the second sentence has been taken (in adding to it a few commas, and of course without the final exclamation point) from a paragraph of the *body* of the article dealing with the means of obtaining better knowledge of man: "For example, a study of human typology must be developed. This knowledge is indispensable to pedagogy and professional orientation. We must *also* [omitted by Nay] take on the problem of the formation . . ." (*France*, p. 686). Alexis Carrel is actually talking about the way in which personality *is* fashioned by a physical environment (a largely commonplace theme nowadays), and then, later, at the end, he salutes the renewal of scientific activity in the France of 1942 (this is thus a self-congratulatory note). We are rather far, in this article, from a Dr. Frankenstein who would be an early advocate of genetic manipulation planning to reshape the hereditary character of his fellow citizens overwhelmed by the defeat of 1940 . . .

53. [*Translator's note*: Acronym for "Service d'Ordre Légionnaire." This was a select group of highly militant officers of Pétain's "Légion Française de Combattants" or "French Legion of War Veterans," the organization with which Pétain sought to unite all veterans under Vichy's patronage. The leader of the SOL was Joseph Darnand, who would later be the head of the Milice, which was created out of the SOL. From its inception, the SOL was fervently loyal to Vichy and the National Revolution, and virulently anti-Semitic and anti-Communist.]

54. Noël de Tissot, "Nos ennemis," *France*, p. 669. Noël de Tissot, who was a professor holding the university degree in science and who served as Joseph Darnand's cabinet head, enrolled in the Waffen SS in October 1943 and was later killed on the Eastern front. Cf. Delperrié de Bayac, *Histoire*.

55. *France*, p. 670.

56. Ibid., p. 671.

57. Pierre Péan, in his book *Une jeunesse française, François Mitterrand, 1934–1947* (Paris: Fayard, 1994), pp. 127 and 270, quotes long excerpts of another text by François Mitterrand which was intended for number 8 of *France. Revue de l'État nouveau* in March 1943, "The Carpenter of Orlathal." Péan had found the manuscript in the archives of the censorship office of Vichy's Ministry of Information (National Archives, F41 208). This piece expresses the feelings that brought the prisoner Mitterrand closer to his German employer, who was a veteran of the Battle of Verdun. Seen in the line of his previous articles, it proves nothing, except perhaps that in early 1943 François Mitterrand had indeed maintained close ties to Gabriel Jeantet and official Pétainist circles while at the same time making contact with the resister from the ORA, something that moreover was already known. However, Pierre Péan is mistaken in writing that this article was published in March 1943 (p. 292, in his chapter on the Francisque), for when one checks the record, one sees that *it was never published*, for reasons that it might have been worthwhile to probe, given the importance granted to some of François Mitterrand's youthful writings. It is thus possible to question the validity of certain commentaries made during the controversy of the autumn of 1994, in which commentators based their conclusions solely on their reading of Pierre Péan's book without having consulted the original sources—which Péan had had the great merit of digging up—and without proving either a textual or contextual critique. Thus in her article in *Le Monde* that we have cited, Claire Andrieu seems to believe that the text in question had indeed been published. This is doubtless a nuance, but nevertheless an important one, given the political issues and the stir created at the time by these "revelations."

58. By virtue of the laws of May 26, 1941, and October 16, 1941. Cf. Françoise Gaspard and Gérard Grunberg, "Les titulaires de la Francisque gallique," in *Le Gouvernement de Vichy 1940–1942. Institutions et politiques* (Paris: Fondation nationale des sciences politiques/Armand Colin, 1972), p. 71ff.

59. Article 5 of the Francisque Statute, a decree dating from July 31, 1942, in the *Journal officiel de l'État français*, 24–25 August 1942.

60. [*Translator's note*: The "Action Française" was a group of viscerally antidemocratic and anti-Semitic monarchists led by Charles Maurras. With his newspaper of the same name, Maurras had spearheaded the extreme Right's press attack on the Third Republic and such figures as Léon Blum during the 1930s.]

61. [*Translator's note*: Upon taking office as Prime Minister in June 1940, Pétain addressed the nation over the radio in a famous speech in which he announced that the fighting with Nazi Germany had to cease and that he was offering himself up personally to the service of his country. This image of Pétain as father figure/savior would reappear in many if his subsequent messages.]

62. Ibid., Article 2.

63. Henri du Moulin de Labarthète, *Le Temps des illusions souvenirs (juillet 1940–avril 1942)* (Genève: Les Éditions du Cheval ailé, 1946), p. 288.

64. Françoise Gaspard and Gérard Grunberg, "Les titulaires," p. 73.

65. Pierre Viansson-Ponté, *Lettre ouverte aux hommes politiques* (Paris: Albin Michel, 1976), p. 53.

66. [*Translator's note*: The French television network "Télévision Française 1."]

67. Cf. Pierre Jouve and Ali Magoudi, *François Mitterrand, portrait total* (Paris: Carrère, 1986), p. 163.

68. According to the little boxed column in the daily newspaper *Est républicain*, which relates the substance of the President's remarks in its 1 April 1987 issue.

69. *Écrits de Paris*, January 1966.

70. [*Translator's note*: François Mitterrand opposed Charles de Gaulle in the presidential elections held that year in France.]

71. Michel Picar and Julie Montagnard, *Danielle Mitterrand, portrait* (Paris: Ramsay, 1982).

72. Giesbert, *Mitterrand*, p. 43.

73. Plenel, *La Parte d'ombre*, p. 385.

74. Péan, *Une jeunesse française*.

75. Lewin, *Le Retour*, p. 37.

76. Excerpt from an interview with Éric Conan in *L'Express*, 16 July 1992.

77. *Ma part de vérité*, pp. 23–24.

78. Cited from Wieviorka, *Nous entrerons*, pp. 343–44. We have borrowed heavily from this extremely well-done book. Chance would have it that this work came out right in the middle of the Touvier trial and the heavy focus on some of the things François Mitterrand said about the Bousquet and Touvier cases has caused people to overlook the wealth of material that this book contains for anyone who wishes to grasp the difficult history of the Resistance legacy.

79. Ibid., p. 348. This excerpt is the full response to one of Wieviorka's questions: "In your opinion, must Vichy nowadays be condemned in its very principle?"

80. Several people close to the President have confirmed this aspect of things. All one has to do to prove it is to see his reactions to the appeal of the "Comité Vél' d'Hiv' 42" or to the legal proceedings against his former collaborators or former Vichy officials (cf. chapters 1 and 2).

81. About this indulgence, see chapter 3 of this book. About his ties with Bousquet, see Pascale Froment, *René Bousquet* (Paris: Stock, 1994), and Péan, *Une jeunesse française*.

82. These paragraphs come from the afterword to the second French edition published by Gallimard in 1996.

83. See the biography by Pascale Froment, *René Bousquet*, which was also published right in the middle of the Mitterrand affair. Although incomplete, this study retraces the career of the former Secretary General of the Police in Laval's government.

84. [*Translator's note*: The "Croix-de-Feu" (literally, "fire crosses") were the largest of the militaristic "leagues" that formed between the two world wars in France and which cultivated a highly nationalistic patriotism. Attracting a large number of veterans of World War I disgruntled with the Third Republic, their public gatherings and marches with torches were somewhat reminiscent of Fascist rallies. Colonel La Rocque was the charismatic leader of the Croix-de-Feu. Henry Rousso points out that during the war, he was arrested by the occupying forces and deported to Germany.]

85. We are referring to "Pèlerinage en Thuringe. Notes d'un prisonnier de guerre," in *France. Revue de l'État nouveau*, no. 5, December 1942, and "Sur la route qui mène en France," in *Métier de chef*, no. 23, April 1943. Another piece, "Le char-

pentier de l'Orlathal," was originally scheduled to come out in March 1943 in *France. Revue de l'État nouveau*, but, for reasons that remain unclear, *was not published*, contrary to what Pierre Péan indicated in his book (p. 270: see also this chapter, "The Mitterrand Generation"). We must specify that the two articles from the journal *France* (both the one published *as well as the other one*) had been included in the first volume of François Mitterrand's political writings, which were published at the time when he was the Union de la Gauche's candidate: *Politique. Textes et discours. 1938–1981* (Paris: Fayard, 1977). The piece that appeared in *Métier de chef* was extensively cited in the biography written by Franz-Olivier Giesbert, *François Mitterrand ou la Tentation de l'Histoire*. In both cases the most important references that would allow us to identify with great accuracy the (Pétainist) character of these journals are missing: Pierre Péan thus contributed a useful piece of information (even if it is partially erroneous) regarding "Le charpentier de l'Orlathal." It is nevertheless difficult to claim, as did certain commentators, that the presentation of these texts constituted a "revelation." (See notes 48 and 57.)

86. [*Translator's note*: Mitterrand is shown shaking Marshall Pétain's hand.]

87. [*Translator's note*: The term "Pétainiste" indicates adherence to Pétain's stridently authoritarian and reactionary ideology and to the agenda of the "Révolution Nationale," whereas the term "maréchaliste" refers to someone rather superficially taken by the aura and personality of Pétain.]

88. Pierre Péan, *Une jeunesse française*, pp. 187–88.

89. See in particular the editorial by Jacques Julliard, who demanded the resignation of the President in the newsmagazine *Le Nouvel Observateur* of September 15, 1994. See also the editorials of the daily newspaper *Le Monde*, which harped heavily on this key.

90. Cf. Henry Rousso, *The Vichy Syndrome*, p. 183ff.

91. Jean-Marie Colombiani, "Ne pas banaliser Vichy," *Le Monde*, 9 September 1994.

92. Alain Rollat, "M. Mitterrand et le Maréchal," *Le Monde*, 23 July 1992. The article targeted by these remarks was published in *L'Express*, 9 July 1992.

93. We base this assertion on testimony taken from his entourage, in particular within the office of the President's chief of staff, in September 1994.

5. THE RESISTERS (PP. 156–74)

1. [*Translator's note*: "Our Century on the Move."]

2. [*Translator's note*: "The Great Recruitment."]

3. Thierry Wolton, *Le Grand Recrutement* (Paris: Grasset, 1993).

4. "Paroles de résistants" ["Resisters speak out"], broadcast live from the Centre d'Histoire de la Résistance et de la Déportation in Lyons on May 19, 1993, on the fiftieth anniversary of the creation of the CNR ["Conseil National de la Résistance," or "National Council of the Resistance"] on May 27, 1943, by Jean Moulin.

5. Pierre Laborie, "Historiens sous haute surveillance," in "Que reste-t-il de la Résistance?" special issue, *Esprit* 1 (January 1994): pp. 36–49.

6. Nowadays there are other ways of making a travesty of the memory of the

Resistance. This is illustrated, for example, by the holding of a highly publicized colloquium in Lyons, in October 1992, which tended to present the clandestine struggle as one that had largely been carried out by foreigners or "Jews" who thus supposedly confronted an "Eternal France," which was assumed to be intrinsically Pétainist. This sort of mistake is clearly a disservice to both history and memory. (See the published acts of the colloquium: Émile Malet, ed., *Résistance et mémoire. D'Auschwitz à Sarajevo* [Lyon: Passages/Hachette, 1993].)

7. For the most recent of these works, see in particular: Jean-Marie Guillon, *La Résistance dans le Var. Essai d'histoire politique* (State Doctorate thesis, Université d'Aix-Marseille I, 1989); Olivier Wieviorka, *Une certaine idée de la Résistance: "Défense de la France" 1940–1949* (Paris: Le Seuil, 1995); Laurent Douzou, *La Désobéissance. Histoire d'un mouvement et d'un journal clandestin: "Libération-Sud" (1940–1944)* (Paris: Odile Jacob, 1995); and Anne Simonin, *Les Éditions de Minuit 1942–1955: le devoir d'insoumission* (Paris: IMEC Éditions, 1994). The Institut d'Histoire du Temps Présent, the Centre de Recherches et d'Études de la Seconde Guerre Mondiale de Bruxelles, and several French universities have, between 1993 and 1997, organized several conferences about the "Resistance and the French": see Jean-Marie Guillon and Pierre Laborie, eds., *Mémoire et Histoire: la Résistance* (Toulouse: Privat, 1995); Jacqueline Sainclivier and Christian Bougeard, eds., *La Résistance et les Français. Enjeux stratégiques et environnement social* (Rennes: Presses Universitaires de Rennes, 1995); Robert Frank and José Gotovitch, eds., *La Résistance et les Européens du nord* (two volumes) (Bruxelles: Centre d'études et de recherches historiques de la Seconde Guerre mondiale/IHTP, 1994–1996); François Marcot, ed., *La Résistance et les Français. Lutte armée et maquis* (Besançon: Annales littéraires de l'Université de Franche-Comté, 1996); Laurent Douzou, Robert Frank, Denis Peschanski, and Dominique Veillon, eds., *La Résistance et les Français: villes, centres et logiques de décision* (Paris: IHTP-CNRS, 1995); Jean-Marie Guillon and Robert Mencherini, eds., *La Résistance et les Européens du sud* (Aix-en-Provence: UMR TELEMME, 1997). In the bibliography of this book can be found a series of titles of an historiographical nature which provide a glimpse of recent work done in the field. We should point out here the article by Jean-Pierre Azéma and François Bédarida, "L'historisation de la Résistance," in *Esprit* 1 (January 1994): pp. 19–35.

8. Daniel Cordier, *Jean Moulin, l'inconnu du Panthéon*, vol. 1, *Une ambition pour la Républic, juin 1899–juin 1936* (Paris: Jean-Claude Lattès, 1989); vol. 2, *Le Choix d'un destin, juin 1936–novembre 1940* (1989); vol. 3, *De Gaulle, capitale de la Résistance, novembre 1940–décembre 1941* (1993). Three more volumes, covering the years 1942–1943, are planned.

9. [*Translator's note*: "Committee on the History of the Second World War."]

10. [*Translator's note*: "Institute of Contemporary History."]

11. See Jacques Semelin, *Sans armes face à Hitler: la résistance civile en Europe (1939–1943)* (Paris: Payot, 1989), and "Qu'est-ce que résister?" in *Esprit* 1 (January 1994): pp. 50–63.

12. This is particularly true for the essential work of the resister, historian, and lawyer Henri Noguères, which was for a long time a basic reference on the subject and which was for the most part based on personal testimony: Henri Noguères (in collaboration with Jean-Louis Vigier for the first two volumes and with Marcel Degliame-Fouché), *Histoire de la Résistance en France*, 5 vols. (Paris: Robert Laffont,

1967–1981). Other major works have withstood the progress of historiography in better condition. For example, the work of Claude Bourdet, *L'Aventure incertaine* (Paris: Stock, 1975), remains not only an exceptional personal testimony, but also a first-class historical work.

13. On the question of personal testimony, see the recent clarification published by the Institut d'Histoire du Temps Présent: Danièle Voldman, ed., *La Bouche de la vérité? La recherche historique et les sources orales, Les Cahiers de l'IHTP* 21 (November 1992).

14. However, the repeated meetings of historians and witnesses in the context of seminars and other university colloquia have turned out to be something unique, for many of these witnesses have taken great strides in the direction of the historians in trying to understand their frame of mind and their detachment. As far as the historians are concerned, they have paid attention to these men and women, and have acknowledged their entire legitimacy in coming to express themselves in the scholarly setting (if we leave aside the voices of a few hotheads—who are always isolated —who feel that historians should have no right to study these subjects). There are few domains of historical research into highly contemporary matters in which one can find such synergy between living memory and scholarly memory. At times, the encounter of the protagonists of history with historians can give rise to great tension, as was the case in July 1997 in the "Aubrac affair": certain historians had sought to shed light on the murky areas still surrounding the two famous resisters Raymond and Lucie Aubrac. See the series of articles published by the newspaper *Libération* on July 9, 1997, and the following days.

15. In his reconversion to the profession of history, he found the support of the most solid specialists, beginning with Jean-Pierre Azéma. It can be pointed out that the case of Daniel Cordier is not an isolated one. A few other protagonists of this era have, in recent years, followed the same intellectual itinerary. This is true of Jean-Louis Crémieux-Brilhac, former secretary of the Propaganda Committee of the Free French in London and author of *Les Français de l'an 40*, vol. 1, *Oui ou non?*; vol. 2, *Ouvriers et soldats* (Paris: Gallimard, 1990); and of a *Histoire de la France libre* to be published by the same company. This is equally true of Adam Rayski, who wrote in particular: *Le Sang de l'étranger. Les immigrés de la MOI dans la Résistance* (Paris: Fayard, 1989) (in collaboration with Stéphane Courtois and Denis Peschanski) and *Le Choix des juifs sous Vichy* (Paris: La Découverte, 1992).

16. About that incident, see the highly documented recent update by Dominique Veillon and Jean-Pierre Azéma, "Le point sur Caluire," in Jean-Pierre Azéma, François Bédarida, and Robert Frank, eds., *Jean Moulin et la Résistance en 1943, Les Cahiers de l'IHTP* 27 (June 1994): pp. 127–43 (these are the acts of a day-long session organized on June 15, 1993, by the Institut d'Histoire du Temps Présent: "Juin 1943: la Résistance et ses enjeux.")

17. Pierre Laborie, "Historiens," p. 39.

18. This text was published in its entirety in the last published volume of Cordier's biography of Jean Moulin, along with most of the known variations and an exhaustive (fifty-page) dossier on the subject (*Moulin*, vol. 3, pp. 1286–1335). The citations are excerpts of a version that reached the offices of the Free French in London, on July 10, 1941 (pp. 1287–89). In his doctoral thesis, Jean-Marie Guillon published the complete text of another version that had been found at the Depart-

mental Archives of the Var. Finally, excerpts of this text were published in *Le Monde*, 7 November 1989, with a commentary by Jean-Pierre Azéma: "Contre une histoire pieuse" ["The Case Against Pious History"].

19. [*Translator's note*: On July 3, 1940, the British, fearing that the powerful French fleet would fall into German hands following France's armistice with the Nazis, issued an ultimatum to the French ships stationed at the port of Mers-El-Kebir, near Oran on the Algerian coast, ordering them either to disarm or to join forces with the British. After the commanding Admiral Gensoul's refusal, the British opened fire, sinking three major war vessels and killing some 1,300 French sailors. This incident fueled anti-English sentiment and rhetoric in France. The reference to the Senegalese city of Dakar recalls the failed attempt of de Gaulle's forces to win this important port in the French Empire over from Vichy to the Free French on September 23–25, 1940.]

20. Statement made by General Maurice Chevance-Bertin, in an interview given to *Le Monde*, 25 November 1989.

21. Frenay, *La Nuit finira*.

22. [*Translator's note*: "Notebook," and, in this context, "diary."]

23. [*Translator's note*: "Civilian and military organization."]

24. Wolton, *Le Grand Recrutement*, p. 12.

25. From that standpoint, we can salute the recent publication of an intelligent history of espionage done by an author diametrically opposed to "historical investigators": Alain Dewerpe, *Espion: une anthropologie historique du secret d'État contemporain* (Paris: Gallimard, 1994).

26. [*Translator's note*: Maurice Thorez was Secretary General of the French Communist party from 1934 until 1964.]

27. [*Translator's note*: "Red Orchestra."]

28. Wolton, *Le Grand Recrutement*, p. 376. In an appendix, the author gives the interrogation of Léopold Trepper in its entirety. This is a document whose authenticity is not disputed. However, the author does not indicate exactly where it comes from.

29. Thierry Wolton has given this bit of information (which is not without interest) not in his book but after the book's publication in an interview given to *Figaro-Magazine*, 6 February 1993, in a featured article published with the photo of Jean Moulin on the magazine's cover: "L'incroyable dossier. Jean Moulin agent soviétique?" [The Incredible Dossier. Was Jean Moulin a Soviet agent?] These documents can also be found in the appendix to Wolton's book.

30. [*Translator's note*: Acronym for "Direction de la Surveillance du Territoire," literally "Central Agency for Monitoring (French) Territory," or the rough equivalent of the FBI.]

31. Stéphane Courtois, "Jean Moulin et les communistes," an interview with Véronique Sales published in *L'Histoire* 166 (May 1993): p. 12. The author articulated doubts and criticisms about the notion that Jean Moulin could have been a "Soviet agent," but he feels that Thierry Wolton brings "completely new data" to the question. (Ibid.) There is no proof that this testimony by Maurice Panier emanates from the DST, especially since another rumor contradicts that allegation, which does not get us anywhere: this is moreover the trademark of all so-called secret history! That being said, however, Stéphane Courtois has done Thierry Wolton's readers a big favor, since, in this interview, which deals with the history of the

Communists during the war, he is the one who presented the sources on the subject with the greatest clarity.

32. Daniel Cordier, "L'histoire en danger," preface to vol. 2 of *Moulin*, p. 61ff.

33. In the magazine *Globe*, 16 March 1993, as cited by Cordier, *Moulin*, p. 63.

34. Thierry Wolton, "La mémoire contre l'histoire," *Commentaire* 16, no. 62, (Summer 1993): p. 265.

35. Stéphane Courtois, "Archives du communisme: mort d'une mémoire, naissance d'une histoire," *Le Débat*, November–December 1993.

36. Stéphane Courtois, "Jean Moulin," p. 14.

37. Cordier, *Moulin*, vol. 3.

38. Pierre Vidal-Naquet, *Le Trait empoisonné. Réflexions sur l'affaire Moulin* (Paris: La Découverte, 1993), p. 76ff. About this same preposterous assertion, see also François Bédarida, "L'histoire de la Résistance et l'"affaire' Jean Moulin'," in Azéma, Bédarida, and Frank, *Jean Moulin et la Résistance*, p. 161.

39. Bédarida, "L'histoire de la Résistance," pp. 159–160.

40. Jean-Pierre Azéma, "Jean Moulin et la Résistance: essai historiographique," in Azéma, Bédarida, and Frank, *Jean Moulin et la Résistance*, pp. 9–17.

41. [*Translator's note*: Jean Moulin's ashes now repose in the Pantheon in Paris, having been solemnly transferred to this site of national honor under the presidency of Charles de Gaulle in late December 1964.]

42. Annie Kriegel (with Henri-Christian Giraud) in the previously cited feature article of the *Figaro-Magazine*, 6 February 1993; "Remue-ménage chez les historiens," *Le Figaro*, 25 May 1993.

43. [*Translator's note*: François Furet was perhaps France's preeminent historian of the French Revolution, who has recently written a major book about the rise and fall of the Communist credo (*Le passé d'une illusion*). He died in 1997.]

44. François Furet, "Le secret des taupes," *Le Nouvel Observateur*, 18 February 1993.

45. Introductory paragraph to Wolton, "La mémoire contre l'histoire," p. 265.

46. Raymond Aron, "Existe-t-il un mystère nazi?" *Commentaire* 7 (Autumn 1979): p. 342.

47. Wolton, *Le Grand Recrutement*, p. 12. There is nothing that would let us think, as he claims in a rather pitiful self-defense provided in response to Daniel Cordier's criticisms, that "this sentence concerns the period prior to June 1941, when the USSR was the best ally of Nazi Germany" (*L'Express*, 10 June 1993). The sentence appears on the contrary to apply to the *entire* wartime era. And given the book's general tone, it is highly implausible that it could have been simply a poor choice of words.

48. This is in essence the theory put forward in a recent book written by General Giraud's grandson: Henri-Christian Giraud, *De Gaulle et les communistes* (Paris: Albin Michel, 1989). Although it was unnoticed by the general public, it is nowadays used as a reference by the new anti-Gaullist front (its author, along with Annie Kriegel, cosigned the previously cited feature article in the *Figaro-Magazine* dealing with the book by Thierry Wolton, who drew largely upon Giraud's theory). On these subjects, one should instead read Stéphane Courtois and Marc Lazar, eds., *Cinquante ans d'une passion française. De Gaulle et les communistes* (Paris: Balland, 1991).

49. On this subject, in addition to Daniel Cordier's work, see the recent book by

Philippe Buton, *Les Lendemains qui déchantent. Le Parti communiste français à la Libération* (Paris: Presses de la FNSP, 1993). This book gives an edifying example of the proper historical use of Soviet archives.

50. Thibaud, "La République et ses héros," p. 65.

51. Ibid., p. 66.

52. Jean-Pierre Azéma, "Des résistances à la Résistance," in Jean-Pierre Azéma and François Bédarida, eds., *La France des années noires*, vol. 2, *De l'Occupation à la Libération* (Paris: Le Seuil, 1993), p. 242. On the subject of the first acts of resistance, see the moving text by Bertrande d'Astier de La Vigerie, *Notes de prison (15 mars–4 avril 1941)*, edited with an introduction by Laurent Douzou, *Les Cahiers de l'IHTP* 25 (October 1993); see also H. Roderick Kedward, *Resistance in Vichy France: A Study of Ideas and Motivations in the Southern Zone, 1940–1942* (New York: Oxford University Press, 1978).

53. [*Translator's note*: Where, of course, General de Gaulle had his headquarters.]

54. Thibaud, "La République et ses heros," p. 76.

55. Stanley Hoffmann, "Histoire et mémoire," *Commentaire* 52 (Winter 1990–1991): p. 810.

56. This is the image used by Paul Thibaud in another article devoted to the memory of the war: "La culpabilité française," *Esprit* 1 (January 1991): p. 27.

6. SO WHAT IS THE TEACHER UP TO? (PP. 175–96)

1. [*Translator's note*: Acronym for "l'Union des étudiants juifs de France."]

2. [*Translator's note*: In the French lycée system, this is "la classe de première," which is the year before the final year in which the students prepare for the baccalaureate exam.]

3. Maryse Souchard, *Le traitement de la Shoah dans les manuels d'histoire des classes de première* (SCP Communication, 1993), p. 5 (of 77). Several newspapers printed excerpts without offering the slightest criticism.

4. Ibid., p. 7.

5. Ibid., p. 61.

6. This information was kindly provided by Jeannie Bauvois, who will soon, at the Université de Grenoble, defend a doctoral thesis on the comparative history of the teaching of history in secondary schools in France and Germany.

7. [*Translator's note*: Between Laval and Pétain. For many years during the 1950s and 1960s, the notion that Laval was the instigator for all the iniquitous policies of Vichy and that Pétain did his best to protect France's vital interests and gain time was widely accepted, thanks largely to the work of the historian Robert Aron (now discredited).]

8. [*Translator's note*: Darlan succeeded Laval as Marshall Pétain's Prime Minister in February 1941, remaining in office until April 1942, when Laval returned to power.]

9. A. Bonifacio, *Histoire. Le monde contemporain* (for the classes of the final year of the lycée) (Paris: Hachette, 1966), pp. 110–11. This excerpt, which remained practically unchanged until the 1981 edition, constitutes half of the paragraph devoted to Vichy and the occupying forces. In addition, the chapter contains two

other paragraphs of the same caliber dealing with "The French Resistance" and "The Maquis and the partisan war [in France]." In other words, there is three times as much space devoted to the Resistance as to Vichy and the Germans.

10. [*Translator's note*: Drancy was an internment camp in the northern suburb of Paris that served as a staging ground for deportations to Auschwitz.]

11. These two examples, which have been taken respectively from textbooks put out by the publishers Nathan (1976 and 1981, p. 224) and Hatier (1975 and 1980, p. 110), are quoted by Serge Klarsfeld in *L'Enseignement de la Choa* (Paris: CDJC, 1982), pp. 42–43.

12. A.-J. Bernard et al., *Le Monde du XXe siècle* (for ninth grade classes) (Paris: Magnard, 1980), p. 57 (of the 1981 edition). We thank the historian Jacques Dupâquier for having called our attention to this book. N.B. the *numerus clausus* was enacted in the universities against students by virtue of the law of June 21, 1941, after the second Jewish Statute (dating from June 2, 1941). Cf. Claude Singer, *Vichy, l'université et les juifs. Les silences et la mémoire* (Paris: Les Belles Lettres, 1992). As for the internments, they affected for the most part foreign Jews.

13. These directives can be consulted in the publications of the Centre National de Documentation Pédagogique (CDNP), 1987.

14. [*Translator's note*: The Institute of Contemporary History.]

15. For technical reasons, the World War II era may once again be placed on the curriculum for the final year of lycée.

16. [*Translator's note*: French lycée students take the French language and literature portion of the baccalaureate exam after the eleventh grade, before their final year at the lycée.]

17. [*Translator's note*: There are several quite different types of baccalaureate degrees that French students can earn, including literary, technical, and scientific. Accordingly, the curricula required for each respective baccalaureate exam vary greatly from one field to another.]

18. Jeannie Bauvois, dissertation in progress, Université de Grenoble.

19. From 1986 to 1989, until the most recent reform, World War II "popped up" several times on the baccalaureate exam, in the written section of the history and geography test: 7 out of 45 history questions, in 1986; 12 out of 57, in 1987; 10 out of 47, in 1988; 14 out of 60, in 1989, for an average of about 1 out of 5 over this four-year period. This information was provided to us by Jeannie Bauvois, as well as Bernard Pénisson and Jean-Henri Calmon, in Poitiers, whom we thank for their kind assistance. For more complete information, refer to *Les Annales du bac*.

20. Here are some examples of test questions appearing on this exam given at the end of the ninth grade in the regional district of Nantes: "The Genocide (1942–1945)," study of documents (1981); "The Defeat of 1940 and the Vichy Government," study of documents (1987); "The Nazi Order of Things in Europe from 1939 to 1945," essay (1988); "The United States and World War II," essay (1988); "The Outcome of World War II," essay (1993). This information was provided by Rémy Foucault, a respondent from the Mayenne region, and Gérard Boeldieu.

21. [*Translator's note*: The error is both more subtle and more understandable in French, which reads "*Quoiqu*'il arrive" (instead of "*Quoi qu*'il arrive").]

22. Stéphane Khémis, in his letter of August 1, 1988, cited in the case (number 12, 844) brought before the Conseil d'État on August 6, 1991.

23. Dominique Veillon in her letter of March 8, 1989, which was cited in the same case as above.

24. Letter sent by the superintendent to the head of the administrative tribunal of Caen on May 17, 1989, in the same case cited above.

25. [*Translator's note*: "Quoique" and "quoi que."]

26. Jean-Pierre Ponthus, "Paper in Response to the Letter of the Superintendent of the Caen Regional District, Dating from October 11, 1988," cited in case 12, 844. We should add, incidentally, that in March 1990, the regional district of Dijon gave to ninth-grade classes, for the National Resistance and Deportation Contest, a composition topic on de Gaulle's call of June 18 which quoted the well-known phrase as follows on the printed sheets: "*Although* it may happen, the flame of the Resistance . . ." ["*Quoiqu*'il arrive, la flamme de la Résistance . . ."].

27. Pierre Lostis, letter to the Ministry of Education, October 18, 1989, ibid.

28. See *Les Déportés d'Avon*, first published in 1988 by the school, then by La Découverte in 1989. Based on archival documents and on personal testimony, the study recounts the history of the middle school in 1944. The preparation of this special action project created a veritable local dynamic, with lectures, exhibits, and so on. This is an example that has been featured in media reports; others have remained unknown to the public, except locally. Some of these special action projects are described in Kantin and Manceron, *Les Échos de la mémoire*. We should also point out the original work of Jean-Pierre Levert, a history teacher at the lycée Jean-Baptiste Say, in Paris, which he wrote with two former students of the school: *Un lycée dans la tourmente. Jean-Baptiste Say 1934–1944* (Paris: Calmann-Lévy, 1994), which illustrates the current commitment of teachers and students to combine research and teaching on the subject of World War II.

29. Without entering into a full-scale discussion of the basic problems posed by this film, let us quote a statement by Raul Hilberg, the great scholar of the history of the Holocaust: "This film by Resnais, which has been so widely praised, is an erroneous and dangerous presentation of the facts. The gas chambers seem to be intended for Belgian, French, or Dutch prisoners, without the Jews being mentioned a single time" (*L'Express*, 24 February 1993). For an analysis of the film, see Richard Raskin, "*Nuit et Brouillard*" *by Alain Resnais. On the Making, Reception, and Functions of a Major Documentary Film* (Aarhus, Denmark: Aarhus University Press, 1987); Claudine Drame, *Les Représentations du génocide et des crimes de masse nazis dans le cinéma en France (1945–1962). Contribution à l'étude de la formation d'une mémoire* (thesis for the DEA diploma, EHESS, June 1992); Wieviorka, *Déportation et génocide*.

30. This information was provided to us by Jeanne Gillot-Voisin, a teacher in Dijon, whom we thank for her assistance. See her doctoral thesis, *Les Répressions allemandes*, pp. 486–87.

31. [*Translator's note*: As explained by Henry Rousso in *The Vichy Syndrome*, "resistancialism" consists of systematically overemphasizing the role of the Resistance, both in terms of its representativeness and in terms of its military significance. During the immediate postwar period, former members of the Resistance often seemed to claim a special privilege to occupy key political posts and thus to take charge of public affairs.]

32. For example, Serge Berstein and Pierre Milza, authors of the final-year textbook published by Hatier (1993 edition), recently found it hard to write a history

that was still smoldering: an official complaint from the Academy of Serbia reproached them for having mentioned in their book what could be found printed in black and white in the international press for almost two years, namely the Serbian practice of "ethnic cleansing" in Bosnia (see *Libération*, 17 February 1993).

33. This documentation is nevertheless one of the major innovations of our country's textbooks, which are widely admired abroad: "The Czech reader of French textbooks is constantly amazed with the inventiveness and thought demonstrated in the use of graphic and typographical means toward didactic ends" (Michaela Rampouchova, "Les Manuels tchècques et français de 1985 à 1993. Représentations de la Seconde Guerre mondiale et de la Résistance," *La Nouvelle Alternative* 32 [December 1993]: p. 25).

34. Souchard, *Le Traitement de la Shoah*, p. 10.

35. Ibid., p. 25.

36. Ibid., p. 10.

37. Ibid., p. 41.

38. [*Translator's note*: Paul Reynaud was Prime Minister during France's military debacle of May–June 1940. Before resigning, he argued in favor of military capitulation against Pétain, then an honorary government minister, and army chief General Weygand, both of whom favored armistice. This debate occurred on June 13, 1940, in the château of Cangey in the Tours region, where the government had fled from the German onslaught threatening Paris.]

39. The survey of June 1990 dealt with two distinct sample groups: those from 18 to 44 years of age, and university students along with lycée students in the eleventh grade and the final year. It was published in the daily newspaper *Le Monde*, 14 June 1990, and in Kantin and Manceron, *Les Échos de la mémoire*, with a commentary by Philippe Bernard. The survey of September 1992 was conducted on a group of young people of 15 to 24 years of age (the detailed breakdown was very kindly provided to us by the UEJF).

40. *Surveys* (journal put out by the IFOP [Institut Français de l'Opinion Publique]), 3–4, 1976, and *Le Figaro-Magazine*, 17 May 1980: these were two surveys about the memory of Philippe Pétain. See Henry Rousso, *The Vichy Syndrome*, chapter 7.

7. The Future of an Obsession (pp. 197–211)

1. As was the case for the Gypsies in France, whose fate was admittedly little known until very recently: cf. note 44, chapter 3.

2. [*Translator's note*: This is an allusion to the highly publicized book by Bernard Henri-Levy, *L'Idéologie française*, which depicted right-wing, anti-Semitic nationalism as a dominant strain of thought in nineteenth- and twentieth-century literature and politics.]

3. Cf. Dr. Pierre Moutin and Dr. Martin Schweitzer, *Les Crimes contre l'humanité. Du silence à la parole. Études cliniques* (Grenoble: Presses universitaires de Grenoble/Fondation pour la mémoire de la déportation, 1994).

4. It is perhaps this tendency that explains the popularity and success of the book by Daniel J. Goldhagen, *Hitler's Willing Executioners. Ordinary Germans and*

the Holocaust (New York and London: Alfred Knopf, 1996), inasmuch as this book has, rightly or wrongly, been seen as a reaction to the "historicization" of the Holocaust favored by many historians, especially those of the "functionalist" current of thought.

5. The most recent example is the removal of street signs bearing the name of Alexis Carrel, especially in Paris where, on March 16, 1994, several associations (Ras l'Front [literally, "We're sick of the Front," the National Front being Le Pen's party, an anti–Le Pen, anti–National Front group], the Parisian federation of the LICRA ["Ligue Contre le Racisme et l'Antisémitisme," League Against Racism and Anti-Semitism], and others) stripped the name from this street of the fifteenth arrondissement, after city hall refused to consider their request. We need not be concerned about Alexis Carrel, whose stands on the subject of eugenics do not deserve to be remembered for posterity, even though the case brought against him often is based on imaginary accusations (such as the notion that he was "Vichy's great exterminator of crazy people"). But what are we to think of this other example: In March 1994, the Parisian federation of the Socialist party protested against the presence of a plaque in the lobby of the Ministry of National Education listing the ministers, including those of the Vichy regime, who had held this position. The plaque was thus taken down under orders from Minister of Education François Bayrou; this was right in the middle of the Touvier trial, and Steven Spielberg's film had just appeared. This initiative was probably awkward, at the very least. But we can ask ourselves: if the same plaque had been placed there without the names of the Vichy ministers, would there not have been watchful people there to protest longly and loudly about this "lapse of memory"? There is one last example which can only be put into the category of the absurd. In October 1992, the president of the League Against Racism and Anti-Semitism of the Centre region requested that the mayor of Courtemeaux (in the Loiret regional department) modify the name of the place called "La Mort-aux-Juifs" [Death of/to the Jews], for this name constituted an "insult to the victims of Nazism." In view of the refusal of the city council, the regional leader of the League Against Racism and Anti-Semitism alerted national headquarters in order that the matter might be brought before the Conseil d'État. It was indeed necessary for "big History to sweep away the little local history." However, it is widely acknowledged that this name is one of the rare traces, in the region's scenery, of the pogroms that had taken place there in the Middle Ages . . .

6. Daniel Lindenberg, "Guerres de mémoire en France," *Vingtième Siècle. Revue d'histoire* 42 (April–June 1994): pp. 77–95. This is an article that goes beyond simple observation and puts forth proposals for "inventing a pedagogy of memory." We owe much to this article.

7. Thibaud, "La République et ses héros," p. 65.

8. Nicolaïdis, "La Nation, les crimes et la mémoire," p. 89. The author is talking about the historians who are scholars of Vichy.

9. "Ideological" history, from this angle, recalls the joys of "flipper" or pinball: "It's more fun to compete!"

10. [*Translator's note*: The New Right.]

11. [*Translator's note*: General Giraud had remained loyal to Vichy until the German invasion of the southern, previously unoccupied zone, in November 1942. Imprisoned for voicing opposition to Vichy's docility in the face of this invasion, he

later escaped to North Africa and joined with the Allies, all while retaining the reactionary values of Pétain's "National Revolution."]

12. By "professional historians," we mean those who, due to their professional vocation, fall under standards of ethics and responsibility in the spreading of knowledge, and also under rules for scholarly cross-checking and assessment: these are rules and principles that certain people either do not know or refuse to obey, whether they hide behind the label of "investigative historical reporting" or any other unconfirmed label of the sort.

13. On the role of the historian in contemporary intellectual debate, one can refer to Olivier Mongin, *Face au scepticisme (1976–1993). Les mutations du paysage intellectuel ou l'invention de l'intellectuel démocratique* (Paris: La Découverte, 1994). The first chapter of this book is entitled, "La consécration de l'historien" [The crowning (installation into office) of the historian]. After criticisms come the praises . . .

Bibliography

This bibliography, being very succinct, lists only the books and articles dealing with the memory, the aftermath, and the historiography of the period stretching from 1939 to 1945, in particular the most recent works. We have put particular emphasis on the topics discussed in this book. We have not listed works on the war in the strict sense, except when they include chapters on memory or historiography. This bibliography was completed for the American edition.

THE MEMORY OF THE OCCUPATION IN FRANCE

"La Deuxième Guerre mondiale 1939–1945. Récits et mémoire." *Le Monde*, coll. "L'Histoire au jour le jour," 1994.
Le "Fichier juif." *Rapport de la commission présidée par René Rémond au Premier ministre*. Paris: Plon, 1996.
"Les Générations." Special issue, *Vingtième Siècle. Revue d'histoire* 22 (April–June 1989).
"Les Guerres franco-françaises." Special issue, *Vingtième Siècle. Revue d'histoire* 5 (1985).
"Il y a cinquante ans . . . L'obsession du passé?" Dossier. *Les Nouveaux Cahiers* 120 (Spring 1995): pp. 4–15, and no. 122 (Winter 1995).
"Mémoire des guerres et des résistances en Tchéco-Slovaquie, en Europe centrale et en France." Dossier. *La Nouvelle Alternative* 37–38 (March and June 1995): pp. 3–36 and 18–38.
"Présence du passé, lenteur de l'Histoire. Vichy, l'Occupation, les Juifs." Special issue, *Annales ESC* 3 (June 1993).
"Le Président, Vichy, la France et la mort." Dossier. *Esprit* 11 (November 1994).
"Que faire de Vichy?" Special issue, *Esprit* 1 (January 1994).
"Que reste-t-il de la Résistance?" Special issue, *Esprit* 1 (January 1994).
"Symposium on Mitterrand's Past." *French Politics and Society* 13, no. 1 (Winter 1995): pp. 4–35.
"A Time to Remember." Special issue, *Contemporary French Civilization* 19, no. 2 (Summer/Fall 1995), edited by Nathan Bracher.
"The Vichy Syndrome." Dossier. *French Cultural Studies* 19, no. 2 (Fall 1995).
Andrieu, Claire. "Managing Memory: National and Personal Identity at Stake in the Mitterrand Affair." *French Politics and Society* 14, no. 2 (Spring 1996): pp. 17–32.
Avni, Ora. *D'un passé l'autre. Aux portes de l'histoire avec Patrick Modiano*. Paris: L'Harmattan, 1997.

Azéma, Jean-Pierre. "La Guerre." In *Pour une histoire politique*, edited by René Rémond. Paris: Le Seuil, 1988.

Barcellini, Serge, and Annette Wieviorka. *Passant, souviens-toi! Les Lieux de mémoire de la Seconde Guerre mondiale en France*. Paris: Plon, 1995.

Barriere, Philippe. *L'Élaboration de la mémoire grenobloise de la Deuxième Guerre mondiale*. Master's thesis, Université des sciences sociales de Grenoble, 1991.

Bartov, Omer. "Martyr's Vengeance. Memory, Trauma, and Fear of War, 1918–1940." *Historical Reflections/Réflexions Historiques* 22, no. 1 (Winter 1996): pp. 47–76.

Borne, Dominique. "L'Histoire du XXe siècle au lycée. Le nouveau programme de terminale." *Vingtième Siècle. Revue d'histoire* 21 (January–March 1989) with responses in 23 (July–September 1989).

Burrin, Philippe. "Vichy." In *Les Lieux de mémoire, t. III: Les France, vol. 1: Conflits et partages*, edited by Pierre Nora, pp. 320–45. Paris: Gallimard, 1992.

Combe, Sonia. *Archives interdites. Les peurs françaises face à l'histoire contemporaine*. Paris: Albin Michel, 1994. [To be read as a clinical symptom of current aberrations in discourse about Vichy.]

Cornette, Joël, and Jean-Noël Luc. "'Bac-Génération' 84. L'Enseignement du temps présent en terminale." *Vingtième Siècle. Revue d'histoire* 6 (April–June 1985).

Courtois, Stéphane. "Luttes politiques et élaboration d'une histoire: le PCF historien du PCF dans la Deuxième Guerre mondiale." *Communisme* 4 (1983).

Drame, Claudine. *Les Représentations du génocide et des crimes de masse nazis dans le cinéma en France (1945–1962). Contribution à l'étude de la formation d'une mémoire*. DEA thesis, EHESS, June 1992.

Faligot, Roger, and Rémi Kauffer, *Les Résistants. De la guerre de l'ombre aux allées du pouvoir (1944–1989)*. Paris: Fayard, 1989.

Farmer, Sarah. *Oradour: arrêt sur mémoire*. Paris: Calmann-Lévy, 1994.

Frank, Robert. "La mémoire empoisonnée." In *La France des années noires, t. II: De l'Occupation à la Libération*, edited by Jean-Pierre Azéma and François Bédarida, pp. 483–514. Paris: Le Seuil, 1993.

Haft, Cynthia. *The Theme of Nazi Concentration Camps in French Literature*. Paris and The Hague: Mouton, 1973.

Heinich, Nathalie. "Sortir du silence: justice ou pardon?" and Henry Rousso, "Sortir du dilemme: Pétain, est-ce la France?" in "Sur la responsabilité des crimes de Vichy," *Le Débat* 89 (March–April 1996): pp. 190–207.

Herberich-Marx, Geneviève, and Freddy Raphael. "Les Incorporés de force alsaciens. Déni, convocation et provocation de la memoire." *Vingtième Siècle. Revue d'histoire* 6 (April-June 1985).

Hoffmann, Stanley. *Decline or Renewal? France Since the 1930's*. New York: Viking Press, 1974.

———. "Battling Clichés." *French Historical Studies* 19, no. 2 (Fall 1995).

Institut d'histoire du temps présent. *La Mémoire des Français. Quarante ans de commémorations de la Seconde Guerre mondiale*. Paris: Éditions du CNRS, 1986.

Kantin, Georges, and Gilles Manceron, eds. *Les Échos de la mémoire. Tabous et enseignement de la Seconde Guerre mondiale*. Paris: Le Monde Éditions, 1991.

Kimmel, Alain, and Jacques Poujol. *Certaines Idées de la France*. Frankfurt: Diesterweg, 1982.

Koreman, Megan. "A Hero's Homecoming: The Return of the Deportees to France, 1945." *Journal of Contemporary History* 32, no. 1 (January 1997): pp. 9–22.

Kritzman, Lawrence, ed. *Auschwitz and After. Race, Culture, and the "Jewish Question" in France*. New York and London: Routledge, 1995.

Lagrou, Pieter. *Heroes, Martyrs, Victims. A Comparative Social History of the Memory of World War II in France, Belgium, and the Netherlands, 1945–1965*. Doctoral dissertation, Katholieke Universiteit Leuven, 1996.

———. "Victims of Genocide and National Memory: Belgium, France, and the Netherlands 1945–1965." *Past & Present. A Journal of Historical Studies* 154 (February 1997): pp. 181–222.

Lalieu, Olivier. *La Déportation fragmentée. Les anciens déportés parlent de politique 1945–1980*. Paris: La Boutique d'Histoire Éditions, 1994.

Laroche, Jacques M. "A Success Story in French Popular Literature of the 1980's: *La Bicyclette bleue.*" *The French Review* 60, no. 4 (March 1987).

Lavabre, Marie-Claire. "Du poids et du choix du passé. Lecture critique du *Syndrome de Vichy.*" In *Histoire politique et sciences sociales*, edited by Denis Peschanski, Michael Pollak, and Henry Rousso, pp. 265–78. Bruxelles: Complexe, 1991.

———. *Le Fil rouge: sociologie de la mémoire communiste*. Paris: Presses de la FNSP, 1994.

Lewin, Christophe. *Le Retour des prisonniers de guerre français. Naissance et développement de la FNPG, 1944–1952*. Paris: Publications de la Sorbonne, 1986.

Lindenberg, Daniel. "Guerres de memoire en France." *Vingtième Siècle. Revue d'histoire* 42 (April–June 1994), pp. 77–95.

Lindeperg, Sylvie. *La Seconde Guerre mondiale dans le cinéma français (1944–1969): Les écrans de l'ombre*. Paris: CNRS Éditions, 1996.

———. "La Résistance rejouée. Usages gaullistes du cinéma." *Politix. Travaux de science politique* 24 (1993): pp. 134–53.

Maurel, Stéphane. *Aux origines de la Fédération nationale des déportés et internés résistants et patriotes (FNDIRP) 1944–1946*. Paris: Éditions de la FNDIRP, 1993.

Mazzucchetti, Denis. *Le Front national et les "années noires": gestion d'un souvenir*. DEA thesis, IEP de Paris, 1991.

Morris, Alan. *Collaboration and Resistance Reviewed: Writers and the Mode Retro in Post-Gaullist France*. New York: Berg, 1992.

———. *Patrick Modiano*. New York: Berg, 1996.

Namer, Gérard. *Batailles pour la Mémoire. La Commémoration en France de 1945 à nos jours*. Paris: Papyrus, 1983.

Nicolaïdis, Dimitri, ed. *Oublier nos crimes. L'amnésie nationale, une spécificité française?* Paris: Autrement, 1994.

Nora, Pierre. "Gaullistes et communistes." In *Les Lieux de memoire, t. III: Les France, vol 1: Conflits et partages*, edited by Pierre Nora, pp. 346–393. Paris: Gallimard, 1992.

Ory, Pascal. "Comme de l'an quarante. Dix années de 'rétro satanas.'" *Le Débat* 16 (November 1981).

Péan, Pierre. *Une jeunesse française. François Mitterrand, 1934–1947*. Paris: Fayard, 1994, and Paris: Livre de Poche, 1995.

Racine-Furlaud, Nicole. "18 juin ou 10 juillet: bataille de mémoires." In *50 ans d'une passion française: De Gaulle et les communistes*, edited by Stéphane Courtois and Marc Lazar, pp. 197–215. Paris: Balland, 1991.

Raimond, Pierre-François. *Un exemple de politique publique de la mémoire: la Délégation à la mémoire et à l'information historique*. DEA thesis, IEP de Paris, 1994.

Renault, Didier. *La Représentation de la collaboration et de la résistance dans le cinéma français (1954–1969). Enjeux de mémoire*. DEA thesis, EHESS, 1991.

Rigoulot, Pierre. *Les Enfants de l'épuration*. Paris: Plon, 1993.

Rioux, Jean-Pierre. "Le Procès d'Oradour." *L'Histoire* 64 (February 1984): pp. 6–17.

Rousso, Henry. "La Seconde Guerre mondiale dans la mémoire des droites françaises." In *Histoire des droites en France, t. II: Cultures*, edited by Jean-François Sirinelli, pp. 549–620. Paris: Gallimard, 1992.

Taubmann, Michel. *L'Affaire Guingouin*. Lucien Souny, 1994.

Théolleyre, Jean-Marc. *Procès d'après-guerre*. Paris: La Découverte/*Le Monde*, 1985.

Thibaud, Paul. "La Culpabilité française." *Esprit* 1 (January 1991): pp. 23–30.

———. "La République et ses héros. Le gaullisme pendant et après la guerre" in "Que reste-t-il de la Résistance?" Special issue, *Esprit* 1 (January 1994), pp. 64–83.

Todorov, Tzvetan. *Les Abus de la mémoire*. Paris: Arléa, 1995.

Varaut, Jean-Marc. *Le Procès Pétain, 1945–1995*. Paris: Perrin, 1995.

Veillon, Dominique. "La Seconde Guerre mondiale à travers ses sources orales." *Questions à l'histoire orale, Les Cahiers de l'IHTP* 4 (June 1987).

Wahl, Alfred, ed. *Mémoire de la Seconde Guerre mondiale, Actes du colloque de Metz, 6–8 October 1983*. Metz: Centre de recherche histoire et civilisation de l'université de Metz, 1984.

Wieviorka, Annette. "Les déportés ont-ils témoigné?" *Bulletin trimestriel de la fondation Auschwitz* 27 (January–March 1991), pp. 7–23.

———. *Déportation et génocide. Entre la mémoire et l'oubli*. Paris: Plon, 1992.

Wieviorka, Olivier. "La Génération de la Résistance." *Vingtième Siècle. Revue d'histoire* 22 (April–June 1989): pp. 111–16.

———. *Nous entrerons dans la carrière. De la Résistance à l'exercice du pouvoir. Claude Bourdet, Jacques Chaban-Delmas, Michel Debré, André Dewavrin, Pierre Hervé, Daniel Mayer, Pierre Messmer, François Mitterrand, Christian Pineau, René Pleven, Gaston Plissonnier, Maurice Schumann, Georges Séguy, Pierre-Henri Teitgen*. Paris: Le Seuil, 1994.

Wilkinson, James D. "Remembering World War II. The Perspective of the Losers." *The American Scholar* (Summer 1985).

———. "A Choice of Fictions: Historians, Memory, and Evidence." *Publications of the Modern Language Association of America* 111, no. 1 (January 1996): pp. 80–92.

Wood, Nancy. "Memorial Militancy in France: 'Working-through' or the Politics of Anachronism?" in "Fifty Years after the Holocaust and the Second World War." *Patterns of Prejudice* 29, nos. 2–3 (April–July 1995): pp. 89–103.

HISTORIOGRAPHICAL PROBLEMS

Azéma, Jean-Pierre and François Bédarida, eds., with the collaboration of Denis Peschanski and Henry Rousso. *Le Régime de Vichy et les Français*. Paris: Fayard,

1992. Part one: "L'Historiographie de Vichy d'hier à aujourd'hui" by Jean-Pierre Azéma, Bernard Laguerre, Renée Poznanski, and Olivier Wieviorka, pp. 23–74.

Azéma, Jean-Pierre, and François Bédarida. "Vichy et ses historiens" in "Que faire de Vichy?" Special issue, *Esprit* 5 (May 1992): pp. 43–51.

———. "L'Historisation de la Résistance" in "Que reste-t-il de la Résistance?" Special issue, *Esprit* 1 (January 1994): pp. 19–35.

Bédarida, François. "L'Histoire de la Résistance. Lectures d'hier, chantiers de demain." *Vingtième Siècle. Revue d'histoire* 11 (July–September 1986): pp. 75–89.

Hoffmann, Stanley. "Histoire et mémoire." *Commentaire* 52 (Winter 1990–1991): pp. 808–811.

Laborie, Pierre. "Historiens sous haute surveillance" in "Que reste-t-il de la Résistance?" Special issue, *Esprit* 1 (January 1994): pp. 19–35.

Lévy, Claude. "La Résistance juive en France. De l'enjeu de mémoire à l'histoire critique." *Vingtième Siècle. Revue d'histoire* 22 (April–June 1989): pp. 117–28.

Martens, Stefan, "'Drôle de Guerre'—Occupation—Épuration: Frankreich in Zweiten Weltkrieg." *Neue Politische Literatur* 37 (1992): pp. 185–213.

Munholland, Kim. "Wartime France: Remembering Vichy." *French Historical Studies* 18, no. 3 (Spring 1994): pp. 801–820.

Peschanski, Denis. "La Francia di Vichy o la Francia sotto Vichy? Sguardi sulla storiografia." *Ricerche di Storia politica* 8 (1993): pp. 75–82.

Rousso, Henry. "Où en est l'histoire de la Résistance?" In *L'Histoire, Études sur la France de 1939 à nos jours*, pp. 113–33. Paris: Le Seuil (Collection "Points-Histoire), 1985.

JUSTICE AND CRIMES AGAINST HUMANITY

Le Procès de Nuremberg. Conséquences et actualisation. Collection de droit international de l'Institut de sociologie de l'Université libre de Bruxelles, no. 22. Bruylant/Éditions de l'ULB, 1988.

Arendt, Hannah. *Eichmann in Jerusalem: A Report on the Banality of Evil.* New York: Viking, 1963.

Dobkine, Michel, ed. *Crimes et humanité. Extraits des actes du procès de Nuremberg, 18 October 1945–1er October 1946.* Paris: Romilliat, 1992.

Finkielkraut, Alain. *La Mémoire vaine. Du crime contre l'humantié.* Paris: Gallimard, 1989, and Collection "Folio," 1991.

Frossard, André. *Le Crime contre l'humanité.* Paris: Laffont, 1987.

Grynfogel, Catherine. *Le Crime contre l'humanité, notion et régime juridique.* 2 vols. Ph.D. diss., Toulouse I, 1991.

Mertens, Pierre. *L'Imprescriptibilité des crimes de guerre et contre l'humanité. Étude de droit international et de droit pénal comparé.* Bruxelles: Éditions de l'ULB, Centre de droit international de l'Institut de sociologie de l'Université libre de Bruxelles, 6, 1974.

Mota, Joachim Jorge de Magalhães, and Gunnar Nerdrum. "État des procédures judiciaires en cours diligentées pour crimes contre l'humanité. Rapport de mission, France, 14–19 octobre 1990." *La Lettre de la Fédération internationale des droits de l'homme.* Special issue (January 1991).

Reisman, W. Michael, and Chris T. Antoniou, eds. *The Laws of War. A Comprehensive Collection of Primary Documents on International Laws Governing Armed Conflict*. New York: Vintage Books, 1994.

Taylor, Telford. *The Anatomy of the Nuremberg Trials: A Personal Memoir*. New York: Knopf, 1992.

Truche, Pierre. "La Notion du crime contre l'humanité. Bilan et propositions" in "Que faire de Vichy?" Special issue, *Esprit* 5 (May 1992): pp. 67–87.

Varaut, Jean-Marc. *Le Procès de Nuremberg: le glaive dans la balance*. Paris: Perrin, 1992.

Wexler, Leila Sadat. "The Interpretation of the Nuremberg Principles by the French Court of Cassation: From Touvier to Barbie and Back Again." *Columbia Journal of Transnational Law* 32, no. 2 (1994): pp. 289–380.

Wieviorka, Annette. *Le Procès Eichmann*. Bruxelles: Complexe, 1989.

———. *Le Procès de Nuremberg*. Rennes & Caen: Mémorial de Caen/Éditions Ouest-France, 1995.

THE TOUVIER, BOUSQUET, AND PAPON AFFAIRS

Golsan, Richard J., ed. *Memory, the Holocaust, and French Justice: The Bousquet and Touvier Affairs*. Hanover, N.H.: University Press of New England, 1996.

Lambert, Bernard. *Bousquet, Papon, Touvier, inculpés de crimes contre l'humanité. Dossiers d'accusation*. Paris: FNDIRP, 1991.

The Touvier Affair

Bédarida, François, ed. *Touvier, Vichy et le crime contre l'humanité: le dossier de l'accusation*. Paris: Le Seuil, 1996.

Flory, Claude. *Touvier m'a avoué*. Paris: Laffont, 1989.

Gaurichon, Stéphane. *L'Affaire Touvier (depuis 1989)*. Criminal law thesis, Université de Poitiers, 1993.

Greilshamer, Laurent, and Daniel Schneidermann. *Un certain Monsieur Paul. L'affaire Touvier*. 2d ed. Paris: Fayard, 1994.

Henne, Jean-Pierre. *Un étrange combat. Méditations sur l'affaire Touvier*. Bouère: Dominique Martin Morin, 1995 [By the Chief Judge of the Court of Criminal Appeals of Paris who signed the ruling in favor of dismissing the charges on April 13, 1992.]

Jacubowicz, Alain, and René Raffin. *Touvier. Histoire du procès*. Paris: Julliard, 1995.

Klarsfeld, Arno. *Touvier, un crime français*. Paris: Fayard, 1994.

Moniquet, Claude. *Touvier, un milicien à l'ombre de l'Église*. Paris: Olivier Orban, 1989.

Pinto, Roger. "L'Affaire Touvier. Analyse critique de l'arrêt du 13 April 1992." *Journal du droit international* 3 (July–August–September 1992): pp. 607–623.

Rémond, René, et al. *Paul Touvier et l'Église*. Paris: Fayard, 1992.

Touvier, Chantal, and Pierre Touvier. *Lettre ouverte aux représentants du peuple français suivie de 20 documents inédits*. June 1976.

Touvier, Paul. *Lettre ouverte au grand juge suivie de ce qu'avait à dire mon avocat en Cour de cassation*. June 1976.

————. *Mes crimes contre l'humanité*. Imprimerie SPT, November 1979.

Trémolet de Villers, Jacques. *Paul Touvier est innocent*. Bouère: Dominique-Martin-Morin, 1991.

————. *L'Affaire Touvier. Chronique d'un procès en idéologie*. Bouère: Dominique-Martin-Morin, 1994.

Wexler, Leila Sadat. "Reflections on the Trial of Vichy Collaborator Paul Touvier for Crimes Against Humanity." *Law and Social Inquiry. Journal of the American Bar Association* 20, no. 1 (Winter 1995): pp. 191–221.

The Bousquet Affair

"Le dossier Bousquet." *Libération*, supplement to no. 3776, 13 July 1993.

Aouizerate, Cyril. *René Bousquet. Biographie d'un collabo*. Paris: Éditions du Forum, 1993.

Froment, Pascale. *René Bousquet*. Paris: Stock, 1994.

Husson, Jean-Pierre. "L'itinéraire d'un haut fonctionnaire: René Bousquet." In *Le Régime de Vichy et les Français*, edited by Jean-Pierre Azéma and François Bédarida, with the collaboration of Denis Peschanski and Henry Rousso, pp. 287–301. Paris: Fayard, 1992.

The Papon Affair

Boulanger, Gérard. *Maurice Papon. Un technocrate français dans la Collaboration*. Paris: Le Seuil, 1994.

Matisson, Maurice-David, and Jean-Paul Abribat. *Psychanalyse de la Collaboration. Le syndrome de Bordeaux: 1940–1945*. Marseille: Éditions "Hommes et perspectives," 1991.

Slitinski, Michel. *L'Affaire Papon*. Paris: Alain Moreau, 1983.

THE MEMORY OF NAZISM AND OF THE GENOCIDE ON AN INTERNATIONAL LEVEL

Although this topic is treated only incidentally in our book, it is indispensable to know that it has, for several years now, given rise to a considerable output of publications—a symptom of a phenomenon that concerns not only France—of which we will only give a quick overview here; for the most part, these are French and English works.

"L'Allemagne, le nazisme et les juifs." Dossier. *Vingtième Siècle. Revue d'histoire* 16 (October–December 1987).

"I crimini nazisti, la memoria, l'Europa di oggi." *Passato e Presente* 34 (1995): pp. 15–36.

"Fifty Years after the Holocaust and the Second World War." Dossier. *Patterns of Prejudice* 29, nos. 2–3 (April–July 1995).

"Histoire et mémoire des crimes et génocides nazis." *Bulletin trimestriel de la Fondation Auschwitz*. Special issues 36–37 (April–September 1993); 38–39 (October–December 1993); 40–41 (January–June 1994); 42–43 (July–September 1994); 44–45 (October–December 1994); 49 (October–December 1995).

"Interrogations allemandes." Dossier. *Le Débat* 45 (May–September 1987).

"La Mémoire d'Auschwitz." Dossier. *Esprit* 9 (September 1980).

"Mémoire du nazisme et RFA et RDA." Dossier. *Esprit* 10 (October 1987).

"Mémoires juives." Dossier. *Le Débat* 82 (November–December 1994). [See in particular: Jean-Michel Chaumont, "Connaissance ou reconnaissance? Les enjeux du débat sur la singularité de la Shoah," and Georges Bensoussan, "Histoire, mémoire et commémoration. Vers une religion civile," as well as the interviews with Théo Klein and Alex Derczansky.]

"Penser Auschwitz." Special issue, *Pardès* 9–10 (1989).

"La Querelle des historiens allemands vue de l'Est." Dossier. *La Nouvelle Alternative* 13 (March 1989).

L'Allemagne nazie et le génocide juif. Paris: EHESS/Gallimard/Le Seuil, 1985.

Au sujet de Shoah de Claude Lanzmann. Paris: Belin, 1990.

L'Enseignement de la Choa. Comment les manuels d'histoire présentent-ils l'extermination des Juifs au cours de la deuxième guerre mondiale? Paris: Centre de Documentation Juive Contemporaine, 1982.

Devant l'histoire. Les Documents de la controverse sur la singularité de l'extermination des Juifs par le régime nazi. Paris: Passages/Cerf, 1988.

Ayçoberry, Pierre. *La Question nazie. Essai sur les interprétations du national-socialisme (1922–1975).* Paris: Le Seuil (Collection "Points-Histoire"), 1979.

Bartoszewski, Wladyslaw T. *The Convent at Auschwitz.* New York: G. Braziller, 1990.

Bartov, Omer. "Intellectuals on Auschwitz: Memory, History, and Truth." *History and Memory. Studies in Representation of the Past* 1 (Spring–Summer 1993): pp. 87–129.

———. *Murder in our Midst. The Holocaust, Industrial Killing, and Representation.* New York and Oxford: Oxford University Press, 1996.

Bartram, G., et al., eds. *Reconstructing the Past. Representations of the Fascist Era in Post-War European Culture.* Keele, England: Keele University Press, 1996.

Bédarida, François, ed. *La Politique nazie d'extermination.* Paris: IHTP/Albin Michel, 1989.

———. *Le Génocide et le nazisme: histoire et témoignages.* Paris: Presses-Pocket, 1992.

———. Gervereau, Laurent, ed. *La Déportation. Le système concentrationnaire nazi.* Nanterre: Éditions de la BDIC, 1995. [Catalogue of the exhibit of the same name in the Museum of Contemporary History, with a chapter on memory.]

Broszat, Martin, and Saul Friedländer. "A Controversy about the Historicization of National-Socialism." *Yad Vashem Studies* 19 (Fall 1988): pp. 1–47.

Buruma, Ian. *The Wages of Guilt. Memories of War in Germany and Japan.* New York: Farrar, Straus, & Giroux, 1994.

Dawidowicz, Lucy S. *The Holocaust and the Historians.* Cambridge, Mass.: Harvard University Press, 1981.

Diner, Dan. "Historical Experience and Cognition: Perspectives on National-Socialism." *History and Memory. Studies in Representation of the Past* 2 (Fall 1990): pp. 84–110.

Erler, Gernot, Rolf-Dieter Müller, et al. *L'Histoire escamotée. Les tentatives de liquidation du passé nazi en Allemagne.* Paris: La Découverte, 1988.

Friedländer, Saul. "The 'Final Solution': On the Unease in Historical Interpretation." *History and Memory. Studies in the Representation of the Past* 1, (Fall–Winter 1989): pp. 61–76.

———, ed. *Probing the Limits of Representation: Nazism and the Final Solution.* Cambridge, Mass.: Harvard University Press, 1992.

Gittelman, Zvi. "History, Memory, and Politics: The Holocaust in the Soviet Union." *Holocaust and Genocide Studies* 5 (1990): pp. 23–37.

Grosser, Alfred. *Le Crime et la mémoire.* Paris: Flammarion, 1989.

Hartmann, Geoffrey, ed. *Bitburg in Moral and Political Perspective.* Bloomington: Indiana University Press, 1986.

———. *The Shapes of Memory.* London: Blackwell, 1993.

———. "Public Memory and its Discontents." *Raritan. A Quarterly Review* (Summer 1994): pp. 24–40.

Hayes, Peter, ed. *Lessons and Legacies: The Meaning of the Holocaust in a Changing World.* Evanston, Ill.: Northwestern University Press, 1991.

Hilberg, Raul. *The Politics of Memory.* Chicago: Ivan R. Dee, 1996.

Husson, Edouard. *Une culpabilité ordinaire? Hitler, les Allemands et la Shoah.* Paris: François-Xavier de Guibert, 1997.

Klarsfeld, Serge, ed. *Mémoire de Génocide.* Paris: Centre de documentation juive contemporaine/Association des Fils et Filles des déportés juifs de France, 1987.

Langer, William L. *Holocaust Testimonies. The Ruins of Memory.* New Haven, Conn.: Yale University Press, 1991.

LaPierre, Nicole. *Le Silence de la mémoire. A la recherche des juifs de Plock.* Paris: Plon, 1989.

Maier, Charles S. *The Unmasterable Past. History, Holocaust, and German National Identity.* Cambridge, Mass., and London: Harvard University Press, 1988.

Marrus, Michael R. *The Holocaust in History.* Hanover, N.H.: University Press of New England, 1987.

Miller, Judith. *One, by One, by One: Facing the Holocaust.* New York: Simon and Schuster, 1990.

Paggi, Leonardo. "Per una memoria europea dei crimini nazisti." *Passato e Presente* 32 (May–August 1994): pp. 105–117.

Pollak, Michael. *L'Expérience concentrationnaire. Essai sur le maintien de l'identité sociale.* Paris: A. M. Métailié, 1990.

Posner, Gerald L. *Hitler's Children: Sons and Daughters of the Third Reich Talk About Their Fathers and Themselves.* New York: Random House, 1992.

Segev, Tom. *The Seventh Million: The Israelis and the Holocaust.* New York: Hill & Wang, 1993.

Sheftel, Yoram. *L'Affaire Demjanjuk. Les secrets d'un procès-spectacle.* Paris: Jean-Claude Lattès, 1994.

Sichrovsky, Peter. *Born Guilty: Children of Nazi Families.* New York: Basic Books, 1988.

Szafran, Arthur Willy, and Yannis Thanassekos. *Un deuil perpétuel.* Bruxelles: Éditions du Centre d'études et de documentation de la Fondation Auschwitz, 1995. [Special issue of the *Bulletin trimestriel de la Fondation Auschwitz* 46 (January–March 1995).]

Vidal-Naquet, Pierre. *The Jews: History, Memory, and the Present.* New York: Columbia University Press, 1996.

———. "Le défi de la Shoah à l'Histoire." *Les Temps modernes* 507 (October 1988).

———. *Réflexions sur le Génocide*. Vol. III of *Les Juifs, la mémoire et le présent*. Paris: La Découverte, 1995.

Young, James E. *The Texture of Memory. Holocaust Memorials and Meaning*. New Haven, Conn.: Yale University Press, 1993.

ON HOLOCAUST DENIAL

"Négationnisme et révisionnisme." Special issue, *Relations internationales* 65 (Spring 1991).

Finkielkraut, Alain. *L'Avenir d'une négation. Réflexion sur la question du génocide*. Paris: Le Seuil, 1982.

Fresco, Nadine. "Les Redresseurs de morts." *Les Temps modernes* 407 (June 1980).

Lewin, Roland. "Paul Rassinier ou la conjonction des extrêmes." *Silex* 26 (1984).

Lipstadt, Deborah E. *Denying the Holocaust: The Growing Assault on Truth and Memory*. The Hebrew University of Jerusalem, 1993, and New York: Plume, 1994.

Rousso, Henry. "La Négation du génocide juif." *L'Histoire* 106 (December 1987), pp. 76–79.

Steinberg, Maxime. *Les Yeux du témoin et le regard du borgne. L'Histoire face au révisionnisme*. Paris: Cerf, 1990.

Taguieff, Pierre-André. "La Nouvelle Judéophobie. Antisionisme, antiracisme et anti-impérialisme." *Les Temps modernes* 520 (November 1989): pp. 1–80.

Vidal-Naquet, Pierre. *Assassins of Memory: Essays on the Denial of the Holocaust*. New York: Columbia University Press, 1992.

Index of Names

UNIVERSITY PRESS OF NEW ENGLAND publishes books under its own imprint and is the publisher for Brandeis University Press, Dartmouth College, Middlebury College Press, University of New Hampshire, Tufts University, and Wesleyan University Press.

LIBRARY OF CONGRESS CATALOGING-IN-PUBLICATION DATA
Conan, Eric.
  [Vichy. English]
  Vichy : an ever-present past / by Eric Conan and Henry Rousso ;
  translated by Nathan Bracher ; foreword by Robert O. Paxton
      p.   cm. — (Contemporary French culture and society)
  Translation of the 2nd ed. published in paperback: Paris :
  Gallimard, c1996. (Collection Folio/histoire ; 71)
  A sequel to Henry Rousso's Le syndrome de Vichy. Paris : Seuil,
  c1987.
  Includes bibliographical references and index.
  ISBN 0–87451–795–8 (cloth : alk. paper)
    1. France—History—German occupation, 1940–1945. 2. World War,
  1939–1945—Moral and ethical aspects. 3. Vichy (France)—Politics
  and government. 4. Politicians—France—Attitudes. 5. War crime
  trials—France. 6. War crime trials—France.   I. Rousso, Henry,
  1954– . II. Series.
  DC397.C5913   1998
  944.081'6—dc21   97–44597